I Am My Father's Son

DAN HILL

I Am My Father's Son

A MEMOIR OF LOVE AND FORGIVENESS

HarperCollinsPublishersLtd

Published by HarperCollins Publishers Ltd.

First edition

For the sake of compression, some of the characters that appear in the
book are composites of people the author has known, and some events
appear out of precise chronology. In addition, the names of many figures,
and in some cases details about them, have been changed.

Lyrics to "McCarthy's Day" are reprinted courtesy of McCauley Music.

HarperCollins books may be purchased for educational, business,
or sales promotional use through our Special Markets Department.

HarperCollins Publishers Ltd
2 Bloor Street East, 20th Floor
Toronto, Ontario, Canada
M4W 1A8

www.harpercollins.ca

Library and Archives Canada Cataloguing in Publication
information is available upon request.

ISBN 978-1-55468-190-7

RRD 9 8 7 6 5 4 3 2 1

Printed and bound in the United States

To my father, Daniel Grafton Hill III,
and my mother, Donna Mae Hill.

PROLOGUE

1969: The Sample

Not that this is anything to brag about, but I may well have been the only teenager in the history of the Western world punished for not masturbating. As the sound of Dad's oversized feet clomped their way up the stairs and lumbered purposefully towards my bedroom, I braced myself for another of our confrontations. Still, I was in no way prepared for the perverse twist this, our third major argument in as many days, would take. Trust me, if I'd possessed advance knowledge of the screwball Q&A Dad was going to put me through I would have handily escaped out my bedroom window, always left open just in case. After all, any self-respecting teenager would have eagerly risked breaking an ankle over one of my dad's inquisitions.

Thwackkk! The door flew open, smashing against my bedroom wall and bouncing right back at Dad. He flicked out the big, broad palm of his hand with the speed and deftness of a seasoned boxer, steadying the door and then closing it behind him as if to say, "Whatever's about to go down between us stays in this room."

Then he said, in his patented Dad snarl, "Where is it, boy?"

"Where's what?"

"You know what I'm talking about."

"Sorry, Dad, I don't."

For once I wasn't lying. The kind of stuff I concealed from my old man wasn't really the sort of thing that could be found stashed away in my room, like, say, a skin magazine (Dad had been buying me *Playboys* since I'd turned eight), or his coveted World War II pistol, or a twenty-dollar bill he'd left sitting on his bedroom dresser. My secrets, my sweet little acts of rebellion and betrayal, were way cooler than that.

"Look up at me when I'm talking to you. And stop slouching over that daggum guitar of yours."

I tilted my head ever so slightly in his direction, careful to make sure his face was still out of my line of vision.

"That's better. Now, I'm talking about that sample of yours. The one you promised Dr. Peters you'd produce and have on his secretary's desk last week."

"Oh, that." I mumbled, straining to keep the "Oh God, here we go" out of my voice. This was going to get ugly. Beyond ugly. And Dad was just getting started.

"Stop your stalling, boy, and tell me, right this instant, where that sample is."

"I lost it."

"You're lying through your teeth, boy."

Something about the way my dad leaned on the word "boy," the way he used it as a kind of punctuation to cap off one of his insulting harangues, always pissed me off more than the harangue itself. "Boy" was what white officers called lowly Negro privates like Dad in the U.S. Army during World War II. And now, a quarter-century later, "boy" was what Dad called me to remind me that I was, and would always be, his subordinate. Still, boy or no boy, it occurred to me that I might just be able to take him. I was fifteen, on the high school wrestling and cross-country

Dan Hill

teams. Dad was forty-five, overweight, overworked and diabetic. But then I thought about how quickly he'd intercepted the bounce-back of my bedroom door. I knew from experience that his hands were big and fast, and I'd been on the receiving end of his out-of-nowhere slaps enough times to know better than to knuckle it out with him.

"There you go, daydreaming again. Get that moony look out of your eyes and start listening, carefully." Dad paused here, just to make sure his words were having the intended effect. They were.

"Danny, we both know that Dr. Peters gave you that deposit cup two weeks ago. I want your sperm sample in that cup and in his office by the end of the week. No ifs, ands or buts."

Just hearing that dreaded word, "sperm," made me shout out in protest: "No way I'm doing *that*. You can't make me. I don't care if I'm sterile. I don't wanna have kids anyway."

Saying that would wind Dad up even more, but I sure as hell wasn't going to tell him the real reason why Dr. Peters wasn't going to get his precious little sample out of me: I hadn't masturbated. And the closest I'd come to being sexually active was sneak-reading Dad's paperback copy of *Candy*, memorizing the juicy parts and reciting them to my thunderstruck classmates over the phone. Although, truth be told, even if I had been more, well, experienced, I would have put off delivering what my doctor had so breezily ordered. To see Dad go apoplectic at the thought of his first son possibly being sterile was high entertainment for me. I was, after all, Daniel Grafton Hill the Fourth, the eldest of three kids—the extension of the Hill family legacy rested on my shoulders, or, to be blunt, on my so far unproven ability to coax a sperm sample out of my reluctant body. Talk about pressure. Especially since, according to Dad, the Hill family was a superior species. "Hills were born to be extraordinary," he'd trumpet around the house with that mad grin sweeping across his face. After all, his PhD-toting father, Daniel Hill Jr., in his capacity as dean of the Howard University School of Religion, had moved in the highest circles of the "Negro elite," arranging in the early sixties for such luminaries as Dr. Martin Luther King Jr. to speak at his school. ("Continued success in the noble work that you are doing," the great human rights leader had written Granddad in a thank-you letter that kicked off a correspondence between them.)

Well. What Dad, currently the first director of the Ontario Human Rights Commission, was demanding of me could hardly be considered "noble." *What about my human rights?* I thought, as Dad, inching closer to me, clenching and unclenching his hands, hissed, "I'm warning you, boy, you're in no position to tell me what you will or won't do, so don't get sassy with me or I'll slap you sideways."

If this was meant to intimidate me, it had the opposite effect, as Dad's blows were never preceded by a warning. With him, violence and surprise came in the same package.

"I'm not trying to be sassy, Dad. I'm just saying that there's not a chance I'm gonna deliver a sperm sample for that perverted Dr. Peters."

Dad removed his glasses and slid them into his shirt pocket. I'd inadvertently issued him a challenge. Big mistake. He took a few seconds to mull over his response. Then he smiled. Not a good sign.

"I'm not wasting any more time on this foolishness. You've spent the whole daggum summer flat on your back with that crazy virus of yours."

"It's called orchitis, Dad."

"Call it whatever you want, your testicles were swollen up to the size of grapefruits. Your mother and I were worried sick about you. I don't know what you were doing at that summer camp up north, but it sure as hell wasn't pitching tents. This is not about you or your precious privacy. As your father, it's my right to know whether or not you're sterile."

"Jesus, Dad, I'm fifteen years old."

"That means you're old enough to picture what I'm about to say. If you don't have that sperm sample ready by the end of the week, you're gonna be bundled up in a straitjacket and dragged into Dr. Peters' office. Then you're gonna be strapped face down onto a cold, metal table with your legs forced wide apart, while the doctor gives you a prostate massage."

"What's a prostrate massage?"

"Prostate. It's what medics did to soldiers in the army when they needed a sperm sample. Once a doctor's finger winds its way deep into your raised hindquarters and makes contact with your prostate, you'll have an involuntary orgasm."

Dad snapped his fingers in front of my face, as if to drive home the horrifying image of me in the throes of some spastic orgasm, courtesy of Dr. Peters' frighteningly nimble, hairy finger.

"Trust me, son, once Peters is through with you, you'll have produced enough sperm to fill a milk bottle."

I blinked back at my dad, stupefied. For some reason, all I could think was that I'd never be able to drink a drop of milk again.

"Anyway, it's your choice, son. Either deliver that sperm sample on your own or the doctor lends his helping hand."

Dad's voice had softened, to the point of being almost cheerful. Like he'd done me a real favour by giving me these options. Then, acting as though this ridiculous conversation had never taken place, he brightly announced, "Don't forget, Danny. Dinner's at six sharp. I'm making my special meatloaf. Your mother's favourite."

With that he was out of my room. Trust Dad to storm into my room like some Black Marquis de Sade, batting around preposterous and disgusting threats, only to saunter out minutes later masquerading as Betty Crocker.

As if I hadn't been through enough that summer, laid out on my back with that just-kicked-in-the-balls feeling day in and day out, balancing an ice pack that leaked freezing water all over my scrotum. The rare times I'd risked the agony of walking, I'd tenderly cupped my elephantine testicles with both hands, convinced that if I didn't they'd burst right through the stretched-to-the-breaking-point sack of skin and drop, *ka-plunk,* like bowling balls, to the floor.

When I'd finally got better, Dr. Peters had checked me over and determined, in his clinically pinched tone: "I have to tell you, Danny, that there's some rather disturbing evidence of asymmetry down below." Then he ordered the sperm test, yanking a plastic cup out of one of his cupboards and handing it to me as if it were some sort of special bonus that came with visiting your friendly neighbourhood doctor.

How Dad got wind of this remains a mystery. I was long past the age of needing a parent to take me to the doctor. I don't mean to come off as paranoid, but at times I could have sworn he had spies everywhere, financed by some secret government payroll, who kept track of my every move. Why couldn't Dad be more like my pleasantly oblivious mom, who knew nothing about my post-orchitis "asymmetry" or the doctor's sample orders?

Suffice it to say that everything about my dad was way over the top, larger than life and outrageous in the extreme. Worse still, his need to control everyone around him, whether within our family or off at work—he was forever bragging about the size of his staff—rarely met with any kind of resistance. Alas, I was the sole exception that proved the rule. I delighted in defying him at every twist and turn, although usually my rebellion came in an indirect and sneaky form. Unfortunately, a sperm sample was a pretty black-and-white order, and, short of enlisting a "pinch hitter," either I complied with Dad's command or I faced the consequences.

However, since almost everything that leapt out of Dad's mouth was, if not an outright lie, an inspired exaggeration, I sensed that Dad's talk of me being kidnapped and deposited onto the doctor's examining table was just that: talk. I'd become something of an expert at sifting through and weighing his threats. Even the word "prostate" sounded suspect: yet another of Dad's elaborate made-up words. Surely, if such a revolting piece of anatomy actually existed, I would have heard of it by now, being that I possessed a pretty advanced sexual vocabulary. What I lacked in raw experience I made up for in literary research: Harold Robbins, D.H. Lawrence, Henry Miller, Anaïs Nin—hell, when you're hungry for knowledge, you don't discriminate. Whatever, prostate or no prostate, Dad's threat of what basically amounted to anal interference in the name of our family's future left me more than a little rattled.

At least I'd been smart enough to stay seated on my bed, hunched over my guitar, throughout most of our little showdown, thus denying Dad the satisfaction of seeing my face flush a deep sunburned red at the thought of Dr. Peters bearing down on me with his gloved, wiggling middle finger. With respect to the daily dust-ups between Dad and me, any victory that came my way, however small and fleeting, gave me the strength I needed to keep my side of the war going strong. Now that he'd finally left my room I could get back to working on my new song. It was about a half-Black teenager who drops out of high school and leaves home to become a famous singer. Aside from that, it wasn't really autobiographical.

As I predicted, Dad never followed through on his threat to have me dragged like a prisoner into Dr. Peters' office to endure the unendurable. Knowing all along that he couldn't force me to comply with his demand, his real punishment for my refusal was not a prostate massage but the threat of it. Indeed, the bizarre scenario of being kidnapped and deposited on Dr. Peters' "massage" table left me wrestling with a mortifying image that spooked me for months.

Dad, no doubt satisfied that I'd suffered the appropriate consequence for my disobedience—absolute humiliation—never mentioned the sperm sample again.

CHAPTER 1

Mom's Pregnant Appendix

The story leading up to my birth goes something like this: when Mom told Dad she was going into labour, Dad responded by stroking her pregnant stomach, her roundness swallowed up by his massive palm, and cooing, in his honeyed voice, "Relax, Donna, it's probably just a gas bubble."

Mom apparently responded to Dad's homespun diagnosis by snapping, "Honestly, Dan! I think can tell the difference between labour pains and gas."

Only Dad, with his wide-open brown face and melt-the-world smile, could make the term "gas bubble" sound romantic. According to my mom, he fervently believed that every affliction known to man sprang from somewhere deep in the bowels. Still, Dad continued his caressing—likely to soothe himself as much as my mother that this was a false alarm. Because, gas or no gas, my dad wasn't ready for my mom to give birth. Not only was my mom just eight months pregnant, but

I was totally unplanned. Perhaps he believed that as long as his wife's pains were little more than, say, undigested avocado, then his indomitable will could put off her labour indefinitely.

Dad wanted to get his PhD before becoming a father, and Mom, barely twenty-six, was just getting the hang of living in Canada.

They'd met only fifteen months earlier and were still swept up in the heady, "everything is new and exciting" stage of their relationship. So why complicate things by starting a family so soon? Though neither ever said as much to me, the timing of my arrival, while not necessarily disastrous, was hardly convenient.

Mom had finished work at the Ontario Planning Council the day before going into labour and had been looking forward to taking the next four weeks off. She'd read up on pregnancy and labour, proudly sharing her newfound knowledge with anyone who'd listen. But the pains that woke her Saturday morning didn't come close to fitting the description of the labour pains she'd read about in her books. Still, Mom, tenacious and tough as she was tiny, hung on until noon before calling her obstetrician at home. "Come in after dinner," came the doctor's unhurried reply, which Mom heard as, "Suck it up, toots. Hold on till I've finished eating."

"You'd think I'd called him to complain about a hangnail," was how Mom later described the doctor's dismissive tone, making it eminently clear to her that, doctor or not, this guy was a first-class jerk. She'd met him at a monthly prenatal clinic. The clinic was free and my parents were poor, with no family doctor or health coverage. So Mom was hardly in a position to challenge the doctor's mealtime routine. But her pains weren't adhering to any convenient timetable. They were getting worse, like nothing she'd ever felt before. However, despite knowing she might very well give birth at any time, while dealing with a husband in denial and a doctor who seemed to expect her to give birth according to his meal schedule, Mom didn't complain. That was not her style. "It's not as if complaining would've made the pain any better," she would explain later, in that dry, logical way of hers.

Dan Hill

Dad checked Mom into emergency at 7:00 p.m. Despite the waiting area being next to empty, they sat there, ignored, for half an hour. Then an hour. Then ninety minutes. By the time the doctor finally appeared to take Mom back to the examining room she was too buckled over in agony to catch the look in his eyes. *That look.* But Dad couldn't miss it. He shifted his two-hundred-plus pounds uncomfortably in his chair as he watched the doctor take in first his white-skinned, waiflike wife, whose bulbous stomach, seemingly tacked onto her diminutive frame, gave her the appearance of a lost teenager—and then him: big, lumbering and imposingly brown.

Two more doctors appeared.

"Maybe it was the hospital's idea of a security measure," wondered Mom, when thinking back on it. "I mean, from no doctors anywhere in sight for hours, to suddenly three doctors, once word spread of this pregnant white woman with a Black husband . . ."

All at once the three doctors started poking my mom—here, there and everywhere—and asking the obvious "Does this hurt, does that hurt?" kind of questions. Finally, one of the doctors placed his hand on her belly and said, "That feels like a real labour pain to me."

To which the eminent senior doctor replied: "She's too early to be in labour. She's having an appendicitis attack. We're going to operate for appendicitis." The other two doctors, outranked, looked down at the floor.

They anaesthetized Mom, and Dad was told to go home. A doctor was as close as you could get to God in 1950s Toronto. But Dad, a not-so-recently converted atheist, knew that something wasn't quite right. Still, he did the math. American Negro. Caucasian, Canadian doctor. Well, thank goodness his wife was white. Maybe, just maybe, all the hostility was directed at him. Which, if true, suggested that once he was out of the picture, the doctors would get down to the business at hand: taking care of his wife. At any rate, in the fifties, men did not hang around delivery rooms when their wives were giving birth. Or having their appendices removed. So Dad reluctantly left the hospital, assuming that he'd return the following morning to be greeted by a newborn baby and an exhausted, but happy, appendix-free wife.

My dad was more wowed by the status of the professional class, i.e., doctors and lawyers, than my mom, who, in her true iconoclastic fashion, thought everyone was full of shit until proven otherwise. And, more to the point, she was the only woman there among all those males. *Medical degrees or not,* she must have been thinking, *what the fuck do any of them know about labour pains?*

At least Mom was unconscious when Dad left the hospital. He wouldn't have been able to leave her had she still been awake. Still, Dad surely felt the strangest kind of loneliness, leaving her in the hands of these doctors. Other than his work or studies, he chose to spend every waking and sleeping second with his wife, doting on her like a love-struck puppy, as if he still couldn't believe how lucky he was that she had agreed to move to Canada with him, a country where she knew no one. "Married or unmarried?" had been her only question.

They'd been married for almost a year now.

On the drive home, my dad must have tried to brush aside his doubts. About the obstetrician. About the hospital. This was Canada, after all, not America. He'd spent most of the last five years studying and working in Toronto, a city he'd described in a letter to his parents as "splendid but still tainted." People were not so aggressively racist here. Or, as Dad went on to observe, it was a country that practised "discrimination of a more subtle, insidious nature than I've seen in the U.S. . . . it exists in the snide remarks of a potential employer or the sly but highly polite way in which you are refused a room."

And so Dad, opting for Toronto's subtlety over America's blatant racism, had adopted Canada as his permanent home, thrilled that his new bride was quick to share his guarded enthusiasm for this "splendid but tainted" city. In coming here, she'd trusted him completely. Did that blind trust weigh heavily on him as he drove his ancient Plymouth down deserted University Avenue? Was his hope that his wife and baby would be properly cared for eclipsed by a sense that something was a little off about the doctor? Did he explain the feeling away as paranoia, a leftover from the racism of his U.S. Army days ?

Maybe Dad couldn't bring himself to look at the bed when he opened the door to their tiny basement apartment. Maybe the thought of laying down without her beside him on a mattress that, for the first time, would have felt way too big, was what caused him to trudge over to his desk, where a full bottle of whiskey was sitting. Dad would later claim, with vaguely sheepish pride, that he was still clutching the bottle to his chest when the phone call from the hospital woke him from a drunken sleep, several hours later.

The appendectomy was completed by one in the morning. When Mom woke up in the surgery recovery room to searing pain, she started wailing to anyone within earshot that she was still in labour. The nurses called for a sedative, perhaps hoping to shut her up.

"Oh yes, it's possible you're in labour," the doctor allowed grandly, after checking on her. Then he left as quickly as he had appeared, without sharing his revised diagnosis with any of the nurses. Mom, too exhausted to scream anymore, was left alone, whimpering—from being cut open and stitched back together, from labour pains and worst of all, from not knowing if there was an end to this torture.

As Mom's water broke, one of the nurses, unable to see the trace of the fluid due to Mom's swaddling of bandages, started to scold her for deliberately urinating.

"I believe you're in labour, but don't tell anyone I told you this," a nurse's aide whispered, like she'd made some breakthrough discovery, once the first, clucking nurse had disappeared. "Don't push," she continued, wheeling Mom into an elevator.

"I have to push!" Mom groaned, weakly.

She was whisked into the labour room in the obstetrical ward upstairs. "The baby's head is right there," someone yelled, and Mom was promptly rolled right back onto the stretcher and rushed into the delivery room. Someone yelled "Scrub!" and Mom croaked, "I wanna have a natural delivery," just as the anaesthesia was clamped over her face. The doctor, worrying that, among other things, the new stitches from Mom's appendectomy might not hold, did an episiotomy. I like to think that I played a small in part keeping her stitches intact, as I slid into the world the morning of June 3, 1954, weighing only five pounds.

Dad, upon returning to the hospital, caught in the grogginess between fading drunkenness and rising hangover, was taken aside by one of the three doctors who had originally examined Mom.

"I witnessed your wife's operation and read the report. Her appendix was perfectly normal," he said. But as the obstetrician waltzed in, the doctor's revelations faded into a scratchy, deferential cough.

"Well that wasn't so bad, was it?" the obstetrician offered, looking blithely down at Mom.

It's hard to know what Dad made of all this. This was one story he never spoke about directly, which, given Dad's penchant for wild tales, can be interpreted any number of ways. Instead he cloaked the entire episode in his usual grandstanding humour, throwing the focus of Mom's delivery back onto himself. "I left your mother in the hospital that night and curled up with a big bottle of whiskey. In no time flat I downed the whole bottle. Passed out slumped over my daggum study desk. Ha ha ha. Next thing I know I'm back in the hospital the following morning and there you are—heaven's sakes alive—born a whole month early. You were so itsy-bitsy they damned near stuck you in an incubator. Imagine that."

As always with Dad, his style of storytelling—brashly triumphant, his face swallowed up in a huge lopsided grin—easily upstaged the substance. If Dad appeared to find downing a whole bottle of booze holed up in his one-room flat hilarious, as a child, I found it heroic.

Mom, par for the course, was perfectly content to let Dad tell the story of my birth from his comic-book perspective. But how did Dad honestly feel about his wife having her "perfectly normal" appendix removed while she was in labour? Did he feel guilt or shame for abandoning his wife to a night of unimaginable hell? Or did he even see it that way?

My guess is that Dad couldn't bear to think about it, choosing instead to cover Mom's tired face in loud kisses and let himself be swept up in the excitement of being a new father with a healthy baby and a wife who had managed, miraculously, to come through this nightmare in one piece. Still, when the doctor beneath Mom's obstetrician told my dad that his wife's appendix was perfectly normal, Dad must have allowed himself to believe, if only for an instant, that he'd fallen short as a husband of properly protecting his wife. He never made that mistake again. For the rest of his life, he was her self-appointed protector, her unshakable armour, hovering over her like a second shadow.

I didn't get Mom's side of this story, in all its lurid detail, until a few years ago when visiting her at home. I didn't dare ask her if she felt as though her husband had abandoned her that night. That would have brought our discussion to an abrupt end, with my mom glowering at me as if I'd blasphemed my father. And really, I loved that she was so unfailingly loyal. It reassured me. Surely, if she loved him so deeply that she couldn't stand to hear me or anyone else question, even indirectly, his character, that had to say something about my father as a man. As a husband. As a father. And naturally, Mom's protectiveness, her ferocious loyalty, extended to her children as well. Typical for Mom that she managed to tell the story of my birth and tie it all together with an improbably upbeat conclusion.

"Danny, you must have picked up on the terror I went through right before your birth. You could hear me begging for help. Feeling utterly alone. This is why you turned out to be such an extraordinarily sensitive child."

Mom smiled at me adoringly as she said this, as if all that she went through at that hospital was well worth it. But feeling uncomfortable with being called an "extraordinarily sensitive child," I quickly changed the subject: "How could a doctor, an obstetrician at that, possibly confuse labour with an appendicitis attack?" I kept hoping that if I questioned her story enough times, she'd finally give me a different answer. That she'd eventually smile and say, "I admit it, Danny. You got me. I was just kidding." Or, better still, "Your father tossed that doctor out of the way, saved my appendix in the nick of time and then delivered you with his bare hands."

But Mom's answer never changed. "That doctor needed to practise."

"Practise what?"

"You know what I'm talking about, Danny. The doctor, the obstetrician I mean," she said, pausing to sarcastically draw out each of the syllables, "needed the experience of performing an appendectomy on a pregnant woman."

I've thought about this so often, wondering if it possibly could be true, that the obvious question didn't occur to me right away. Maybe because that kind of premeditated cruelty, particularly when it concerned my mother, was too awful for me to consider. Nevertheless, one day, when I was backing out of my mom's driveway, and she was waving goodbye in that little-girl way of hers, I suddenly wondered if my mom's needless appendectomy had been a kind of punishment for being a pregnant white woman married to a very big, very confident Negro in 1954. I didn't know then and I don't know now, but just the idea of it sends chills down my spine.

Whatever the impetus for that night's harrowing events, Mom's unnecessarily difficult labour and birth of me seemed to serve as an indicator for the type of family we would eventually become: outsiders, wary of the world hovering just beyond our doorstep, forever suspicious that its motives ran counter to our collective and individual well-being. Our only recourse was to question everything, be it Mother's Day or the Lord's Prayer, the domino theory or Boy Scouts. To survive in such a world was challenge enough, but to thrive, to leave an indelible mark, you had to embrace cunning and gamesmanship, balance brains and bravado, while always remaining on the highest alert. If you didn't, sooner or later you'd find yourself flat on your back and defenceless, waiting for the world to reach in and rip you apart from the inside. Just because it could.

A Brief (Well, Not That Brief) Explanation

After a long and courageous struggle with diabetes, and an infection-induced coma, my dad passed away in 2003. The morning after his death I sat, hunched over, with my forehead resting on my arms and my arms pressed flat on my piano keys. Music had always been my healer, my therapy, in the face of all manner of personal disaster, humiliation or, as in this case, irreplaceable loss. But not that morning. When my piano yielded up little more than watered-down Billy Joel imitations, I turned to my guitar. The same guitar I'd purchased thirty-one years before for four hundred dollars, that being all the money I earned from my first recording session when I was signed as an artist to RCA Records.

"Boy, it's a crying-out-loud disgrace for you to throw that kind of money away on a bloomin' guitar. You're a high school dropout, making a buck eighty-nine an hour at the civil service. Donna, try talking some sense into this hard-headed kid of ours, he's gonna spend the rest of his life in the poorhouse."

The memory of Dad's yelping blended into my guitar chords. The well-worn Martin D-35 had travelled around the world with me more times than I could count, coaxing thousands of songs out of my fingers over the years. Most of those songs haven't amounted to all that much. Not that it matters, since right from the beginning, I've written songs simply because I've had no other choice. Nevertheless, a handful of my songs have earned me enough money to ensure that I'll never have to bother with a real job, indeed, more money than I'd have ever dreamed possible when I started composing at fourteen, holed up in my bedroom, a temporary haven from Dad's high-spirited teasing. I've never tried to add it all up, but it's safe to say that the combined unit sales of all my songs (between my own numerous albums and all the international artists who have recorded my songs) is in the range of one hundred million. This means that I fall asleep every night and wake up the following morning a few bucks richer, simply because somewhere, on some radio station, TV channel or movie screen, one of my songs is being performed. Or ringtoned. Or lampooned. Or someone in Germany, Japan or Argentina is purchasing a Britney Spears, Celine Dion or Tina Turner CD that I had a hand in writing, which means I'll eventually receive—*ka-ching*—a royalty.

But the morning after Dad died, all my pipeline royalties seemed pretty meaningless. All the songs I'd cast out into the world—hits, misses and the somewhere in-betweens—weren't going to bring him back. Still I pressed on, the familiar hiss of my tape recorder sounding like an ancient kettle on the boil, knowing that the alternative, sitting alone with my thoughts while staring blankly at my untouched instruments, would leave me all the more susceptible to a blackness of mood that could easily consume me. Anything, even writing lousy songs, was better than that.

"It's okay," I caught myself saying, "you don't have to write a hit today. Write something just for fun. A title. Or the opening chords to an intro."

As I mechanically strummed away, juggling time signatures like Sinatra juggled women—"Try 12/8," I told myself, sounding more like a used car salesman than a songwriter, "Streisand's always been a sucker for faux European waltzes"—snippets of past conversations with Dad whirled around in my head, variations really on the same old theme, over and over, year after year. I'd phone him, out of my mind with excitement over what I considered to be my latest career breakthrough, thinking that finally I'd done it, I'd pulled off the impossible: I'd accomplished something that would finally make Dad proud of me.

1972: "You won't believe this, Dad. I've just been offered a recording contract with RCA Records."

"That's right, boy, I don't believe you for a second. You're lying through your teeth, like you always do."

1973: "Hey Dad, guess what? I just finished meeting with Harry Belafonte in Manhattan. He wants to record some of my songs."

"Donna, it's that head-in-the-clouds son of ours, Danny, on the phone. He made it back from New York City in one piece. Now he's making up some nonsense about doing some business with Harry Belafonte."

1979: "Dad, sorry if I'm calling so late. It's only nine o'clock here in L.A. 'Sometimes When We Touch' is becoming one of the biggest songs of the decade here in America. My managers tell me I can retire on this song."

"Wake up, Donna. Get this! Danny thinks he's gonna go down in family history as the first Hill millionaire."

"Dad, I never said anything about being—"

"Ha, ha, ha!" Dad's laughter cuts off my backpedalling. "Son, you know your mother and I don't trust those managers of yours. If I were you, I'd watch them like a hawk. And remember, any money they actually fork over to you should be banked and collecting interest. So you can help pay for your brother and sister's university education."

"I'm already doing that, Dad."

"Good. Keep it up."

Dad pauses to take in something Mom is telling him. I can make out a stern, "Quiet, Dan. Listen for once." This is followed by the muffled sound of brief quarrelling, before Dad resumes with a rather forced, "Your mother wants to know if you have any other news."

"Well, yeah, I've just found out that I've been nominated for a Grammy."

"You're getting a Grammy? As a songwriter? Wait till I tell your grandpar—"

"No, as male vocalist of the year. And I haven't won the Grammy, I've only been nominated."

"They're not giving out any awards for songwriting?"

I'm tempted to say, "That's right, Dad, the Grammys only award singing," but, sensing that Dad is laying a trap here and that, really, he knows the Grammys have a songwriting category, I confess, lamely, that I haven't been nominated as a songwriter.

"How did that happen? Hills are born to be great writers. Danny, I've told you since I can remember: pretty voices come and go like yesterday's news. But words, words last forever."

In a perverse way, I came to look forward to Dad's skepticism regarding my music. His off-the-cuff putdowns, his unwavering cynicism, was part of what made him Dad, and a big part of what made me, to use Dad's mocking term, "the first Hill millionaire," with an eventual Grammy award as a producer (sorry Dad, never got one as a writer, yet), five Junos and countless gold and platinum albums. If trying to win Dad over had been a big part of the driving force behind the forty-nine-year war between us, it had been a war I'd come to secretly enjoy as much as outwardly despise it. The rivalry, the never-ending push and pull, the constant battles, helped define who I was. It was what drove me. And it was never supposed to end. Except that it did end, on June 26, 2003, at 3:42 in the afternoon.

"Goodbye, Dad." My brother Larry's words, uttered the very instant Dad slipped away, had sounded so casual, so eerily conversational— as though our father had simply strolled off to the store to buy one of his disgusting Cuban cigars and he'd be back in no time—that it took a beat or two before they registered. *Goodbye, Dad.* Larry's words kept echoing, pinging, softer and softer, turning over in my head, until I finally let them in, only to realize that they were the saddest words I'd ever heard.

The whole family was crowded around Dad in Toronto's St. Michael's Hospital. His intubator had been removed several hours earlier, leaving him to breathe on his own. He'd been in a coma for more than a week. He would only be able to breathe unassisted like this for a short while. And then he wouldn't be able to breathe at all.

A monitor attached to the wall above his bed displayed his vital signs. A few minutes earlier, my wife had pointed to the screen, showing me in furtive sign language that Dad's steadily slowing heart rate spiked whenever Mom stroked his hand or arm. Why did she have to show me this? What did his spiking heart rate mean? That even as Dad lay dying, his love for his wife, my mother, was still a force, an unstoppable force, unto itself? For the next few hours we watched Dad's heart rate and blood pressure blip up and down on the screen, the numbers gradually, inexorably dropping lower and lower. It made me think of watching TV as a child, with Dad warning me in that take-no-prisoners voice of his that my daily allotted half-hour of television time was quickly coming to an end. Only now it was his time coming to an end. I almost expected his voice to boom out with one last speech, one final command. Instead, without warning, the numbers abruptly disappeared and the screen went black. And just like that it was over.

Somehow I'd anticipated this, felt a foreshadowing, and had stepped aside so Larry could slip in to lean close to Dad and touch him one last time before the unthinkable happened. Because really, despite all of the years building up to this, it was unthinkable to me that Dad could ever, would ever, stop living. *Goodbye, Dad.* Larry's words had jolted me on so many levels that I found myself blinking back floating stars as I stared, numbly and silently, at the blackened TV screen, willing it to turn on again. I blinked again. Then I realized that everyone was crying. Everyone, that is, except me. Dad had taught me, as the oldest child, to always remain strong, stoic, especially when everyone around me is losing it. But who was I kidding? We were all lost now. Lost behind our hospital masks and goggles and gloves and gowns, courtesy of the SARS scare that had recently swept through Toronto. So I couldn't see the tears. I could only hear the sobs, slowly rising to wails.

I turned and reached out for Mom. She looked impossibly, heart-breakingly small. Like she might disappear. Breaking hospital protocol, she removed her mask. Then she leaned over Dad, tucked her delicate and petite hands underneath his wide, brown shoulders as if to steady herself and kissed him tenderly on the forehead as I'd seen her do thou-sands of times before. "Goodbye, sweet, sweet man," she said, softly. Then I held her and we all walked out of the room.

A week later, and still, every time I closed my eyes and started stumbling onto a few desultory chord progressions, that final, terrible moment came back to me. I sure as hell was not going to write a song about that. And somehow, I didn't think the uplifting ditty that the Backstreet Boys needed to rescue their career would be spilling out of me that day, if ever again. I gently placed my guitar down on the piano bench. What was the point in writing a big ol' hit song, when, after the fact, there'd be no one for me to phone about "a big, fat, juicy royalty cheque"—

that's how Dad described them when he was in one of his rare chari-table moods—and no one telling me to "pipe down" when I'd phone, excited, demanding that Dad switch the radio station from his beloved CBC to the latest pop or country station, to catch my new single.

As time passed and I still couldn't finish a halfway-decent song, I began to worry. What if, when Dad died, all the music in me shrivelled up and died along with him? I had to do something. Without songwrit-ing, I was a forty-nine-year-old man with no skills and only a grade twelve education. I hadn't worked—in the traditional sense, meaning a boss, structured hours and a fixed paycheque—for close to thirty years. The good news was my annual royalty flow meant I never really needed to work again. That was also the bad news.

I've always wondered what happens to those guys who rob a bank and move to Mexico with more money than they can spend in a life-time. The movie always ends with the outlaws kicking back on some beach, throwing back margaritas, flanked by briefcases jammed with cash. So what do these newly rich badasses do for the rest of their lives? From my perspective, that's when the real movie begins.

In a way, my real movie began not so long after Dad died, when, finding myself still creatively washed out and looking for something to do, I ended up buried in the Archives of Ontario building in downtown Toronto. Due to my father's groundbreaking work in human rights and Canadian Black history, he had been convinced to donate his papers to the federal and provincial governments. These papers included not only his professional notes, but seventy-plus years of personal correspon-dence. It was this personal correspondence, something I'd always sworn I'd never look through while Dad was alive, that I was most interested in. These letters represented the contents, the stages, of Dad's life—his world, his secrets, his self-destructive behaviour as a teenager, his time in the U.S. Army, his much-talked-about successes, his never-mentioned failures and humiliations, and all points in between, revealed, betrayed if you will, in his own words. Some of Dad's letters were so old—a brief and quite obviously coerced note in his six-year-old scrawl to his grand-parents thanking them for a birthday present—that merely touching the original paper it was written on felt like an offence, a violation. It seemed possible that these razor-thin sheets of paper might come apart in my hands, not unlike the wings of a moth caught between a child's curious fingers.

Dad's startling letters might never have come to light had it not been for my sleuthlike brother stumbling across them while staying with our grandparents in Washington, D.C. A typical teenager (like me) would have given them a perfunctory glance, tossed them indifferently back into their dusty, indexed boxes and continued rummaging through the nooks and crannies of my grandparents' basement hoping to discover—what else—a discarded *Playboy* or trashy novel. But Larry, following in Dad's footsteps as indefatigable family historian and showing early signs of his future stint as a newspaper reporter, scooped up all of Dad's letters, spent days reading and sorting them chronologically, and presented them to our flabbergasted dad many years later as a surprise birthday gift.

I can still recall the hush that fell over our family once Dad, upon tearing through Larry's immaculate wrapping job, discovered what he'd assumed was safely hidden from public view: a deeply intimate record of his innermost thoughts, his sometimes rash decisions along with their brutal consequences, spanning hundreds of pages and several decades, including, most notably, his U.S. Army letters from the years 1942 to 1946. To look at Dad's scowling face, one might have thought Larry had just given him a lifetime's honorary membership in the Ku Klux Klan.

The year was 1980. Dad had just turned fifty-seven. I'd recently returned from performing in Japan and was living, 24–7, for my pop music career. To my typically self-involved way of thinking at the time, I was too busy making history to want to waste my time wallowing in anyone else's, least of all Dad's, family history. So, I paid little attention to Dad's stony silence, assuming his reaction was similar to mine: who in their right mind would choose to waste their time reading musty old letters they'd written half a century ago?

Now, only a few years younger than Dad was then, I've come to understand the significance of family history. But it wasn't until I fell under the spell of Dad's letters that I understood just how fully Dad's family history shaped and moulded him into the man, the husband, the human rights activist and, most significantly to me, the father he ultimately became. Which of course influenced, for better and for worse, the man that I've become.

The months leading up to, and immediately following, Dad's death, I'd become untethered, downing a bottle of wine every night alone in my living room while the world around me slept, careful not to let anyone (particularly my wife and son) see me sloshed. In case the wine wasn't enough to render me sufficiently numb, I'd throw back a couple of prescription sleeping pills and wait for the nothingness to neutralize all that inconvenient, stultifying sadness. By the time I came to the next day, the darkness would have returned: spreading, intensifying, threatening to pull me under. The afternoon that I sat in the government archives building, slowly peeling back the layers, the pages of my dad's life, I began, very slowly, to see my way out of the darkness and back into the light. My greatest shot at surviving, of moving on with my own life after Dad's death, was to do what I'd always done. Write. But not songs this time. Only a book could come close to capturing the story of Dad and me. His journey. And mine. How our lives intersected, crossed over and ran parallel as we jostled, challenged, inspired and jockeyed for control. Of ourselves. Of each other.

Every family has its attendant dramas, its unique set of horrors and tragedies, triumphs and unsolved mysteries. I was determined—obsessed actually—to figure out, through writing this book, what it was that made Dad's and my relationship so bloody peculiar and yet so universal. So spectacularly and unintentionally funny and so heart-crushingly sad. I wanted to figure out why he felt so compelled to dominate me (and everyone else in his circle of loved ones) through brilliant and slyly unexpected manoeuvres of cruelty, humiliation and emotional blackmail, and then, without warning, turn inspiring and loving in ways that made me feel as though I could achieve anything.

To honour Dad's favourite quote, "A man has as many selves as he has situations" (which he attributed to an old sociologist), I interviewed many family members, former employees and co-workers of Dad's, and several of Dad's close friends, people who had known him and seen him operate in just about every capacity and situation save one: father. That was my job. Their impressions, recollections of and experiences with Dad, while always vivid, moving and frequently entertaining, rarely coincided with, and often contradicted, mine.

No son can be objective about his father. And certainly a man as complicated as my father defies easy, conventional analysis. I suppose in a way this is Dad's final, posthumous challenge to me. And so, for me to even attempt to unravel my father's many selves, I must start from the beginning: Dad's beginnings. But just one last thing before this, his story, our story, unfolds. As I fell under the spell of writing this book, tumbling deeper and deeper into Dad's captivating, moving and astonishingly secretive life, an unexpected bonus slowly unfolded before me, like a precious gift. I felt, ironically, closer, more connected to Dad, as he sprang back to life in these pages, than ever before.

CHAPTER 2

Dad's Family History

D ad never told me that his maternal great-grandmother, Genevieve Coakley, worked as a seamstress in President Grant's White House. For a man who lived to tell stories, outrageous stories, most of which revolved around the extraordinary achievements of generation upon generation of Hills, this was a rather curious omission. But there was a reason why the story of Genevieve Coakley was too outrageous for even Dad to talk about. It was too odious to bear repeating. After all, what dad in his right mind would tell his little boy that his great-grandmother, at sixteen, had been raped?

It gets worse. Apparently, Dad's great-grandmother was raped by a white man who also worked in the White House. (The identity of the rapist is not known.) The rape resulted in Dad's great-grandmother giving birth to a daughter, my dad's grandmother Marie Coakley, in 1876. Marie was raised to believe that her grandparents were her parents, and that her sixteen-year-old mother was her older sister. She didn't discover the truth until she was an adult.

"I am not a bastard child!" Marie was reported to have screamed, recoiling in shame, when one of her aunts finally confronted her with the truth.

How does a Black, teenaged girl born into slavery manage to get a job working in, of all places, the White House? Well, it certainly helped that Genevieve Coakley had an unusually enterprising father, Gabriel Coakley. He had petitioned for, and was granted permission to purchase, his entire family's freedom in 1862 for $3,300, when Genevieve was a little girl. (Some of the more "lenient" slave masters allowed their slaves to work at paying jobs in the evenings and weekends, once their regular duties had been completed.) Barely two years into his new life as a free man, Gabriel Coakley, along with a small group of recently freed Blacks, somehow wrangled a meeting with President Lincoln. During the brief meeting, Coakley asked President Lincoln for permission to hold a fundraiser on the White House lawn to help fund the building of St. Augustine's Church. President Lincoln granted this permission, allowing the event to take place on July 4. Both Lincoln and his wife, Mary Todd, participated and made donations, inspiring everyone else to make generous donations as well. And so, beyond Gabriel Coakley successfully raising funds for what turned out to be Washington, D.C.'s first Black Catholic church, a significant connection was established between his family and the White House, which likely resulted in Gabriel Coakley's daughter Genevieve working in the White House as a seamstress.

I don't tell the story of how Dad's grandmother Marie was conceived, or the cover-up that followed, to suggest that what happened in our family was, from a historical vantage point, particularly unusual. It's hardly breaking news that the rape of Black females, whether slaves or several generations removed from slavery, was frequently committed by white males in power. (Despite former president Thomas Jefferson's denials, DNA evidence confirms that Sally Hemings, a slave of Jefferson's, bore six children fathered by someone in the Jefferson family. Recent research has all but proved that it was Jefferson himself.) I tell this story because the rape by a white male of a Black female, particularly, but not exclusively, when resulting in a pregnancy, can set off a ripple effect of shame that impacts generation after generation. This is certainly not to suggest that white-on-Black rape represents the only cause of racial self-loathing. Nor do I claim that the cover-ups, the secrets or the "passing" as white or, equally destructive, the unacknowledged, elevated social status of lighter-skinned Blacks at the expense of Blacks of darker complexions, can be traced solely to one heinous incident lurking, unacknowledged, in the past.

There is also another side to one's contradictory feelings about being Black, whether light-skinned or dark-skinned or the thousands of shades in between. The best chance of surviving with any semblance of dignity, while protecting against future victimization, is to achieve. And to never stop achieving. Call it compensation, a way of establishing, as best one can, some distance from past humiliations, whether exacted the year before or generations past.

I am not so foolish as to suggest that this phenomenon is exclusive to my family, nor is it exclusive to any particular race. Nevertheless, this is my story, my family's story, and race plays a huge role. With that in mind, I will skip a few generations, leaping from my great-grandmother Marie's birth in 1876 to my father's, a half-century later.

My dad was born in Independence, Missouri, in 1923. Officially christened Daniel Grafton Hill III, in order to avoid name confusion he was nicknamed Buddy by his maternal grandfather, Dr. Thomas W. Edwards. The nickname proved prescient; from infancy on he remained fiercely loyal to his sisters, appointing himself, frequently to their annoyance, their protector and comrade. His unflagging devotion to his family, combined with what his youngest sister, Doris, characterized as his "great, spontaneous sense of humour," meant the nickname stuck with him for the rest of his life.

My dad's paternal great-grandfather, Richard Hill, had been born a slave in Maryland, but in the late 1800s managed to buy freedom for himself, his wife, Demias Crew, and their family. Daniel Hill I, my dad's grandfather, was born into freedom a few years later. The youngest of ten children, he was still a toddler when his mother died, leaving his overwhelmed father little choice but to send young Daniel to live with a white Quaker family. The practice of Black parents shipping one of their young children off to live with a "benevolent" white family was common at this time, as it afforded the Black child a valued opportunity to enjoy the advantages of a solid education, something that would have otherwise been unattainable. Daniel's departure was unusual in the sense that white families preferred taking in girls rather than boys, for the reason that Negro girls were viewed by whites as more acceptable and less threatening than their brothers. Young Daniel, however, more than earned his keep while growing up with his adopted Quaker family, taking on the lion's share of the household chores and earning top grades in high school and later at Storer College in Harpers Ferry, West Virginia. Upon graduating from Lincoln University he became a minister at the Bethel African Methodist Episcopal (AME) Church in Baltimore.

My grandfather was the second Daniel Grafton Hill (Dan II, as I'll call him), and, determined to follow in his father's footsteps, he also became an AME minister, eventually getting his doctorate in sacred divinity and serving as the dean of the School of Religion at Howard University in Washington, D.C.

My grandmother, May Louise Edwards, came from a prominent Catholic family that included doctors and dentists. Belonging to the small class of Black professionals was of utmost importance to May's parents, as it was a rare and prestigious position for Black Americans. All the more reason for May's mother, Marie, to make sure that the shameful (and damaging) details of her parentage would never come to light. Anxious to ensure that her children not do anything to jeopardize their upper-class status, Marie made every effort possible to steer them clear of middle-class or lower-income Blacks, while encouraging them to interact with lighter-skinned, bourgeois-leaning Negroes. Marie's obsessive class consciousness all but derailed my grandmother May's marriage to the much darker skinned Dan II, who came from an "undesirable" (as in middle-class) family. In the long run, however, Marie's dramatic interventions made my grandparents all the more inseparable. Even the story of how they were introduced is the stuff of old-fashioned, sepia-toned movies.

"When I met your grandfather he looked so handsome and dignified in his World War I officer's uniform," Grandma May always told us, implying that this was the way Granddad was dressed the first time the two of them met. But May had been introduced to my grandfather once before when he'd dropped by her house to meet up with one of her brothers. Since he wasn't in military uniform that first time, he barely made an impression. When Dan appeared at May's house the next time outfitted in full military regalia, she never suspected that this dashing display was for her benefit. This time May was smitten. That Dan II was an officer, a highly esteemed achievement for a young Negro at that time, undoubtedly added to his regal bearing.

As for Dan II, he always swore that "I fell in love with your grandmother the moment I saw her. And I've loved her ever since." It came as little surprise that he said those same words during their sixtieth anniversary celebration; everyone knew that this was one of the few stories Granddad didn't alter with each telling.

"Oh shush," May would always whisper with a bashful smile in response to Granddad's romantic outpouring. A glance at any of Granddad's letters to May, written when he served in France as a second lieutenant during World War I, exemplifies both his love for his young bride and his droll humour. "Dearest Little Girl," he wrote in August 1918:

> I have been able to visit the post office daily only to find nothing from the States. I guess there is mail here somewhere for me but as usual there often happens to be a tie-up at one of the bases; then again a Deutsch submarine gets in a lucky shot occasionally and thereby sends a few loving letters to the bottom to be censored by "sea-weed" and "sharks" . . . I am just about as crazy as I can be to hear from you and the home folk . . . my opportunities [to write] will decrease in the future, but you must

*never weary or despair of hearing from your boy . . . Take good
care my little girl, May, my wife.*

Your boy, Dan

Whenever my dad told me stories about his parents, he tended to
spare the mushy stuff and cut right to the heart of the action: "My poor
mother! Right after she eloped with my father he was shipped off to
fight the Germans in World War I. He killed a lot of enemy soldiers in
close quarters, in dagger-to-dagger combat."

"That's enough, Dan," Mom would interject, steering the subject
to something more child-friendly. "Did you know, children, that when
your grandfather was in the war your grandmother May graduated
from Howard University with a degree in English literature? She had to
keep her marriage a secret or Howard University wouldn't have allowed
her to continue her studies."

Tales of Grandma's university triumphs didn't stand much of a
chance next to Granddad's fight-to-the-death battles in the trenches of
France. Especially since the number of "German victims" who died at
Granddad's hand kept changing each time Dad told us these blood-
and-guts stories. The closest Granddad himself came to disclosing what
really happened in those trenches was in the last years of his life when
he'd cry out each night in his dreams, reliving whatever unspeakable
horrors he'd experienced.

Dad never explained that his parents eloped because May's parents
profoundly disapproved of Granddad, or rather what Granddad represented. Had they known of their daughter's intention to marry a non-
Catholic "cursed" with a complexion several shades darker than May's,
they would have done everything in their power to have prevented it.
Dan II returned from fighting overseas only to find himself immersed
in another, less noble battle: trying, against overwhelming odds, to win
his in-laws' blessing. Still weak from being gassed by the Germans during his service—he'd spent weeks in a Paris hospital recovering—this
was hardly a welcome homecoming. Anxious to appease his in-laws, he

promised never to become a Methodist minister like his father, a promise he promptly rescinded once his strength (and resolve) returned.

This broken promise was quickly and cannily exploited by May's mother, who pressured May to leave her minister husband, going so far as to offer her gifts and large sums of money if she capitulated. May, frustrated by the constant moving (an occupational hazard for a rookie Methodist minister), gave in to her mother's bribes a few times, taking the children and moving back to Jersey City to live with her parents. But these separations never lasted long. One day, tired of being caught in a tug-of-war between mother and husband, May stormed out her parents' door for the last time, declaring, "I'm taking my children and moving back in with my 'heathen husband.'" From then on, Dan II and May stayed together, and, from all I could gather (first-hand, as well as from Dad's innumerable stories, cross-referenced with scores of family letters), they enjoyed an unusually affectionate and loving marriage.

My father grew up in a strict, protective and extremely close-knit household. Since their father was a minister, Dad and the other children rarely had to be reminded that they had a reputation to uphold. Dad had three sisters: Jean was the oldest, Margaret came second, and Dad next, followed three years later by Doris. The children grew up in the 1920s and 1930s, through America's worst economic turmoil and depression. Fortunately, thanks to their parents' higher education and tireless work ethic, they were largely shielded from the blatant racism and grinding poverty that faced so many Black Americans. The neighbourhoods the children grew up in were well integrated, with surprisingly little in the way of outright racial tension. "There wasn't a lot of poverty in the communities we were raised in," Doris explained. "You didn't see street people. They had people who rode the rails . . . we used to call them tramps . . . but among those there were not many Blacks." But relative economic stability did not always spare Blacks from what could be the most insidious racism of all: that from within their own community. When Dan II was transferred to minister in Portland, Oregon, the all-Black congregation was reluctant to accept him because he was so dark. Only when his far fairer-skinned wife joined him a few weeks later did the church eventually come to open their hearts to Dan II.

During America's post–World War I period, opportunities for a Black person to obtain a higher education were extremely limited. Either you were forced to drop out of school at an early age to find work in order to support your family, or you were denied entry into college by racist admission policies. If you managed to make it through high school and be accepted into university (usually a Black college), chances were that the tuition fees would be unaffordable. Dan II and May were among the exceptions to this rule, part of what the Black sociologist W.E.B. Du Bois termed "the talented tenth." Their good fortune made them all the more determined to remain low-key and down to earth. They considered getting decked out for Easter not only pagan but downright cruel, as it would serve to remind people from more modest backgrounds of their economic struggles. Materialism was frowned upon. "It was a simpler life back then," Doris recalled wistfully. "We never wanted for anything, but possessions were not so important. We had what we needed and were content with that. Coming out of the Depression, we, and everyone we knew, lived frugally."

Each child was assigned certain chores, done before they were allowed any "social time." Saturday mornings were spent house cleaning, with the understanding that—if and when the mopping, sweeping and washing were up to snuff—they could attend the afternoon matinee, a favourite family activity. The many chores weren't divided along gender lines, which left my dad to excel as the most gifted cook and gardener of the children. May and Dan, while sharing few of the sexist attitudes of this era, nevertheless had one hard and fast rule concerning Hill males and females: "The gentlemen always protect the women of the family."

The high point of the day was dinnertime. After leading the family through prayer, Dan II would entertain everyone with lively stories about some of the characters in his church. "Today my temperamental church organist announced she wasn't in the mood to perform for the Lord," he'd begin. "I had to scramble from the pulpit to the pipe organ so I could accompany the choir, and then sprint back to the pulpit when the song was over to resume my service." In between helpings of chicken and collard greens, the children got a sense of what was going on in the outside world: everything from politics to details of Dan II's work, to May's experiences as a social worker and board member for Planned Parenthood. (May's work with Planned Parenthood caused more than a few people in the community to regard her as a woman who championed "casual relations.") May, never one to shrink in the face of public opinion, insisted that the children embrace independent, progressive thinking, even if that invited the odd raised eyebrow.

Questions from the children were not only expected but demanded, with each child encouraged to express his or her own opinion on the various issues of the day, provided they could back it up with intelligent, cogent logic. Surprisingly, religion was a flexible topic, with the children encouraged to read about all kinds of faiths and, ultimately, form their own opinions about their spiritual direction.

Dan II's strong presence in the community meant that there was always some member of the congregation looking out for his children. This proved to be something of a mixed blessing for my dad, as the people in the community—whom he referred to as "no-good, nosy busybodies"—never hesitated in reporting to his parents if there was the slightest cause for concern.

Punishment, when merited, came swiftly. My father, the most irrepressible and rambunctious of the children, received the bulk of the discipline. Dan II would take him into a room, close the door and commence with the spanking. Dad would start bawling before the first blow landed, not so much out of fear but to alert his sisters, knowing they'd quickly rally to his defence. The three of them would huddle against the door in the hallway, wailing at their father to stop. "Would you girls like some of the same?" Dan II would inquire as he walked out of the room, glaring down at his daughters, wiping his hands as if to cleanse them of the unseemly whomping he'd just laid on his son's backside, the three girls scattering like frightened mice.

When Dan II moved his family to Denver, Colorado, his lungs, still compromised by the lingering affects of his wartime exposure to mustard gas, couldn't adjust to the higher altitude. The decreased oxygen level at that elevation left him feeling as if he could barely breathe. His doctor told him his only chance of recovery was to leave the mountains for at least six weeks, or until his circulation improved. The Methodist bishop reassigned Dan II to a church in Kansas, where May's uncle Jessie, who taught at the Black college there, agreed to take him in. But my dad refused to let his father leave without him. At three years of age his temper tantrums were already legendary; one of his most effective attention-getting tactics was to bang his head on the floor with such force that he'd frequently knock himself out. Unable to see his son so anguished, Dan II agreed to take his son to Kansas with him. Uncle Jessie provided much more than mere lodging for Dan II and his son.

"Uncle Jessie was able to talk to my father 'man to man,'" Doris later disclosed, taking great pains to explain that Dan II, who'd been secretly suffering from postwar trauma (not a recognized disorder at this time), was able to confide in Uncle Jessie. It's likely these "man to man" talks were the real cure Dan II needed. Six weeks later he returned home, never to suffer from the mountain air again.

Throughout the mid-twenties and early thirties, the Hill family moved frequently, as Dan II found himself constantly being reassigned to different churches in various small towns. "The one thing you can rely on in life is change," Dan II would tell his children. Because the congregations in these towns couldn't afford to contribute anything in the way of money to the church offering, Dan II would frequently supplement the family income by putting on concerts for the local community. Admission would be nominal: a nickel, or sometimes a loaf of bread, or a chicken.

Dan II, a splendid, self-taught musician who could play back on the church organ virtually any song he heard, usually performed alongside May, who was also an accomplished pianist and vocalist. Together they'd fill the church auditorium with uplifting Negro spirituals. Dan II would always add a little local spice by writing and performing humorous songs dealing with issues or gossip germane to his town and congregation, frequently improvising new lyrics. On many occasions, the resulting laughter would continue for so long that he'd be forced to kill time with a long harmonica solo. The people in these small towns, rarely exposed to concerts or shows of any kind, regarded the Hill concerts as major events.

As the Hill family continued to pick up and move, each new home became a meeting place, attracting people from every conceivable background. Dan II kept in contact with a wide variety of Howard University alumni, among them Black writers and entertainers who, being shut out of hotels and restaurants when travelling, would lodge with anyone who might have the room to take them in. This meant that on any given evening, Blacks travelling through the area might show up for dinner, lodge with the Hills for a day or two and then move on to the next stop. These visitors included Langston Hughes and the great lyric tenor Roland Hayes.

During the direst period of America's Great Depression, parents with children also came knocking at the Hill door, begging for scraps of food. My young dad learned the art of making quickie peanut-butter sandwiches—handing them out to all takers under the protective eye of his mother.

Through the constant parade of people drifting in and out of Dad's life as a boy came a powerful message: If you're Black and educated you can rise above the barriers of racism and be anyone you choose to be. Conversely if you're uneducated, you could well end up like one of those beggars, existing on handouts from strangers.

But generosity had its limits. When a thief started making off with the bottled milk that was delivered before sunrise to every front doorstep in the neighbourhood, Dan II decided to act. Early one morning, after staying up all night waiting in the darkened front hall, he spotted the culprit—a clinking, weighed-down potato sack slung over his shoulder—scooping the bottles of milk off the front porch. As Dan II flung open the front door, the thief scuttled across his lawn. After repeatedly warning the thief to stop or he'd shoot—whereupon the thief picked up the pace—Dan II squeezed the trigger of his World War I .45 pistol twice: *Pop! Pop!*

Two shots, sounding like distant hand claps, were immediately followed by milk spilling out of the potato sack, and the thief sprawled on the front lawn traumatized but unharmed, howling out his surrender.

Emulating his father's heroics, Dad decided to take up target practice in the basement with his own BB gun. One careless trigger pull resulted in all the basement windows being blown out, thanks to the wild ricocheting of the little bullets. Dan II chose to spare his son the usual beating and instead confiscated his BB gun.

But Dad's predilection for mischief, the more devious the better, wasn't easily discouraged. One night he decided his father's pre-dinner prayer needed a little upstaging. After excusing himself to use the bathroom, Dad snuck into the living room and plopped a risqué recording entitled "A Preaching Blues" onto his parents' Victrola. As the saucy double entendres tumbled out of the speakers, Dan II raced to the record player, snatched the "obscenity" off the turntable and smashed it to pieces.

Fortunately, Dad's impossibly cheery, relentlessly funny nature saved him from staying in anyone's bad books for very long. More than a few times, Dan II was seen winding up to give his son a stiff swat, only to pause in mid-strike in an effort to suppress a rising chortle. But while Dan II used his humour to defuse various community, church and household tensions, Dad's humour was intended to produce precisely the opposite effect. Dad was looking to cause trouble: sprinkling a large dose of sneezing powder on his unsuspecting grade four classmates or stealthily dipping an unsuspecting girl's pigtails into his inkwell. His teachers tended to overlook his pranks because, at Dan II's insistence, Dad had been moved up two grades and was assumed not to have developed the maturity to match his intellect.

His parents knew that the most effective way to keep my dad out of trouble was to occupy him with chores. His favourite task was lighting the gas furnace in the church an hour before each service. One day when he was ten, he turned on the gas and waited too long to light the furnace. The furnace exploded, the blast hitting him square in the face and blowing him several feet in the air. Somehow, he was able to drag himself to his feet and stagger home, where his sister Jean took one look at him and fainted. Dad limped to the sink and dunked his entire face in cold water. This was not the accepted remedy back then, but it was a quick and effective treatment that saved his face from permanent disfigurement. Already, Dad was demonstrating quick thinking during a crisis far beyond his years.

Dad's spunk never got in the way of his loyalty and affection for his sisters. He was especially fond and protective of the youngest, Doris, applying something of a double standard when it came to how he thought she should behave. After graduating from elementary school, Dad made a habit of dropping by to ask Doris's teachers how she was getting along. The teachers, bemused that one of their most unruly students had recast himself as his little sister's de facto parent, eventually told him to stop worrying, that Doris was making out just fine without his constant supervision.

Doris's agreeable temperament held up surprisingly well under her big brother's over-attentiveness. The upside was that he included her in everything: insisting to the disgruntled boys in the neighbourhood that she be allowed to participate in after-school touch football games and marbles competitions, and taking her by the hand to Saturday matinees. Indeed, Dad could go from tough to tender and back again within minutes. One weekend afternoon as the two of them were walking up the stairs of a movie theatre, a boy sneered at Doris, hissing, "Nigger." *Whoppp!* Almost before the epithet had registered, the boy's mouth was greeted by a hard and fast smack courtesy of Dad's right hook. *Bomp, bomp, bomp,* the dazed boy tumbled down a few stairs, and Dad and Doris continued walking into the movie theatre as though nothing had happened.

Being ever watchful of Doris didn't discourage Dad from inviting her to take part in some of his riskier excursions. By eleven years old, Dad had taken to sneaking out of the house to drive his father's car in the middle of the night, at first limiting his travels to the backyard, where he could gradually get used to the feel of the clutch and the stick shift. Once he'd mastered this new skill, he patiently passed it on to eight-year-old Doris, sitting her on his knee so that her tiny arms could reach the steering wheel. In no time they were driving in tight little circles in the backyard. But as Dad's confidence grew and he started taking the car for midnight spins around the block, Doris, game and impressionable though she was, refused to join him.

As the Hill children approached adolescence their individual characters became even more defined, their respective strengths subtly contributing to the collective personality of the family. Even though Dad may have never matched his eldest sister Jean's academic excellence, Margaret's impressive creative abilities or Doris's musical gifts, he was the family spark plug: funny and fearless, dynamic and unpredictable.

While part of Dad's spunk sprang from his genetic makeup, he was also finding his own way to rebel against the strict conformity of the intellectual, upwardly mobile Negro middle class. Some Black parents believed that in order to blend in and succeed in mainstream society, you had to out-white the whites: be more polite, more driven, more intelligent and educated, more punctiliously clean. There was always that nagging imposter syndrome tugging, lurking just beneath the skin. One crude act, misused word or lapse in manners, and you'd be seen for what you really were: a rag-clad, classless, dark-skinned interloper. At any moment, for any reason, you and your family could be hurled back to where you came from: some master's plantation, or the White House working as a teenaged seamstress, at the mercy of powerful white men.

Certainly, the flawless behaviour demanded of the Hill children was not exclusive to upwardly mobile Blacks in the 1930s. But still, rules of etiquette in the Hill household were rigid to the extreme. There were to be no "boarding-house reaches"—stretching your arm across the table to grab the salt shaker; no "short stopping"—helping yourself to salt before passing it on; no singing or raised voices at the table or unseemly bodily noises of any kind; no "lazy man's load"—carrying too many dishes from the dinner table to the kitchen sink to save subsequent trips; and absolutely no shows of gluttony. "My job is to nourish you, not to fill you up," was May's quick rejoinder should anyone dare to ask for a second helping. Evidently, too much of anything—food, clothes, material things or even attitude—revealed a weakness of character.

If Dad embraced his parents' values and manner of thinking, he also felt the need, from time to time, to strike out against them. At first this was limited to shenanigans at home, but as Dad grew older, he began pushing the limits beyond the four walls of his house.

Dad's best friend as a teenager was a boy nicknamed Mushmouth, due to his enormous lips. Mushmouth delighted in Dad's daredevil impulses, constantly matching them and challenging Dad to up the ante. When the two of them turned sixteen, they frequently went out on double dates with various girls. If and when Dad's behaviour and schoolwork met the family standard of excellence, his father would sometimes let him drive his car—a rare privilege for a Negro boy in his neighbourhood.

One Sunday morning, Dad dropped his father off at church with the understanding that he'd return to pick him up at the end of services. Unbeknownst to Dad's parents, he and Mushmouth had a double date lined up and, armed with "daddy's car," they were determined to make the greatest possible impact on the two girls, whom they barely knew. After picking up their dates and cruising around town a few times, Dad, deciding the girls weren't sufficiently impressed, ramped up the charm. After instructing Mushmouth to hand out a couple of cigarettes, Dad, with one hand on the wheel, turned his head to wink at the two startled girls in the back seat and gallantly offered to light both their cigarettes. When the girls' looks of surprise turned to horror, Dad swung his head around just in time to see another car right in front of him. *Ka-bang!* He'd crashed his father's car into another car stopped at a red light.

Mushmouth and the girls, unhurt and wanting no part of any messy consequences, scrambled out of the car and fled. The driver of the stopped car, incurring minimal damage and having no insurance, drove off. Dad's father's car, however, was destroyed, leaving Dad no choice but to abandon the vehicle at the side of the road and walk back to his father's church. His father stood out front, waiting impatiently.

"Where did you park the car, son? Don't dilly-dally," his father asked, exhausted from a long day of leading services.

Dad's punishment bore the markings of his father's unassailable and, under the circumstances, remarkably even-handed logic. Not only were Dad's driving privileges suspended indefinitely, he was not allowed to sit in the front seat of any car for an entire year.

Despite the Hill family's relative middle-class comfort, there were always stinging reminders that as a Negro, you were a second-class citizen. An outdoor recreational pool was a stone's throw away from where the family lived in Portland, providing welcome relief to all, seven days a week. All, that is, except Negroes, who were allowed to swim for only one hour a week in water that hadn't been replaced for several days. Immediately afterwards the pool was drained and refilled so that the non-coloured could swim in water free of any "Negro contaminants." At home, Dad's capricious sense of fun at all costs, grating as it sometimes could be, provided his family with a welcome distraction from the shadowy unpleasantness, or worse, of the world beyond their four walls.

Inevitably, as Dad moved into his teenage years, his behaviour began to carry a whiff of rebellion, self-destruction and troubling indications of a rising temper. He was sucking up two packs of cigarettes a day and enjoying all-night drinking binges with his buddies. When he returned home in the early hours of the morning, his abstemious father would greet him at the front door and testy verbal exchanges would ensue. A few times they came close to blows, with May having to intervene and separate them.

One night Dad got so drunk that he passed out, and his friends, unable to revive him, deposited him like a sack of flour on his front porch, rang the doorbell and bolted. Dad's father dragged him to his feet, slapped him awake and steered him into the foyer. Then he propped him up in front of the full-length mirror and forced him to take a look at himself.

"I want you to see just how pathetic you are. Anyone could take advantage of you in any way they see fit. You're totally helpless, worse than a baby. You're a disgrace."

Dan II's message rang out loud and clear. In the world that Dad would soon be venturing into, the worst thing that you could do was to leave yourself vulnerable, to be in any way out of control.

At seventeen, Dad left home to study at Lincoln University in Pennsylvania, where he boarded with his father's youngest brother, Joe, and his family. Lincoln, an all-Black school, had become a proud tradition for the Hill family, and the knowledge that both his father and grandfather had graduated from this highly regarded institution weighed heavily on my dad. To make things worse, his uncle Joe was a dean who taught English literature and was so caught up in his image as the erudite English professor that he was nicknamed, scornfully, "the Black Englishman." Soon my dad would be stigmatized as "the professor's boy." Joe's preening arrogance, combined with Dad's parents' expectation that he follow in the footsteps of other "Hill scholars," proved all but intolerable for my father, as this, his first letter home from Lincoln in 1941, bears out.

> *I have come to the conclusion that I do not like the prevailing*
> *pressure. I would much rather be a student, just an average*
> *student whose uncle was not the dean of the university . . . I*
> *am even called by everybody the little Dean. I hope that I am*
> *not stepping out of line when I say this but when . . . [Uncle*
> *Joe] implies that I am stupid because I have not read* Hamlet,
> *I do not particularly like the remark . . . I am continually being*
> *reminded by everybody (and when I say everybody I mean*
> *everybody because there is not a single person on this campus*
> *that does not know me), that I am Dean Hill's nephew and*
> *that I must get a straight A average . . . The main reason is*
> *because Uncle Joe is a very hard and heartless man. The other*
> *day [Uncle Joe] kicked a very good friend of mine out of the*
> *class and gave him an F for the day, simply because he did not*
> *have a necktie on. I must myself have a necktie on at all times,*
> *and I must walk on my toes or the balls of my feet in the house.*
> *He insists that I sleep too much, and that I should read some*

of Shakespeare's plays instead of going to bed between 9–10–11 o'clock every night. He is trying desperately to make me a cultured, and refined man. I cannot whistle, sing crazy swing tunes, wear T-shirts, jeans, or lounge around. When I come home you will not know me.

If Dad had found the rigorous rules of the Negro bourgeois oppressive at home, what he encountered at Uncle Joe's house was much worse. The usually winning aspects of his personality—endless enthusiasm, disarming (albeit irreverent) humour, unstoppable energy—were being met with scorn, and his intelligence questioned. No wonder he was awfully homesick for, as he wrote, his father's "informality and joking manner, and the good old home atmosphere."

Uncle Joe's expectation that you were a loser if you didn't excel academically wasn't all that different from Dad's parents' views. But Dad's parents constantly reassured him that he had the right stuff to succeed. Uncle Joe did the opposite, always suggesting to Dad that he was rather dim.

Despite doing well (if not breathtakingly so) in school, Dad's intelligence was of a type that didn't readily come alive in academic surroundings. It thrived in those many grey zones that resisted easy categorization. Dad's smarts—alert to a fault and highly intuitive, imbuing him with a preternatural ability to read people while wisely pretending otherwise—weren't readily measurable.

Uncle Joe's strict manner and hostility towards Dad may have been a mask for Joe's own personal problems. A secretly addicted gambler who had racked up enormous debts to the mob, Joe attempted to defraud the university in an effort to pay his debt. Shortly after my father returned home from Lincoln, Joe's house was bombed and he and his family fled to Liberia—thanks to Dan II's connections—until things settled down.

Had Dad been aware of Joe's assorted transgressions he might have been less vulnerable to his uncle's taunts. As it was, Uncle Joe managed to touch on Dad's greatest fear, that maybe he wasn't smart enough where it ultimately mattered the most: college and from there, the ever-competitive, ever-racist workplace.

The anguish that pours out of my father in the following letter to his dad speaks to an unsettledness that is universal to all teenagers.

> *I have not quite found myself as yet, if you know what I mean, I think I would like to [quit school and] work for a year in California [or] I could get a job working for the Matson Steamship Company as a cabin boy or a cook's aide. The ships go to Samoa, the Fiji Islands, and the South Sea Islands. You know that I am going onto 18 and am fast becoming a man. You might think that all of this stuff I am writing is bunk, but before you do I urge you to think about me and see if you can't remember what kind of boy I was. As you recall I was never a good student. I got along with people pretty well but I never was too serious about anything. I do not have a major at Lincoln because I am still confused about what I want to do, and what I want to become. At any rate, Dad, I do not want you to over estimate me and build yourself up and then get an awful letdown . . . If I do not make the grade it will not be because I did not try, but it seems to me that I put twice as much time on the subjects that the other boys seem to get with a snap.*
>
> *Your son,*
> *Buddy*

Not only was Dad unsure of his place in the world, it was becoming increasingly difficult for anyone to gauge where the world, at large, was headed. While many Americans believed that they were safe from the conflicts and slaughter unfolding across the Atlantic (and Pacific), all that changed on December 7, 1941, when Pearl Harbor was attacked.

"The news knocked me off my feet, and took me completely unaware," Dad began a letter to his father, written on the day of the attack.

Wait, I have just heard an open declaration of war by Japan against the U.S. and Britain. This mess is too darn close to our homes and loved ones. Listen Dad, I want to lay the facts down to you hard and cold . . . You cannot Tell What These Japanese might do. Right now our country is at war, and I am afraid that there might be a bombing of the pacific Coast. Prices will go sky High, and I do not want to be in the East when so much trouble is going on near my home . . . You can believe it or not, but this war is a very serious thing, and my business isn't to be in school here, but to be at home with the rest of my family.

It's a given that, as attached as he was to his family, Dad wouldn't want to be away from them during the most catastrophic event of his life to date. But he was also looking for a way out of university. The Pearl Harbor bombings gave him the perfect excuse to drop out of school. Within weeks, he'd moved back home to live with his parents in Oakland, where he found work as a welder in the shipbuilding industry. The job was deemed vital to America's war effort, and he could have easily avoided being drafted into the army so long as his foreman granted him the status of a "necessary worker." But freed from the constraints of Uncle Joe's rules and relieved to be out of the academic pressure cooker of Lincoln, Dad's commitment to work was upstaged by his whirlwind social schedule. Dad's new nickname was Party Boy, drawn from the new group he ran with, called the Red Wine Boys.

Dad repeatedly ignored warnings from his boss that he would lose his necessary worker status if he continued to miss work or show up late and badly hung over. As a result, he lost his special status and was drafted into the U.S. Army in 1942. He was eighteen years old.

CHAPTER 3

Hill Kids Are Extraordinary

"How come you never get into any fights, boy?" Dad yelps, tossing aside the fingerpainting I've presented to him, courtesy of my kindergarten art class. Although I know Dad's half kidding—his voice turns higher and more singsongy when he's having me on—I can tell he's also genuinely concerned that I haven't been in a shoving match, let alone an all-out brawl. He's put on that exaggerated frown face again, a sign that he's about to light up the kitchen with one of his performances.

"Dan," Mom chimes in, "what's the big hurry? Danny's not even six yet."

"He's at an age where he's gotta know how to defend himself. What if somebody goes after Larry or Karen? Daggum, someone's gotta show him how to look out for his brother and sister."

Mom issues one of her big sighs. She knows that when Dad's winding up to give me one of his lectures, there's not a thing she can do to stop him. Just the same, she sneaks me a reassuring "don't take your father too seriously" wink.

"Every day after school, my little sister and I would walk through the tough Italian neighbourhood," Dad says. "And every day some kid would call me a nigger and I'd have to say to Doris, 'Sis, hold my glasses for me,' and then, *pow!*" To demonstrate, Dad smacks the kitchen wall with the open palm of his hand with such force that dishes everywhere start rattling. The noise makes me jump. "I'd beat the kid halfway to tomorrow and come home with my clothes in tatters. My mother would be so cross with me she'd make me sew the clothes back together myself."

Dad's got the transistor radio tuned to an upcoming heavyweight boxing match, and to warm up for the broadcast he's shadowboxing, weaving and ducking and dancing across the kitchen, his considerable size making the floor vibrate and hum. I can't take my eyes off him. As he juts out his fat lower lip, pretending to mock an imaginary opponent, Mom and I are overcome with laughter. Anything that puts Dad in a good mood—a "swinging" Basie record, smoked oysters dipped in his special hot mustard mixture, a well-tended garden, a big American sporting event—sweeps me and the rest of the family right up along with him. The opposite is also true. Now Dad abruptly stops his mugging and turns serious.

"Son, promise me you'll protect Larry and Karen. Don't you ever let anyone lay a hand on them."

I nod obediently, ashamed to tell him that the idea of fighting anyone, for any reason, frightens me.

"Give me your hand, son."

Dad forms my fingers and palm into a fist and shows me how to lean into a punch. The heat of his mitt-sized hand makes me feel bigger and stronger and braver. I don't want him to ever let go.

"That's it, boy. See, you're getting the hang of it now."

I hear the smack of my scrawny fist against the wall before I feel the throbbing in my knuckles. It takes me another instant to realize my closed hand produced this whacking sound. Mom's standing between the two of us now, shaking her head with a resigned smile, as if she's torn between loving the high drama of Dad's delivery and disapproving of its message.

Dad's already on to another story.

"When I was eight years old, my father had been asked to give a speech to my public school during 'Brotherhood Week,' about the importance of racial harmony." I've heard this one before, but Dad can spin the same yarn a hundred times and still make it riveting. "My father arrived at the principal's office to find me and a white boy looking all dishevelled and bloody, sitting there awaiting our punishment."

"Was your father mad?" I ask, trying to imagine the impossible: Dad as a young boy, cut and bleeding all over the principal's office.

"My father would have given me a whupping on the spot, had I not explained that the white boy beside me had called me a nigger, leaving me no choice but to beat him up."

I had yet to realize that Dad was simply passing on his father's trick of instruction, right down to the preacher-like inflections. Any message, which in this case was "Know how to protect yourself against anyone trying to drag you or your family down, even if that means breaking a few rules," had greater impact when wrapped in a compelling story. Then again, almost everything Dad said came out in story form. For all I know, some of them may have even been true. Several months after Dad's shadowboxing display, he fired off this nifty piece of fiction to his parents:

Newmarket 1960
Danny starts school in the fall and is currently going through
the period of fistfights with the local boys. He holds up fairly
well—has been told to defend himself but never to initiate
brawls unless someone strikes him, Larry or Karen first.

My parents and I had moved from Toronto to the small town of Newmarket, an hour's drive north of the city, where they'd purchased their first house in a new subdivision for thirteen thousand dollars in 1955. Larry was born there in 1957, Karen, one year and three days later.

At that time Newmarket was surrounded by lush farmland. Most of its eight thousand occupants were British, many of whom had moved there after the war to work at Avro, and later, De Havilland, building fighter airplanes. Aside from Dad, there was no hint of colour anywhere in this bedroom community, unless you counted the red and orange speckled leaves that lit up the woods and forests once the cooler weather came. While I was oblivious to the endless canvas of white faces, the same could not be said for my mother or for Karen, who was born with the darkest complexion of us three kids. At least once a week, someone would approach my mom when she was out grocery shopping with my sister and say, "How very kind of you to have adopted that little brown-skinned girl," refusing to accept the possibility that this very brown-skinned girl could have come out of my very white-skinned mother. Eileen, our next-door neighbour and Mom's best friend, was approached to sign a petition to have us thrown out of the neighbourhood.

I had no inkling about race, or the fact that Dad was the only Black man in this small town, until we acquired our first television in 1959. One Saturday morning, I saw a cartoon in which grotesque creatures with bugged-out eyes and the blackest of skin shimmied around in a jungle with what looked like human bones sticking out of their hugely swollen mouths. They were hurling captive white men into boiling pots of water, smacking their drooling, anaconda-sized lips in anticipation of a delicious meal. My four-year-old mind whirred like a toy top, trying to categorize these odious not-quite-monkey, not-quite-human creatures as they bounded about, semi-naked and chattering unintelligibly.

I dashed down the hall and into my parents' room, dragging my barely awake father out of bed and into the living room. "What are they, Daddy?"

Dad looked at the TV and slapped my little, pointing finger away from the screen.

"Owww," I cried. Not from the pain—when Dad hit to hurt, I knew it—but from the sick sensation that I'd done something really bad.

"Skin! Skin! Skin!" Dad screamed at the creepy, dark creatures licking their dreadful lips.

What did he mean, "skin"? Dad's yelling—that tended to be Mom's specialty—frightened me. But his incessant repeating of "skin"—no other word escaped his mouth—left me immobilized. My eyes darting back and forth between Dad and the crazed activity on the TV screen, all I could figure was that "skin" related to the cartoonish creatures' inky-black colour. Did something about their black skin make them crave human flesh? White-skinned flesh? But what did this have to do with me? As Dad continued to yell at the TV and then me, I couldn't figure out what I'd done wrong.

Mom tore into the room, her white bathrobe flapping off her sides like half-formed wings. "Shit," she said. "Damn it, Danny, turn off that TV right now and get back to bed."

Later that day, when he had calmed down, Dad explained that the cartoon was making fun of Negroes.

But what were Negroes? Dad complicated things further by telling me that he was a Negro. Which made me and Larry and Karen Negroes as well. But, for some reason, not Mom. And that because the TV station did a bad thing, I wasn't allowed to watch that channel until Dad got them to stop showing those kinds of cartoons. And by the sound of Dad's stern words over the phone—"Don't eavesdrop, Danny," Mom scolded—that might not happen for a long, long time.

This left only one other station: CBC, the boring channel. When Mom caught me watching the banned channel at a friend's house, I got in a lot of trouble. Dad had a talk with my friend's parents. I wasn't allowed over there anymore. Not only that, now I wasn't allowed to play at anyone's house that watched the banned channel. Which eliminated every kid whose family owned a TV. I didn't mention to Dad that being a Negro wasn't much fun.

That was the first time I'd deliberately disobeyed Dad. It started a pattern that would hound the two of us for the rest of Dad's life: Dad would issue a rule and, sooner or later, I would find a way to break it.

Luckily, Dad wasn't piling up the rules back in those early Newmarket years. Between his work, his studies and his commute to Toronto and back every day, he wasn't around that much during the week. Mom always said that because Eileen lived next door, the week flew by. "We're like sisters," I heard Mom tell someone over the phone. Even though having a best friend next door could take the edge off Mom's temper, especially since she and Eileen could smush their combined six kids together like one big family and do a lot of stuff together, I could still be a major thorn in Mom's side. Every morning started the same way: "Danny, get out of the house. Get some exercise. Find something to do. You're not allowed to come home till it gets dark outside."

This being 7:00 a.m. and all, I knew that meant by midday she'd be in a better mood, passing out graham crackers with peanut butter, listening critically as I sang the jingle, "Kraft peanut butter tastes fresher in the jar than peanuts in the shell," ready to pounce whenever I muffed the melody so she could sing it back to me with perfect tone and pitch. But first thing in the morning, with Dad already long gone, Mom might have felt overwhelmed with three little kids crowding round her in the kitchen. I didn't make things any easier, the way I bounced around all over the place, poking (well, actually plowing) Larry in the stomach and laughing in amazement when he couldn't breathe, or tying together Karen's pigtails from the back, which, just as I'd hoped, started her blubbering. The next two sounds I'd hear were Mom swinging open the front door with one hand and smacking my rear end with the other.

I was always happy to get out of the house. Newmarket in the fifties was like an extended playground, a dream place for a child like me to wander about and explore. There was little in the way of urban development and acres and acres of unexplored woods that a child with half an imagination could easily lose himself in. When I was growing up, parents didn't have the fear of strange adults lurking in bushes ready to pounce on their unsuspecting children. And other than the friendly milkman, who always gave me a free bottle of cold chocolate milk, Newmarket wasn't exactly swarming with people back then. Most days, I could play in the woods down the block from my house and not see another living soul the entire day. I would return home only when my arms were sore from hours of digging up the nearby woods for buried pirate treasure, and my hands reeked from the overpowering odour of the dead rats that I'd scoop out of the smelly pond and swing like prizes over my shoulder to present as gifts to my strangely unappreciative mother.

Mom was always in a better mood on the weekends, when Dad was around. This meant that I could hang around the house pretty much all day, because even with one extra adult in the house Mom didn't feel crowded by us kids. When it was rainy outside, I'd lose myself for hours in what Dad described as "Danny's indoor projects." When I'd finished a difficult puzzle, or constructed a five-year-old's version of Atlantis out of building blocks, Dad would cry out, "Come over here, Donna. Take a look at what our son's done. He's gonna be a great architect some day."

A year later, I developed the knack for fiddling with our rabbit-eared, black-and-white television until the screen boasted marginally improved reception. "Who taught you how to do that, son?" Dad would ask, as if I'd come up with a cure for cancer. "For heaven's sakes alive, where on earth did you get your mechanical genius? Not from the Hill side of the family, that's for sure. Ha, ha, ha."

Every Saturday morning, I'd bike to the corner store and buy an Old Port cigar for Dad, sucking the packaged cigar through its wrapper in my mouth like a lollipop on my return. Dad would drop this drool-soaked, teeth-indented thing as though it were a lumpy turd, braying, "Sit your behind back on your bike and get me another Old Port. If I find even a speck of saliva—" I was pedalling like crazy before I could catch the end of his threat.

Dad's attention and approval was the drug I never stopped craving. On the other hand, when I made him angry, I wanted to disappear, anywhere, and never come back. Dad's moods were like an ever-changing weather pattern; he could be entertaining, jolly, and then, without warning, the smallest thing could set him off. There was only one thing worse than igniting Dad's temper: disappointing him.

One summer Saturday, Larry and I were splashing around in what my parents thought was a shallow lake. Suddenly the top half of my brother disappeared beneath the water's surface, like a duck in search of a meal. "Save him, Danny! Hurry!" Dad yelled. All I could see were Larry's little calves and feet, kicking wildly back and forth upside down, like some zany cartoon. Even from only a few feet away, his flailing legs appeared so unreal that I fell into hysterical laughter, unable to move. Dad, still hollering, bounded fully dressed into the lake, pulling Larry out of the water and up against his chest, hustling him back to safety as my laughter turned to slobbering and bawling. Dad threw me a glance that left me winded.

It had been my third blunder of the day. An hour earlier, as Dad and I visited the public urinal, I'd glanced over at Dad's serpentine penis and asked if he'd ever wished he were a girl. As Dad glared at me incredulously, a soggy pack of matches tumbled out of my bathing suit and hit the floor. I'd discovered them on the beach and, instantly curious, had tucked them away for a later, secret inspection. Dad may have overlooked the matches and me gaping at his penis, but my failing to rescue my little brother was a crime against family. That could not go unpunished.

Dad waited till we got home before he spanked me. I'd flown into my room and had tried to hide between the mattress and the box spring, seized with a black terror.

"You're getting ten smacks, boy," Dad snarled. The sharp, resonating *thwackkk* of his bare hand on my horribly exposed bum made my head feel like it was about to split wide open.

Long after it was over, I remained wracked with feelings of worthlessness. How could I have failed to protect little Larry? I had stood there and laughed while he almost swallowed an entire lake. I swore to myself that I would never let my family down again.

There was one thing that could rescue me from my moods: the music that leapt out of my parents' hi-fi stereo. Indeed, the richest part of my vocabulary came from Dad's extensive collection of Frank Sinatra, Joe Williams and Harry Belafonte records. Sinatra, in particular, struck a nerve. I recognized that sad ache in his voice, the empathetic swirling counterpoint of Nelson Riddle's orchestra. The music spoke to me, calmed and comforted me, infused me with guarded hope; I wasn't so alone after all.

I suspect my parents understood this about me. In a household where almost everything remained decidedly "hands-off" for me, the stereo was the one exception. I loved gently placing Sinatra's *Songs for Swingers* gleaming 33 on the turntable, holding the cartridge just so and balancing the tiny needle on the edge of the vinyl. I'd sit right between the speakers, waiting for the wonderful crackle of the needle on groove to give way to the rushing whoosh of music. I'd sing along, transported into a romantic fantasy world, my voice catching and then matching Sinatra's interval for interval, phrase for phrase, breath for breath.

On my sixth birthday, my parents gave me my very own miniature record player. "Honest to God, boy, all that ever comes out of that mouth of yours these days are songs," Dad chortled. "Have you forgotten how to talk?"

"What your father's trying to say," Mom translated, "is having your own record player in your bedroom may influence you to listen more and sing less."

The opposite happened. My grandparents, more entranced by my singing than my ear-weary parents, gave me two 78 rpm recordings: a cowgirl record with a songstress who dreamily crooned about feeling like a million bucks when she wore a ten-gallon hat, and a singing story about a too-tall fireman who was teased until his height helped him to rescue someone from the tenth floor of a burning apartment building. I enthusiastically sang along with such volume that I'd always be ordered to close my bedroom door.

The narrative driving these songs captivated me as much as the jaunty melodies. What could be more enthralling than the image of an eight-foot-tall fireman discovering heroism as a means of overcoming derision, or outlaw cowgirls taming horses on the American prairies?

That fall I would turn to music more and more for comfort and sustenance. I'd started school.

"Daddy, you and Mommy promised me I would like learning. But I don't like it one bit. So tell the school I'm not going anymore. Please."

"I'll take that under consideration, son," Dad would say, nodding his head with a father's understanding as he headed out the door for work.

The moment I started grade one, Newmarket ceased to be a place of endless, woodsy charm. With school came teachers and other children. And as people took the place of ponds and woods, Newmarket turned gloomy and threatening.

"Time to check for niggers under your fingernails, children!" my teacher, a no-nonsense, ruddy-faced woman, would announce first thing each Monday morning, brandishing her pointed nail file at the class.

Tempted as I was to tell Dad about my teacher's weekly "nigger search" ritual, I was afraid he might get angry at me for not setting my teacher straight. I couldn't remember: was I suppose to fight adults—even teachers—who said "nigger," or was I to limit my slaughter to other kids? As my teacher speared her nail file into the soft flesh of my skin, flicking out the last of those "stubborn little nigger critters," it felt as though I were infected with some awful fungus that all her painful scooping could never get rid of.

Bad enough that school knocked me out of my perfectly constructed imaginary world, but this new world seemed nasty and unrelenting and bewildering, leaving me to wobble through grade one convinced there'd been some terrible mistake, that I'd been dropped off at the wrong place. All this pressure to learn boring stuff on a precise schedule, while fending off brashly aggressive boys and bossy, fusspot girls, left me in a silent state of panic.

Happily, after school, I could always count on the music from my 78 collection to wash over me, building me back up again one song at a time. The sheer physical joy of singing made me feel how I imagined Clark Kent felt when he snuck into a phone booth and changed into his Superman outfit, or the singer of the cowgirl song when she donned her ten-gallon hat and felt like a million dollars: invulnerable. Those kids could crow all they wanted about their adding and subtracting skills, but none of them could sing like me or feel music in the special way I did.

In the summer of 1960, Mom and Eileen returned home extremely late one night, still swooning over the Robert Goulet concert they'd attended in Toronto. Dad, who never liked Mom going to Toronto (or anywhere else that wasn't spitting distance from our house) without his protection, greeted Mom at the front door, livid. The more Mom oohed and aahed about Goulet, the angrier Dad became. I, in turn, felt a kind of roiling jealousy I'd never experienced before. That did it: I was going to be a famous singer, the greatest singer ever, good enough to make Mom swoon, so she wouldn't disappear until the early hours of the morning. When Dad declared, shortly after the Goulet incident, that we were moving out of Newmarket, I was convinced that Mom's night out in Toronto with Eileen was the reason.

Mom, although heartbroken over leaving Newmarket for Don Mills, kept any distaste she may have felt for our new neighbourhood to herself, listening stone-faced as Dad would tell us, in his pep rally voice: "This new Don Mills neighbourhood is chock full of all sorts of opportunities." "Opportunity" was one of Dad's favourite words. But not mine. Because with new opportunities came new expectations, which meant more pressure, which meant, I was convinced, more failures. What if I let Dad down, after all the trouble he'd gone through to move us into this shiny new subdivision?

"Every move we make—to a new house, to a better school—represents an exciting step your father is taking up the career ladder," was Mom's non-answer answer when I asked her how she felt about leaving Newmarket. But I didn't much like ladders.

In time, the power of Dad's determined enthusiasm overrode our fears. We were like a little family assembly line, as one by one, Dad's insistence that we would soon see the superior splendour of Don Mills passed from him to Mom to me, and on down to Larry and Karen, until we were all converted to his way of thinking. Larry and Karen were too young to know much of anything. You could put them on the moon and they'd still play and fight in the same non-stop, irritating way. Mom, however, may have found it unfair how everything from the important stuff—where we lived—to the everyday—which set of lawn chairs to buy—always came down to what Dad wanted. But when Dad wound himself up into one of his deliriously joyous moods, Mom couldn't resist him. She would step back and peer up at him the way a child might gawk at a circus performer.

"Sabina, I'm glad I've found ya . . ." Dad would improvise in a pure, tenor voice to the shy little German girl who'd recently moved in across the street and had yet to make any friends. "I'm comin' on strong, to wrap my arms around you . . . Sabina . . . whoaaa . . . Sabina . . ." leaving Sabina barely able to stay balanced on her tricycle she was laughing so hard, us three kids studying Dad's big lips so we could try to sing along to his ever-changing words, and Mom beaming in disbelief as if she were wondering, "Who is this man? This crazy, brilliant, force of nature who blazes life?"

And so, for a while anyway, Mom's nagging disappointments and annoyances—leaving Eileen behind in Newmarket, Dad's growing absences due to his ever-increasing career demands, his domineering manner—were well worth it. Almost anything was worth it. Because when he was happy, the world—Mom's world, our world—felt utterly perfect and unconquerable.

I'm seven years old and tossing a football back and forth with my dad. We're on the front lawn of Mallow Road Public School in Don Mills. It's an exquisite Sunday afternoon in early autumn. We can see people through the windows ensconced in some kind of Bible study.

"Look at those poor suckers," Dad snickers, tossing me a perfect spiral. "There they are, rotting away, studying the Bible while we're out here playing football. They think we're heathens. But you know something? They're jealous as all get-out. They'd do anything to trade places with us."

Thrilled at the thought of breaking some kind of sacred rule with Dad, I grin defiantly at the people peering out at us from the classroom.

"They're brainwashed," Dad says, reaching up to catch my over-thrown pass with one hand, the football almost disappearing from view as he traps it between his arm and his chest. Then he makes two quick pumping motions in the direction of the Bible class, his feigned throw so brash that I stop breathing, bracing for the sound and spectacle of shattered glass. Catching me gawking, Dad cocks his arm and fires the football hard and fast into my sternum. "Always be prepared," he scolds, as I bobble and lurch, half-winded from the force of Dad's bullet pass, falling clumsily to the ground as the football squirts out of my arms. "Good effort, son."

Hoping for more heathen football games, I took to coming home from my new public school reciting verbatim passages from the Bible. When it came to violence and gore, the Old Testament had it all over the Sergeant Rock war comics my classmates were hooked on.

"Listen to that boy, Donna," Dad would carp. "Instead of arithmetic, all he remembers is his nutty Bible studies. That stuff has got to be taken out of the schools."

I certainly didn't want it taken out of the schools. Bible study was one of the few courses I was acing. The nerve of my parents, not believing in God. While all my classmates were comforted by the notion of heaven awaiting them, I was left to cope with the cold truth. When you died, that was it. Over. The idea that one day my parents would die, that I would die, left me eager to find some kind of loophole.

"But once you've lived a long life, you'll be happy to die," Mom blithely explained. "You'll just close your eyes and say, 'Well, this has been lots of fun but I'm tired now and my time has come.'"

"No, I won't!"

"We'll live on in you. And when you die you'll live on in your children . . ."

"What if a lion eats me? Will I live on in the lion?"

"Danny asks too many damned questions," I overheard Dad tell his dad when Granddad and Grandma were staying with us one Christmas.

Dad, as respectful of his parents' ardent religious beliefs as he was contemptuous of everyone else's, portrayed himself as the picture of tolerance when deconstructing the dilemma of Christianity to his children. "Danny's asking quite a bit about Jesus and God," he wrote his father in 1959.

I answer him as best I can and hope that later I can assist in giving him the broadest and best life experiences available within my means . . . The other day he walked in the house—

*after having a discussion with a Catholic friend down the
street—and announced that he saw God flapping around in
the clouds . . . I told him that this was quite interesting, but
that he should call me out on such occasions, so that I could see
him too.*

But soon Dad, finding early-sixties Don Mills far more Christian
than late-fifties Newmarket, no longer viewed my struggle with religion
as quaint. It wasn't only religion that challenged my parents in Don Mills.
It was an overall conservatism that leaked down through every member
of the community. Even babysitters would tell me I was going straight to
hell for not praying. When my parents came home from their evening
out, it would take all night for them to calm me down. "Heaven and hell,
that's just a bunch of fairytale stuff," Dad would groan. "Donna, that fool
babysitter is not setting foot in this house again."

It didn't take long for most of the babysitters to be barred from
our house due to one transgression or another: too evangelical, too
hawkish on Vietnam, too sports-crazed or anti-Semitic. And I was
to blame for most of my babysitters' firings—they'd have kept their
mouths shut if I hadn't baited them in the first place by trying out my
parents' assorted left-wing beliefs on them. Debating these issues was
good practice for me. I used the word "propaganda"—I loved throwing around Dad's big words—so much during social studies that my
teacher banned the word.

It did feel a little isolating sometimes, having atheist parents
who thought skiing was a pretentious extravagance, believed America
should stay out of Vietnam, regarded Valentine's Day and Mother's Day
as "meretricious, capitalist flim-flam," and turned sniffy at the idea of
going to Florida for Christmas.

"They're all racists in the south," Dad seethed, his contemptuous stare making me feel like the family turncoat for even suggesting
a southern holiday. "Any Negro stupid enough to venture into Florida
deserves what he gets."

"What about the Negro's family?" I asked.

"If they have parents that dumb, they're good as dead anyway."

Just the same, there were some definite perks to growing up with parents who consistently thumbed their noses at the types of activities most other families in Don Mills considered sacrosanct. My parents never pressured me to join the Boy Scouts, an organization that Dad claimed to be fascist and teeming with white supremacists. While I didn't know what "fascist" meant and had pointed out to Dad that maybe no Negroes were in Cubs because there weren't any other Negroes in our neighbourhood, the whole concept of Cubs and Scouts didn't sit right with me. I sat in on a Cub jamboree one evening out of curiosity, and all those kids standing perfectly still in neatly pressed green uniforms struck me as plain wrong. I thought all that mass saluting was some kind of a joke put on for my benefit, until one boy was caught saluting with the wrong hand and told to go home. When all the kids crouched in a tight circle and started howling like wolves I got out of there as fast as I could.

There were times when I felt like Don Mills was one huge inside joke, and for some reason the punch line always sailed way over my head. Everyone else in my class fell off their chairs laughing at the Three Stooges film shown on special "Movie Thursdays," but for the life of me, I couldn't figure out what was so funny. As my classmates streamed into school Monday morning raving about Sunday night's *The Wonderful World of Disney* I'd give a fake nod, recalling Dad's fervently held theory for banning *Disney* from our TV set: "They don't hire Negroes at Disney—except to play the occasional low-life criminal in their asinine movies."

"Face it, you're just weird," Elaine, a freckle-faced girl that I secretly liked, told me after I'd forwarded Dad's wish to have "Ol' Man River" dropped from our choir repertoire for its references to Blacks as darkies. "You go out of your way to find something wrong with everything!"

One of the reasons Dad continued to wave the race flag in our faces was to compensate for the relative racelessness of Don Mills. Not even a decade old, it was one of Canada's first perfectly planned suburban communities, sparklingly sterile with endless immaculate parks and cute cul-de-sacs. In fact, the only thing Don Mills seemed to be missing, other than any hint of culture or colour, was a cemetery, as if any neighbourhood this self-consciously tidy would result in a population that never fell ill or aged.

But what Don Mills lacked in character, it made up for by being ordered and civilized. Here in the suburbs, the school kids didn't seem as raw or tough or downright surly. The mother two doors up from us didn't look like she was going to cut me into pieces and eat me if I so much as glanced in her direction, like Mrs. Peterson did in Newmarket. Above all, the Don Mills kids were bred to be competitive. By and large, no one dared slack off—bad grades stuck to a student like a funky smell.

This was part and parcel of Dad's master plan, as if moving from Newmarket to Don Mills were akin to being promoted from a hockey farm team to the NHL. A letter to his parents in 1961, adorned as always with his formal sociology jargon, handily illustrates how I was expected to rise to the occasion: "Danny is having to work much harder in this Don Mills school; the kids are children of the striving, progressive and middle class and Danny can't lag. I've impressed this on him and he's responding okay." Mom's take on Don Mills, based on this letter to her sister, showed a more sardonic vantage point: "There is a tendency in this neighbourhood to build friendships around bridge clubs and curling. Neither of which I have any tolerance for, alas."

Whether "striving" or "clubbish," Don Mills was all about winning, even if that meant playing dirty sometimes. "If you see an opposing player sprawled out on the ice, crowding your goalie, skate over his hand," commanded my grade three teacher, our hockey coach, as we skated around him in dizzyingly tight circles, "My job is to turn you kids into young men. Now stop leaning on your sticks for balance like a bunch of wooden Indians and start hustling. Move it!"

Dad didn't blink when I informed him of my teacher's "skate over the other guy's hand" order, but the "wooden Indian" comment caused him to fire off a letter of protest to the school principal. Two things that Dad would not tolerate in school were racist comments and any teacher who dared lay a hand on his child. I realize now I spent my years in public school protected by an invisible shield, complete with a blinking sign that only teachers could read, warning, "Touch this kid and his big, brown bear of a dad is going to tear you limb from limb."

I was lucky to be spared, because when it came to discipline, my public school teachers were not only prone to smacking students whom they felt deserved punishment, they doled out just deserts with gusto. "You wretched, wretched child," my enraged teacher would shriek, digging her long nails clear through a classmate's shirt till they found traction in his arms, making it impossible for the scratched and bleeding kid to break free.

Some of the more "enlightened" teachers shunned physical discipline, opting for inspired psychological torture techniques that no kid would dare reveal to his parents. What boy would relive the humiliation of being made to dress up in a diaper and tiny pink bonnet, with a baby bottle stuck in his quivering mouth to keep him quiet, and sit in a baby carriage in front of the class until the school day was finished?

Unlike my father, I made it through my early school years as a goody two-shoes, running all-out with Dad's "Hills are born superior" mantra, scared to let up or even look over my shoulder for a second. Larry was every bit as driven and well behaved, to the point where his grade one teacher called in my nonplussed parents for an emergency meeting to complain that "your overly earnest son is driving himself too hard and overachieving."

"Daggum, Donna, if Larry had straight blond hair and blue eyes they wouldn't be giving his straight As a second glance," Dad harrumphed. "Time for us to get into that school and straighten out that fool teacher."

As for setting his three kids straight, Dad had an effective brainwashing drill that he dragged us through most Saturday mornings.

"Always do your best! Always do your best!" Dad would chant, with my siblings and me obediently singing along, my nine-year-old voice squeaking uncertainly as it tried to match his proud cadence.

"Hill kids are not ordinary kids," he'd declare, his voice foghornloud. "You were born to be extraordinary." Then he'd go on to list the endless triumphs that various members of the Hill family had achieved throughout the generations, often with the word "first" affixed to their specified profession. Aunt Lena wasn't just a gynecologist and psychiatrist—she was the first Black female gynecologist ever to practise out of New Jersey. That I hadn't the foggiest idea what "gynecologist" meant made her profession sound all the more glamorous and important. Our great-grandfather Edwards was no "ordinary" dentist—he was the first Black dentist from the Washington, D.C., area. Lest we miss the significance and prestige of such a lofty profession, Dad would go on to say, "Dr. Edwards was the *first* Black man in all of D.C. rich enough to own a refrigerator."

"Danny and Larry, quick: tell me how much your great-great-grandfather Hill paid to free himself and his family from slavery?"

I balked, feeling crushed under the weight of all the great-great-greats—how could anyone keep track of so many sets of ancestors?—but Larry shouted out, "One thousand dollars!"

"Daggum it, Larry, for winning the smartest Hill child award you get a hard-earned nickel from your broken-down old pappy."

Dad's "family pride" speeches scared me silly. What if I became the first Hill child in history to be considered ordinary?

"What's wrong with you, Danny? Your Flateau cousins are getting straight As!" Dad would rage. One glance at my report card would cause him to look away in agony, my multitude of C-pluses too much of a family betrayal to contemplate. When, midway through second grade, my teacher wrote a note to my parents claiming I needed to stay after class for extra tutoring in "reading comprehension," Dad waved the note in front of my mom's nose as if this was somehow her fault: "Donna, explain to me how Danny can top his class in creative writing and not understand a bloody thing that's going on in the books he's reading?"

"Dan, you know how Danny's mind works: he understands what he wants to understand. But if something doesn't interest him he loses—"

"Donna, we gotta save this boy from that wild imagination of his. You and I are going to see Danny's teacher first thing tomorrow morning to get to the bottom of this."

I didn't like Dad going to the school and making a big commotion. Lately he'd been visiting at least once a month. I wasn't *that* close to failing, but the erratic nature of my grades—an A-plus in music and history followed by a C-minus in arithmetic and science—really got under Dad's skin, as though I was bopping from the top of my class to the bottom just to get him going. Far as I could tell, no other parents made a habit of showing up without warning first thing in the morning to "have words" with their child's second grade teacher. So it wasn't exactly a coincidence that during "family storytime" I shared with my astonished class how Mom, on Halloween night, had yanked down Dad's pants and spanked him for gobbling up most of the candies I'd collected. I had a pretty good feeling that this "bare-bottom whacking," when discussed in the prim and proper setting of Miss Hutchinson's class, would cause Dad some embarrassment.

"It's not nice to lie about your parents," a blushing Miss Hutchinson had stammered, sucking her teeth.

If only I were lying. The sound of Dad's theatrical boohooing, accompanied by the sight of his bared brown behind, stuck with me like a scene from a horror movie. Even though Mom and Dad were goofing around, I didn't find it at all funny, at least at the time. But it was downright hilarious when, halfway through dinner, Dad just about choked on his meatloaf when I let it slip that my storytime confession had resulted in my classmates howling and me being sent to the principal's office.

"Your parents did what?" Mr. Cutcher, the principal, asked, needing to sit down once I'd confessed my misdeed, as though he needed to catch his breath. Then, as though just the thought of such a scandalous act scared him, he ordered me back to class with a whispered: "Make sure you never, ever repeat that story to anyone again."

Up until that point, it had been uncharacteristic of me to risk punishment. But as time passed, my confidence grew; I was figuring out that, with a little forethought, I could break any number of rules—Dad's in particular—without getting caught.

If I was the family sneak, complying with Dad's autocratic rule on the face of things while defying him on the sly, Larry was the great debater, inexhaustibly taking Dad to task over everything from how much TV he could watch to how late he was allowed to stay up at night. "Enough!" Dad would eventually thunder. "Discussion's over!" But Dad always managed to soften his stance with one of his crooked, half-approving smiles. "Donna, that boy's a fighter, he's gonna be another huge Hill success story," he'd say to Mom, in one of those stage whispers even the mailman walking up our front steps could hear.

Karen, thank goodness, was neither a debater nor a sneak. Her sweet temperament provided the balance our house so dearly needed; otherwise the collective Hill intensity would have blown our roof sky-high. Dad, who'd always wanted a daughter, labelled her his Little Love Bug, overloading her with equal measures of protection and affection. It was as if he needed to remind himself, after contending with two obstinate boys, that his "darling little butterball" was actually real. Despite the attention Dad paid to Karen, it never occurred to me to feel jealous, as she seemed to be hard-wired by a different set of genes. Not only was she as well behaved as I was disobedient, she was as gullible as Larry was suspicious.

"Hey, Karen, look at that black beetle with all those crooked legs, don't you think it'd be fun to eat? Really, Larry and I eat them all the time when we're bored."

Crunch. Smack. Drool. Karen would quickly gulp the wriggling beetle down like it was one of those chocolate turtles and then look up at me with that eager-to-please smile, awaiting my next command. Had I asked Larry to eat a bug he would have picked it up and mashed it into my forehead.

When we had company for dinner, usually Dad's jazz-loving, pipe-smoking intellectual friends, Karen would be called on for a song and dance.

"Sing 'A Fine Romance' for us, my little Lena Horne," Dad would request, and Karen would hop off the dining-room chair and channel Joe Williams right down to his sassy baritone, twisting and gyrating her coiled, pint-sized body low to the floor as the dinner guests oohed and aahed at the spectacle of a four-year-old gravelling out the witty jazz classic like a seasoned pro.

As our guests clapped and hollered out their approval, Karen, finding herself at the end of the song and beyond the protective spell of her singing, would clamber onto Mom's lap, as embarrassed as I was secretly impressed by her ninety-second burst of hamming.

Karen shared my singing abilities and outperformed me in school, constantly pulling off marks almost as high as Larry's. But she lacked my attitude, my growing sense of certainty.

I might have thought that Karen's timidity came with being female, except that Mom, while sharing none of Dad's appetite for the spotlight, made it clear that she was no pushover. She was quick to fix her classic "who are you fucking kidding?" face on anyone who dared question her opinion on anything from politics to literature to fashion. But while Karen witnessed her bigger, more rambunctious brothers catching Dad's competitive spark and running with it, our intensity pulling other kids into our orbit, Karen was finding that most girls her age operated in snotty little social clubs with an impossibly exclusive membership.

"Let's play hide-and-go-seek," the leader of the girl clique would suggest to Karen. And Karen, thrilled at finally being included, would be the designated seeker, eagerly covering her eyes and counting to the appropriate number. It would take her half an hour of fruitless searching before she realized that the gang had long since abandoned her, this being their idea of a clever joke.

And so, given Mom's Mighty Mouse pluck, and Larry and I destined to become "obnoxiously relentless Hill strivers," Karen's gentle and uncompetitive nature, her confounding manner of wanting simply to love people and be loved back, struck me as not only wrong, but dangerous. I remained convinced that if I didn't tease my sister out of her vulnerability, it would somehow infect me as well.

As a child growing up under Dad's reign, I figured you could go one of two ways: You could marvel at his strength, while bit by bit determining how to stand up to his dominance, either directly like Larry, or indirectly like me. Or, as in Mom's case a lot of the time, and in Karen's case all of the time, you could be subsumed by the sheer magnitude of Dad, with the understanding that, as a reward for your obeisance, he would always be sweet, loving and tender. Whatever direction you chose, Dad was watching, ever mindful. Sometimes Dad's protectiveness was undetectable (a teacher wisely reconsidering cuffing a Hill child for interrupting his lesson), but more often it could be stifling and embarrassing (the way he wrapped his burly arms around Karen, Larry and me while herding us like wayward cubs across a parking lot and into a restaurant, glaring at the driver of any car remotely in our vicinity to get the hell out of our way). And then there were times when Dad's protectiveness verged on the superhuman.

During the Christmas season of 1963, when our family was driving home from visiting relatives in various parts of the United States, we were involved in a car crash that almost killed us. Mom had wanted to visit her twin sister, Dottie, in Boston, but Dad wanted us to visit his parents and sister Margaret in Washington, D.C., as well as his sister Jean and her family in Brooklyn. So they flipped a coin to see which of them got to choose. When Mom won the coin toss, Dad, being Dad, reinterpreted the rules of the toss and insisted that they visit both sides of the family.

In the car with us on the return trip was my Aunt Margaret. She'd been living with my grandparents, unable to take care of herself since she'd been struck down by mental illness. While the details were pretty murky to my ten-year-old mind, it seemed my grandparents were starting to crack under the constant strain of caring for her. Now Aunt Margaret was coming home to live with us. Margaret sat, barely stirring, beside me in the back of the car—not reacting when I'd sneak glances at her, trying to find signs of this invisible illness we were forbidden to mention. Dad kept telling Mom she was driving too fast, that she should slow down. Dad hadn't wanted Mom to drive at all, but he'd done all the driving up to that point and Mom had finally convinced him that he needed a break. The weather was bad. A cold, light rain was falling, freezing once it hit the highway. Fifty miles from the Canada–U.S. border we hit black ice. The back of our Valiant station wagon went into a fishtail.

Mom, panicking, took her foot off the accelerator and slammed on the brakes. The fishtailing increased; Margaret screamed; the car spun out of control, hitting the guardrail and bouncing off like a toy with a concealed spring. It stopped with its back end sticking out halfway into the right-hand lane of the highway, an easy target for oncoming traffic.

"Drive forward, Donna," Dad yelled. "Hurry! Get the car off the throughway and onto the shoulder." But the car wouldn't start. While the rest of us sat stunned, Dad leapt out of the car and pushed the car with all of us in it onto the shoulder of the highway and out of danger. It happened so quickly that it felt like a dizzying carnival ride gone wickedly askew. We sat on the shoulder, Mom slumped over the wheel, crying, Margaret cradling my sister in her arms, crying, Larry not seeming to react at all and Dad flinging open the doors to the station wagon and, one by one, yanking us out of the car. What a great story to tell my class, I thought, guiltily. On the long, bumpy ride in a tow truck to a roadside motel, Mom's crying seemed to go on forever, counterpointed by Dad's uncharacteristically quiet, calming voice of comfort.

"If not for your father, we'd all be dead right now," Mom used to say, until Dad forbade her and the rest of us to talk about the accident anymore. "I don't think there's another man alive who would have had the power, the presence of mind, to have done what he did."

All Dad cared to say about the throughway incident was "Any father would have done the same thing for his family."

Dad consistently downplayed his size and physical strength, which in turn gave his powers a mythic aura. Even when he shared his stories of teaching men how to box, or throw grenades, in the U.S. Army during World War II, it was his quickness of mind, his mental reflexes that he'd accentuate.

"One time a soldier pulled the pin, cocked the grenade behind his shoulder and froze," Dad told us while we were driving to a campsite for a long weekend, sticking the heel of his right hand into the roof of our Valiant to demonstrate a limb momentarily paralyzed while clinging to a live grenade. "I had to make a mad dash to his side, grab that grenade and throw it away in an instant. Had I waited one more second we'd have all been blown to kingdom come. And you know what that means, don't you, kids?"

"Yes, Daddy," we'd say in unison, strangely chipper under the circumstances. "None of us would've been born."

"That's right. Remember, all of you, he who hesitates is lost."

Of the many sides of my father, this was the one that most inspired me. I couldn't relate to his university degrees and his high-octane career. But his presence of mind, his ability to react on a dime to a sudden crisis and quickly defuse any and all danger with a combination of power and brains, was what stuck with me. That was the kind of man I wanted to be.

CHAPTER 4

The Stocking Cap

Realizing that music wielded an unusual hold on me, and that I would have sung non-stop had it not been for inconvenient school rules, my parents enrolled me in a Toronto conservatory music program. The class was based on the teachings of renowned German composer Carl Orff, whose philosophy was that children's initial exposure to music be recreational, experimenting with primal rhythms and playful percussive sounds. In the sixties, this idea was revolutionary. Regrettably, what appeared on paper to be a refreshing approach to introducing young children to music didn't come out that way in the class.

Twice a week, I was among seven "gifted" kids (we'd had to audition to be selected) herded into a small, overheated room (the furnace in this University of Toronto building was on permanent blast-off) cluttered with hand drums, cymbals, glockenspiels, bongos and enough bells, whistles and wind chimes to supply a hundred New

Year's Eve parties. This appeared too good to be true, a bribe in the making. Any parent with a smattering of empathy can understand that for most eight-year-olds, being subjected to a forty-five-minute drive downtown after a full day of school and then saddled with two hours of music lessons, however revolutionary the teaching, wasn't a whole lot of fun. Especially when you knew that your less gifted but far happier friends were throwing rotten eggs (picked up from the refuse bin behind the local supermarket) at passing cars and then running like the dickens when some old guy leapt out of his front seat and took chase, wheezing obscenities.

All the same, if ever there was an after-school program that would have appealed to me, this would have been it: ten instruments for every student, little emphasis on sight reading or tonality, lots of whacking out noisy rhythms with your hands and nary a violin in sight. There was, however, a fly in the ointment: our teacher, Miss Moon. A neurotic, artsy woman in her thirties, Miss Moon began every class by tartly reminding us that she'd been destined to become a world-famous concert pianist. Tragically, some mysterious injury had prevented her from making a mark on the world. The rest of the lesson was spent with Miss Moon taking out her career frustrations on us. She thrived on spewing ridicule—the more kids she could bowl over with one sweeping put-down, the more she came to life. After three years of being exposed to teachers of varying temperaments, I'd already accepted that misanthropy and teaching often overlapped. What was harder to handle was that I was the only child Miss Moon didn't attack. In fact, she loved me. So maybe I had a quicker intuitive grasp of how to stop a cymbal from ringing—just grab it—big deal. Maybe I'd been (according to Dad) blessed with advanced hand-eye coordination that enabled me to bang across the brilliant, United Nations–coloured xylophone with more of a melodic flair than my fellow students, but again, so what?

Every class wound down with Miss Moon clapping out long, varying rhythms wearing elegant white gloves, making what should have been a *smack, smack, smack* sound like a muffled *shhhd, shhhd, shhhd*. Still, her rhythms were a cinch to clap back, for me, if not for anyone else.

"I've never, in all my years of teaching, come across a boy as musical as your son," Miss Moon told my mom at the end of one of my lessons.

"Danny?" Mom asked, gesturing at me, suspecting that Miss Moon had confused me with some other young Mozart.

"It's not just his beautiful singing tone, but his knowledge of how to use his voice that's so . . . so, well, it's enough to make you believe in reincarnation."

"Reincarnation! That's a bunch of propaganda," I murmured, copying Dad's inflections under my breath.

"I'm an artist," Miss Moon concluded, clutching Mom's elbow as she walked us out of her classroom. "I'm trained to spot budding artists in the making."

Okay, so my artsy-fartsy teacher thought I was "special." I'd known for years that no kid alive—other than Karen—could sing like me. The problem with Miss Moon blabbing on about my "heaven-kissed gift" was that it might lead to a lifetime of after-school music classes—with her.

"But I don't wanna go to any more Orff lessons," I cried, as Mom discussed with me the responsibilities that came with being gifted. Nuts to that. I wanted to do what I'd always done. Rush home to inhale a couple hours of Sinatra records and then, sufficiently energized, scamper outdoors to play football and smash pumpkins.

"We'll talk this over at suppertime with your father," Mom answered tersely.

Predictably, Miss Moon's patronizing pushiness didn't mix well with Dad's personality. When the time came to enrol in the next set of classes, Miss Moon explained to Dad over the phone that she wanted to take me all around the province, displaying my musical genius—and how she was coaxing it out of me—to other Orff teachers and students. Dad nixed that idea, believing that my travelling outside the city, even with a tutor, would damage my already average school grades. Miss Moon interpreted Dad's refusal to allow me to be her "little travelling musical monkey" (as he put it to Mom in that behind-closed-doors voice that I could always overhear) as a personal insult. Finally, between Dad musing aloud that Miss Moon was "a little batty" and me pitching a fit at the thought of suffering through another series of her classes, Dad, over Mom's protests, withdrew me from the Orff program.

With all the regular challenges of raising a family, Mom and Dad let the curse of my gift slide for a year or two, leaving me happily singing on my own, discovering the magic of music in my informal way. My idea of the perfect lesson never changed: listening to Billie Holiday till I had her reedy, mournful style memorized and then singing "My Funny Valentine"—Dad's greasy comb as my microphone—into the bathroom mirror. But then, a month after my tenth birthday, my parents presented me with another one of their bright ideas.

"Danny, you're at an age now where you should be learning to play a musical instrument," Dad said. "You can't let your talent go to waste."

Mom, always one to pour a bit of sugar on Dad's rules, added, "It can be any musical instrument of your choice."

"Okay. I wanna learn how to play the drums."

"Any instrument but the drums," my parents said, both of them flinching.

"Okay, I wanna play electric guitar. Like the Beatles."

"Any instrument but the drums or electric guitar," Dad said.

"How about classical guitar, Danny?" offered Mom. "If you study that for a while and do well, then we'll talk about getting you an electric guitar."

I wasn't against the idea of learning classical guitar, but I suspected this was another one of my parents' attempts at playing up the upper-middle-class, well-cultured family thing. Music not so much a passion or a career choice, but a way of letting your neighbours know that—not unlike smoking a pipe while playing tennis in matching whites—you were terribly refined.

"It's important that the Hill kids have a touch of culture in their lives," Dad would say, conveniently forgetting his childhood bout with culture—three force-fed piano lessons culminating in sore knuckles, a busted ruler and a teacher who decided Dad was a lost cause. Dad had a fixation with culture: eating in ethnic restaurants (even though Dad would manage to get the Indian or Greek or Chinese restaurant to make him a grilled-cheese sandwich), sitting through boring operas and pansy ballet recitals, reading Shakespeare and now this: forcing his son to "master" a musical instrument, all in the name of creating a cultivated appearance.

But I found classical guitar lessons to be a great adventure. Mr. Lemmings, my guitar teacher, had an interesting instruction method. He spent the first two-thirds of the lesson filing the nails of my right hand into lovely half moons—the ideal length to catch the nylon guitar strings just so, to produce that sweet sound. My manicure completed, he'd then produce a thick classical guitar book and begin explaining the fundamentals of reading music. By the time he'd get around to pointing out the differences between the bass and treble clef I'd have tuned him out, distracted by the half-dozen black-and-white photos taped crookedly to his wall. They all featured him in an aggressive crouch, playing Spanish guitar with slicked-back black hair, wearing a tuxedo and a fiendish grin. I imagined a snorting bull was just out of camera frame, about to gore him and his gleaming Spanish guitar at any moment.

I never liked to play in front of Mr. Lemmings, but in the safety of my own room I found the preludes and the etudes evocative, dreamlike and easy to arpeggiate. I'd make up my own melodies and words as I plucked through these exercises on my rented guitar, and my singing improved my playing, or maybe it just seemed that way. Mr. Lemmings always appeared shocked that I'd mastered whatever homework he'd given me, as I must have seemed clueless, stumbling and hacking during his initial instruction. He'd often ask me to play in special recitals, but that was definitely not for me. Much as I loved the classical guitar and its gorgeous, gliding tone, its introspective chord progressions, even its exacting technique, I always knew I was biding my time for the real music: rock 'n' roll and pop.

As I'd suspected, after I'd taken six months of lessons, my parents were already insisting that I entertain the assortment of guests that drifted in and out of our house. "Nothing like some after-dinner guitar music," Dad would say, pointing at me as the new family beacon of culture. Flattered despite myself, I'd sit in perfect classical guitar posture, left foot resting on a six-inch stool, guitar positioned at the perfect angle across my left thigh, and play "Malaguena," boring the dutiful guests cross-eyed. Clearly, Segovia had nothing to worry about.

On my eleventh birthday my parents bought me my first guitar.

"Now that we know you're serious about practising, it's time for you to have your own guitar," Dad explained. Overcome with excitement, I mumbled: "Thank you. This is, like, well, it's the last thing I ever—"

"You never thought your tightwad ol' pappy would spring for something like this, eh boy?" Dad teased. "Still got a few surprises left in me, see!"

"Mmmmm," I said, too busy cradling in my arms the greatest present I'd ever received to concentrate on anything else. One strum of my fingers across the zinging new strings and our living room burst with a majestic *thrummm* that hung in the air for a good twenty seconds.

I took that guitar everywhere with me: school, parties, babysitting. It gave me confidence, an illusion of independence and a slight swagger in my stride. This meant that the clash of wills between Dad and me became more pronounced. Our family had recently moved from our original Don Mills bungalow to a big four-bedroom house in a brand-new subdivision on the other, wealthier side of the Don Valley Parkway. In keeping with this burnished and even Waspier neighbourhood, we were now expected to comport ourselves as immaculately mannered young adults.

This may well have been related to the rising expectations and pressures Dad was now facing in his own life. Two years into his job as director of the Ontario Human Rights Commission, the first of its kind in Canada, his taxing schedule included constant travelling and frequent media appearances. He was a rising star in government, making him a frequent punching bag for right-wing newspaper editorialists blanching at the thought of government-imposed human rights legislation. Left-wing radicals made their own noise, claiming Dad was too moderate. Because Dad, in the early-to-mid-sixties, was the only Black person playing a key role in the Ontario government, he felt all the more pressure to be perfect. He must have sensed the entire Black community holding its collective breath; the better his performance, the more openings there might be for future Black movers and shakers in government. Equally intense was the idea that one little misstep on his part could be perceived by many as "a Negro had been given a chance, and blown it."

Nonetheless, Dad loved all this attention. A negative editorial in the *Toronto Sun* would have him furiously pacing the house, griping about those "nutty reactionaries." "That so-and-so," he'd protest to no one in particular, "he's out to get me." A rave write-up in the *Toronto Star* would have him strolling through the house like a king. When someone started to call in bomb threats to our house, we were warned not to answer the phone. This threat left me feeling more awestruck than anxious: yet another example of Dad's impact on the world.

But bomb threats and the odd accusation of being a Communist sympathizer felt like little more than schoolyard taunts compared to the news he and Mom greeted us with one Sunday morning, after our chores had been completed. We were huddled around Dad in the living room, where we always congregated when a Hill family meeting had been called.

"This is a big family secret," Dad began. "When we first moved into this house, my doctor informed me that I had diabetes. In all the hubbub of moving and getting you kids enrolled in new schools, your mother and I decided to hold back on telling you this news."

But we'd moved back in March of '65. Now summer was long over, and the leaves were changing colours. My parents' logic left me suspicious. *What was this diabetes thing?* To hear my parents go on so furtively made me wonder whether Dad had committed some terrible crime that had to be covered up in order to save our family name. Mom was in the midst of pointing out the symptoms that Dad might exhibit if his sugars were either too high or too low, batting around terms like "coma" and "hypoglycemia" like she was talking about a mild case of the sniffles.

"My father and I became diabetic at precisely the same age," Dad interrupted, noticing that Mom's detailed impaired-pancreas lesson was a tad advanced for us. "And just like you kids, my sisters and I were forbidden to tell a soul. People might jump to conclusions and think that diabetes could interfere with a man's work."

Dad, the king of mixed messages, appeared almost happy to be sharing this disease with his father, even as he was warning us to keep quiet about it. While Larry and I silently took all this in, Karen started crying, managing in between heaving breaths to ask: "Daddy, does diarreas mean you're going to die?"

"Diabetes," Larry and I yelled.

"Don't be silly," Dad said. "You kids know by now that Hills are made of powerful stuff. There's no illness that can defeat us!" Dad paused to give Mom a peck on the cheek, leaving me to wonder if maybe diabetes was like a kind of advanced crossword puzzle that could be solved with sheer brain power. In true camp-counsellor style, Dad concluded our family meeting on a rousing note: "Your grandmother May had throat cancer. The doctors gave her a year to live, tops, and she fooled them all. That was more than thirty years ago and she's still out gardening every day."

Dad's speech left me convinced that there was nothing to worry about. A man of his magnitude seemed immune to all illness, and because diabetes tends to work insidiously—the high blood sugars slowly and painlessly eroding the blood vessels and inner organs—neither Dad nor the rest of us could see the damage it was doing to his body. We did feel the effects of his frequent, unpredictable mood swings, much of which could be attributed to his see-sawing blood sugars. To the outside world, however, Dad's authority, energy and dynamism appeared undiminished. As much as Dad loved and believed in the substance of his work, the resulting attention he received—whether from the media, the higher-ups in government or a neighbour on the street—could leave him pumped for the remainder of the day. I never tired of witnessing these transformations. It was like a switch had been flicked on under his skin; his brown eyes would sparkle and his voice would turn animated, his balmy laughter and rat-tat-tat sentences infecting everyone around him with the same buoyant enthusiasm.

As Dad's career and public profile continued to gain momentum, any talk of his diabetes was discouraged, even within the privacy of our home. In front of us, Dad never displayed any concern over his rival-a-rock-star travel schedule. Indeed, his self-reflection seemed to decrease in direct proportion to his ever-growing career status—or, as he put it, "appreciation in government circles." For a man who actively advertised his disbelief in God, he started to take on an almost godly presence to me, as more and more, none of the ordinary laws of nature seemed to apply to him. It's quite possible Dad believed in his utter infallibility as deeply as I did.

Meanwhile, from the mid-sixties on, our household was in an ongoing state of transition. With three kids in school and Dad darting all over Ontario investigating discrimination cases, Mom had more time on her hands. Lacking a close friend (like her former Newmarket neighbour, Eileen), and more alienated in clean and clubby Don Mills than she let on, she appeared restless, even bored. For the first time I could feel some tension between my parents. Mom, while still going along with Dad's domineering rule, was second-guessing, even criticizing, some of his decisions—to his face and, more disturbingly, to me when Dad was off at work.

"When your father is actually home, he never wants to do anything with me, or take me anywhere, and yet he expects me to stay housebound as well. He's a skinflint, keeping me on too tight a budget, especially now that he's making more money . . ."

I hated hearing this stuff, all the more because it touched on some of the things I was noticing: the Dad I once knew, the ebullient, irreverent and high-spirited Newmarket Dad, was gradually giving way to a cantankerous and often withdrawn Don Mills Dad. A Dad whose growing litany of regulations and behavioural codes struck me as just plain dumb. Okay, some of them were kind of funny: no "putting" (Dad's word for breaking wind) except in the bathroom. The fine for such a lapse in self-control was twenty-five cents. Some of them were annoying: a haircut to start off each month, with Dad ordering me back to the barber if he determined that enough hadn't been taken off.

And then there were the rules that any normal prepubescent kid simply couldn't abide by. We weren't allowed to sleep with underwear on beneath our pyjamas—something to do with it impeding circulation. Dad sometimes implemented surprise bedtime checks. "Out of bed immediately, it's army inspection time. Stand up and slip down those pyjama bottoms, boy. Let me see what you got on underneath."

We were also forbidden to lock the bathroom door. "In case of a household emergency, like a fire," Dad said. Not only did I lock the door, I also propped a chair up against the handle to further impede someone devilish enough (like Larry, who learned this trick from me) to pick the lock with a straightened paper clip. One Sunday morning, after I'd locked the bathroom door to go about my business, Dad decided to pull one of his spot checks. *Bwammm!* Slamming his hand against the door with a force that left the walls shaking, he screamed, "Get up here and open that door right now, boy! On the double!" Shackled by the pants still clinging around my ankles, I stumbled, bent over, to the door and unlocked it. *Whoppp!* Dad struck my face, leaving it branded with the hot imprint of his open palm. Then I hobbled backwards to the toilet. This, I understood, was the natural consequence of me being stupid, of getting caught. Resolving not to be humiliated again, I learned to regulate my bathroom schedule to the hours when Dad was out of the house.

Despite appearances to the contrary, Dad was feeling less and less in charge. With no way of checking his sugar levels at home (self-testing devices were not available in the sixties), and with diabetes meds rife with side effects, the inner workings of his body were volatile and unpredictable. He must have felt as though everything around him was in flux: a wife exhibiting signs of discontent, a job that meant dealing with politicians with suspect agendas, a fast-growing staff to supervise, the mounting expenses of a growing family. And then there was me, intent on playing guitar more and more, and studying less and less.

Dad's defence against all this impertinence was the one thing that remained consistent. Exact control where and when and over whomever he could. Not that I understood any of this when Dad would take Larry and me aside for one of his "special talks." Usually, if he separated us from Mom and Karen, it was a tip-off that things could be getting a little twisted. One of his more notable lectures came about after Larry and I had returned from a month at summer camp. I was eleven years old, already well into puberty, and I had a sinking feeling that this was feeding into Dad's urgency.

"Two of your teenage cousins on your mother's side are pregnant. And Danny, you should know they're not much older than you."

Dad shot me a scathing look, as if this fact somehow implicated me. After I reminded Dad that I'd yet to meet these cousins (although now I wished I had), he said, "Your mother and I have decided that you're at the age now where you should have your own condoms."

What next? Dad subjecting Larry and me to a series of hands-on condom lessons? I mean, nine-year-old Larry or me having sex was about as likely as Dad campaigning for Richard Nixon. But that wasn't the point. We understood that if Dad wanted to hold court and lecture us, graphically, about condom use, he was doing so strictly for his own amusement, so he could watch us wilt in embarrassment. To my relief, Dad didn't turn the condom talk into any kind of demonstration. He simply flashed us a wicked smile and walked away, whistling happily.

"Your father and I know you're experiencing frequent nocturnal emissions," Mom confided, when I begged her to ask Dad to back off with the condom stuff. Surely, shooting off a loaded gun while in dreamland was a far cry from getting some girl pregnant. I mean, c'mon, this was Don Mills, not Haight-Ashbury.

Still, Mom did run pretty good interference. As my voice started deepening, along with all the other fun stuff that signifies the coming of adolescence, Dad threatened to subject me to a whole-body inspection. "To make sure everything is 'coming in' just right," he'd add, by way of justification.

"Mom, can you talk to Dad, please!" would be my first line of defence. But I knew better than to let Dad get to me. As usual, he was just messing with my head, reminding me who was boss. The trick was not to engage him. If you ignored him, his threats would come and go like his endless supply of tall tales, never to be mentioned again.

I was beginning to figure out that our family wasn't what one might consider ordinary. Even Dad's manner of speaking stood out, flitting back and forth, sometimes within the same paragraph, from airily professorial—a Black, liberal version of William F. Buckley Jr. sans the faux Oxford accent—to colloquial and profane. When I slept over at friends' houses, I was struck by how unprepossessing the other fathers appeared, their voices strangely monotone, their descriptions of anything—from politics to work—tepid. Walking home the following morning I could pick Dad out a good block away. He'd be hunched over the garden in our front yard, his ill-fitting straw hat and oversized, dirt-smudged clothes flapping off his body while he tenderly planted his bulbs, singing noisily along to the strains of Count Basie thumping through the living-room window. Did he simply not care how he came across? Was he trying to send our street's property values plummeting? Or was I the only one reacting to him this way: ping-ponging between feeling proud of Dad's extreme behaviour and being mortified by it?

I hated to admit to myself that much of my discomfort over Dad's eccentricities was based on race. The only brown face for miles, his actions—whether born out of his hobbies, tastes or manner of dress and speech—amplified his Blackness. Was this why I sometimes caught myself going in the opposite direction, "whitewashing" my behaviour to better fit in with the neighbourhood? This could be a dangerously easy impersonation, since my skin was neither brown nor white, just that cursed in-between shade, my lips full while not being thick, my hair curly without spinning into kinky little circles. Moreover, I understood that the way I acted could be the greatest determining factor as to whether kids in my neighbourhood saw me as Black or white. I secretly resented Dad for being the one person who could blow my Caucasian cover.

My shame, alas, would deepen in the wake of Dad's constant demands that we, as not only mixed-race children but the children of human rights activists, had a moral responsibility to enlighten people, to disabuse them of their racist inclinations. It was as though Dad thought he could will us into fierce combatants of racism by writing exaggerated accounts in letters such as this one, from 1962, to his parents:

"Donna and I are both exceedingly pleased with [the children's] general development—physically; in the use of language and concepts; and in their unusually developed sense of social justice. They know when they are being wronged, by other parents or siblings, and are vociferous about their rights." It's difficult to imagine Larry, Karen or me being too "vociferous" about anything in 1962, given that I was eight, Larry six and Karen five. I didn't really start coming face to face with racist taunting until a few years later, once we'd moved to the "classy" but seemingly less tolerant side of Don Mills. It was there that I was really given the chance to stand up for social justice—and quietly stayed seated.

I was more than willing, at the know-it-all age of twelve, to dominate poitical debates in the safety of the classroom, rabidly engaging all comers on the issues of the day: school busing, affirmative action, America's foreign policies, etc. But unlike Dad, once I was removed from the cocoon of my classroom and confronted with real-life bigoted behaviour, whether in the schoolyard or on my block, I kept my mouth shut. While everyone traded "nigger jokes" in the dressing room after a hockey game, I'd sit twitching, silently. All I wanted was to shrink into myself, to have my skin turn paler and paler. Meanwhile, Dad's words would stick beneath my skin, reminding me of my unfulfilled obligations. *Stand up to any person who uses words like "Kike" or "Jap" in front of you, 'cause they'll be calling you a "nigger" the second your back is turned.*

People didn't necessarily wait till my back was turned. When I started attending junior high, the cool, older kids would hang around the local plaza after class, sitting on the five-foot wall abutting the corner house and the parking lot, trying their best to look tough. One day the leader of the gang offered me a cigarette. I said yes as casually as possible, knowing I was getting in way over my head. In my eagerness to prove my cool-worthiness, I chomped down hard on the cigarette, leaving it soaked with saliva. After a few fey puffs I handed the cigarette back to the leader, who looked dismissively at the soggy butt and scoffed, "Nigger lips."

"Pardon?"

"Your lips are fat, like a dumb nigger's, that's why you drenched my fuckin' cigarette, you moron," he sneered. As if pre-rehearsed, the entire gang took up his chant, jeering: "Nigger lips! Nigger lips!"

I ran home, tore into my room and slammed the door, feeling a multi-layered shame: shame for being regarded as different, and a deeper, more troubling shame for not having the guts to stand up to their slurs. I would never again look at a cigarette without feeling sick to my stomach.

The angrier I became at my gutlessness outside the house, or my hollow "Black power" rhetoric during classroom discussions, the more resentful I became of Dad—for being Black like him but not being strong and confrontational like him.

My way of shutting all this race stuff out was to lose myself in music. It was the one thing, the only thing that I was fearless about. Mom would sometimes say with a wry laugh that I immersed myself in the arts because it was as far removed from Dad's chosen profession as possible. But in fact I'd simply taken Dad's browbeating influence to always do your best, to be hugely successful, and filtered it through the lens of what I considered my natural calling: to be the greatest singer-songwriter ever.

In the same way that Dad, as a teenager, ferreted out kids who shared his formidable party-hearty spirit, and Larry, the brainer, sought out other deep thinkers at his elite private school, it wasn't long before I stumbled across other kids who, like myself, turned to creativity to carve out their own sense of belonging. The Don Mills I grew up in may have been back-breakingly straight, but if you dug a little deeper there were also some brilliant kids—quietly iconoclastic—lost in their own world of books, music and imagination.

I met Matt McCauley in grade seven. His father, Dr. William McCauley, was one of Canada's top television and film composers. Matt grew up sitting next to his father on the piano bench, captivated by the sight of his father's fingers coaxing melodies out of his nine-foot Steinway grand. By the time Matt and I became friends, he could play every instrument under the sun, better than any other kid I knew. He also had a recording studio in his house and a Moog synthesizer, something most of the world had never heard of in 1967. We started spending hours in his studio, making demos of my songs, dissecting every note of every hit song on the radio, turning each other on to artists that ran the spectrum from Frank Zappa and Jimi Hendrix (his choice) to Laura Nyro and Simon and Garfunkel (mine). Matt, already an advanced composer and arranger, viewed writing songs and making records as an exact science, whereas to me music was all about passion—the less trained, the more organic, the better.

Matt had the kind of looks that most Don Mills boys would kill for: tall and slender, with waves of dark curly hair and eyes so fiercely green they seemed catlike. The poster boy for the ideal-looking white kid, he'd acted in numerous TV commercials and a few CBC dramas. Interestingly, his striking appearance didn't prevent him from becoming the school's outcast. An unabashed nonconformist, Matt was proof that if you didn't act like everyone else you were treated like an alien species, regardless of your skin colour. All the boys hated him—and for good reason. Not only was he a brilliant musician, but in a "nice" neighbourhood where modesty about one's abilities was the accepted rule, Matt had little problem reminding everyone that he was brilliant, and then some. By the time we were both fourteen, Matt was being subcontracted to score scenes in assorted movies and TV series that his father was too busy to compose. And he wasn't shy about letting everyone in the school know that he was making more dough in one cushy studio session than all the other kids in his class combined, who were slogging it out with their paper routes through black February mornings.

But Matt's worst flaw was that every girl in every class was in love with him.

In Don Mills, boys didn't object to another guy being a stud if he was a star quarterback. But there was something suspect about a decidedly unathletic guy who attracted girls simply because he slung around a lot of fifty-dollar words and could take a recording studio apart and put it back together again, improved, without even glancing at a manual.

"Don't worry about what the guys in our school think of you," I'd say, when Matt complained to me about feeling excluded. "These guys hate the Beatles for the same reason they hate you."

"'Cause I'm a genius."

"Nah. They couldn't care less about that. They just don't like that the girls are all horned up by the thought of you being a genius."

"That's a pretty nebulous distinction, if you ask me. But if that's true, then how come you're not jealous of me?"

"Because you can't sing or write songs like me. Besides, having half the school love you and the other half hate you—man, that's way too much pressure."

Matt considered this, his mouth tightening into a patronizing moue before countering, "I can compose music better than you. You recycle the same half-dozen chords in all your songs. It's just that your words are so good that people forget how redundant your music can be."

I had learned to take Matt's haughty observations in stride, retaliating with gibes of my own when necessary. I can't imagine any two Don Mills kids more bent on one-upmanship. But like many creative and competitive collaborations, this worked to our advantage. We tacitly understood that our respective talents were as different as they were complementary. Matt's penchant for scribbling complex orchestrations on a napkin in the junior high cafeteria left me feeling a twinge of inadequacy, until I remembered my knack for writing: by fifteen I was already getting articles published in Toronto newspapers like the *Telegram* at twenty-five dollars a pop, and winning essay contests, along with their cash prizes, in local periodicals such as *Contrast* (a Black newspaper), leaving some people accusing me of plagiarizing. Still, we turned everything into a competition, right down to the whose-family-is-smarter contest.

"You have a way with words, I'll give you that," Matt would concede, "but my grandfather wrote all the *Hardy Boys* books. What did your grandfather publish?"

"Well, my mom's dad wrote *Great Moments in Pharmacy*, which was even spoofed in *Mad* magazine."

"Sounds like a real cliffhanger, that one," Matt sniffed.

But no matter how much we pissed each other off, we understood that we were stuck with each other. I benefited from the free run of Matt's recording studio, along with his invaluable production and arrangement help. And my natural grasp of pop music, from its deceptively simple song structure to its subtle vocal inflections, grounded Matt, while giving him a fresh outlet for his classical music training. We grudgingly respected each other and, more importantly, related to the other's dubious status of being misfits by Don Mills standards.

Treated as precocious by his parents, Matt's eccentricities were nurtured and encouraged when he was at home. Watching Dr. McCauley beam as his son played his latest TV score left me so uncomfortable, so consumed with envy, I sometimes had to leave in the middle of Matt's performance. Unlike Matt, home was becoming the last place I'd go to be reminded that there was no shame in being different. Home was the one place where my growing reputation as "the kid with the guitar" couldn't distract me from feeling that, from the colour of my skin right down to the way I perceived things, I was very much alone.

As I read more Black literature and became increasingly aware of racial politics, I was beginning to notice that some of Dad's messages concerning racial pride were not simply mixed, they were downright scrambled. Dad could be the proudest, baddest Negro in the world and then do something that indicated that our Blackness needed to be tamed, watered down and reined in.

Late one evening, I was reviewing chords to a pop song in the kitchen. Appointed to accompany the school choir the following weekend, I was halfway through the Turtles' "Happy Together" when Dad appeared, pulled up a chair and sat down beside me. He waited until I completed the song before speaking. Not a good sign.

"Son, your hair has started to get way out of control. You're at the age now where you're going to have to wear a stocking cap to bed at night."

"Huh?"

Dad quickly yanked a hair out of my head and placed it in front of me on the kitchen table.

"Hey, what's your problem?"

"Watch your mouth, boy, or I'll smack it sideways."

Trying to ignore him, I watched this single brown strand of hair loop into a kind of broken figure eight, contrasting rudely with the table's bright white surface.

"You see that, son," Dad said, affecting the tone of a science teacher, "your hair's way too curly. Nobody wants hair *that* curly. Wearing a stocking cap at night will straighten it out right away."

I swept the disgusting, twisted, black hair off the table. The guitar bobbled on my lap. As I steadied it, I could feel my Adam's apple slowly rise and expand. It was already too big. Dad had said it was because I hit puberty so young and sang too much, but damned if it didn't always swell up in my throat to the size of a squash ball when Dad got to me.

Dad rolled the stocking cap over my head—I knew better than to resist—and pulled it down over my ears so that they were scrunched up hard against my head, then sauntered out of the kitchen.

For three years, as I'd tug, pull and drag it over my unruly curls, Dad's gift of the stocking cap was a nightly reminder that, because I was Black, I was different. And that, as much as this difference was something to embrace, you couldn't embrace it too much, or else.

CHAPTER 5

Dad's Army Years

The tremendous volume of my father's letters, combined with his unremittingly confessional writing style, was at times too much for me to handle. Reading them made me feel as though I were a child again, listening to Dad tell us about some of his harrowing army experiences. *"One morning, my sergeant punished me for a minor infraction . . ."* I could hear his voice as I began shuffling his army letters into chronological order. Dad had unspooled his "crime and punishment" story in all its stupendous detail during our cross-Canada camping trip in the summer of 1962.

"It had been my turn to get my barracks up, but I'd slept through my alarm. That meant big trouble for me." Knowing that Dad was about to face serious punishment had Larry, Karen and me fidgeting in the back seat of our station wagon, too spellbound by Dad's continuing play-by-play to take in the beauty of the Rocky Mountains as they flashed past our windows.

"In full uniform, under the blazing Oklahoma sun, I had to strap a hundred-and-thirty-pound backpack over my shoulders. Then I was forced to dig a ditch several feet deep. Once I'd finished digging, I had to walk one hundred yards down field where I was given a thimble—"

"Are you certain you want to tell the kids this story, Dan?" Mom asked. But her objection was two or three gruesome details too late.

"I was ordered to scoop water out of a barrel with this itsy-bitsy thimble, walk one hundred yards back to the ditch and spill the remaining drops out of this thimble and into the hole. I had to do this till the ditch was filled. But I kept fainting." At this point, Dad started talking faster. Something in his hurried cadence felt horribly wrong. Bending over, head between my knees, I stared at the candy wrappers on the car's dirty floor mat so no one would see me wrestling back tears.

"My sergeant revived me, stood me back up on my army boots, pried open my mouth, stuck a salt tablet down my throat and made me keep going. I ended up fainting so many times I lost track. But I learned my lesson. I never slept in again."

Bolting up from my slumped-over position in the back seat, I had to fight back an impulse to throw my arms around Dad's neck and shoulders, and protect him. It didn't matter that the damage to Dad had already been done. I needed, somehow, to undo it.

Now, as I sat slumped over a long metal table in the archives building, lost in Dad's army letters, that strange protective reflex was being reawakened, leaving me feeling as powerless as I did forty-five years ago in the back seat of our family station wagon. To cope with all the messy emotions these letters provoked in me, I stayed dryly task-oriented, spending my first day in the Ontario archives building skimming and then listing the letters that were to be copied and sent to me. When, two weeks later, Dad's letters were couriered to my house in a box as big as a suitcase, I felt sick with excitement. Actually, more sick than excited. What had I gotten myself into? The box containing so much of Dad's life sat on the table, where it remained unopened for a few days.

What are you waiting for, boy? I could almost hear Dad cry out. *Stop pussyfooting around! GET TO WORK!* Still, I stalled, circling that bigger-than-life box once or twice each day, slowly inching closer, feeling guiltier the longer I put off the inevitable.

Although a musician who'd made my entire living stripping emotions bare in song, microanalyzing the unspoken minutiae of human relationships, there was a part of me that didn't want to scrape beneath Dad's inscrutable surface. I'd always wanted him to remain more archetype than actual flesh and blood. Anything but human: even his flaws I preferred to see as big and overblown, full of bravado and ballyhoo. So why dive into the back pages of my father's life now? Was it a missing part of Dad I was looking for, or something lost, buried, inside me?

By the end of the week, as the box on the dining-room table started taking up more and more psychic room, Dad's badgering voice clanged on: *Time to be a man, son. No more running away from your responsibilities.* Unable to bear that voice anymore, I made myself a pot of coffee, upended Dad's box of letters on my dining room table and dove in.

In the early forties, despite months of monkeying around all night with his fellow Red Wine Boys and showing up late (if at all) the next day for work, Dad couldn't believe that his foreman had finally made good on his threat and removed him from the protection of necessary work status, leaving him eligible for the U.S. draft. The army had reacted immediately, sending Dad a notice to report to its headquarters in Portland in ten days to undergo a physical. Barring the army doctors detecting cancer or sickle cell anemia, Dad was weeks away from being drafted. This was the last thing Dad wanted. He'd grown up with a father who'd been constantly plagued by war-related illnesses and injuries, a father who'd refused to disclose even the vaguest details about his experiences in the trenches, which had disabused my dad of any romantic notions of combat. All the more so since after patriotically fighting for his country, Dan II's reward had been to return to an America every bit as racist. While my father was by no means blind to the horror of Nazi

Germany's death march across Europe, accounts of Hitler's pogrom, an ocean removed, failed to have the immediate impact of the racism he was experiencing in America. Furthermore, although the majority of Americans believed they were fighting the Nazis to maintain the democratic freedoms inherent in their country of origin, Dad most certainly understood that there was a lot about the American way of life that was neither democratic or free, or worth fighting for. At eighteen years of age, Dad articulated what a lot of Blacks were feeling in one of his early army letters to his parents: "It seems that the Negroes are not going to tolerate anymore prejudice. I am with them and would just as soon clean up on these crackers here as to go overseas."

But above all, four years in the U.S. Army meant four years without serious partying. As a teenager recently liberated from college (and his supercilious Uncle Joe), nothing—not a Methodist minister father, a sheltered upbringing or a work foreman who warned him repeatedly not to show up late or else—was about to stand in the way of his devoted drinking, clubbing and skirt chasing. Only the army had the capability of reining in what Dad's parents were starting to view, with considerable alarm, as their son's increasingly wild behaviour.

The extreme turn Dad's life was about to take took some time to sink in. In the meantime, he purposely flunked his IQ test and then, for good measure, malingered through his physical. Exposed to this type of ruse every day, the army demanded that Dad begin his four years in the military at the end of the month, in Monterey, California.

Twenty years later, Dad would leave Larry, Karen and me laughing till our stomachs hurt, detailing some of the more novel methods soldiers used to get kicked out of the army.

"I had a buddy who got himself thrown out of the army by tying a hot dog to a long piece of string and dragging it behind him everywhere he went—"

"A hot dog?!" the three of us squealed.

"Yup! That daggum hot dog followed him to the outhouse like a trained poodle, even lay beside him on his pillow, stinking up the whole barracks . . ." Dad paused, scrunching his wide, flat nose until it twisted into a kind of deformed pretzel. Then, as if stumbling into the grossest of bathrooms, he issued two loud, shuddering sniffs.

"Ewww, Daddy, stop doing that thing with your nose, it's like we can smell it!"

"You kids wanna know the last place he dragged that smelly hot dog?" Dad asked, in a playful chirp.

"Yes. Yes. Yes."

"My buddy, crazy like a fox, skipped into his psych evaluation looking over his shoulder at his flea-bitten hot dog on a string and yelping, 'Here doggy doggy, woof woof, come on pooch, come come!' Then he fell to his knees and started petting and kissing that sorry hot dog. The army turned around and threw my buddy's behind, hot dog and all, on the first bus back to his hometown."

Not understanding the "crazy like a fox" point to Dad's story didn't prevent me from finding the whole loony act fascinating, all the more so after Mom commented, in her ho-hum style, "Dan. Come on now. Are you sure that wasn't yours truly slinging that hot dog on a string, acting like a mad hatter?"

Now, almost half a century later, as the pages of Dad's life in the service unfolded before me on my dining-room table, it occurred to me that Mom's teasing may well have had an element of truth to it. Maybe Dad was the hot dog slinger, only his little caper, rather than earning him an army exemption, landed him in trouble. Sadly, the first letter that tumbled out of the archive box suggested that trouble clung to Dad like a second skin during his years in the army.

Fort Sill, 1943
Dear Family:

> *... The army is indeed a strange and hard thing to understand for it operates at times with feelings towards no one ...*
> *I have caught particular h—— ever since I have been here at Fort Sill. Other of my buddies had left and gone to camps of advancement all over the country. Yet Buddy Hill remained*

here stuck; working K.P., doing Guard duty, cleaning toilets,
doing clean up, flunky and humiliating work for white officers;
taking insults, abuse . . .

If boarding at Uncle Joe's had forced Dad, for the first time, to live in a world that was not always just, but often downright mean and cold-hearted, that was merely a taste of what he was in for during the next four years. While serving his country Dad would be blindsided by the full and implacable force of racism, U.S. Army–style. His letters home draw a vivid picture of a man retreating into comforting childhood memories, late at night, as a way of coping.

Dear Mom:

Many times I lay in my bunk thinking about the times you
would rub me down when I was in bed with a cold. All of those
things that you did for me will never be forgotten. I guess it's
when a boy is out on his own, bucking all kinds of situations,
that a boy's deepest appreciation of his parents comes.

Throughout his time in the U.S. Army, Dad relied heavily on writing letters to his parents, opening his heart in a startling manner, as a way of maintaining his sanity. Growing up with three sisters and a doting yet independent-thinking mother, it surely was a shock to the senses to be hurled into a regiment of men, all Black and primarily from the south, whose life experiences were completely different from Dad's. Most of the army's southern Blacks, poorly educated thanks to a segregated school system, had been subjected to a far more virulent form of racism and poverty than anything Dad had ever been exposed to. This meant that they were less likely than a relatively privileged northern Negro to be shocked by the army's systemic racism.

Dad, at a loss as to what to do, reverted to his parents' teachings, using his logic and intelligence to question and challenge some of his army superiors' orders. While this thinking may have helped him in civilian life, it most certainly worked against him in the army. Dad was caught between being too educated and not quite educated enough. A university education would have enabled access to the Officer's Commission School, and graduation from OCS would have put him in a rank well above the Black sergeants who delighted in making privates, particularly privates with *attitude,* suffer. On the other hand, having no education would have made him seem less threatening to his immediate superiors. Dad understood the advantages of playing down his advanced schooling to his less privileged army peers: "I do not speak of the fact that I am fairly well educated because if I did my comrades would feel as if I were above them for some of them *can not read or write* . . . I wrote a letter home for a soldier yesterday." But his constant striving to better his military rank made him stand out, in the worst way possible, among his more passive southern comrades: "I went to see my Battery Commander today in order to find out what the delay was in sending me before the Board of selecting officers."

Dad's early service consisted of basic war training exercises: topping the list was the care and feeding of guns and ammunition of every conceivable sort, and later, marksmanship training. The firearm exercises were followed by endless hours of fitness drills, from calisthenics to marathon march-hikes (all the more onerous due to the hundred-plus pounds of equipment weighing down the backpacks) through the hottest and coldest of weather. If several hours of daily regimental marching, in endlessly changing formations, didn't sufficiently break the soldiers down, the constant barking intimidation that hounded them, courtesy of the ever-present, ever-critical Negro sergeants, certainly had the desired demoralizing effect. These marches were also designed to prepare the soldiers for field training trips, complete with camouflaged snipers crouched in the darkness. *Pow, pow, pow*—like deranged bogeymen, these snipers would jump out of the woods to greet an exhausted soldier. The crackling explosion of blanks inches from their faces was known to give even the most resolute of men "loose piles." And if the snipers didn't sufficiently discombobulate them, the land mines placed randomly in the ground, charged with varying (but never full) levels of explosives, could easily injure anyone whose boot landed in the wrong place.

At first Dad tried to convince himself and his parents that he could make the transition to selfless soldier. The following letter, written from Fort Sill, Oklahoma, in February 1943, was still early in his army career, when he undoubtedly wanted to present a positive spin to his loved ones.

Dear Mom and Dad,

. . . My days of individualism are over, I am beginning to realize that I am part of a group. Living, eating, sleeping, learning to fight side by side with my companions makes me realize that when I do wrong, the group as well as myself suffers. When I do right and strive to get ahead, the group advances.

But as the novelty of Dad's new environment wore thin, it became obvious that a private's life was a life of abuse: the physical labour alone, be it ditch digging, latrine and fence building, or constant cleaning and polishing of everything from army boots to shower rods, rivalled that of prison chain gangs. Sure, a soldier earned money, but what was the good of money when you couldn't spend it? For one thing, the towns surrounding the various army bases weren't hospitable to Black soldiers, populated with, according to one of Dad's letters, "nothing but dirty, illiterate, tobacco chewing white trash with their prejudice. So, you see I would rather not to take a pass . . . By confining myself to the camp I eliminate the possibility of getting into unnecessary trouble." Should a Black soldier decide to venture into hostile "white trash" territory, he'd be allowed to leave base only from 5:30 till 11:00 p.m. (Forty-eight-hour furloughs were few and far between.) The closest town was usually at least five miles away, and buses travelling into these towns refused to pick up Black soldiers, while the restaurants and movie theatres would also shut them out.

Hard as it was to witness the full-on prejudice that hovered outside the base, it was the racism inside the segregated Black barracks that most wounded Dad. The army operated on a kind of plantation system that plucked the "best behaved," less independent-thinking Blacks—Uncle Toms, if you will—out of the throng of privates, and gave them the rank of sergeant—provided they kept the potentially uppity Negro soldiers, privates like my father, "in their place." Dad's newly minted army superiors took an instant dislike to what they viewed as a lippy northern Negro, sparing no opportunity to punish him. A 1943 letter to his mother shows the hostility was mutual: "Woe be unto those hypocritic, two-faced rotten Negroes who have tried to block you . . . Jealous, selfish, backbiting Negroes are a detriment to their race, as well as to society."

Both inspired and haunted by his father's officer status (Dan II had been one of over a thousand educated Black men invited to enlist in a military camp in Fort Des Moines, Iowa, where he was trained as an officer shortly before World War I), Dad was determined to earn this honour as well: "My application for OCS [Officer's Commission School] is going in again, and again, until they finally admit me. They will soon tire of seeing me popping up in their Lily White Faces." These "lily white faces" were the white officers who decided who'd be admitted into OCS. In Dad's mind, these officers were the army's de facto slave masters, the ones who yanked the strings of those "hypocritic, two faced rotten Negro" sergeants. And yet, Dad's letters suggest that his greatest outpouring of rage and loathing was directed at himself. He acknowledged as much when he promised in a letter to his parents, "I will soldier to my utmost, because the pressure is on me and I must succeed. I am beginning to get that mental drive and inspiration that I had while at Lincoln. I lost it when I came home, due to my constant playing around, but it is coming back."

Upon realizing that no amount of fake injuries or lunatic impersonations was going to exempt him from service, Dad resolved to make the best of his situation, straining at times to affect a measure of pride. This was, after all, World War II, when a certain status came with being a soldier. If not on the base itself, certainly from the outside looking in, from a civilian's vantage point (notwithstanding the racist exclusion of Negro soldiers by the local population), he was one of his country's protectors.

I guess I'm not doing anything that thousands of others
are[n't] doing in their all out sacrifice . . . I am making out in
great style here. I feel as if I can really soldier for the army. My
shoes shine so hard that they look like a mirror . . . There's one
thing that is essential in this man's army, and that is a sense
of humor, without it you are lost . . . the other night at retreat,
the bugler messed up the call something awful . . . the whole
company was laughing. Well it ended up in the captain giving
us hell for laughing at retreat, and the bugler was made to
practise his call behind closed doors all night.

Dad would soon find out that a sense of humour might offer the odd diversion, but not much more. It seemed that just as he was developing a sense of camaraderie with his fellow soldiers, he'd find himself or one of his new buddies transferred to another base in another state. (Part of the army's grand scheme was to constantly shuffle around the Black soldiers: taking poorly educated sharecroppers from the south and depositing them in the north, while dumping Blacks from the north into southern camps, all the better to disorient and render them vulnerable.) This left my father with little choice but to turn inward, embracing, for the first time in his life, books and ideas. For a young man formerly known as Party Boy, who'd confessed only the year before in a scribbled note to his father that he'd "not quite found himself yet," this represented quite a turnaround. After updating his father on the relative merits of scholarly texts running the gamut from E. Franklin Frazier's *The Negro Family in the United States* to fifteenth-century Persian mathematician and philosopher Omar Khayyám, Dad summarized, "I have found that constant reading of novels, fiction, history and poetry has done a great deal to keep my spirit up. By doing this I hope to never let my interest in further education leave me."

This new commitment led Dad to rewrite and ace his IQ test, giving him the opportunity to enrol in a number of classes, which led to several teaching jobs: everything from basic health classes to self-defence to marksmanship and munitions training. The army was reinforcing the one hard and fast rule that Dad's parents had always stressed: without higher education, particularly as a Negro, you are lost. Eager to let his parents know that he had finally come to see the wisdom of their ways, Dad wrote, "I took an exam for officer's candidate school in artillery and passed. Two white boys and three colored took the exam. Only three passed. I was one . . . At any rate I am not stopping at anything short of a pair of bars. Lieutenant D.G.H. at 19 is my goal."

As soul-destroying as the U.S. Army could be, Dad's sheer effervescence, though sometimes blunted, was never far from the surface. His letters home could seem like notes from a Boy Scout camping excursion. Musing that all things positive in his life were the direct result of his parents' loving tutelage, he wrote, "Oh yes, I made third highest out of 60 Negroes on the Rifle Range . . . the Lieutenant asked where I learned to shoot. I took great pride in telling him that my father was an officer in the last war. Taught me all I knew about shooting . . . Ask Dad if he remembers the time I shot all those ducks in the shooting gallery." His outpouring of affection could also be generous:

Dear Mom,

> *. . . I keep [your] picture in my wallet, beside the dime Dad gave me that he carried in the last war. The dime with your first name and his first name on both sides. Little things like that mean the world to me and give me things to remember, memories that are worth living for.*

But the more Dad reached out for the comfort of family memories, the more he was reminded of his father's prestigious officer ranking in the previous world war. Which would then leave him panicked at the thought of not living up to his father's achievements. Panic would soon give way to anger at a military system that remained determined to block his every effort to get ahead, and also, increasingly, at himself (a letter to his mom goes so far as to describe his past behaviour as "moody, apprehensive, and evil").

As stir-craziness got the better of him, Dad abandoned his vow to avoid the local towns and took a five-hour pass to Lawson. Once there, he was reminded why he was better off staying on base, where, at least, his enemies were a known quantity. "We had a minor race riot in the town outside of camp . . . I really saw southern bigotry, hate, prejudice and ignorance with my own two eyes, plus a little violence. Things are really brewing down here and I expect the lid to be blown off soon. A Negro officer is being forced to relinquish his commission due to friction with The Whites."

Through the ongoing swirl of white-on-Black antipathy, Dad continued to see becoming an officer as his one chance of rising above the fray, his only shot at redemption for his previous reckless behaviour. But redemption would not come easily. "My [battery] commander is a highly prejudiced, self centered man . . . He knows that I have qualified and he cannot hold me back much longer. I forced the issue, so soon my break for college or OCS will come."

Instead the army would turn Dad's ambitions against him, while methodically draining him, one defeat at a time, of his youthful braggadocio. In June 1943, still awaiting his acceptance for OCS, he informed his mother that "the other day they let 12 Negro boys out of OCS . . . not giving any reason for the dismissal at all. They were all splendid men. They told me it's hard to write and tell the folks back home about it." It's as though he is preparing her, and himself, for the inevitable. That it would be but a matter of time before he would join the disgraced ranks of "splendid men."

For most young men, the years aged eighteen to twenty-two bring with them a litany of dramatic changes. It's hard, really, to think of any other four years that are suffused with so many questions, so much in the way of re-evaluation. Without question, it was my father's religious views that underwent the most radical change. All evidence suggests that he went into the army a Christian and left the army an atheist. Initially, he kept his growing skepticism at bay. From Fort Sill, Oklahoma, he wrote, in 1943:

Dear Mom,

*I wish to thank you again for the bracing, helping letter that
you wrote to me when you mailed the check . . . those few
scripture quotations and your telling me how I must stay close
to God, helped me a great deal. Up until that time I had been
a mighty discouraged, downhearted, beaten in spirit, young
man . . . If I haven't found the way, yet . . .*

Your devoted son,
Buddy

But from this point on, Dad's references to religion, which had
been a consistent and positive theme in letters home during his first
year of service, all but disappear, to be replaced by statements like these,
written in early 1945: "I do not place my trust in anything any longer,"
and "these last few days have seen me nearly lose faith in everything that
is supposed to be just and fair in the army."

If the seeds of his religious skepticism were likely planted early on
in his army career, his letters home suggest that it wasn't until he was
well into his third year of service that his faith abandoned him completely. He'd finally had his big break. At first it had looked so promising:
against what had felt like impossible odds, he found himself accepted
into the Army Specialized Training Program (ASTP).

Dear Mom,

*I valiantly tried for an army program called ASTP Army
Specialized training program. Your I.Q. must be 115 or over
and you must have a high school or college education for all of
the phases. [If and when you pass intense questioning from] a
stiff board of superior officers, the army temporarily dismisses
you from active service and sends you to colleges and universi-
ties all over the country . . . if you have made good grades,*

you are able to apply immediately for OCS in Military Intel-
ligence . . . I tried and tried to get this chance to continue my
collegiate training but some white officer in my immediate
Battery did not send my request in, nor did he send my I.Q. in
which alone qualifies me for the program . . . without notifying
my superior white officers, I went to the Headquarters of my
center to see one of the biggest men . . . I told [him] my aim [of
getting into the ASTP]. He was surprised that I had gone by
unnoticed by my immediate officers, and immediately he put
my name on the list to come before the examining board. One
week later . . . I met the board with a salute . . . After stiff ques-
tioning and debate they accepted me. My days of dog life have
ceased. I will be leaving to go to a College to be classified.

Dismissed from active service, Dad was transferred to West Virginia where he was enrolled in several college courses the army had
offered as options. Given that this was the first time in two years that
Dad was interacting with civilians, notably female civilians, it's impressive that he was able to concentrate at all on his studies. Though thoroughly disgusted with every aspect of army life, Dad understood all
too well the cachet of showing up for class in full military uniform. As
he polished his army boots each morning in preparation for his grand
school entrance, the image of his mother swooning over his father,
decked out in full World War I attire, must not have been far from his
mind. Within weeks Dad met a fellow student, Jo, and fell in love. In
a year they were married. And, like so many unfortunate events that
bedevilled my father during his army tenure, after his marriage crashed
and burned, less than twenty months later, he resolved to never speak
about it again.

I needed a break from reading Dad's army letters. It felt like I was inhab-
iting him, cheering on his triumphs and then ducking in anticipation
of his defeats. "Goodness, Dad, you're wearing me out," I mumbled as
Dad's letters kept coming. Fortunately, his constant ever-judgmental

references to his sisters never failed to provide me with some comic relief. To be sure, his fussing was all too familiar.

"Oh yes, by the way, Marge did not get married," Dad, as town crier, informed his mother, although how he would know more about his sister's marital status—considering he was locked away on a remote army base in Oklahoma—than his mother left me puzzled. "This makes three times she jumped from boy friend to boy friend. She ought to get wise to herself, and know what she is doing and what she wants." A few letters later Dad took Margaret to task directly, beseeching her to "make good at home, make the grade, the family is counting on you. Go to college, study, come out the finest social worker ever . . . I'm sacrificing my future, [so] you don't have to do it, don't let me down sis."

"How on earth did Dad become so bloody condescending, so young?" I wondered out loud. It was easier to dwell on these peccadilloes because they distracted me from the bigger picture: even though I didn't know how Dad's big break—being one of a select group of soldiers accepted into the ASTP—would pan out, I had that knotted feeling in the pit of my stomach, the sensation we all get when we know that our favourite character in a movie is about to get slammed. Coward that I was, I tossed all of Dad's letters back into the archive box and hauled it over to my mom's house. It was my intention that the two of us could talk, on the record, about Dad's life in the army.

"How long is this interview supposed to take?" Mom asks, guardedly. Mom's doll-like delicateness catches me by surprise every time I enter her house. (How very weird, that it's no longer Mom and Dad's house.) In my mind, I always picture Mom as bigger, a whole lot bigger, than she really is. So it takes me a few long seconds to reconcile my mental image of Mom—that of a hard-edged, independent woman who'll cuss you out as quickly as she'll hug you—with this delicately framed, white-haired woman who sweetly kisses me on the cheek and offers me some of her fresh-picked raspberries, even as she steels herself for the Interview from Hell.

Dad's presence is everywhere, dwarfing everything. As I walk through the living room, my eyes land on the framed photograph of Dad receiving the Order of Canada from Governor General Adrienne Clarkson. Dad received this award in 2001 for his outstanding work in human rights and Canadian Black history. By then Dad's health was deteriorating far too rapidly for him to travel to Ottawa, so the governor general came to the house for the ceremony. I automatically scan the wall for images of the virile, omnipotent Dad I worshipped as a child. There it is: a perfectly mounted photograph of him, decked out in his imposing World War II U.S. Army uniform. He looks impossibly handsome, with his ramrod-straight posture, serious salute, thin moustache and playful brown eyes. A photo of his own father hangs only inches away, looking eerily similar—just one war, one generation removed.

As I place my tape recorder in front of Mom and put it through its requisite testing, I joke about how foreign it feels for me to cast myself in the role of interviewer. I've always been the interviewee, the one who imperiously stares down the reporter, waiting for his first move, pondering which truth, or lie, or combination thereof, to tell. Mom laughs.

"You've always been a very good liar, Danny," Mom says, like she's giving me a true compliment. I remind her that Dad was an excellent teacher in this regard.

"Touché," she says. Good, she's starting to relax. But the interview gets off to a rocky start when I ask Mom whether some of Dad's anger at his army experiences may have influenced his behaviour as a father.

"I'm not saying your dad wasn't mean, Danny," Mom says, frowning in response to my theory. "If you and Larry insist that he was, well, I guess you both can't be wrong. But I have to say, honestly, I never really noticed that side of him." With that, Mom shoots me one of those cut-the-psychobabble-crap looks. Then she shuffles within inches of my tape recorder, sees that the cassette is running and the red light is on and asks, "Did I ever tell you kids about the time your father tried to kill a vicious army sergeant?"

"What?!"

Mom gazes at me suspiciously, as though, really, she has told me about this event, it's just that I, in my typically absent-minded fashion, have forgotten all about it.

"You've never mentioned this, Mom. I have a feeling I would've remembered."

Mom stares back at me, still unconvinced. "Your dad didn't offer up a lot of details."

"No problem, just tell me what you can remember."

"All I remember, Danny, is that he crawled onto the roof of a two- or three-storey building and dropped a big boulder on this sergeant's head."

"You mean, he hit the bastard?" I realize, too late, that I've asked this with too much enthusiasm.

"Oh no, the boulder missed. I think the sergeant had hunched over to light a cigarette and that saved his life."

"Jesus. Was Dad caught?"

"Of course not. You think we'd be having this conversation if your father had been caught?"

What's weirder, I wonder: Dad's alleged murder attempt or Mom's blasé attitude about the whole thing? I take a letter of Dad's from the archive box and read it to Mom, explaining that it was addressed to his mother in 1943: "Tell Dad that I have a Top Sarge [who] is a hard, evil Negro. I strictly keep out of his way because he conducts a reign of terror on these Negroes."

"I'd like to see that letter, Danny."

"Sure, Mom. But why? You think I'm inventing this?" I'm joking, but Mom isn't smiling.

"Actually Danny, your father didn't talk that much about his time in the army."

I interpret Mom's comment as a gentle way of telling me that she doesn't care to talk any more to me about Dad's army period.

"Imagine," Mom muses, "all three of you children, writers. What are the chances?"

I have a feeling that, at this moment anyway, Mom would have been a lot happier if we'd all been plumbers.

Back at home, I pick up the letters where I'd left off: right after he'd informed his parents of his acceptance into the ASTP. Six months passed before Dad wrote another letter to his family—an unusually long silence.

Dear Family:

When I came home on furlough I was under the complete impression that I would be returned to Engineering School. You were all quite proud of me . . . though now you are entitled to feel any disappointment that you may in me.

The inevitable had happened: Dad had become one of those "splendid Negro men" faced with the task of informing his family of his shameful fall from grace. That Dad owned up to his failure and his resulting sense of humiliation, with such gut-wrenching honesty, undoubtedly moved his parents to be far more concerned about his plunging mood than his not making the grade.

I and 18 other men had been ordered to return to the field under a special request from my mathematics instructor who said that we had not successfully passed his course and could not be recommended to study further in mathematics. This one subject completely eliminated me from school. I had passed all other subjects . . . This failure, which is the same as disgrace to me, knowing the embarrassment my family must have gone through, hurt me worse than anything I have ever had to take in my life. It took the pep and spirit out of me and I did not know how to meet it for I've never failed completely, nor ever intended to fail in any enterprise I undertook on my own power.

Dad still had two more years left to serve in the army. His letters home during this period were largely variations on the same theme: due to his dogged striving for advancement, a sliver of opportunity beckons, a door opens a crack only to be slammed in his face. Dad never did get into officers' school. Realizing that his chances of army advancement at this point were slim to none, his behaviour started to turn openly defiant. What more did he have to lose? This would have been the time Dad may have entertained fantasies of revenge. And if nothing else, this cryptic letter to his father was enough for me to imagine Dad crouched over the edge of a tall building under cover of night, about to use a sergeant's head as target practice.

Denver, 1944.

They tried their best to shanghai me . . . There are many many things I must tell you only in person . . . The only time that I'll be able to give you the complete low-down on this incident that occurred is when I see you. (For obvious reasons, I'm not even mailing this letter from Camp because though letters are not opened or censored in the zone of the interior, I don't put it pass these ——s to try it. Jo is mailing it for me from the college. You talk about a tight mouth Negro. My girl really doesn't know the spot I was in this week.)

Right after reading his son's letter, Dan II, sensing impending disaster, caught the first train to Denver, where Dad was then posted. Over and over Dan II pleaded with his son to remember where he was—the army—and who he was being commanded by—people who had the power to do whatever they wanted to anyone of inferior rank, without fear of consequences. "You keep rocking the boat like this and you're going to get killed. If you think you'd be the first soldier in the army to disappear without explanation, you're mistaken."

It may well have been the combination of Dan II's timely counsel and his elite status as a World War I officer that saved Dad from imploding. Rather than someone contemplating murder, Dad comes off, in the letter he wrote immediately following his father's "prop up" visit, sounding more like an appreciative young son.

1944
Dear Dad,

. . . I want you to know that the few hours that I enjoyed spending with you did a great deal to pull me out of a rut that had nearly swallowed me up. I had been struck by so many adversities . . . Without a shadow of a doubt, I feel that you are as great a DAD as any son could ask for . . . I think there is a fair chance of my getting out of this thing called Quartermasters [and] into an OCS in the Army Ground Forces. I will not, however, start on my plans until you notify me as to what you think I should do . . . I'll continue to plod under all circumstances.

As Dad "plodded on," his buddies, "the last of the old ASTP men," were shipped overseas, one step closer to engaging in direct battle with the Nazis. While his family was naturally relieved that their Buddy would be spared the possible fate of Dan II in World War I, or worse, my dad was left with the stigma of being one of the few soldiers held back.

When Dad's term was finally over, at the age of twenty-two, he transitioned into civilian life a markedly changed person. Entering the army single and ambivalent about his further education, he left the army married and deadly serious about pursuing higher learning. He was also, due to the lowest-rung jobs that were forever meted out to him (his hard-labour punishment, while unimaginably demanding, paled compared to the class disgrace that went along with it), contemptuous of any kind of manual labour. This was a far cry from his days at Lincoln University, when he'd write to his dad about possibly working as a "cabin boy or cook's aide, for awhile on a ship at sea." In the place of his former teenaged whimsy was a deliberate young man with, as his December 1945 letter to his dad indicates, "a definite program ahead . . . My entrance in Columbia, an economical apartment in Jersey, and . . . I will work labor only as a means to get more money to stay in college and support a wife."

Dad left the army totally disenchanted with any and all things associated with America. However, if the army planted a knee-jerk cynicism in Dad that would only crystallize over the years, it also gave him what can only be described as a four-year wake-up call providing him with a focus, drive and discipline that he lacked before being drafted. Dad re-entered civilian life in 1945 with the understanding that his ultimate profession would consist of trying to educate the ignorant and in doing so eradicate, to the best of his ability, America's racial inequities.

A part of Dad, however, would always remain incensed over what he witnessed and experienced during his army service. In later years, Dad's anger festered beneath his brashly mischievous persona, manifesting itself in unexpected flashes of cruel behaviour: his teasing edgy and dark, his manner of manipulation as effective as it was strategic. Of course these resulting traits were understandable, born out of self-protection. In many respects, it's a testament to my father's resilience (not to mention his parents' unwavering, unconditional love and support) that he survived his four years of service with so few visible scars. More than a few of his Negro army buddies committed suicide—some by direct means, others through prolonged alcohol and drug abuse—once they became civilians.

Dad learned the hard way that to be Black, uneducated and in the army is to be at the bottom of the food chain. You are always at someone else's mercy. You are never in control. More importantly, Dad understood that the army was a crude microcosm of American society at large, leaving him determined to never again relinquish control to any person, institution or religion. There was only one surefire way to ensure this: whenever possible, he would control everyone else. And yet, the army did give my father one great gift: his life's calling.

CHAPTER 6

Children Are Resilient

Most of the reasons behind Dad's increasing displays of temper were easy for me to grasp. Children always know more about what's going on with (and between) their parents than they're given credit for. Frequently, I'd overhear Mom pleading with Dad to not drive himself so hard at work, to watch his diet (the diabetes meds caused weight gain and increased appetite), to get out of the house so they could take up their old habit of strolling the neighbourhood and, my personal favourite—to *stop picking fights with Danny.* Dad's beleaguered response, "Once I'm finished with this case, Donna, things will ease up," was never that convincing. So long as there was discrimination there'd be no shortage of cases, so long as there was food Dad would overindulge and so long as there was school there'd be report cards, most of which carried the same message from my teachers: "Danny's grades could be much better if he . . ."

Much as I thought I understood the myriad pressures facing Dad, I didn't know the half of it. One by one, all but a few of my adult female relatives, on both sides of the family, were being diagnosed as manic-depressive. It seemed that when Dad wasn't paving the way for improved human rights legislation, or browbeating his kids into becoming world-class scholars, he was darting off to the rescue of one of his ailing sisters. He single-handedly policed his sisters' sanity and, really, if anyone was capable of pulling off such a feat it would most certainly have been Dad, even if that meant delegating some of this responsibility to Mom and, indirectly, us kids.

When Dad's sister Jean had a breakdown in 1958, he immediately offered to take in several of her children, insisting to his mother that:

> *Financially and in terms of space, I have never been in a better position to assist than now. My working hours are extremely flexible [and] left up to my discretion . . . I have fixed my den up considerably and could absorb two kids with no difficulty whatsoever (and more by grabbing off a few cots from the Canadian Army Surplus) . . . I can readily afford to come down and transport the children to Newmarket personally.*

Jean recovered from her episode that same year—"episode" being the family euphemism for a temporary crack-up—and, a few setbacks notwithstanding (once she accused a callow male psychiatrist of being a "doctor of dubious degree" and socked him in the mouth), enjoyed a long and healthy life. Dad's sister Margaret was not so fortunate.

"Family looks out for each other," Dad explained to me when Aunt Margaret first came to live with us. I was in grade three. "Remember, Danny, the strong take care of the weak. That means the males in the Hill household always protect the females."

Suddenly I felt myself grow in stature. Dad was including me in some special pact. Meanwhile, Mom didn't have to say a word for me to sense that she wasn't overjoyed with this arrangement. Dad, after all, was constantly on the move, scampering all over the province, if not the country, attending some high-level government convention or another. That meant Margaret, who never seemed to sleep, was left in Mom's care, with the three of us kids tiptoeing around the house on our best behaviour, saddled with extra chore duty to keep the household, as Dad said, "running efficiently." I'd come home from school and Margaret, as beautiful as she was phlegmatic and fat, would be keeled over in Dad's living-room chair, as if drunk from unhappiness, crying hard and long while listening to Ella Fitzgerald sing "Shiny Stockings."

"Why is Aunt Margaret always so sad and lonely?" I asked Dad, so disturbed by this display of adult suffering that I was willing to break his cardinal rule of not discussing Margaret's problems.

"It's all her children's fault. They're spoiled rotten and they constantly run roughshod over her," Dad said, shooting me a dark, accusing look. After doing a quick inventory of my recent misdeeds—dropping Larry's toothbrush down the toilet and causing it to overflow, then blaming the whole brouhaha on him and not copping to my crime till Larry was severely spanked—I looked anxiously in Mom's direction. Dad let the silence build as I stared down at my hands. Once satisfied that I'd stewed in my own guilty juices for long enough he resumed:

"Margaret's mean-hearted husband left her for another woman at the first sign of her illness. And this after my sister had worked night and day to put him through medical school."

There was real hate in Dad's eyes, and for a moment I felt anxious for Margaret's "mean-hearted husband," fearing for what would happen if he chanced to run across Dad. Then I felt like a traitor for worrying about such a bad man instead of my aunt.

"Now that my sister's husband has made all this money," Dad paused on "money," making it sound like the most vulgar, hideous thing in the world, "now that he's a rich doctor, he's taken custody of their two children. That man destroyed my sister. Margaret was happy as could be before she came across the likes of him."

A couple of weeks into Aunt Margaret's stay with us, I returned home from school for lunch to see an ambulance, red lights flashing and sirens wailing—just like on TV—parked in our driveway with the motor running. I pushed through the throng of neighbours whispering and pointing on my front lawn, and tiptoed through our suspiciously wide-open front door. Margaret was being carried out of the living room by two ambulance attendants who'd somehow managed to hoist her up onto a long white stretcher. She looked like she was sleeping, her mouth open in the shape of a lopsided O, most of her massive breasts and thighs spilling out from under a torn, undersized bathrobe.

"She's overdosed on sleeping pills," Mom was sobbing to Dad over the telephone. Deciding I wasn't that hungry, I returned to the calm of my school playground, where I announced to my classmates swinging on the monkey bars that my aunt had just committed suicide. Sure, it was only an attempt, but I didn't know that at the time, and it came as little comfort when Mom explained later that evening that most suicides don't succeed. "Don't worry Danny, they're only a cry for help. Just the same, do not discuss this with anyone."

How trying to kill yourself was a cry for help was way beyond me, yet another example of the confusing logic adults used to explain away bad things. And family loyalty—i.e., keeping secrets, never a strong suit of mine—could only go so far.

Inserting a word like "suicide" into my vocabulary brought forth wonderful reactions. As the days passed and I went into greater and greater detail on the dangers of swallowing too many sleeping pills, kids and teachers gaped at me, trying to determine if this story was yet another in a series of my magnificent lies.

"If you're lucky and don't die, you wake up as a vegetable."

"What kind of vegetable?" one of my freaked-out classmates asked.

"That's enough, Danny!" my teacher snapped.

Margaret was back living with us within days of her overdose. "They upped her medication," Mom explained, "so she'll feel happier." But Margaret didn't seem much different to me. She cried a little less and slept a little more. And she stopped listening to "Shiny Stockings."

For the next month or so, I felt safer out of the house playing sports, momentarily free of whatever mysterious mental-illness germ seemed to be circulating through our air vents.

"Children are resilient," I overheard Dad say to Mom late one night, shortly after Margaret returned to Washington, D.C., to live with my grandparents. Although Margaret continued to stay with us sporadically throughout my childhood, when she wasn't visiting, I did my best to block her out of my thoughts.

To my way of seeing things, mental illness, divorce and being a Negro were part and parcel of the same equation. Margaret was guilty of all three, and from where I stood, the combination of divorce and brown skin was a perfect recipe for a nervous breakdown. Thus, the last thing I ever worried about was Mom succumbing to madness. She was happily married and white.

Just watching how she greeted Dad when he came home from work gave me the impression of a couple that, due to the armour of each other's love, would always be safe from any kind of harm. Dad always made the same staged entrance, ringing the doorbell twice and waiting for Mom to answer. His winter or suit jacket would be folded neatly over his left arm. When Mom greeted him he would kiss her, first on the cheek and then all over her face and neck, with a big sloppy, slurping sound. She'd quietly soak up his wet smacks, all the while remaining perfectly still and expressionless, as if voluminous, soppy kisses were something a wife had to endure. We all knew, however, that this was a pose put on for our benefit, and that she really loved Dad's public display of disgusting, touchy-feely love. "Your Dad's the most affectionate person I've ever known," she used to tell us, as if she still couldn't quite fathom it. Sometimes, when Dad let Mom go and she took his coat and hung it in the closet, I could catch the faintest hint of a smile on her face. Which is why her descent into madness took me totally by surprise.

Other than helping Dad edit his speeches, articles and papers, Mom rarely worked outside the home once we moved to Don Mills. This was exactly as Dad wanted it. His frequent boast—"Your mother is in charge of the family bookkeeping. She pays all our bills promptly and keeps our chequing account in perfect order"—articulated Dad's idea of the perfect job for Mom. But whenever he praised her for her impeccable book balancing, she'd scrunch up her face to indicate that she felt patronized. Here she was, an unusually intelligent, energetic woman in her thirties, with children at school all day and a husband out of town or returning home exhausted late at night.

In 1965, Mom immersed herself in a summer teaching program. The course was a year of teachers' college crammed into six weeks, something the Ontario government had recently set up for "mature women" who, according to Mom, "had lived a little." When the school year started in September, Mom interned with a veritable revolving door of teachers, moving from class to class before getting a chance to connect with either teacher or students. Mom found the entire experience a nightmare. Her assigned school was in a poor area peppered with tough, demanding kids and teachers who, in Mom's view, ranged from awful to indifferent, giving her precious little exposure to good teaching. Draining as her school day was, the hours of preparation she had to put in each night for the following day's class left her feeling under siege. This, in turn, led to Dad's biggest problem with Mom teaching: not so much that she was working during the day, but that at night, when he wanted to talk to her about *his* work, Mom was unable to give him the time and support he'd grown accustomed to.

"Dan, please, can't this wait," Mom would say. "I'm working on tomorrow's lesson plan."

With twelve years of marriage behind them in which Mom had faithfully followed Dad's lead, giving him whatever invaluable feedback and attention he needed, exactly *when* he needed it, this represented, from Dad's vantage point, an unwelcome change in their relationship. It didn't take long before his hurt feelings turned from sulky to openly hostile. Of the two parents, Mom had the sharper tongue, something that proved to be her best weapon whenever Dad needed to be reeled in. Conversely, Dad's power with Mom didn't display itself verbally; a husband with his presence rarely needed to use harsh words to exert his will on his wife. This is precisely why Dad's stinging late-night condemnation shook Mom to her very foundation: "You're a failure as a wife and a mother."

Neither my siblings nor I were present when Dad unloaded this on Mom. That, however, did not stop Mom from repeating those nine eviscerating words to us, ad nauseam, in the weeks leading up to her unravelling. Rightly or wrongly, I came to believe that one sentence was what eventually broke her. She started coming home from school talking so fast and loud my head would hurt. "The other teachers are horrible. They've given up on the kids. The kids are out of control because a lot of them come from rough homes. I'm the only one who cares enough to get through to them."

Mom could go on for hours like this. I'd follow her at a safe distance, mumbling "uh huh" or "oh no, that's awful," as she darted all over the house, straightening a picture, dusting a lamp, folding and refolding a sweater; she seemed too agitated to stay in one place for more than a second. Just as I was getting the hang of tuning her out, she'd start to complain bitterly about Dad.

"He doesn't want me to work or be independent in any way. Now that I've started teaching, I could really use his support. But it's like he wants me to fail."

It was one thing for me to sometimes despise Dad, but I couldn't bear to hear someone else say anything bad about him. And now, whether Mom expressed her anger to Dad's face or behind his back, it didn't flare and quickly subside, the way it used to. What was worse was that her complaints were no longer limited to specific actions or inactions of Dad's, but went deeper, cutting to the core of his shortcomings as a man. Dad would respond in one of two ways, by tuning her out or throwing up a smokescreen of deflective humour.

Earlier that year, Dad had objected to the moaning sounds Mom made when my friend Don gave her a quick shoulder and neck massage. Mom quickly went on the offensive. How dare he sexualize such an innocent gesture? After calmly taking in her response for a while, accepting, with feigned diffidence, all the zeitgeist terms—"chauvinist," "hung-up," "sexist"—Dad finally asked, "How would you feel if I went up to Don's mom and said, 'How ya doing, Mary?' and started patting her behind, like this, *pop-pop-pop-pop*?" By way of demonstration, he began whirling his mitt-sized brown hands into cupped scooping gestures, like he was playing the congas upside down. He staged a lascivious look, nostrils flared like upside-down thimbles, his mouth making revolting, sucking sounds. With everyone laughing too hard to continue, the argument was over. Advantage: Dad.

But lately, even Dad's madcap routines could do little more than provide the odd moment of comic relief—like a diversion in a horror movie just before the bloodletting starts—in the face of Mom's scary mood swings.

Trudeau-mania was starting to sweep the country. My parents were staunch NDPers. So Dad wasn't exactly thrilled when Mom taped a sexy picture of a Speedo-clad Trudeau diving into a pool to their bedroom wall. Dad took the picture of Trudeau down. The next day Mom bought a nude painting of a woman and hung it in our living room. Dad, claiming it was too provocative, demanded she take it back and get a refund. The next morning during breakfast, Mom lashed back at him with profanity-strewn invective so extreme that it made every insult Dad had tossed my way over the years sound like constructive criticism. Dad, who sat there quietly absorbing Mom's vicious outpouring with a grim expression, explained to me later that night that he had no other choice. Nor would I, he emphasized, if she chose to lash out at me. "It hurt, son, but I couldn't criticize her. She's extremely fragile and anything I might've said against her could have destroyed her. You have to be very gentle with your mother."

The day before Mom was finally taken away, Larry and I got in a fight over a bowl of cottage cheese and applesauce. In our struggle the bowl slipped from our fingers and crashed onto the kitchen floor. We jumped back, startled by the *thwackkk* of the bowl breaking into pieces and the oozing of cottage-cheese-speckled applesauce everywhere. But Mom's reaction startled us far more than the broken dish. It was as if that bowl were the final straw. When she finished screaming at us, she started sobbing with a forcefulness that didn't seem human. I always hated seeing Mom cry, but this seemed to come from a darker, forbidden, place. This wailing person staring back at me, through me, seemed altered, totally unrecognizable. That got to me more than all her crazy, fast talk, all her yelling and swearing and crying combined. Suddenly it felt like someone or something had scooped out my insides.

Dad had warned me to tread softly around Mom. To protect her and help her and be extra attentive. And my response was to pick a fight with my brother over a silly bowl of cottage cheese and applesauce. It was my fault when she went away.

The day Mom left, I was playing ball hockey on our driveway with a classmate. I remember Dad seeming as agitated as Mom seemed subdued while he slowly escorted her out of our house, down the front steps and into a car. His car? A hospital car? Was there another adult, a hospital official, helping Dad? I don't recall. I did everything in my power to erase the particulars surrounding Mom's departure. What I do remember is trying my hardest not to pay attention to my parents, keeping my eyes glued to the tennis ball on our recently paved driveway, stick-handling ardently, careful not to utter a sound. I could hold it together so long as I didn't have to look up at anybody. At eleven and a half years old, I was becoming something of a pro at remaining, on the outside at least, stoic in the face of the emotional unravelling of family members.

We were never told when Mom was coming home, or even if she was coming home. I don't recall any of us asking, either. We were scared of what the answer might be. What had happened to make Mom turn out like this? Why had it happened? Could she be fixed? Could it happen again? I kept all those questions to myself, as, I imagine, did Larry and Karen, since we never talked about Mom among ourselves. Some things were just too awful to talk about. Our collective behaviour, always pretty good, became perfect. Maybe because Larry and Karen, just like me, felt responsible for Mom's hospitalization and believed, like me, that if we went from merely good to outstanding Hill citizens she would somehow get better and be returned to us. And then all would go back to normal. When Dad brought back a letter Mom had written to me from the hospital I was scared to read it, terrified that she would put into words what I considered to be the horrible, unspoken truth. That I had pushed her over the edge. But instead:

1966
Dear Danny,

*Daddy will probably be in to visit me soon, and I promised
yesterday that I'd have a note for each of you. Take a good, long
look at the picture on the front, as well as the "notes" on the
back of this note paper. It might be useful in a history work-
book. Oh yes, if I'm in for a long stay, tell Mrs. Anderson [my
teacher] I'll be glad, in fact grateful, for a chance to translate
that French pamphlet on Champlain's first settlement at Port
Royal. Please practise up on one of your classical guitar preludes, and polish up on Michelle and Yesterday . . .*

Happy New Year!
Love, Mom

We three kids took on the cooking, cleaning and all the household
chores. Dad would visit Mom twice a day without fail. At lunchtime he
brought flowers. After work he'd commute home, supervise the three
of us, checking that our chores were properly carried out ("I'm gonna
give this the old army test now," he'd warn, wetting his middle finger
and then running it over top of the shower rail, checking for dust) and
that our homework was ready to be tackled. Then he would quietly and
gently braid Karen's hair. After supervising Larry and Karen's bedtime
routine, he'd drive back downtown to visit Mom in the evening.

Whenever he included us on one his visits, Dad would forewarn:
"Don't ask your mother any questions or let her talk for too long. She's
easily worn out." His face would always light up the moment he saw
her, whether tucked away in bed, sedated, or sitting in one of the arts
and crafts rooms. He always had some kind of present for her: a book,
chocolates, magazines, makeup. He'd made sure we'd all written her
letters, offered as our small tokens of love. At first the three of us would
stand back at a safe distance, unsure of how she would react to us.
Sometimes she talked in spooky, elliptical riddles. Other times she'd

be too tired to say much of anything. But she always seemed happy to see us. By the end of each visit, Dad's visible affection for Mom would slice through our fear. We'd inch closer to Mom's bed, saying little as she told us about her day.

I never talked about Mom's situation to anyone in my neighbourhood. And no one, not teachers or friends or even the mouthiest kids at school, mentioned a thing about my mom to me. That was definitely one of the good things that came with living in Don Mills. People knew better than to talk about stuff like this.

At home, my constant singing and guitar playing helped fill the space left by Mom's absence. "Come on in here, just for a second, I gotta play you something," I'd say to anyone unlucky enough to get within a few feet of our front door. The mailman, the meter reader, the kid collecting for the *Toronto Star*—no one was spared my latest rendition of "Yesterday." Everyone patiently indulged my spontaneous "stop everything and listen to me" performances. Even Dad didn't discourage my growing penchant for dragging total strangers into our living room and subjecting them to my Beatles interpretations. In a small way, the music that sprang out of my guitar helped lighten some of the shadows that had crept into the house when Mom was taken away from us.

Before long, I was being asked to perform at parties and school functions. I jumped at the chance, inhaling every syllable of praise, every infinitesimal glance of approval, using it as fuel to practise more, to sing better.

Mom returned home after several months, drugged and sluggish. Dad insisted she go everywhere with him. "He knew the key to my recovery was to get me out of the house, to keep me in motion," Mom told me, not long after she felt better. "'C'mon, we're going to Windsor,' he'd say. And when I'd resist, he'd announce, 'I have to investigate a case there and I don't want to drive all that way alone.' I'd always agree, knowing it took more energy to refuse your dad than to go along with him."

Grandfather Bender, still riding high on the recent successful publication of his book, *Great Moments in Pharmacy*, tucked some articles on the efficacy of lithium in treating manic-depression into the auto-graphed copy he mailed us.

"Three things saved your mother's life," Dad said, once Mom's health started to improve. "One: lithium. Two: an outstanding female psychiatrist. Three: she had three children and a husband who loved her."

"You three kids," Mom later claimed, "were all that held me back, in my darkest moments, from ending it all. I knew you guys needed me."

If my view of women changed after Mom's breakdown—that women were fragile and in constant need of protection from men—my view of men, and more specifically of husbands and fathers, changed as well. Maybe Dad did hasten Mom's breakdown, or maybe, judging from our family history, Mom's breakdown would have happened in any event. But what remained beyond speculation was Dad's behaviour once Mom fell ill. Indeed, if anything positive could be gleaned from Mom's hospitalization, it was simply that a man, a real man, is always there, without fail and whatever the circumstance, for his family, for his wife. Always. Whether that means pushing a station wagon with your three kids, wife and sister out of the middle of a New York throughway and safely back onto the shoulder, or visiting your wife in the hospital twice a day with flowers in one hand and chocolates in the other, you do it. Because that's what men, husbands, fathers do.

CHAPTER 7

The Secret Marriage

As I continued to dig into my father's life, sometimes assuming the lofty role of interviewer, there was one thing I was discovering. The good stuff, the fascinating information, would invariably come tumbling out at the most unexpected times. Because I became aware of so many highly charged areas of Dad's life once he was no longer alive, sometimes I could feel myself assuming the role of an impartial biographer, reviewing and writing about a person of historical interest whose time on earth never overlapped with mine. But something would always jolt me out of my removed interviewer persona, leaving me feeling vulnerable and amateurish, and on the verge of saying, "Hey, back up—this is my father you're talking about!"

I hadn't expected my interview with Jim Maben, one of Dad's closest friends when they were flatmates studying at the University of Toronto in the early 1950s, to contain any truly shocking revelations. So much for expectations.

"I'm sorry, Danny, I really should have asked. Did you know your father had been married before?"

Given that this was one aspect of Dad's life that he refused to discuss with me, I was shocked that he'd talked to Mr. Maben, or anyone in Canada, about it. Still, I covered up as best I could, offering my best nod of reassurance.

Up until that point Jim Maben's tales of living with my father had been interesting, even entertaining, while reinforcing much of what I already knew about the magnetism of Dad's personality. I could easily relate to Mr. Maben, along with the other college flatmates, seeing Dad as a guru figure. "He opened our minds to social issues and attitudes that had hardly occurred to us," had been Mr. Maben's recollection, after explaining that he and the other students were "sheltered white kids, so skinny and poor that the prostitutes would take pity on us and leave us sandwiches."

Mr. Maben and his small-town friends, hungry for knowledge of the outside world, were mesmerized by this educated Black American, an atheist son of a Methodist minister, fresh out of the U.S. Army. Mr. Maben described a bunch of guys sitting around in a dark room while Dad "held forth with story after story. No one else spoke. We just sat and listened."

Admittedly, Mr. Maben's discovery that Dad could easily go from cult leader status to "one of the boys" caught me off guard a little. "Once, someone made the rare and unfortunate mistake of arguing a point with your father, only to find himself tied up in knots by his common-sense logic." Finally, realizing he couldn't defeat Dad in a debate, the flummoxed opponent challenged him to a wrestling match. "He figured that if he couldn't overcome Dan intellectually, he would do it physically," Mr. Maben remembered. "So they wrestled. And Dan won that one too."

And then, perhaps sensing he'd softened me up, Mr. Maben would drop a real shocker on me, likening some of Dad's academic pursuits to, say, Alfred Kinsey's landmark study on human sexuality. Dad had become fast chums with a fellow tenant, a Black musician from the

States who'd earned a reputation as a wanton womanizer. Mr. Maben had walked into this musician's room one night without knocking and discovered the landlady of the house being orally gratified by the musician, with Dad standing over the two of them, studiously jotting notes down on a piece of paper, drolly commenting on how he was going to incorporate his latest research into his next sociological thesis, the theme of which was purportedly how long it took this particular woman to achieve orgasm.

Feeling at this point that perhaps I should conclude this interview lest any more undue surprises leave me stuttering, I shut off my tape recorder, said my goodbyes and began gathering up my "biographer tools." But talking about Dad had triggered something in Mr. Maben, as though he'd time-travelled back to 1951 and didn't want to return to the present day. Stroking his Santa Claus–like beard and tightly crossing his legs, he began gently rocking his small upper body, his eyes narrowing as though accessing some long-buried memory. And then, motioning for me to turn on my tape recorder, his voice cracking with emotion, he began to tell the story of a painful breakup he'd gone through while rooming with my father.

"I was constantly afraid that I was going to run into her, she lived just around the corner. I was going through misery, real misery. And your dad sat me down one time and told me, 'I know what you're going through because this happened to me.'"

Dad had then proceeded to reveal the story of his own disastrous first marriage and how it had crashed and burned, resulting in unspeakable heartbreak and disgrace. Dad's startling revelation had a deep impact on Mr. Maben: "That was so meaningful, so helpful to me at the time. There was a guy that I really bowed down to and the same thing happened to him and he survived. And I've remembered that and loved him for it."

As had happened so many times before when interviewing people about my father, I was struck by how memories well over half a century old seemed so fresh and raw. Mr. Maben had become so increasingly emotional, telling me about his breakup and Dad's most generous response, that the story within the story—Dad's first marriage—didn't resonate with me till I left his Oakville apartment and began the long drive home. As the miles flew by, the hypnotic effect of the highway's white lines blurring together became an unlikely video backdrop to the strains of Buffalo Springfield's "For What It's Worth" as it rattled through my car radio. And for the rest of the drive old family images, intercut with all too candid conversations, tugged at me.

The year was 1968. I remember it being cold outside. Dad was away on a six-week tour of human rights conferences that took him to such faraway places as Iran. My mother, my siblings and I were having dinner at the Sharzers', who were close friends of my parents. Mr. and Mrs. Sharzer were talking to Mom about the usual boring adult stuff, and I was kicking Larry's foot under the table, just for something to do, when I heard Mom say, " . . . Dan's first wife."

I looked up at Mom from my dinner plate, convinced I'd heard her wrong. Then I looked over at Larry and Karen. Same shocked reaction. Did Mom really just refer to Dad's "first wife"?

"Don't give me that deer-in-the-headlights look, Danny. It was no big deal. The marriage barely lasted a year."

Suddenly it felt like I wasn't going to be able to hold down the food I'd just eaten. Could this be Mom's idea of a joke? She'd had a bit to drink, so maybe her sense of humour had taken a left turn. In a not so subtle attempt to change the subject, Mrs. Sharzer asked me a question about songwriting. But Mom, knowing that she'd opened some kind of forbidden door, if only a crack, decided to tear it off its hinges.

"Your father was just a kid in the army. Happened all the time to kids in that situation."

Mom's speech was deliberate and slower than usual, a typical effect after two glasses of wine. She didn't tend to drink as much when Dad was around. The stricken look in Larry's eyes from across the table made me want to slap him. Didn't he know better than to let his emotions show so openly? I mumbled something about having to get home to finish off some homework.

"Let me get your coats," Mrs. Sharzer quickly offered, excusing herself from the table.

I found myself jumping several steps ahead in my mind, plotting how I was going to coax the rest of this story out of Mom. *When she's alone, once Larry and Karen are in bed, and before she's totally sobered up. That will be my only chance. Once Dad gets home she won't talk, and there's no way I would ever risk asking Dad about this.*

On the short drive home, Larry, Karen and I chose silence over our usual bickering and jockeying for Mom's attention.

"Why are you guys so quiet? What's gotten into the three of you?" Mom asked as we slipped wordlessly out of the car.

Alone in my bedroom, guitar in hand, I tried, unsuccessfully, to make sense of Mom's latest family news bulletin. Since Dad was never particularly discreet about the transgressions of his friends and associates, I'd foolishly assumed that he was also forthright about his own life, past and present. Even his "secrets" he made a big deal of. "I'm not telling you my salary," he'd boast, though it had never occurred to me to ask. "Or what your mother and I have saved. But we're doing extremely well."

How could Dad be so quick to reveal, with abundant enthusiasm, his childhood misadventures, his backroom battles with politicians, stories of our cousins' teenaged pregnancies, my mother's father's serial adulteries and resulting nasty divorce, and yet never get around to mentioning that he'd been married before? What was next, Mom blathering at the next dinner party about my various half-brothers and half-sisters?

I cornered Mom with my questions later that night, as this was usually the time she seemed a little lonely and welcomed conversation. Dad had never been gone for this long before, and it seemed that with each day, Mom became a little sadder, a little more unstrung.

"Don't ask me about this, Danny," she replied wearily, "not now. As it is, I really don't know that much about your father's first marriage, it's not something we waste time talking about."

But I hammered away at her, knowing that if I didn't press on, I'd be up all night, wondering, imagining and driving myself crazy. Finally growing weary under the relentless barrage of questions, Mom offered me a snapshot version of Dad's first marriage. If the reasons for Dad's marriage didn't shock me—"He was young and lonely and scared of being shipped to Japan and killed"—her explanation for his divorce certainly did.

"Your father had his parents send her all the money he'd saved up—and he'd saved lots—from his years in the army, plus all he'd earned from his year of welding and shipbuilding before that, so he and his new wife could build a life together once he got out of the army. But she squandered it. Every last penny. And then demanded more. Would you like to know what she needed the extra money for?" *Here it comes, my punishment for asking too many questions.* "She was fooling around on him." Mom was on a roll now. "She got syphilis or gonorrhea, and drugs that cured those diseases back then were very expensive."

Forty-some years later, after interviewing family members and extracting piecemeal details from Dad's assorted friends and colleagues, the story behind Dad's first marriage was still spotty, leaving me to return, once more, to my most reliable and vibrant source of information: Dad's letters from the 1940s. Dad's announcement of his imminent engagement to Jo was filled with organizational details.

> *We should be able to become engaged now. If I don't run into*
> *any difficulty, I should draw enough money to get the ring.*
> *All I need is two months and we can lay what plans that are*
> *necessary for anything in the future. This will enable me to go*
> *back to New York and talk to her Dad . . . She has been helping*
> *me to lay my plans to complete my education under the G.I.*
> *bill of rights. If she can finish her work in chemistry, take some*
> *graduate work, save money and plan, then she will be in a*
> *position to help me finish my studies in Sociology. The govern-*
> *ment will send me to school, pay for my books and give me*
> *$75.00 a month for subsistence if I'm married.*

By early 1945, however, Dad was unable to contain his euphoria any longer and went on at length about his fiancée's many attributes, before ending his letter on a note of foreboding:

I was counting on this payday in April to buy the ring . . . I had written to her father for his consent. I met him at her home in Brooklyn last January . . . She has been acclaimed by students and papers alike as one of the most beautiful girls on the campus. Her constant companionship, intelligence and love for me have kept me out of trouble many times . . . Whatever I do and wherever I go, she has given me the stimulus and the will to make it and come out on top . . . I did not want to tell you about these things until we announced our engagement . . . Circumstances and coming events make it necessary for my family to know the innermost secrets of my heart.

Two months later, Dad wrote to inform his parents that he was now a married man, making no mention as to why they weren't invited to the ceremony. (Quite possibly, Dad, knowing that his parents eloped, may have wanted to repeat family history.) He requested that his parents send him all the money and bonds he'd saved up as a soldier, announcing that he was going to merge all his savings with Jo's account in Brooklyn. Dad mentioned Jo in only two more letters, revealing as much in what he chose not to share as in the murky details he disclosed:

December, 1945

When you didn't hear from me for such a long time, you surmised that something was wrong. It looks as if you were right. I was ankle deep in trouble at the time . . . "Jo" has had to go through some fairly rugged ordeals and I haven't been able to be by her side and help like I should. Out of a condition like this it is only natural that other problems should arise. Conflict

in thinking, in ideas and ideals had to be ironed out to our
mutual satisfaction . . . There is a great deal more that I would
like to tell you . . . [when] I put an appearance in Washington
D.C. I will be able to talk to you, Father and son.

January, 1946

Don't be disappointed if Jo and I don't come to Washington
to school . . . many factors enter in that would not make the
adventure suitable to all concerned. We plan to rent a room and
kitchenette in Brooklyn, N.Y. until we can do better. We have
both agreed conclusively to live away from all our relatives.

Reading between the lines, I have to assume that Dad sensed that
the end of his marriage was fast approaching (it may well have already
been over at this point). This, coming right on the heels of his stunning
army failures, must've been almost too much to bear.

True to form, Dad's parents came to his rescue, taking him on a
two-week driving trip through New England, gently boosting his morale
and shoring up his confidence. Granddad had, among other degrees, a
master's in counselling, and his extraordinary ability to offer comfort
and strength in the face of calamity was practised on his children to
wonderful effect, as much as it had been on his congregations.

Dad never mentioned his first wife to his children for the same
reason she was never again referred to in any of his letters. That way Jo,
and by extension, his first marriage, had never really existed.

The closest Dad and I came to discussing his first marriage was immediately following his return home from Iran. Still smarting from Mom's
explanation, the last thing I wanted to do was talk to anyone about this
ever again, especially to Dad. He waited till everyone else in the house
was sound asleep before coming into my room.

"Son, you are never to ask your mother about my first marriage.
That's none of your business. That's no one's business. You've upset your

mother a great deal with all your questions. At your age, after all your mother was going through, you should know better than that."

He was gone before I had a chance to say anything, leaving me to feel like some peeping Tom caught sneaking glances into people's private lives. Dad's implication that my nosiness might land Mom back in the hospital produced the desired effect, leaving me so overwrought about upsetting her that I stopped thinking about Dad's secret marriage. It had been my responsibility, with Dad away for so long, to keep the household humming along perfectly. Not so much to ask, really, of the eldest child. Especially given that the worst part of discovering Dad's secret marriage had little to do with the marriage itself. The worst part was how, and why, it had been revealed. Mom's little bombshell wasn't about Dad at all. It was about Mom beginning to unravel again. While it would be stretching things to say I was happy Dad had finally returned home, I certainly was relieved. Dad was the glue Mom needed. He was the only person capable of keeping her various fractious selves from splintering into a million pieces. He could put her back together again. And he did. But I couldn't help but think that, as usual, I had failed where Dad had succeeded. He had stepped up, as the man of the house, where I had badly stumbled. There was still a lot I needed to learn from Dad, much as I hated to admit it.

Fresh out of the army and a bad marriage, Dad's overzealous social life picked up where he'd left it. Only now he had learned the art of balancing work and play. He finished his undergraduate degree at Howard University (on the American G.I. Bill) and graduated with high enough marks to earn a scholarship to study at the University of Oslo in Norway for a year in 1948.

Dad found Norway to be a refreshingly gentle and engaging country. There were no buses belching exhaust in his face as they rumbled by carrying only white soldiers. All restaurants and hotels welcomed him; Norwegian children would run up and touch his skin, exclaiming delightedly, "Brun Norska, Brun Norska" (brown Norwegian). He didn't mind feeling like "the only Negro in Oslo," as he put it, so long as he didn't feel judged by the colour of his skin. After completing his courses in international government in Oslo, Dad returned to America, where he lived in Ann Arbor, immersing himself in graduate studies at the University of Michigan.

In a letter home Dad showed that while his interest in race relations remained as keen as ever, his perspective had become more analytical and measured. He realized that the racial divisions polarizing America needed to be addressed and eradicated by working within rather than outside of the system: "The Negro Under-grad students seem to isolate themselves from the inter-racial organizations on this campus. They follow a pattern of self-segregation that nauseates me. This pattern, exhibited by the so called Future Negro intellectuals, is surely detrimental to integration on the part of the two groups."

Within a year, Dad, running low on savings, took a brief break from school, getting a government job in a Detroit social welfare agency. The applicants were predominantly Black, poor and unemployed. However much Dad wanted to assist the applicants most in need, he found that his hands were tied. Essentially, his role in the welfare agency was to clog up the system by throwing up as much bureaucratic red tape as was necessary to delay, interminably, any kind of government assistance. When an indigent family with sixteen kids was deemed eligible for welfare money, Dad's supervisor, determined to forestall payment indefinitely (sixteen children represented a lot of government money), kept sending Dad back to visit the family. Each visit meant more forms—many unnecessary and redundant—for the household to fill out. Predictably, the illiterate parents, ground down by the weight of all the endless bureaucratic paperwork, and discouraged and humiliated, gave up their claim. Realizing that his job amounted to little more than window dressing, Dad's frustration gave way to despondency. Dan II, intuiting his son's despair once again, immediately drove to Detroit to see him.

"You are not blessed with the temperament to live in the U.S.," his father warned. "Get out before this country destroys you."

Taking his father's advice, Dad mailed off applications to the University of Mexico and the University of Toronto, vowing to attend whichever university responded first. Within weeks the U of T sent back its notice of acceptance. And so, barely a month after his father recommended that he leave America, Dad moved to Toronto to begin his master's degree at U of T.

Like many immigrants, my father saw Canada as a blank slate, a new world on which he could project all his ambitions and dreams of glory, without any of the baggage that defined his country of origin. Canada also meant that he could be within striking distance of home, and yet far enough away to be out of the ever-watchful eye of family. Dad's first letter to his parents, in 1951, offers a telling distinction between American and Canadian discrimination: "There is one great difference between Toronto and an American city of comparable size and that is, that discrimination can be fought and the battle won in Toronto with greater facility. All of the things that I'm seeing and feeling now will enable me to write a better doctoral thesis and to give a more objective opinion of this city."

In 1952, after receiving his master's degree in sociology at the University of Toronto, Dad, running low on cash, returned to Washington, D.C., for a year. He lived with his parents and taught sociology at Morgan State College in Baltimore, a Black, liberal arts school. His salary—three thousand dollars for a whopping five courses—was half that of a typical professor for double the course load. But at least he was following his pledge to stay clear of manual labour.

While teaching at Morgan State, Dad went to visit a woman on campus whom he'd befriended in Norway, where she'd been studying on a similar scholarship program. Sitting beside this woman on the front steps of her co-op was one of her roommates—my mom.

"His gaze fell upon me" is how Mom always puts it, her voice dropping slightly over those five words. Then, as if catching herself before sounding too maudlin, she quickly adds, "Especially the bottle of rum I was sharing, which I'd just brought back from a holiday in Puerto Rico."

Mom had moved to Washington, D.C., to work for Democratic senator Herbert Lehman. She was twenty-four, Dad, twenty-nine. In pictures and in old family movies from that period, they look impossibly beautiful, their striking appearance magnified all the more by their compelling physical contrasts. Dad's trademark smile displayed a pure and absolute delight for life—like he was on to something great and vaguely wicked that the rest of us could only guess at. Mom was tiny and fiery, her whiter-than-white skin giving her an almost translucent glow. But beyond her incandescent allure loomed a not-so-distant ferocity. "Judge me at your peril," her eyes always seemed to say.

My parents first dated in January 1953, and Mom, while enormously attracted to my father, was well aware of his reputation as a ladies' man.

"At the beginning, our relationship wasn't really defined," Mom used to tell us. (We never tired of hearing this story.) "But when your father discovered I'd had a date with someone else, he became upset and started to take me a lot more seriously." Mom's definition of serious left little to the imagination. Announcing their engagement that March, they prepared for a June wedding.

Now came the tough part: Mom had to inform her family. Mom assumed her father, George Bender, the more reactionary of her parents, would completely disown her but that her mother, Ruby, divorced and single since 1948, would support her decision. Her father responded first, in a letter in April 1953:

My Dear Donna:

Well—we can always count on Donna to do something original! While your announcement came as a surprise—since you made no mention of the matter when I was down there—I can't say I was wholly unprepared for it—as I have been aware of the possibility of such an interest developing, for some time. While I may as well admit that it isn't exactly what I would have wished for you—I quit trying to run your life when you

were 18—and I shan't try to now . . . I would like to have an
opportunity to talk to you about your marriage, and your
future; and to meet, if possible, Dan. Also, I'd like to meet
his father if that can be arranged . . . I think you know there
won't be any scenes . . . There is one point that I want to make
clear—you are my daughter, and I shall welcome your hus-
band as I have other kin by marriage; and my house will be
open to you and your husband and future family at any time.

Within weeks, Dan II played the perfect host to Mom's father, grandly escorting him around the Howard campus, where he was now associate dean of theology. Mom's father, suitably impressed, wrote letters to his three other children defending Mom's decision to marry Dad.

While relieved to have her father's blessing, Mom believed that his support was influenced by the fact that she was the first of the Bender tribe to accept his new and significantly younger wife. But Mom's brothers, Frank and Bob, owed their little sister no such favour. Frank's letter, coming right on the heels of her father's, warned her that she and Dad would be shunned by both the Black and white races. And what about their children? Should they be so reckless as to start a family, they would surely live to see their sons and daughters grow up to hate them. For no child could withstand the pressures of having two parents of two different races.

Not surprisingly, Mom's relationship with her brothers went from remote to nonexistent once she married Dad. There were rumours, fuelled by Dad, that they wanted Mom locked up in an asylum, a scenario that Dad found curiously amusing, as if this kind of family backlash somehow gave Mom an almost heroic status. While Mom's twin sister, Dottie, liked my dad, she too worried about the public reception of their marriage. Assuming that Mom and her husband could never live in the States, she said, "What are you going to do next? Move to Sweden?"

Mom's mother, Ruby, was badly shaken by the news of her daughter's upcoming marriage to a Black man. Since her divorce, Ruby had been inconsolably lonely and desperately looking to remarry—and she thought she'd finally found a likely candidate. Believing that nothing would kibosh the chance of her own marriage faster than the news of her daughter marrying a Negro, Ruby begged my mom to put off her wedding. Mom refused, and as predicted, Ruby's relationship ended the moment she revealed the news to her male friend that her daughter was about to marry "outside of her race."

The reaction to their marriage from Dad's side of the family was significantly less dramatic. As far as Dad's parents were concerned, marrying a white woman was tame in comparison to his drinking and carousing. That Mom's family was Congregationalist, a religion fairly close to Methodism, combined with her graduating from Oberlin College—the first U.S. college to admit Blacks—were huge points in her favour. Further boosting Mom's pedigree was her long employment history with the Cleveland Civil Rights Coalition, as well as her present volunteer work with the Congress of Racial Equality.

While it's likely that Grandma May was surreptitiously thrilled at acquiring a Caucasian daughter-in-law—for the same culturally ingrained reasons her parents had been upset that she'd married a darker-skinned Negro—Mom regarded this kind of racial theorizing as offensive.

"Your dad's parents would have been thrilled if my skin was purple," she'd snap. "What mattered to them was that your dad was finally settling down." Mom would wait for her stern correction to sink in before adding, most firmly, "Your father wasn't marrying me because of, but in spite of, being white."

My mom, not one for gushing outpourings of sentiment, was saying in her typically hardboiled style that she and Dad married for precisely one reason. Love.

CHAPTER 8

My First Love Song

"You're lying through your teeth, boy." By the time I turned fifteen, Dad probably flung this accusation at me several times a week. Ninety-nine percent of the time he was dead on. (The other one percent I'd been merely exaggerating.) But why was it that he could lie with impunity whenever the urge hit him yet act as though I had a behavioural problem when I just covered up a minor disobedience? At fifteen, music was taking up almost all of my free time, to the point where Dad had forbidden me to take part in what he termed any "musical misadventures" after school hours. Toronto was being taken over by the folk music scene, and there were hundreds of coffeehouses and church auditoriums where, every night of the week, I could wait my turn along with dozens of other folkies for the opportunity to get onstage to sing a few of my songs. I'd tell my parents that I was studying at a friend's house or at the school library (Dad was out of town so often that when he was home, he was too exhausted or preoccupied to cross-examine me), and then hitchhike downtown or bus it to a suburban church to perform.

Usually I was teaching classical guitar to some kid en route to these gigs, so lugging my instrument everywhere didn't arouse suspicion. But in the excitement leading up to these performances I didn't always get my story straight, which meant Dad would catch me in a lie—usually when my so-called study buddy called the house looking for me.

When a girl I had a crush on, Amanda, invited me to join her at an all-night party with the cast of *Hair,* the biggest rock musical to have ever hit Toronto, I bloody well made sure I had all my bases covered.

"Remember, Steve, no matter what, I'm spending the night at your place. If my dad calls, I'm already asleep. I've been trying to make out with Amanda for a year and the closest I got was barfing all over her when I drank too much gin that afternoon we skipped school. No way I'm going to blow it this time."

"Everything's hunky-dory, Danny. You're covered. Just call me from the party and tell me about all the cool drugs."

I was too proud to tell Steve the truth: Amanda was just using me. She knew, as did everyone in my school, that I'd auditioned for the cast of *Hair* and would have made it had the casting directors not found out at the last minute that I'd lied about my age. No cast member could be under seventeen, and I'd convinced everyone, until they demanded proof during the final set of auditions, that I was two years older than I really was.

Hair was a cultural phenomenon. All the more so in my neck of the woods, because, unlike sophisticated cities like New York or L.A., Toronto in 1970 was pretty provincial. A rock musical that celebrated "free love" and what can only be described at the time as a scandal of epic proportions—full frontal nudity—left the local media and public shocked and titillated. The auditions were held at the Masonic Temple in downtown Toronto, a huge, gothic building that left me feeling small and insignificant when I walked down into the dank basement. I was one of thousands of people waiting for a shot at being a part of a musical that we thought would turn us into big stars.

I'd selected "Yesterday" as my audition song. This was a tricky choice because I was certain a lot of other singers would be choosing it as well. But I also knew the song's stirring melody brought out the best qualities in my voice, and I'd played it hundreds of times on the guitar. I took for granted that I'd be nervous—something I'd been getting better at controlling thanks to all my hours of coffeehouse performances—and was smart enough to know that an easy song like "Yesterday" would hold up well to any bouts of stage fright.

"Where did you learn to sing like that?" one of the three casting directors asked, looking up at me as I did my best casual "lean against the grand piano" pose.

"I dunno. I write songs, so I guess I'm just—ah, you know—always singing."

My performance, near perfect, had ended with me stumbling over the mic cord during my post-song bow.

"If you get a callback come prepared to sing whatever we throw at you."

I got the callback and nailed the audition. What could be easier than singing "Aquarius"? I'd spent the last month or so singing this and all the other songs from the *Hair* soundtrack album in my music class.

"Okay, we've assigned a part for you to learn for the next audition."

My singing had taken me this far, now I had to concentrate on acting. Jogging through the front door, I handed Mom my script, guiding her to my highlighted lines, which I had yet to read.

"Look at this, Danny, they've offered you the role of the homosexual."

"What!?"

Mom looked pleased as punch. Like this was a great honour.

"Don't worry, Danny, it's probably because you'd be the youngest cast member and you look the least masculine."

This was supposed to make me feel better? Too embarrassed to talk, I started singing the song that came with my role. Barely ninety seconds long, the melody was a cinch, but the multisyllabic lyrics, most of which

I'd never heard before, were a mouthful. The one word I knew, "mastur-bation," I hummed through, this being Mom I was singing to and all.

"That's very good, Danny." Mom was laughing. Inappropriately.

"Mom, what do all these words mean? 'Sodomy,' 'cunnilingus,' 'pederasty,' 'fellashee—'?"

"That's 'fellatio,' honeybun, the *a* is like 'ay' not 'ah.'"

After correcting me, Mom went on to calmly explain the meaning of these words.

"No. Stop," I said, as Mom was going into detail about "cunnilin-gus." "What kind of weirdos do this stuff? I sang that song over and over on the bus on the way home. I could have been arrested."

"Don't worry, dear," Mom said. "Very few adults understand the meaning of those words."

Well then, how on earth had she learned them? I wasn't going to ask.

Each time I survived another cut for *Hair* and was called back for another audition, I'd rush to a payphone and share the news with Dad. Dad's response never varied: "If you wanna stand naked as a jaybird in front of all of Toronto, well, that's your business, son. But remem-ber something: you're gonna be scrambling in and out of your hippie-dippie jeans a dozen times a night. So you better make damned good and sure you've greased your zipper." Dad knew me well enough to understand that, while I would've been more than happy to view nudity onstage from the voyeuristic remove of the audience, I wasn't too keen on exposing my wonders in full view of thousands of people a night.

At my final callback, upon surrendering my birth certificate, I was scolded for lying about my age and wasting their time. Then they told me to get lost, with a pie in the sky promise that they might consider me for an understudy role if the show was still around in two years.

As consolation (and entirely due to my parents' connections), the *Toronto Telegram* published an article I wrote describing my half-dozen *Hair* auditions, and paid me more dough than I netted from weeks of guitar teaching. My story in the *Telegram* gained me some extra popu-larity at school, which resulted in girls like Amanda, normally way out of my league, reassessing my dateworthiness.

And so, the night I was supposed to be sleeping over at my friend Steve's, I went down to the Royal Alex theatre, snuck through one of the fire exits after the show and managed to bluff my way backstage. Amanda, the high school babe who'd invited me to meet her for what I assumed would be an all-night orgy, was nowhere to be found. No one I talked to had heard anything about a cast party. Disconsolate, I called Steve, needing a place to stay.

"Your Dad called here a couple hours ago and told me to tell you to 'come home and face the music,'" Steve told me, clearly shaken up by whatever else my dad said to him.

It turned out that Amanda had called a few hours after I'd left the house for my "sleepover." Whether Amanda was as clueless as she was gorgeous or a sadistic prankster didn't much matter. Either way the message she passed on to my dad couldn't have been more damning: "Would you tell Danny that I won't be able to meet him downtown for the all-night cast party?"

When I arrived home Dad and I went through the same old circle game. He'd start with the inquisition, I'd respond with increasingly improbable lies and he'd come back with a snarling, "You're still lying, boy. Smarten up and start talking before I slap the truth right out of your mouth."

Dad could have saved us both a lot of time had he revealed that Amanda had phoned him and blown my cover. But that would have made things too easy for me and too boring for him. Finally, after he dropped the "Who's Amanda?" bomb, I fessed up, busted, broken and awaiting Dad's verdict.

"Your mother and I know how badly you wanted to make *Hair*. So we can understand why you'd want to go to their cast party. So we're not going to punish you. This time. But don't lie to us anymore."

The thing about Dad was, just when you thought you had him figured out, he'd throw you a curve ball.

Soon after publishing my *Hair* story, the *Toronto Telegram* published another article I'd written, entitled "On Being Black" (based on how I felt being raised Black in Don Mills), paying me enough money to allow me to purchase a couple months' worth of pop albums. My newspaper publications, combined with banging out biweekly opinion columns for my high school newspaper, had my English teacher taking me aside for one of those inevitable career lectures: "The music business is too risky. Stick to writing. You'll always be able to find work in journalism."

But I was only pulling off A-pluses in his class because I wrapped up my mandatory course poems in pretty guitar chords and melodies, thus distracting him from my "poor me" lyrics. Dad, as leery of my prose skills as he was my songwriting, glanced at my A-plus in English and advised, "Forget about poetry and start knuckling down on your maths and sciences."

"Math and science aren't gonna do much for my singing career," I sniffed.

"My Uncle Bill was also a brilliant writer and poet," Dad answered, managing to make the word "brilliant" sound tragic. Not knowing, till that very moment, that Dad actually had an Uncle Bill, I gaped back, curious, but knowing better than to ask any questions.

"Poor Bill, he was best friends with James Baldwin and Langston Hughes. But that didn't help him much in the end. He died destitute and disgraced."

Baldwin and Hughes. Damned if there wasn't something about their names that made me uneasy.

"Okay Dad, you got me, what happened to Uncle Bill?"

"You didn't know?" Dad asked, watching me fall into his trap.

"Know what?"

"Uncle Bill was a homosexual." Dad eyeballed me frostily, lest the connection between writer and homosexual was lost on me. This wasn't the first, and by no means the last time, that Dad would suspect that I might be gay. When I was eleven, I had been desperate to win the attention of girls. Along with my deepening voice had come a keen awareness of my body's emerging flaws. Deciding the time had come for me to develop a he-man body, I purchased magazines of musclemen and taped their pictures to my bedroom wall. There they gleamed and glistened—serving as motivation, with their shaved, waxed bodies and bulging, Popeye muscles—wearing leopard-skin bikini briefs.

The next day, Dad (tipped off by Mom) flew into my room, took one look at my new male role models and ripped the pictures off the wall.

"What's got into you, boy? Don't you dare start getting all funny on me! I never wanna see those kind of pictures on your wall again."

He marched off with the photographs crumpled in his hands like some kind of contraband.

"Donna, Danny's going into junior high soon. It's time to buy him some more *Playboys*," Dad's voice gibbered up from the kitchen, over the quick and decisive hand shredding of my eight-by-ten glossies of steroid-chiselled musclemen. Mom started to object. Dad quickly countered, his voice dropping in volume so that all I could pick out was "homosexual leanings." At eleven years of age, I had yet to really twig to what "homo-sexual" meant. Now at fifteen, I understood Dad's implied warnings and laughed them off, keeping my focus on my music and songs.

With my resolve building daily, Dad and I, being the eldest males in the household, began to assume the roles of two superpowers locked in a cold war. This left us reaching out for allies—Larry, Karen, Mom—to buttress our respective sides. My siblings, preferring to stay neutral, developed a sixth sense for when Dad and I were about to get into the thick of things. "Danny, get in here, on the hop!" Dad would bray from the kitchen, and Larry and Karen, who'd been sprawled across the couch listening to me play my latest song, would take off up the stairs, disappearing into their bedrooms. Trying as it may have been for my siblings—always steeling themselves for the next father-son land mine to go off, anxious to improve on their already impeccable behaviour to make up for their older brother's offences—Mom bore the brunt of Dad's and my power struggles.

Mom, unable to flee to her own bedroom like Larry or Karen, was an unwilling spectator forced to sit at ringside till the latest breaking father-son spectacle had run its course. As a teenager I was too selfish to think of how hard it must have been for her, watching two people she loved deeply cause each other so much pain and aggravation. The following excerpt from Mom's diary, written in 1970, offers a glimpse of what she was forced to endure. On this particular night I'd been competing in a songwriting contest downtown called the Davenport Music Festival. I'd won third place, along with six hours of free time in a state-of-the-art recording studio. (The following year I was awarded first place.)

Dan comments that Danny is very late. The audition was supposed to be at 7, now it's past 11 . . . Dan is fussing and fuming. Talks about a "trend" being established, of being out on school nights. I submit that it is no trend. He decides that since Danny has been out two school nights in a row (movie at school Wednesday night, this audition Thursday night), he should therefore spend Friday and Saturday nights study-ing. Danny gets in at midnite. He messes around (eating) for 10–15 minutes. Dan yells for him to hurry up. He comes up. I ask how the audition went. He says the adjudicator said he did the Joni Mitchell thing badly; but when he sang his own song, completely different—great meaning, great message, great communication. The adjudicator—connected with CHUM— urges him to write out the lyrics and music and send it to him—he'll try to get it published. The audition and adjudica-tion took till 11, so Danny's arriving home at 12 wasn't really unreasonable. Dan tells him to bring home all his school books because he's going to have to study Friday and Saturday, from 7 to 9:30. Danny says, quietly but firmly, that he'll bring home the books he likes and study what he likes for as long as he likes. Dan is mad.
"Don't get lippy with me."
"I'm not being lippy—but that's what I mean."
"I'll ground you, and take away your guitar."
"Ground me. I'll play someone else's guitar."

Dan is furious. He jumps out of bed. I, who have been silent
through this, beg, "Dan, keep cool."
Dan grabs Danny's guitar and brings it into our room. "He
can't get away with that, being lippy with me."
I'm close to tears. I close the bedroom door. "Can't you see
what you're doing? If you take away everything important,
why should he do anything we want?"
"As long as he lives here, and I'm supporting him, he won't talk
to me like that."
"That's just it—in two months, he'll be 16. He won't have to
stay here, he won't have any reason to stay here."
Dan scoffs: "He'd never leave home. He doesn't have the guts."
I say, "When you were seventeen, you nearly punched your
father in the mouth. How can you be so angry when he's sim-
ply said, quietly and without violent words, that he's going to
do what he feels is important?"
Dan brushes that aside: "He'll do as I say. He won't be lippy
with me."

What Mom fails to mention in her diary was that she banished Dad from the bedroom that night. This was the only time in all the years I'd lived at home that I'd known Mom to do this. My guitar was back in my room the next day.

As is typical of many parents, Dad's difficulties with my career choice in particular, and me in general, were not so openly expressed in letters to his friends and family. In fact some of his observations regarding my so-called development revealed a degree of optimism: "Danny received his report card a while back and came within *one point* of receiving first class honors." Upon catching himself in a gross misrepresentation—or maybe he got my report card confused with my sister's—he allowed a bit of his frustration with me to show through: "Danny sings (or rather groans) for his friends and plays a good game of chess. He's turning out to be quite a fine boy in spite of some of the headaches he gives to me."

Still in the close quarters of our house, Dad was careful not to offer any signs of encouragement for fear that it would doom me to chasing an impossible dream.

Until I could win his approval, Dad was better off avoided. My bedroom was just a few feet down the hall from his and Mom's, which meant that whenever I risked singing at a decent volume, Dad would barrel into my bedroom saying something to the effect of, "Cut out that racket, now! Or I'll chop up that guitar with an axe and use it as firewood."

My solution was to practise high-volume singing down in the relative isolation of the basement. I was entering my Led Zeppelin stage, which meant I had to sing so crazy loud to keep up with Robert Plant's keening tenor. One Sunday morning, I was down in the basement reviewing the chords to Led Zeppelin's "Babe, I'm Gonna Leave You." I loved the song's haunting A-minor descending chord progression, as it reminded me a lot of the classical guitar exercises I used to practise. Sailing over the galloping guitar part was the steady, dramatic rise of Robert Plant's vocal. Plant's Olympian performance was a great lesson in the importance of vocal dynamics, range and control, something I was determined to emulate.

When I hit the song's climax, where Plant screams like he's possessed, over an impossibly high C, I quickly replaced my guitar with a pillow, singing into it with all my might. But when I removed the pillow from my face and opened my eyes, Dad was standing right over me.

"Have you finished your homework, son?" An accusation disguised as a question. This was how it always started with him.

"Yup."

"You're spending too much time on that blasted guitar. You're throwing your life away on this music foolishness."

"I'm practising for a fashion show at my school. They're paying me ten dollars to perform in between the runway events."

The idea that I could make money through music seemed to further antagonize him. Like the difference between smoking pot and dealing it.

"Time to face the hard cold facts, boy. Accept your limitations. You're never gonna be a Bruce Cockburn."

I was about to tell Dad that I couldn't care less what he thought of me, or my music. But I couldn't risk speaking. Dad would have picked off that dumb tremor in my voice and realized he'd really hurt me. *You're never gonna be a Bruce Cockburn.* That was really hitting below the belt.

"Put down your guitar and get cracking on those schoolbooks, this instant. I don't wanna hear so much as a peep coming out of this basement, or I'll come back and personally put a stop to the noise."

Dad continued to glare down at me, waiting, daring me to make the mistake of saying something even remotely disrespectful. Slowly and deliberately, so as not to appear too intimidated, I placed my guitar back in its case. At that moment, I honestly and truly hated him.

As I got older, I tried my best to make sense of Dad's many inconsistencies: Hills were "blessed with superior genes," but when it came to music, I had to be aware of my limitations; playing sports was "a waste of a good mind" (Dad had forbidden me to participate in school sports, though naturally I did anyway), but watching them on television was allowable. "Look at that, Donna! Whoopee!" he'd yip while viewing an NFL game, knowing that if he called out Mom's name enough times, she would come into the family room and stand beside him for a few minutes. Mom understood that the real entertainment lay in watching Dad watch football: he'd hop up and down on the couch like a child on a serious sugar high, hurling all sorts of outrageously comical comments at the players, coaches and refs till he lost his voice.

Even Dad's constant crowing that "Hill kids and straight As are inseparable" was frequently undermined by his need to put us in our place. Imagine Larry's confusion when Dad discovered he'd decided to write the entrance exams to UTS (University of Toronto Schools), an elite private school for the academically gifted.

"Trust me, son," Dad had scoffed, "you'll never pass the test." Larry had no intention of actually going to UTS, but being blessed and cursed with "Hill Competitive Instinct Disorder" he needed to prove that he could pass the test. Which he did. Not surprisingly, Dad enrolled Larry at UTS despite my brother's protests.

Meanwhile, Dad's consistent dismissal of Larry's and my respective abilities throughout our adolescence caused us to dig even deeper, fervently hoping that one day our achievements might impress him, or at least earn his attention. If this was part of Dad's master plan, it worked. Just like Dad with his dad, I wanted, more than anything else in the world, to make him proud. The critical difference between Dad and me as teenagers, however, was this: Dad constantly told his father that he desperately wanted to earn his approval and respect. Never would I have opened myself up to Dad in this way. "Don't lie to me, boy," Dad scoffed, when, at eighteen, I informed him that I'd been offered a recording contract with RCA. I wasn't going to let up in my quest to be a famous singer until I made Dad eat his words.

There was more fuelling my ambition than figuratively shaking Dad by the throat and saying, "I'm here! I'm worthy. Honestly, I'm not the fuck-up you think I am." The idea of girls, adoring girls, gazing up at me and my guitar with their half-closed eyes suffused with desire, well, yes, that definitely put some extra oomph into my singing. And, just like Dad's approval, that kind of female reaction was not exactly on the immediate horizon. It would be too convenient to blame my sad lack of action on Dad (rather than my overbearing intensity, which sent girls running in the direction of the more rugged, silent and strong football types), but nonetheless, Dad's before-its-time safe sex speech hadn't made intimacy sound all that appealing.

One morning, as a way of spicing up our Sunday family breakfast, Dad decided to share with us the army's advanced method of treating venereal disease back when he was enlisted.

"The cure back then for VD was a big fat needle straight into the head of the penis."

"Oh no! Stop!" I coughed, gagging on my breakfast.

Encouraged by my choking, Dad passed me a glass of water before continuing. "This was followed by the patient resting his member on a level surface. Then the doctor would smash a hammer down on the head of the penis in attempt to force out what remained of the disease. The soldiers would beg to be left to die from venereal infection rather than undergo the cure. Two weeks later, they'd be back in the clinic with another infection, facing another juicy needle and the bonk of a hammer."

If Dad's method for scaring his kids off sex was as original as it was crude, well, what else was new? Beyond not wanting to sound prudish (Dad saw himself as something of a libertarian), he knew that the more typical "sex is wrong" approach wouldn't have worked, and, beyond that, it lacked any theatrical punch. Dad's gruesome scare tactics notwithstanding, to be fifteen in Don Mills in 1970 was akin to living in a sexual wasteland. When I departed on a high school choir trip to Washington, D.C., one of my female classmates was branded a slut because she was seen, briefly, in the hallway of our hotel in her flannel pyjamas. It didn't matter that the only skin showing happened to be on her feet and face; this was considered, by my God-fearing classmates, unrepentant sexually provocative behaviour.

The combination of all these influences—Dad's hellacious VD images, a sex-paranoid community, my shyness when it came to approaching girls and my extensive knowledge of erotic literature— managed to contribute to my archaic thoughts on girls and sex. I don't claim to be the only boy at that time who'd managed to divide potential girlfriends into two immaculate compartments—one for sex (however unlikely), the other for unblemished, platonic love—it's just that, as I did with everything, I took this Victorian notion to the extreme.

The latter category, that of the airbrushed, untouchable kind of undying love, was reserved for a girl named Cynthia whom I'd met when I was fifteen, not long after I'd been betrayed by Amanda. I first saw Cynthia, who'd recently moved to Toronto from St. John's, Newfoundland, at a junior high school dance. Despite a cast on her right leg she was dancing so fluidly, and with such unreserved joy, that I couldn't take my eyes off her. In my school, dancing was the one situation, the only situation really, where a girl was allowed to be sexy without fear of being judged. But Cynthia was the only girl on the dance floor who appeared unconcerned, oblivious to everyone around her. For the rest of the night I stood in a shadowy corner of the gymnasium, content to do nothing but watch her dance. I didn't dare approach her. That would have ruined everything. She was too perfect. I fell in love with every song she danced to that night, even ones I'd previously hated.

A month later she contacted me. A mutual friend had given her my phone number. She was a competitive track athlete and needed a running partner. (I'd recently made my school cross-country team— keeping this news from Dad—and was one of its better runners.)We agreed to meet every weekday at 7:00 a.m., for a three-mile run.

A month is an eternity to nurture a crush when you're a fifteen-year-old boy with enough testosterone to power a team of racehorses. So, when I waited for Cynthia to fly out of her front door for our first Monday-morning run, I was determined not to like her. Amanda had taught me that if I allowed myself to feel too much I'd just wind up horribly disappointed.

"G'morning, Danny, don't you just love running in the rain?"

"Huh? Oh yeah, right . . . it's raining."

I'd been so caught up in my track star posturing that I could've been standing in the middle of a hurricane and I would have scarcely noticed. Not the first impression I was aiming for.

"Whatever happens, Danny, don't let me slow you down. If you want to run faster, I can hang back. Don't feel like you have to wait up for me."

I hadn't expected a sprinter (a female sprinter, no less) to attack a three-mile course with the aggressive confidence of a middle-distance runner, particularly after recovering from a broken ankle. Too out of breath to waste any on conversation, I tried focusing on Cynthia's running form.

Only Cynthia didn't run so much as glide, her arms swinging loosely by her side, a far-off smile never fading form her face. As the miles flew by, Cynthia talked and I grunted, hurting too much to make out a thing she was saying. Fifteen minutes into our run, Cynthia, unable to maintain any semblance of running protocol any longer, took off up the last, long hill on our course. I tried gamely to stay with her but after a few choppy strides I slowed to a trot, praying the lactic acid that was turning my quads into sludgy cement would let up. As Cynthia's sculpted sprinter's legs picked up speed with each quick turnover, I considered telling her she was going to have to find another running partner.

For a fifteen-year-old male ego, it's difficult to feel attracted to someone who's left you feeling woefully inadequate. Cynthia's muscled legs looked pretty amazing as she torqued into her finishing kick, but not in that typically feminine way. I knew I was reaching for flaws, exaggerating and even inventing imperfections along the way, but still, after some serious effort, I managed to convince myself that she wasn't quite my type.

At an age when other girls affected all manner of gestures and attitude, Cynthia seemed so natural that it struck me as almost unnatural, like she existed on another plane than the rest of the kids at our school. While everyone I knew sweated over their marks, their interfering parents, their future, their lack of girlfriends or boyfriends, Cynthia didn't appear concerned about much of anything. Everything seemed to come absurdly easy for her—marks, popularity, good looks, filthy-rich parents—which normally I would have used against her. Except that she appeared unaware of her unearthly advantages.

Her disarming ability to get anyone to open up to her, often in the most touching ways, fascinated me. All the more so because she avoided ever revealing anything significant about herself, deftly answering questions with questions.

Little by little, our running dates spilled over into other activities. Nothing to get cocky about, as most of our get-togethers revolved around me dropping by her place once a week and listening to records. After just one or two listening sessions Cynthia understood my musical tastes so well that she could predict what songs on the radio I'd like or hate. Matt was the only other person who could do that, but unlike Matt, who went out of his way to hate my favourite singers just to pick a fight, Cynthia always loved the same stuff as me. Could her love of music possibly extend to musicians? In my dreams. To imagine Cynthia feeling any kind of romantic stirrings for anyone was beyond me, as she took wholesome to a whole new level. It was one thing for Cynthia to never swear, but when someone else did, her face went blank, as though—*pfff*—she'd instantly wiped the profanity out of her memory.

I knew I was in trouble when I started looking forward to our morning runs a little too much. Her brown hair frizzed out just like mine when it rained, and I could pick out her smile as she ran down her street to meet me, even on the darkest, dreariest February morning, when the sun was still an hour from surfacing.

"Find a fault, find a fault," I kept telling myself each day as our run came to an end and I found myself already impatient for the following morning.

Finally, she gave me something to hold against her: she was totally disinterested in current events. "What would my parents think?" I caught myself wondering one day, following our first argument.

It happened after I'd played her a protest song I'd written about America's involvement in Vietnam. Cynthia usually loved hearing me play and sing, but this time she just sat across from me looking distracted, as if she wanted to be somewhere else.

"Don't mind me, Danny," she said apologetically, once I'd finished, "it's just that I like your more positive songs."

I channelled my hurt into self-righteousness, telling her I thought that Nixon should be tried as a war criminal, for murder.

"You can't say that, Danny," Cynthia answered, appalled. "President Nixon has children. He's a devoted father and husband. Someone like that can't possibly be a murderer."

I started to snicker, thinking she was having me on.

"What's so funny, Danny?"

"Nothing. I was just wondering how Nixon would feel about his kids fighting in Vietnam."

"Don't be silly. President Nixon has girls. Girls can't get drafted."

It was as if Cynthia possessed some kind of weird filtering aura, so that all potentially sinister things conveniently escaped her awareness. But the problem was, much as I wished otherwise, I liked that about her.

It wasn't until Cynthia casually told me, towards the end of one of our runs, that she and her family would shortly be returning to live in St. John's, that I had to confront my utter foolishness. How could I have allowed myself to get sucked into feeling so much for this person?

"Oh, I forgot, Cynthia—I can't run with you tomorrow. I gotta study for a math exam."

At my words, Cynthia came to a full stop in the middle of the sidewalk and stared at me, as though she was waiting for me to say something else. Angry at her news and confused by the emotions it triggered in me, I abandoned her on the sidewalk and took off down the street, running as hard as I could. When I got home I rushed up to my bedroom, picked up my guitar and wrote a song. Really, it wrote itself. It was the first love song I'd ever written.

I agreed to Cynthia's request that we run that weekend, even though it meant cancelling several hours of teaching guitar. We ran faster than usual that morning, as if we both wanted to get it over with.

"Is everything all right, Danny?" Cynthia asked as we flopped on her front lawn, post-workout, gently stretching out each other's hamstrings. This was the only time we ever allowed ourselves any physical contact.

"I've been thinking about this new song I just finished writing," I answered.

"Can you play it for me, I mean right now?"

"Yeah, I guess." On the way to my house, Cynthia peppered me with the usual questions—"What was the song about, when did I write it, what was it called?" She was the only person I knew who seemed more excited about my songwriting than I.

Relieved that everyone in my family appeared to be still sleeping, I led Cynthia into my basement, where she sat on the bottom stair. Grabbing my guitar I squeezed in beside her.

As I closed my eyes and started singing, I tried to convince myself that perhaps Cynthia wouldn't think my new love song was about her. For instance, McCartney's "Yesterday" could have as easily been written about losing his mother, as, say, breaking up with a girl. But my lyrics were as specific and inelegant as McCartney's were universal. Into my second verse I sensed my song was backfiring, badly. Trying to change my words on the spot I froze, hummed a few lines and then reverted to my clumsy musical confession. Before my last guitar note faded, Cynthia tore out of my basement and the house, nearly tripping over my incredulous dad, who'd chosen the worst moment possible to sit on the front porch puffing on his Saturday-morning cigar.

"Daggum, son, what did you do to that poor little girl?" Dad cackled as I burst out the door and looked forlornly down the street for signs of Cynthia, who had already swung right at the bottom of our hill and disappeared. "Heaven's sake alive, I never knew a white girl could run that fast!"

"Dan, stop it, right now. No more teasing Danny about girls, you know how sensitive he gets," Mom scolded, catching the tail-end of the commotion.

How did I manage to end up with parents like this?

On our final run, Cynthia and I channelled the building tension between us into a punishing pace that left us both bent over, sucking and wheezing, when we pulled to a stop in front of her house. What I did next just kind of happened. Still bent over, I pulled the ring off the third finger of my left hand and presented it to Cynthia. The ring itself was nothing much, tiny blue and green beads haphazardly strung together—some of the beads were even missing—but it had always been special to me. As I awkwardly slid the ring up the third finger of her right hand, I felt her palm go clammy and limp.

"It's too late to get involved, Danny," she whispered, looking sadder than I'd ever seen her before. Then she gave my hand a slight squeeze before springing up the stairs to her house and out of my life, still wearing my ring.

The following week, I couldn't bear to jog by the house where she used to live. How could I be so badly broken up—everything, eating, running, even songwriting, seemed unbearably dull since she'd left—over a girl who was never going to be more than a running buddy? She'd always described me to her friends as "nice" and "sweet," the worst two words a girl could say about a boy. Why did I keep writing songs about a girl I'd never see again? Why not simply write songs for Princess Grace of Monaco? I was learning that you can't choose what songs you write.

And my new love songs were way better than that first one I'd mistakenly played her. I owed it to myself to send her the lyrics, so she could see that I was improving. It was no big deal, she'd asked me to write her and keep her updated on all my singing projects. And if I was going to go to the trouble of sending her my latest songs, I might as well send a little note along with them. Within a month of Cynthia's departure, we began exchanging letters every week, a correspondence that would continue for five years.

CHAPTER 9

Dad's Career Soars

1954
Dear Dan & May—

You will have gotten Buddy's letter, and heard the sad news. Our boy's morale is pretty low right now, and he really needs encouragement. His professors all feel he should keep on, but of course it's pretty difficult for him to get started again. I've been trying to encourage him to dig into his research, and he's beginning to do that. What worries him most is time—and the pressure he feels to start earning a steady income. I keep trying to minimize the latter and to assure him that we'll make out all right, for I fear that once he gets involved in a regular full-time job, he will lose sight of this major goal.

Mom's "sad news" was the mixed feedback Dad had received from the three sociology professors reviewing his PhD dissertation, which was entitled "Negroes in Toronto, a Sociological Study of a Minority Group." The professors believed Dad's thesis, while relevant and full of well-researched and interesting statistics, didn't go into enough specific detail about the actual day-to-day lives of individual Negroes. This meant that Dad, who'd assumed his dissertation was complete, had a lot more fieldwork left to do; he'd have to spend time, and a lot of it, not simply interviewing but living with Black individuals and families. To Dad's mind this was a major setback. How could he spend weeks living with families scattered across the city, earn a living and be an attentive father, not to mention husband? Something had to give. Dad was torn between two powerful Hill male traditions: supporting your wife and family versus joining the select ranks of educated elite. His choice, made clear in a letter to his parents, may have been the only responsible one, but that did little to assuage his sense of conflict: "Unfortunately, my thesis and graduate work are standing still and I am making absolutely no progress in this direction, I feel the necessity to do so many things both in the home and in the community that the PhD seems to be fading into the far distant, untouchable horizon."

Part of him must have despaired that he was once again living through a variation of his failures in the army. Of trying to follow in his father's footsteps and running into barriers as insurmountable as they were unfair. Dad, however, was not one to repeat past mistakes. Grounded by his family responsibilities, he was also married to a woman who matched his unflagging loyalty, a woman who believed in his thesis, shared his career vision and had the brains and patience and tact to nudge him forward with equal measures of love, support and advice.

On the one hand, Mom reassured Dad that, PhD or not, he had all the work he could possibly handle and then some. At the same time, Mom busied herself behind the scenes to keep Dad's eye on the distant prize. She secretly enlisted relatives on both sides of the family to give her five or ten dollars for Dad's birthday, so she could set up a "Desk-for-Dan fund" to "perk him up and get him back to concentrating on his work."

Mom's role of invisible, unofficial collaborator proved to be the extra gear Dad desperately needed to stay on task. So long as Dad was working, studying side by side with Mom, it took on the form of a shared project, more than a hobby but less than some onerous never-ending project. Suggesting ways he could humanize his thesis, Mom also played secretary, typing and editing his work.

Still, over the next few years, with all that was going on, Dad's dissertation languished. By 1958, he was commuting several hours a day to Toronto, working full-time at the Social Planning Council (SPC) and studying and writing exams related to his university courses. He'd come home each night to an exhausted wife and three very young kids, all clamouring for his attention. In the back of his mind, he must have known he couldn't put off his thesis forever. But as with any long, challenging and potentially life-changing project, the longer he avoided taking it on, the more overwhelming it felt to take charge of it again.

Eventually his faculty advisor said, "Hand in your finished dissertation by the end of the summer or you'll have to start your PhD all over again from scratch." This was exactly the kind of deadline Dad needed. He agreed to stop working full-time while managing, in his inimitable fashion, to procure a five-hundred-dollar grant from the University of Toronto. Dr. S.D. Clark, happy that his favourite student was finally buckling down, persuaded the head of SPC to give Dad the summer off, with the understanding that he'd return to work in the fall, once his PhD was completed.

Dad spent the summer of 1959 immersed in the Black community of downtown Toronto, where he interviewed and often lived with people in settlement houses. He visited railway porters, a teenager working at a luggage store, Blacks who had just immigrated to Canada and Blacks who had been here for generations. Dad's letter to his father shows just how well his research was paying off:

> During the month of June I was trying to discern the "way
> of life" of Negro families in the most depressed—physically,
> economically, morally—district in Toronto. I have practically

lived with a lower class family as I chummed around with
a young man who grew up in the area. I've been in dives,
pool halls, beer parlours, destitute houses and have talked
to all types of people. The people have accepted me—Black
and white—so long as I'm with Duke (my friend) and I've
amassed what I feel to be valuable information. Never did I or
have I used pencil or paper in front of the people in "the dis-
trict" but have used the technique of casual participation and
easy conversation—devoid of the normal interview approach.
I find this technique most fruitful and less damaging to the
relationship I am trying to establish.

Dad would stay up for hours each night writing down all he'd uncovered while his memories were still fresh. The five-hundred-dollar grant was spent on a daytime nanny so my parents could stay on schedule. Dad's professors, impressed with this new thesis material, rewarded him with assignments usually doled out to professionals with far greater experience. Between giving weekly college lectures on the "Sociology of Deviant Behaviour" and working with a research team on a study of chronic alcoholics, Dad somehow found the time to complete his improved thesis. And in 1960, after what seemed like an endless struggle, Dad was awarded what must have surely felt like the proverbial (and literal, in terms of how it would impact his future salaries) pot of gold at the end of the rainbow. Finally, just like his father, Dad had his coveted PhD.

If I try, I can still remember the commotion that swept through our Newmarket home once Dad's accomplishment sank in. As a six-year-old, I studied my parents' moods avidly, quick to understand that when they were happy I could get away with a lot more stuff—leaving my toys all over the place for Larry and Karen to trip over, interrupting Dad's reading or Mom's telephone conversation without receiving an icy "wait your turn" stare—than when they were anxious or unhappy. The period immediately following Dad's PhD passed like one sustained celebration. People streamed in and out of our Newmarket house, bearing gifts, wearing funny hats and saying strange things like, "Now you're a 'Fud,' Dan," and "Do we have to call you 'doctor'?" Parties would blend into more parties with semi-rude diagrams and illustrations plastered across our bathroom door. Towards the end of each night dozens of people would holler: "Speech, speech, speech!"

"Oh Dan, not this again," Mom would pretend-groan. "We all know what you're about to say!"

"Shush, woman!" Dad would roar, his voice soaring over the cacophony of clinking glasses and alcohol-infused chatter. He drew Mom tight up against his side and waited for her head to rest against his shoulder.

"Okay, Dan, you've set the stage now," Mom observed, meaning the room had, on cue, fallen silent.

"Daggum, as you can all see, I married myself one hard-headed woman. My pappy always told me, 'Buddy, the key to happiness and success in life is to marry a woman smarter than you.'"

"Hear! Hear!" the guests chanted.

Pausing deliberately, Dad tenderly straightened out Mom's hair. Then he said, "Without this woman I would never have made it through the University of Toronto. And I would never have received my PhD. So let's toast Donna, the smartest, most loving woman in the world."

"I don't know when I'm ever going to see this man now," Mom added, once the hooting died down. "He was already working so many jobs before this big degree. Now he's going to be so busy that I'm going to forget that I ever had a husband."

"Actually, Donna, now he's gonna work half the time and get paid twice as much!" someone in the crowd yelled out.

I remember this slew of PhD parties so vividly because they reflected the very best of what Newmarket symbolized to Dad and Mom, and by extension, our entire family. The shared momentum a couple feels building a life together hummed through our house. There was the unspoken, satisfying sensation of all things falling into place. The challenges and setbacks my parents had encountered during their early years in Canada could have easily divided them. But instead they drew closer. If they were, in a sense, outliers in this country, it was as they preferred it. It made them appreciate each other, as well as their small and quirky circle of socially conscious friends, even more. In their unassuming way, my parents defined themselves by how they didn't fit into the prevailing culture that exerted its invisible hold on most of southern Ontario.

Not so long ago Dad had been an alienated, envenomed divorcé working in an ineffectual welfare department in Detroit. Now the world appeared wide open and welcoming, vibrating with promise and possibilities. A PhD was a rare achievement for a Black man in Canada in 1960, and it provided Dad with a status usually reserved for doctors and lawyers. As a sociologist, he understood all too well the importance of symbols when he declared, "No one will ever be allowed to call me Dr. Hill. I'm no doctor. I don't want any special title." Within a year, however, everyone other than his closest friends and relatives referred to him as "Dr." And he never objected.

Much as Mom boasted that Dad hardly needed a PhD to give him a step up in the work force, she must have known that Dad's employability was never the real issue. The name Daniel Grafton Hill III carried with it tremendous weight, responsibilities and traditions. Now Dad could deservedly call himself his father's son.

As for Dad's sense of contentment at this time, his 1959 letter to his parents confirms that he'd found, for a while at any rate, as perfect a balance as any man could possibly hope for: "I think at 35 years, I can truthfully say that my childhood lesson was well learned—love and devotion of family and home. This, mixed with what I feel is a proper balance regarding material and social values has made my new family life with Donna and kids both easy and enjoyable. Problems either melt away, become reconciled or are lived with in an atmosphere of love, warmth and mutual respect."

While education was one highly effective way of transcending the colour barrier in the 1950s, Dad understood that geography played a determining factor as well. The general rule that the further north you ventured, the less oppressive the racism was a major reason why he'd moved to Canada. Compared to what he'd experienced as a soldier in America's Deep South, Toronto's "polite racism" at times intrigued and bemused him. For instance, when my newlywed parents had tried to rent a basement apartment in Toronto, the landlord would typically take one look at the two of them and apologize, claiming the apartment had just been rented. This was obviously a lie, but from Dad's point of view, it still beat the American south, where miscegenation was against the law.

Since a typical Canadian wouldn't admit to being racist, Mom simply had to show up at an apartment for rent with a Caucasian friend and leave a deposit, and then Dad would take the place of her Caucasian friend a few weeks down the line, when it was time to move in. But as Dad's educational credentials became more impressive, even incidents of polite racism lessened. Class trumped race in almost every situation.

This sometimes lulled me into almost forgetting that Dad (and by extension, I) was Black. But that could be dangerous. Because then something unexpected would happen to remind me that the world was not quite as oblivious to colour as it seemed. Like when Dad spent the night in the Don Jail.

It was Dad's first post-PhD job, working at the Addiction and Alcoholism Research Foundation, that landed him in trouble. His first assignment at the foundation was to lead a study on the phenomenon of revolving-door addicts. Why did so many alcoholics land in jail, serve a term, get released and then end up back in jail again? Dad, who was well acquainted with the warden of the Don Jail, obtained permission to interview several alcoholic inmates in their cells. One Saturday evening, halfway through one of Dad's prison interviews, a new guard started his shift. When Dad was ready to go home, the new guard wouldn't let him out of jail, claiming he was a prisoner who was using the interviewing sociologist disguise as a clever ruse to escape. The warden had gone out of town for Thanksgiving weekend. So Dad spent the night in the slammer while Mom paced the kitchen, stretching the phone cord to the breaking point, waking up everyone she knew, trying to track Dad down. When Dad finally stomped through the front door, it was already morning.

Dan Hill

"If the warden hadn't placed a call to the jail to check on things, no telling what might have happened to me. I could have been locked up in that place till kingdom come." Dad was spitting out his words at such a clip that I was missing most of what he was saying.

"But Dan, how could the guard have possibly confused you for . . ." Mom asked, unable to even say the word "prisoner."

"He knew damned well I was no prisoner," Dad fulminated, his clothes wrinkled and foul smelling, his usually baby-smooth face displaying a hint of whiskers. "It must have driven him round the bend to see an educated Black man interviewing a white man in prison."

Dad would eventually rejig his "night in jail" experience, sometimes going so far as to claim he'd escaped by picking the lock on his cell with his pen and tiptoeing by the snoring prison guards. There were two messages I absorbed from all of this. One: Part of coping with any bad luck thrown your way is to turn it into a funny story where you always—facts be damned—emerge triumphant. Two: All the professional status in the world could never guarantee Dad complete protection from the "crime" of being a Negro. Dad, and therefore all of us, were like animals roaming a giant game reserve, and no one knew when the bars would arbitrarily be slammed down, enclosing us in an invisible prison.

Dad's best defence was to never stop achieving.

Not long after Dad's prison stint, in 1961, he wrote a letter informing his parents that "the offers are pouring in for employment." After meticulously detailing a whole slew of job prospects (listing them in order of status), Dad allowed a glimpse of his vulnerability to show through, something he was less and less prone to do as a middle-aged man: "Undoubtedly my PhD-enhanced job opportunities made the future for myself and family more secure . . . I want time—and a badly needed rest before moving on to the next plateau. I have been extremely tired and weary lately and sometimes wonder if the strain of the last two years isn't catching up with me. I try not to think of it too much."

It's likely that Dad was unknowingly sharing with his parents the early symptoms of his undetected diabetes. Regrettably, the closest he would come to getting some of that "badly needed rest" was writing about it. As always, his hastily scrawled comments about his insidious fatigue and wanting to spend more time with his family were tucked into one or two lines at the bottom of the page, once the latest news concerning his career had been catalogued.

Dad's first big break came as a result of Mom's behind-the-scenes connections. In 1962, after hearing that the Ministry of Labour was looking for someone to start up the Ontario Human Rights Commission, Mom phoned an old work associate who happened to be a close friend of the deputy minister of labour, Tom Eberle, and advised, in her usual direct manner, "You tell Tom Eberle that no one's better qualified than Dan Hill."

The first Dad heard of this conversation was when Eberle contacted him for a job interview. ("I didn't want to get your father's hopes up" was Mom's reason for keeping Dad in the dark.) Within weeks of being interviewed, Dad officially became the director of the very first human rights commission in Canada.

During Dad's twelve-year reign at the Ontario Human Rights Commission (OHRC), he generated hundreds of news stories and newspaper headlines. One in particular sheds some light on the prevailing attitude towards minorities at the time: "Negro and Jew Spearhead March by Indians."

It's doubtful that, back in 1965, the readers of the *Winnipeg Tribune* would have considered this front-page headline to be anything out of the ordinary. My father, the "Negro" in question (the "Jew" was one of his closest work allies and the future head of the Canadian Civil Liberties Association, Alan Borovoy), taped this headline to his office wall, where it remained a source of mirth and inspiration for many years. Incidentally, the facts behind the headline were accurate. Dad and Borovoy had surreptitiously bused Natives from northern Ontario into the town of Kenora, where their protests about hideous living conditions on their outlying reserves would catch the eye of the national media.

If nothing else, this headline indicates exactly how resistant the media and public were to the rights of minorities back in the sixties. The overall philosophy could be compared to many Americans' views on gun control today. The idea that a restaurant or hotel owner could be denied his right to determine whom to serve, or rent an apartment to, was looked upon as an affront to personal liberty. Neighbours would accost my father in a grocery store or on our street and screech, "What about my civil liberties! It's my democratic right to hire whomever I want!"

This was precisely why Dad was the perfect fit for the commission. He was a rabble-rouser who loved confrontation. Better still, because he was building the commission from the ground up in a country where no such agency had previously existed, he didn't have to worry about following existing structures or protocols. Dad's early days at the OHRC consisted of him, his secretary and his rusted-out Volkswagen—the antithesis of civil servant bureaucracy. Emboldened by the Ministry of Labour's promise that he was free to conduct his start-up agency without any kind of political interference, Dad spent upwards of ten days out of most months driving all over the province setting up regional offices and investigating cases of possible discrimination.

Unlike a lot of professionals in the field of human rights, Dad could go from combative to charming, from deadly serious to slapstick funny, depending on the situation. How fitting that his combination of incorrigible mischief and considerable powers of coercion was put to such good use—especially when traditional methods failed to bring an alleged discriminator around.

One of Dad's early cases involved a boathouse owner in Chatham who refused to rent fishing boats to Blacks. Dad countered by convening a public hearing. The boathouse owner had no way of knowing that Dad had a special gift for transforming public hearings into community events. Upon arriving at the hearing, the first thing the boathouse owner noticed was that almost everyone in the audience was Black, courtesy of Dad's expert recruiting skills. During an especially withering cross-examination, the boathouse owner folded. Dad, suspicious of the man's resolve, quickly called for an adjournment and pulled a bunch of Black people from the audience and into the judge's chambers, where he arranged for them to immediately put deposits down on fishing boats for the summer. Some of the Blacks balked, claiming not to like fishing. "That's irrelevant," Dad said. "You're going fishing, and that's that."

The best anecdotes about Dad's work adventures came to my attention when his friends dropped by our house. There was always a parade of human rights types drifting in and out of our living room: an assortment of university professors, lawyers, left-leaning politicians and people who worked for Dad at the commission. They were, by and large, a serious bunch, huddled over glasses of scotch, puffing absentmindedly on pipes, discussing (and as the alcohol kicked in, shouting and swearing about) the Big Issue of the moment: Vietnam, the race riots in America's inner cities, the Cold War, whether Prime Minister Trudeau was a true enemy or ally of the "cause." It was as if the fate of the world lay in the hands of these dozen or so friends and colleagues of Dad's, and if someone left our house harbouring the wrong opinion about something we were all doomed. Whenever things got too tense, usually when the last drop of alcohol was consumed, Dad would break the mood by launching into one of his stories. Whether summarizing some human rights case he was fighting in court or spinning some tale about his army days, he showered his attention democratically, his eyes dancing from person to person. He never failed to entertain, his laughter sailing above the debating voices, bathing everyone in warmth.

Often Dad had me bartend his little get-togethers. Nothing pleased me more as a sixteen-year-old than getting his earnest, intellectual friends plowed out of their minds. As the evening wound down, Dad, slightly tipsy, would start bragging about my musical gifts. "Danny must've picked it up from his grandfather," he'd laugh. "Now go grab that guitar of yours, boy, and treat us to one of your latest protest songs."

I'd get my guitar and be singing for Dad and his friends within seconds, before Dad could have a change of heart. But my moment of glory was always short-lived. Midway through the first chorus of my latest masterpiece, Dad, unable to contain himself, would shout out, "When did you write that, son?" expecting me to explain the song's origin and continue singing without dropping a beat.

His friends, reacting to me as though I were the first teenager on earth to sing an original song—while simultaneously playing the guitar no less—would pounce on me with the inevitable question once my song was completed: "Are the lyrics autobiographical?"

I'd just finished a seven-minute, two-chord first-person epic about a boy who, ostracized from society, had clubbed a man to death.

"Yup," I'd answer, so intoxicated by all this high-powered attention that I'd managed to forget that "autobiographical" and "biographical" don't mean the same thing.

"He's a human rights songwriter," Dad would pipe up, as if that somehow justified my homicidal leanings.

"Ahhh. Of course," someone in the group would say, as they all nodded thoughtfully. Then, before I assaulted his friends with another marathon minor-chord dirge, Dad would revert to form, saying, "Danny, time to start cleaning up."

Usually, the last guest to leave Dad's rousing get-togethers was Alan Borovoy. Dad and Borovoy became acquainted in the late fifties when Borovoy was just a rookie lawyer. They were both getting their feet wet as professional activists, or, to use Borovoy's term, "shit disturbers." A good decade younger and greener than Dad, Borovoy took immediate note of Dad's ability to flatter people without coming across as unctuous. If there was one thing that people in power shared, it was an inordinate amount of vanity, something Dad loved to exploit. When, early on in their friendship, Borovoy expressed concern that his bosses at the Jewish Labour Committee wouldn't allow him to pull off some of the more radical things he wanted to implement, Dad's solution was "Make a dinner for them and honour them. You do that and they won't pay any attention to the things you're doing; the dinner's going to be uppermost in their minds."

Physically, Borovoy and Dad were compelling opposites. Borovoy, a bundle of wiry intensity, his small, darting eyes upstaged by thick eyebrows and a jockey's lithe build, perfectly offset Dad's deceptively easygoing, lumbering physicality. Together, their irreverence and rascally spirit crackled through our house, standing in sharp contrast to their outer, public demeanour as no-nonsense human rights activists. An avowed bachelor, Borovoy would have Dad in stitches over his misbegotten romances, while clearly enjoying the helter-skelter family atmosphere of the Hill household. Above all, the two of them shared a Machiavellian philosophy when it came to advancing the cause of human rights. According to Borovoy,

> [Dan's] instincts, his judgment was so good. We were doing
> God's work but we were also having an incredible lot of fun
> with the whole thing. I remember once saying to him, "Dan,
> if there is a frontal way you could solve a problem with the
> government or an anal way, you'll always choose the anal way,
> simply because it's more fun for you." I believed in his integrity
> completely, even as I delighted in the amount of skullduggery
> in which he could benignly engage.

Surely, Dad saw a lot of his former self in Borovoy: the unrepentant womanizer, the good-hearted troublemaker, the practical idealist. Dad's own need for a trustworthy co-conspirator had remained unchanged since childhood. Borovoy turned out to be the perfect adult replacement for his younger sister, Doris, or his high school chum Mushmouth.

During one of my teenaged bartending stints I cornered Borovoy, after plying him with a few stiff drinks, and persuaded him to speak at my high school in his capacity as head of the Canadian Civil Liberties Association. This was my rather awkward way of reaching out to my father, trying to connect with one of his closest friends. The afternoon that Borovoy spent at my school was a great success, even though it almost got me a failing mark in history. Enjoyable as it was to watch

Borovoy make a fool out of my pompous, reactionary history teacher during their debate over Trudeau's War Measures Act ("Excuse me for talking while you're interrupting," Borovoy quipped at one point, whereupon my teacher's sputtering was drowned out by the roar of auditorium laughter), it was his handful of stories concerning Dad's work at the commission, which he shared with me during our walks to and from my school, that truly affected me.

Alternating between rarefied professor-speak and lively street slang, Borovoy unspooled the story of Dad dropping everything to drive to the southern Ontario town of Amherstburg to investigate a cross-burning incident. There was enormous concern that this may have been the work of the Ku Klux Klan, a suspicion that was dividing this small city along colour lines. Dad quickly discovered that the Klan had nothing to do with the incident. Rather than packing up and going home, or making provocative speeches to further heighten the festering racial tension, Dad stuck around for a few days, gauging the mood of the community. Using the pressure of the aroused community as a bargaining chip, he convinced the mayor of Amherstburg to set up a committee to find jobs for young Black kids in areas where they had never worked before.

I'd been tempted to respond by mentioning to Borovoy that Dad's conciliatory talents were not quite so obvious in the privacy of our own home. But I became distracted when Borovoy lectured me on the importance of staying in school, wondering, as I walked him to the bus stop, if Dad had put him up to this. I managed to check my indignation over two of Canada's heaviest human rights hitters ganging up on me by focusing on the irony of the situation. Dad might well have been Mr. Selfless Arbitrator in the outside world, but at home he loved nothing more than to stir things up. In fact he was at his happiest when he had the household up in arms.

Despite Dad's impressive negotiating skills, not all of his cases ended in triumph. No one hated losing more than Dad. In 1971, he took a case all the way to the Supreme Court. A Toronto landlord had refused to rent out the apartment in his house to a Black man. Because the apartment did not have a separate entry (the landlord might have to witness a Black tenant cross a shared stairway to get to his flat), it wasn't, technically, a self-enclosed apartment. Thus, according to the law at the time it was not legally an act of discrimination.

The decision came down 5–2 in favour of the landlord. The defeat left Dad deeply upset, all the more so because the Ontario government had insisted that he use a government lawyer in the Supreme Court case. Dad had believed his only chance of winning the case was to use John Sopinka, arguably the top constitutional lawyer for this kind of case in Ontario. (Sopinka went on to be a federal Supreme Court justice.) What angered Dad the most about being saddled with an inexperienced lawyer was his belief that the government didn't actually want to win the case. In Dad's view, it came down to politics. What if the public, thinking the government was stepping into the sanctity of their personal property—in this case by letting an "undesirable" tenant lope through a shared stairway—voted against it in the next election?

Dad didn't publicize his suspicion. But in 1973, when Tom Eberle was replaced by a new deputy minister of labour, Dad felt he had less autonomy at the OHRC and announced his resignation. Dad's official reason for leaving, while diplomatically worded, still manages to convey his enormous pride:

> *I left the Ontario Human Rights Commission after 11 ½ faithful years (the last two as its chairman) . . . It's time to do something else. I stayed with it longer than I had expected to . . . Ontario's human rights laws are the best in the country. We were the first province to give its commission statutory powers . . . It was very rewarding work but I needed a change. Change, change, change— human beings need change.*

Dad was on the verge of turning fifty. His twelve years of work at the OHRC must have felt like one sustained sprint. Had he not stepped down it's conceivable that, given the insistent *tick tick tick* of his diabetes (still a secret to all but his family), he wouldn't have made it to sixty, or even fifty-five. But he couldn't have worked as passionately, nor could he have driven himself as hard, had he not loved what he did.

Like so many highly driven people, Dad was a different man outside the home than he was with us. A man can only have so much charm, his reservoir of diplomacy and playful cajoling can only run so deep. Did my transformation into a brooding, withdrawn teenager contribute to Dad's frequent ill temper when he arrived home? Or was it the other way around? All I know is that my moods were in constant lockstep with Dad's, my antennae expertly tuned to his emotions whenever he marched through our front door. I may have been resentful of Dad's power over me, but because our home felt complete, safe and far more stimulating when Dad was around, I longed for his presence. Even as I hated it.

CHAPTER 10

The Pink Loincloth

In June 1971, the month I turned seventeen, I made the transition from amateur performer to professional. After years of auditioning for rock musicals, I managed to make it right to the end of the selection process. *Urbania* was slated to open at the Poor Alex Theatre on Brunswick Avenue in September. It was co-written and directed by Des McAnuff, a recent high school graduate from Scarborough, who, at twenty, was building a reputation as a precocious theatre talent. (McAnuff, one of the most successful theatre directors to ever come out of Canada, went on to win multiple Tony Awards.)

A rock musical was not the ideal forum for my talents. I made it into the cast because the auditioning panel emphasized singing, my strength, and minimized the acting and dancing. My dancing was so abysmal that no words can begin to convey its massacre of rhythm. Suffice it to say my powers of self-delusion—one of the by-products of being a teenager—considerably outshone my abilities.

When I informed Dad that I would be performing—for really big dough (fifteen dollars a week)—in a downtown theatre production, six nights a week, starting the day I was to return to school, he asked, "Are you saying you expect to be gallivanting downtown, night after night, the same week you start grade twelve?"

"That's right, Dad. If we're lucky the show could run a year, maybe even get picked up for a Broadway production in Manhattan."

"But in theatre, don't many shows shut down quickly if no one shows up to see them?" Mom asked, managing to put my dreams of glory into perspective while reassuring Dad that this little distraction from school could be over before it began.

Dad, sounding anything but reassured, said, "I forbid you to be scampering around downtown at night when you still have your high school education to focus on."

"Well, guess what, Dad? I'm seventeen. Legally, I don't even have to go to school. I can do whatever I want." My hands, folded on my lap underneath the kitchen table, were shaking.

"Then you'd better find another place to live. Because if you can't obey the rules of this house, you don't belong here anymore."

In my head I'd already played out this conversation a dozen times. I'd prepared myself for this moment—Dad kicking me out—but somehow I'd expected more fireworks. But Dad was unusually calm, which meant one thing—he wasn't bluffing. I looked over at Mom, understanding she couldn't go against Dad. Still, a part of me wanted her to feel bad for siding with him, even if she was bound by the rules of our family: the struggle between Dad and me had to take its course. That this didn't lessen her sadness gave me a small measure of satisfaction. Because if Mom was sad, Dad would have to pay.

I wasn't happy about leaving, but I wasn't torn up about it either. To Dad's credit, he'd always remained consistent on the theme of school being the be-all and end-all for Hill kids. Part of me respected him for that.

Then again, I had a backup plan: a family willing to take me in. My most consistent running partner at the time was Brian Maxwell, who had a shot at representing Canada in both the 1976 and 1980 Olympics.

At eighteen, Brian was about to go to Berkeley on a track scholarship. His parents, who'd immigrated to Canada from England in 1956 with Brian and his older sister, Sheila, had arrived in Toronto with next to no money. Their story was the classic tale of carving out a new life in a new country through hard work, penny-pinching and slow, steady self-advancement. The Maxwell parents, thrilled as they were over Brian's college scholarship, had made a decent life for themselves without the benefit of post-secondary education. They believed in the value of old-fashioned "roll up your sleeves and get your hands dirty" work. Although my musical activities didn't fall under the category of hard labour, the Maxwells could see that I was constantly busy, determined to make something of my life. My grit and drive were similar to their son's, and yet thankfully our respective talents were worlds apart.

Despite their modest means, the Maxwells refused to take any rent money from me, even though I was working full-time that summer, in addition to theatre and coffeehouse gigs. Their kindness was extraordinary. Mr. Maxwell, impressed that I'd fixed his neglected Gibson guitar, took it as a sign of my musical genius. Mrs. Maxwell packed lunches befitting an Olympic marathoner for me every day. Many times I'd bring my guitar to the breakfast table, my sad songs frequently making Mrs. Maxwell cry, while Mr. Maxwell, unnerved by his wife's tears, begged me to write some happy songs.

"How did you become such a sensitive boy?" a usually reserved Mrs. Maxwell would wail.

"Don't be fooled, Mom. Danny's not that sensitive!" Brian would complain, dragging me out for a punishing run as payback for scooping up too much family attention.

"My mom may go gaga over your singing, but you know what she told me when I came in third in my last marathon?" Brian would ask.

"Uhhhahhh," I'd respond, while trying in vain to match his repeat sprints up the local ski hill.

"'We drove all this way to watch you place third?' I'm puking on the grass right after my race and my mom's complaining about how I've let her down."

"Uhhhahhh," I'd grunt in sympathy, realizing that the grass always looked greener, or the other family always looked happier, from a distance. Collapsing into a heap halfway up my fourth hill, I'd gradually feel my body recover as Brian hurled himself up five more times—the last three, running backwards.

Once more I'd found myself drawn into the orbit of a talented, highly disciplined kid my age. In between logging one hundred running miles a week and experimenting with carbohydrate loading (consisting of three days of all protein, no carbs, followed by three days of the reverse before competing in a marathon, presumably to prevent hitting the dreaded "wall"), Brian shattered several national records in various distance events. This, the single-minded dedication to achieve something magnificent, rubbed off on me. I wasn't simply competing with myself to write better songs, I was measuring myself against the achievements of Brian (who would eventually go on to invent the Power Bar, selling it to Nestlé for half a billion dollars), or Cynthia, weighing scholarship offers from several U.S. colleges thanks to her ranking as an elite sprinter, or Matt, composing film scores.

Okay, so maybe performing in *Urbania* was a far cry from being the next Gordon Lightfoot, and maybe I didn't mention to my friends the daily chastisement I earned from the cast's choreographer, or the snickers of ridicule from my fellow performers. Just the same, it was a step in the right direction.

During that summer, my parents and siblings drove to the Maritimes on a camping vacation. Dad, fearing I might use the house for a month of non-stop partying, made it clear I was not to set foot on the property. "You're not responsible like Larry or Karen. I trust you about as far as I can throw you!"

Even had I wanted to party, when could I have fit that in? At this stage in my life, a crazy night would have been joining Brian in a pre-competition carbohydrate binge, or arguing with Matt into the wee hours about whether or not Lightfoot had "gone commercial" now that his records were more lushly orchestrated.

Breaking Dad's rule, I took to biking over to the house every Sunday night (my one night off from rehearsing), sitting in his cherished chair and listening to my favourite records with headphones. As the music poured into me, I'd glance up at the family photos on the wall, feeling an unfamiliar ache. What had happened? How did I come to fall out so deeply with my father? What had I done that was so wrong?

Being all alone in the house made me miss my family terribly. Previous summers, Larry and I would compete in three-mile races in our neighbourhood. Because I was bigger and faster, Larry was awarded a head start. The real competition revolved around our intense debates as to the proper handicap: whether Larry deserved a ninety-second jump, or more, or less. Invariably, our arguments lasted longer than the actual race.

"Okay, Larry, I'll give you eighty-six seconds before I start chasing you."

"How do I know you won't cheat?"

"'Cause Karen will keep time."

"How do I know you won't bribe Karen with money?"

"Larry, if you can't trust me or Karen, who can you trust?"

"I trust you just fine. I trust you to cheat your ass off."

But now, without Larry to chase on my summer runs, my three-mile course felt boring. Especially since our last race had been so spectacular, based on its controversial finish. Midway through our course, when I realized I couldn't catch him, I'd hitched a ride and cruised a mile or so until Larry, running like he was gunning for a national record, turned the final corner onto our street. Once I knew he couldn't see me, I'd jumped out of the car, turned the same corner seconds later, and, fresh as a daisy, sprinted past him just as we approached our house. The best part of my "victory" was hearing Larry, who rarely swore, unleash a series of swear words at me—"cheater" being the only non-profanity—that made him sound as possessed as that creepy girl in *The Exorcist*.

Not only did I miss getting my brother's goat, I missed the sound of my mother and sister cheerfully singing along with the pop songs tumbling out of the kitchen radio as they kneaded dough for biscuits. I missed the sound of Dad's snoring, the way it rumbled through our

Dan Hill

house like a freight train, scaring away, as Dad put it, any robbers who may have otherwise thought the house was unoccupied.

"That's the last time I'm going anywhere with Mom and Dad," was how Larry described the family vacation when I called the house. He refused to offer up any details beyond "Danny, if you'd travelled with us, either you or Dad would be dead now."

"It was a lot of fun," Karen summarized. "Too bad we couldn't have stayed out east longer."

"Why don't you ask your father?" Mom said, as I continued my family poll.

When I reminded her that Dad and I weren't on speaking terms, she replied, "You two—Jesus Christ, Danny. Sometimes I want to take you both and knock your noggins together, until some of your common sense is jarred loose."

"Hmmm," I said.

Mom, knowing this was my way of avoiding the subject of Dad and me, asked, "How's your rock musical coming along? Even your father's been asking about it."

"Oh, fine," I lied, before saying goodbye.

How could I admit to Mom that my original claim—that *Urbania* would enjoy a hugely successful run—was as exaggerated as Dad's prediction that it would be the ruin of me? A TV station filming our last rehearsal had caught me stumbling badly as the cast and I ran through one of our dance routines. An understandably irate Des McAnuff threatened to fire me (no budget for understudies, combined with not enough time for Des to write me out of the script, left him stuck with me for the time being) if I messed up one more dance move. When the TV station chose to air ten seconds of the dance rehearsal, naturally zooming in on me flailing like a web-footed drunk, the choreographer tracked me down at the Maxwells'.

"I hope you're satisfied," she said, after Brian handed me the phone.

"Pardon?"

"You're the reason *Urbania* is gonna flop."

Well, what did she expect? Considering that the gist of my performance consisted of dancing in a blazing red halter top, a puny pink loincloth, see-through stockings and ballet slippers, it was a wonder we didn't all get arrested for obscenity. Each evening as I dressed for my performance, I couldn't help but think of Dad's reaction to my wardrobe. I was living the greater part of each day in a theatre environment where I was the only straight man in the entire cast. This was absolutely fine with me, as I figured that left the females in *Urbania*—who were abundantly heterosexual—all the more susceptible to my feeble attempts at flirting. (They weren't.)

"Whatever you do," I pleaded to Larry over the phone, "don't let Dad see this show."

"Why's that?" Larry asked.

Halfway through the description of my dance wardrobe, Larry, dying of laughter, threatened to personally take Dad to see *Urbania*. So he could watch him have a heart attack.

Towards the end of *Urbania*'s run, as attendance fell off and the cheques started bouncing, the women in the cast took to amusing themselves by singling out and fluffing a male performer, minutes before performance time. Since I was the only straight male in the cast, I ended up bearing the brunt of this teasing. As half a dozen women took turns flashing their breasts and bottoms and slithering their hands up and down the inside of my stockinged thighs, I was a goner. When the curtain flew open, I spun into dance mode, the jerky movement popping my rising hard-on through my itsy-bitsy loincloth, lodging it against my sheer stockings. I put on my best "the show must go on" face, noticing with relief that the theatre hosted only a dozen or so patrons. In the seconds it took for my eyes to adjust to the spotlight and see the shadowy figures in the audience take shape, I heard an all too familiar whinny: "Donna!" Only Dad's hysterical voice could slice through the wall of music pounding from the stage. "What did I tell you about Danny? I warned you this would happen."

My loyal mother, knowing this was the show's final week, had decided to show up and surprise me, guilting Dad into joining her. The blood retreated from the centre of my tent-sized loincloth, leaving me to wonder if I'd ever get it up again.

"Son, it's time for you to come back home. Your mother misses you terribly."

"You mean you're not going to try to stop me from performing at night, after school?"

After a martyred *ahhh-hmmm* throat clearing, Dad offered, under considerable duress, "Well, your mother tells me you're still keeping your grades up. Tell you what, son: if you maintain that B average I'll give you fifty dollars at the end of your school year and take you and the family out to a restaurant of your choosing."

So I returned. Reluctantly—the Maxwell parents and I were even closer now that Brian had departed for Berkeley. When I arrived home, Dad was waiting on the front porch.

"You're seventeen years old now, son. Near the same age I was when I entered the army. So I'm going to stay out of your hair so long as you obey the house rules."

"But I was already seventeen when you kicked me out. So why—"

"Chalk it up to a long, relaxing summer, Danny. Nothing like a break to get a little perspective on things."

Dad and I enjoyed a kind of uneasy truce throughout the remainder of the school year. The OHRC's all too public loss at the Supreme Court left Dad, for the first time in his career, shaken, in transition and unsure of his next move. As usual, I paid little attention to what was going on in Dad's world, nor did he choose to share any of his professional disappointments with me. I returned the favour, speaking little of my musical pursuits, knowing that Dad would take it as salt rubbed into his wounds. With the added feature of "professional theatre performer" sexing up my resumé (since none of the club owners had actually seen *Urbania* they didn't know enough to use this as a strike against me), I was finding more outlets for my songwriting, opening up for better-known acts at establishments ranging from Grumbles to Egerton's to the Riverboat. To everyone's surprise, I managed, with the help of supportive teachers who frequently showed up where I was performing, to keep up my marks. As the year drew to a close, I came pretty damned close to achieving the impossible. I passed grade twelve. With a B-plus average. I had officially graduated from high school. (Technically, there was still grade thirteen for Ontario students who wanted to go to university.)

Upon receiving my final report card, I went straight home, took my guitar out onto the front porch and waited for Dad to get home from work. When he finally drove up the driveway in his dark-green government sedan, he looked tired. He slowly unfolded himself from the driver's seat, grabbed his hulking briefcase and closed the car door.

"Don't forget your promise, Dad."

"What are you talking about?"

"You owe me and the rest of the family a big expensive dinner at the restaurant of my choosing. As well as my fifty-dollar prize for pulling off a B-plus average."

"Work out the arrangements with your mother."

Mom booked the restaurant for Friday, four days away. Four days that Dad and I didn't talk. Mom selected the Underground Railroad as our celebration restaurant. It specialized in southern food and was owned and largely patronized by Blacks, all of whom were aware of Dad's work in human rights.

Dad made his typical swaggering entrance, shaking hands with the three owners of the Underground Railroad and asking for their cornbread recipe.

"They gave us the best table in the house!" Dad roared once we were seated, causing everyone in the restaurant to look over at us, disapproving of our "preferred seating." Going out in public with Dad was always like this. Embarrassing.

I ordered the most expensive item on the menu. Though never a big fan of honeyed, barbecued spare ribs, I'd happily muck up my long, classical guitar–groomed fingernails if it produced the required result. Pissing Dad off.

By the time the food arrived Dad was warning me, in his meant-for-all-ears voice, that I was doomed to failure for choosing to turn my back on a college education. I didn't have to look around to know that the entire restaurant was in on our conversation. Playing to the audience, I said, "You don't care about me or my future, you just care about how it will reflect on you and your big-shot image."

"That's a falsehood, boy," Dad growled, scraping his chair closer to mine. "And you know it."

"Can you stop crowding me?"

"Jesus Christ, can't you guys just enjoy the meal and for once try to lay off each other?" Mom pleaded. But once started, neither Dad nor I could be seen backing down. Something about this restaurant, with its sepia photos of American Blacks fleeing slavery into Canadian border towns, combined with my family shrinking in their chairs as Dad and I got into the thick of it, brought back all the years of Dad's disparaging remarks. I was tired of feeling not good enough.

"Face it, Dad. You're too old and set in your ways to do anything daring. I'd be happy to turn down your fifty dollars—donate it to your precious NDP that no one ever votes for—if you'd drink my finger bowl. You and I both know that'd never happen 'cause you're too worried about what people might think."

In a flash, my finger bowl, polluted with oily grease, congealed rib bits and lumpy scraps of napkin, was scooped up and gulped down by Dad. As he brought a napkin to his mouth, he had a look on his face I'd never seen before. As if he was as shocked by his behaviour as the rest of us. Maybe he thought he'd gotten the best of me, but I knew better. It was well worth the fifty bucks to see Dad down my finger bowl while the entire restaurant watched. Because, grossed-out as I was, I knew that this was one of the few times I'd actually gotten to him.

CHAPTER 11

RCA: The Honeymoon and the Deep Freeze

As my eighteenth birthday approached, I couldn't believe that I still wasn't famous. I was running out of time. Matt, a couple months older than me and similarly anxious to kick up his career a notch, generously opened his recording studio to me. But since it was his studio, I was going to have to accept his criticisms. By the end of each session I was ready to clobber him with my guitar, as he took great pleasure in telling me my sense of time sucked, my fingers made too much squeaking noise across my fretboard and I sang with a vibrato so wide you could drive a tractor-trailer through it.

"Don't act like such a little prima donna," Matt said, when I complained. "You're lucky I'm not charging you for all my studio time and musical feedback."

Once the sessions wrapped and I'd mailed out my demo tape to every record company I could find in the Toronto phone directory, I tried to put the experience behind me. I'd been performing to small audiences for years, not bothering to worry about the technical details of rhythm and residual guitar string noise. I wasn't sure if Matt's constant harping was legitimate criticism or just his way of showboating.

But since a great deal of our time was spent arguing the sting of our mutual insults faded quickly. When two weeks passed without any callbacks from record companies, Matt and I, determined as ever, began plotting future studio dates.

"How about the first week in July?" Matt suggested.

"As long as it's in the evening. I'm working full-time at the civil service now."

"Must be nice to have a dad with connections."

"Oh, and like the fortune you make scoring TV shows isn't because of your dad?"

"Hey, my dad's connections are helping you even more than me. Who do you think duplicated all your demo tapes without charge?"

"Thanks, Matt, for the hundred and twenty-third time." I hung up the phone and started to pack a lunch for work. When the phone rang again, I assumed it was Matt, bent on extracting another thank you from me.

"Yeah, what now?"

"Hello?"

"Hello?"

"I have Tim Bayers on the phone for a Mr. Danny Hill. Please hold while I get him on the line."

As Muzac flooded my phone line and the minutes ticked by, I started to suspect that this was another one of Matt's dumb pranks.

"Mr. Hill. Tim Bayers here. My congratulations." Short of Matt somehow recording the strongest Brooklyn accent ever uttered and looping it back to me through some knob on his synthesizer, the voice on the line was legit. "The demo tape you sent me. It's killer. Where did you learn chord changes like that? How old are you?"

"Ah, I just turned eighteen."

Bayers. It took a second for the name to register. He was one of the several A&R reps I'd sent my demos to. I'd recently read in the newspaper that he'd been shipped from New York's RCA headquarters to the Toronto branch, where he'd be in charge of discovering and developing new Canadian talent.

"You sound a shitload older than eighteen on those songs you sent me. Who wrote those songs?"

"Me."

"Who'd you write them with?"

"Me."

"And it's really you playing guitar and singing? Even all the background vocals?"

"Yup."

"When can you get down here so I can see what you look like? And don't forget your guitar."

The RCA offices and recording studio were located on Mutual Street, in the heart of downtown Toronto. Gold and platinum records covered every inch of the walls, the *whoomphhh* of a bass boomed out of the open door of a recording studio, a couple of what I took to be tittering secretaries flocked around a recently signed singer—he looked all of twenty—as his doppelganger swayed from the ceiling in the form of a cardboard cutout. The singer was falsettoing through his scales in a manner resembling the warm-ups my high school choir practised before some big concert. But nothing else about this place reminded me of any high school I'd ever seen. Bouncing the top of my oversized guitar case against my chest, I nervously started arpeggiating finger rhythms in the air.

"Looks like you've got something lethal in there," a leather-miniskirted secretary with knee-high boots said as she strolled by me and seated herself behind a receptionist's desk the size of a small yacht.

"I beg your pardon, are you talking to me?" I asked. She was part-chewing, part-sucking on a long piece of red licorice, which made it hard for me to stop staring. The singer, along with his rapturous followers, vanished into the studio. In an instant the place changed from Alice in Wonderland meets the Playboy Mansion into some forbidding clinical office policed by a knockout receptionist who appeared to be teething.

"So, do you just walk into random offices and stare at people with those Charles Manson eyes, or are you here to see someone?"

"I have an appointment to see Tim Bayers."

"Oh no! You're that guy!"

"Pardon?"

"The guy whose tape Bayers has been playing non-stop. I love you. Can you autograph my body? Anywhere you like . . ."

In the ninety seconds it took her to walk me to Bayers's office, Shirley handed me her phone number, written on RCA stationery.

"There he is, the boy genius behind the demo tape!"

Bayers leapt up from behind his desk and greeted me with a long, cologne-strangling hug. As he stepped back to look me over, the first thing I noticed was his hair. His Elvis pompadour seemed at odds with his roly-poly lumberjack body. Because he slouched as if he'd strained his back, he looked older than twenty-eight, or, as he would later put it, "Twenty-five American."

"Listen to this!" Bayers said, and with a crisp snap of his fingers, he began singing: *"Let your mind paint watercolours, shades of love, shades of time and if our blues should run together . . ."*

"Mr. Bayers, I wrote that back when I was fifteen. I've improved a lot—"

"Hey, stop that! Bayers Rule Number One: NO EXCUSES! Makes you look weak."

"Sorry, I—"

"Bayers Rule Number Two: DON'T APOLOGIZE!"

Anxious that whatever I said would likely trigger a booming correction, I spent the rest of our meeting shrugging and nodding. Bayers didn't talk so much as yell and, just like a song that's played so loud that the volume obliterates the words, I had trouble deciphering what he was saying. His wardrobe looked like a garish billboard advertisement for RCA's prize acts; a Ricky Nelson T-shirt bulged at the waist over his Glen Campbell belt buckle, which held up his tight sequined bell-bottoms that flared over polished brown cowboy boots. His phone rang constantly, each new series of rings causing him to startle in his chair as if he'd received an electric shock. After barking to his secretary to hold all calls he pointed at my guitar case.

"'Nuff talk," he said, implying that I'd been doing all the yapping. "Time to sing for your supper."

I played three songs while he paced back and forth on his white shag carpet. Every now and then he'd thwack out manic rhythms with his fingertips using his thighs as a drum surface.

"You wanna know what I think?" he asked, once I was finished.

Like I have a choice, I thought.

"Brilliant, lame, bullshit. That's how your three songs hit me. But the most important thing is you've got it in you—not just the raw talent, but the smarts to lead with your best song. You knew your last song sucked, didn't you? It's bullshit because it lacked authenticity. Stick to writing about what you know. Don't write songs about Vietnam unless you've been there."

I didn't know what to say, as I'd considered my last song to be my best.

"Don't look so fucking depressed. Songwriting is like being a designated hitter for the major leagues. Don't be afraid to strike out going for the home run. If you're one for three, you're a superstar."

Bayers's iron-clad pronouncements were a lot easier to stomach when they weren't focused on me or my songs. His occasional manner of referring to himself in the third person gave his profession a suspect quality, as though being shipped across the border to discover Canadian talent was akin to a secret mission behind the Iron Curtain. The reality was that his new job was a result of a change in Canada's broadcasting law. The government had recently implemented Canadian content regulations for radio and TV stations. This meant Canadian stations had to play a certain quota of records performed, written or produced by Canadians. Bayers's job was to find artists in Canada to fill this new quota. According to Bayers, I was the answer to his prayers. I made the mistake of telling him I was flattered.

"Bayers Rule Number Three: leave your modesty bullshit at the door! You know you're fucking brilliant, or you wouldn't have mailed me your tape."

When I left the RCA building I called my supervisor at the civil service and announced my resignation. Now that I was months away from being a superstar, I didn't have time to waste working nine to five.

Bayers moved fast, producing an exclusive five-year recording and publishing contract for me to sign within a month.

"Got something for you to look at, Dad," I announced, handing him my contract and trying to hold back a self-satisfied smile.

The contract definitely had his attention, but he frowned as he flipped the pages.

"Hold onto your horses there, son," he finally said, shoving the contract into his pocket.

"Hey, give that back. That's my contract!"

"This isn't a contract, it's a jail sentence. I'm going to send it to my lawyer to look over," Dad said. "There's even a morality clause in here, of all things."

I went ahead and signed the contract without legal advice. So what if it was one-sided? There were thousands of kids my age writing and singing songs, thinking they were the next James Taylor. How many of them had major record deals?

As my A&R man, Bayers hired himself as my producer. Then he hooked me up with John Stockfish, Gordon Lightfoot's bass player, and a few more key Toronto musicians, leaving me to rehearse a handful of my songs that Bayers deemed potential hits. Stockfish treated me like a son, playing me dozens of Lightfoot's work tapes, showing me how much rewriting and re-recording Canada's best-known songwriter put himself through before he deemed his work ready for public consumption. I responded by spending every waking hour writing, then rewriting, song after song. Bayers, impressed by my hard work, rewarded me with my first paying recording session at the beginning of September. I joined the Toronto branch of the musician's union; *de rigueur* for anyone earning money as a studio musician.

The recording session went smoothly. Bayers was pretty passive compared to Matt, leaving the arranging up to me and the musicians, interrupting the takes from time to time to say, "Amazing, fucking amazing!"

"You mean that's the perfect take?" I'd yelp.

"My burger and fries, they taste awesome. Now, one more take, guys, only try picking up the tempo. And Danny, back off from the mic when you hit those high notes. Or I'll end up charging you for a busted compressor."

I pretended to know what a compressor was. With Bayers, it was always better not to ask questions. Which was why I hadn't asked why he'd arranged for this recording session to go down in the middle of the night. Once we finished recording, as the first hint of light started diffusing through the dark and abandoned offices, Bayers asked me to join him for a breath of fresh air on Mutual Street.

"The musician's union showed up at a session here just last week. That's why I booked this recording for the middle of the night. Less chance of them showing up and killing the studio vibe."

"Oh, I was wondering—"

"Thanks to the fuckin' union here I was forced to file tonight's recording as two officially contracted sessions. But my production budget's tighter than Pat Boone's ass. So, once your union rate cheque arrives in the mail, just hand it over to me."

"You mean the entire cheque? I'm supposed to give it back to you?"

"You got it. This is how to get around the fucking union. Otherwise the studio gets closed down and nobody makes records."

Something about Bayers's union scenario didn't quite add up. But I knew he wasn't someone to be messed with. I promised him I'd hand back the cheque. What did I care about the money? I just wanted to be on the radio.

"If you kick back your cheque you betray everything we've raised you to believe in," Dad yelled. What was I thinking, telling them about this? Mom interrupted Dad to say that if I rolled over on this, I was striking a blow against workers everywhere. Outnumbered and out-moralized, I promised my parents I'd keep the cheque. Then I prayed for a mail strike.

"Has that cheque come in yet?" Bayers asked me at the end of the week. We were listening to the rough mixes of my two tracks. I was wishing the songs would play forever, sensing that this might be the last time Bayers and I would be sitting together, listening to my music. I nodded.

"Well, hand it over."

He started to approach me. I backed away from him, not wanting to be within striking distance.

"I can't do that."

"What are you talking about?"

"I can't give you the cheque."

"What do you mean, you can't? We've already gone through this."

"Sorry, but I—"

"Don't fuckin' 'sorry—but' me. You gave me your word. Now you're telling me you were lying? Just give me the fuckin' cheque. Now."

Bayers abruptly wheeled around and hit stop on his big reel-to-reel recorder, cutting off my song. The thin dark tape buckled slightly, made a small *bong* sound like it might break and then evened out.

"Really, Tim, I want to. It's just—"

I'd spent all week trying to memorize my parents' union lecture so I could bravely throw it back in Bayers's face. But now I was drawing a blank. As Bayers's hollering increased, Shirley, the reception-ist, poked her head through the doorway. God, I couldn't just stand there, wilting.

"Well, there are reasons for unions, you know. They're—"

"Who the fuck have you been talking to? Has your big-time-civil-servant-with-a-fat-pension daddy threatened to cut off your allowance?"

"My parents don't know anything about this—"

"Shut up! The sound of your whining makes me wanna fuckin' puke!"

Bayers removed the two reels from his tape recorder and lobbed them into his overstuffed wastebasket.

"Congratulations, you've really fucked me. Now get the hell outta here. If I ever see your fuckin' face again, you better believe it'll be the last time anyone ever sees your fuckin' . . ."

That was the last I heard of Bayers, or anyone else at RCA, for the next six months. I called him but could never get through. No one there, aside from Shirley, would take my calls.

"The best thing you can do is stop calling. And hope that, in time, Bayers cools off," Shirley advised. "And whatever happened between you and Bayers, don't be stupid enough to talk about it."

How could I have blown my one chance at the big time over a union cheque? I could handle failure if my talent didn't measure up, but this had nothing to do with talent and everything to do with me being stupid. I couldn't blame this on my parents. What did they know about the record business?

It felt like everything was collapsing. I couldn't sleep, preferring to stay up through the night writing songs, letters to Bayers (never sent) and letters to Cynthia seeking her advice. I didn't know that my feelings of worthlessness echoed a letter Dad wrote to his parents when he was my age: "This failure . . . is the same as disgrace to me . . . hurt me worse than anything I have ever had to take in my life . . . ." Dad, seeing me on the verge of breaking down, offered support rather than his usual ridicule, comfort instead of "I told you so."

At first, I attributed Dad's gentler nature to the fact that I'd found a new job. Thanks to Brian Maxwell's contacts, I was hired full-time at the Fitness Institute, a club where high-level executives congregated to network in between squash games. But regular employment did little to shake my depression. I'd read about promising artists who managed to self-destruct just as their once-in-a-lifetime moment beckoned. Was that me, I wondered, while on my hands and knees scrubbing out toilets, washing squash court walls and picking up Kleenexes and candy wrappers from the club's front lawn. Rosy-faced businessmen with initials embossed on fancy workout bags dodged me like I was some kind of beggar grasping for a chance to shine their Gucci shoes for spare change. I felt as hungover as I looked, but not from drinking. I'd taken to lifting a couple of Mom's sleeping pills before bedtime. Still unable to sleep, I'd show up for work stumbling about like a stubble-faced zombie.

My shoddy appearance was the least of my problems or, more to the point, the Fitness Institute's problems with me. I destroyed the Fitness Institute's garden by uprooting all the perennials, shrank half the laundry with my overzealous drying and left the squash court floors even more marked-up than before I'd started cleaning them because I'd forgotten to remove my leather-soled shoes. My boss, finally coming to his senses, declared, "You're the most awful worker ever! You're fired!"

I made it home shortly before dinnertime, hustled to my bedroom and took refuge under the covers, refusing to come down to the kitchen when I heard the table being set. The thought of Dad's dinnertime lecture—that without a college diploma, my life would be a blur of Fitness Institute hirings and firings—was enough to take away my appetite.

Knock, knock.

"Can I come in, son?" Dad opened the door a crack, removed his glasses and said, "I've got something I'd like to tell you."

"What's the point, I know what you're going to say."

"Son, I never told you about my first job, once I left the army. I was serving the most expensive steaks in Washington to people on a posh outdoor patio. Some big, fat crows damned near clipped my head—you know how I detest birds—in search of an easy meal. I hauled off and threw all the steaks on my fancy, silver platter in the air at those damned birds. One of the steaks fell smack in the middle of a table serving six people. *Splat*—red wine went flying, staining a woman's white dress, as glasses smashed onto the patio. That ended my career as a waiter. I couldn't stand serving people. Made me feel like a slave."

Whether Dad's flying platter of steaks confession was the truth, an exaggeration, or an outright fabrication was immaterial; what mattered was that Dad was extending a much-needed measure of Hill solidarity. Moved as I was by Dad's commiseration, the greatest surprise came the following morning.

"Marty and I would like to manage you, son."

Marty was a friend of Dad's who used to sing semi-professionally, claimed to have a few friends still in the music industry and was now a successful businessman. Dad, on the verge of leaving the Ontario Human Rights Commission to open up his own private consulting firm, was going to have a bit more time on his hands. But why, after all his taunts about my musical dreams, was he offering to manage me?

"Your mother and I are concerned about you. You seem to have lost interest in everything. You don't go out for runs anymore. And Larry and Karen tell me they never hear you play your guitar." Though he was wise enough to keep this from me at the time, Dad later told me that he feared that I might have to be hospitalized if I didn't find my bearings soon.

I turned down Dad's offer. Much as he wanted to save me, you can't have a rescuer without a willing rescuee, and, as far as the record business was concerned, I was not ready to be rescued. Taking my refusal in stride, Dad appeared to be mulling something else over.

"Son, have you thought about going further up the food chain?"

"What do you mean?"

"The RCA food chain. Bayers isn't the only person working there. He's just some mid-level employee that New York shipped to Canada. Probably because they didn't know what else to do with him."

Grabbing the phone directory, I started looking up the addresses and phone numbers of the different Toronto RCA branches. The main office was located in Don Mills, not two miles from our house.

"Tell me, Danny, who else have you talked to about this?"

I would have pegged RCA's Canadian president as the lenient principal of a private prep school rather than the head of a major record label. Where Bayers was all strut and fury, this man came off as serenely composed, listening without interruption as I related my RCA experience, starting with the quick honeymoon signing and ending with the even quicker falling out.

"I know a lot of this is my fault, for promising to give Tim Bayers back my musician's union cheque." I wanted to go on, to explain that I could have been kicked out of the union and that I'd still have had to pay taxes on this money had I forked it over, but then I remembered Dad's advice: *Don't talk too much, just lay out the facts simply and quickly.*

"You haven't answered my question, Danny. Who else have you talked to about this?"

"No one. I mean, who else could I talk to? No one I know's ever gone through anything like this."

"Exactly. So then, tell me, if it was up to you, where would you like to go from here?"

"All I want is to finish what I started. The two sides are practically done. Just needs my vocals and a few overdubs. Then it can be released as a single. That was always the plan."

The president told me to wait in the lobby. "Don't go anywhere, I'm going to need you back in here in a few minutes."

I'd barely skimmed through a *Billboard* magazine by the time he ushered me back into his office.

"Mr. Bayers and I have just spoken," he said. "We're heading into Christmas season now, otherwise the two of you would be finishing your single next week. You're booked to resume recording with Mr. Bayers when the holidays are over. The second week of January."

The brave pep talks I received from Brian and Cynthia over Christmas were hard to remember once I found myself behind the expensive U 87 microphone preparing to sing my heart out, while Bayers glared at me from the control room. Throughout most of the recording session, he and his recording engineer pretended I wasn't there. While I laid down my vocal tracks, Bayers kept himself distracted with phone calls. Once I'd finished singing and listened to the finished, unmixed record,

I realized that the bass player had made a mistake in the song's final bar. Bayers refused to have the wrong note corrected.

"Please, Tim. The bass is the root of the chord. It's like the bottom just fell out of the song."

"Don't talk to me about fuckin' music theory. That's why you got no soul. You think way too fuckin' much. Anyway, you should know I can't afford to fix the bass. Union costs—I have to pay extra for overdubs."

I offered to pay.

"You're the fuckin' expert on unions, so you should know you have to be a signatory to the union to hire a musician. And you'd be smart to save every penny you got, 'cause your precious little union cheque is all the money you'll ever make in this business."

I was past caring, or hurting, or being scared. Bayers had taught me a tough lesson. There comes a point where either you rally your defences and move on, or you stay a patsy forever.

CHAPTER 12

Feliciano and Belafonte

The tone of Dad's letters to his parents grew more muted as he approached his fiftieth birthday. In a letter written in the summer of 1973, he referred to a couple of major life events—his stepping down from the OHRC and the release of my RCA single—in an almost dismissive manner. But even at his most taciturn, his concerns about my future came through.

Dear Mom and Dad,

I'm busily preparing to establish my own small consulting firm—Daniel G. Hill Ltd.

I'll be president and Donna secretary-treasurer. I'm starting a new life style that should be most interesting. I'll send you the clippings, notices, etc. about my resignation from the

Commission. I really felt it was time for a change. Please note the enclosed clippings about Danny. The record sales have tapered off and reality is beginning to sink in!! However he has the odd engagement in local coffee houses. His closest friends in the music world are all in university. Hope he'll see the light one day.

I was seeing the light all right. Just not the one Dad hoped I might see. Dad's observation that my record sales were tapering off suggests that at some point my record was actually selling. It didn't sell. It bombed. As for Dad's equally disingenuous comment that my close friends in music were all in university, my best friend, Matt McCauley, did not go to university.

At the beginning of June, I celebrated turning nineteen by moving out (this time of my own volition), subletting an apartment in the pleasant Toronto borough of East York. The day I left home, Dad marked my departure by ripping all the pictures and posters off my bedroom wall, cleaning out my mounds of stuff and turning the room into his office.

"Your father wanted to wipe out any evidence of your existence," Mom told me when she phoned to recommend that I come by and pick up my memorabilia before it was tossed out with the garbage.

When I expressed surprise she said, "I don't think you understand just how hurt he is by your decision to do nothing with your life except music."

"And what about you, Mom?"

"I admire your guts, Danny. I really do. But what's going to happen to you now? Your RCA single never got played on radio."

"Still, RCA didn't drop me. What do you think that means?"

"How should I know, Danny?"

"Bayers messed up the production of my single. The quality of the recording was so bad radio did me a favour by not playing it."

"If you say so, Danny."

Sounded like I wasn't fooling Mom any more than myself. The

single's A-side, "Peter Pan" (the title says it all), possessed nothing in the way of memorable chorus, containing such unfortunate lyrics as, "Peter Pan would trade his wings for the mixed-up joy love can bring." Motown greats Holland-Dozier-Holland could have thrown all their production wizardry at my song and it still would have bombed. For a kid fresh out of high school, I fell into my RCA contract displaying flashes of promise as a songwriter, but by professional standards my songs were pretty average.

But I learned fast. Being exposed to a higher level of songwriting talent is like playing tennis with a superior opponent. You get better. And tougher. During my honeymoon period with RCA I ran into a select group of artists who had either written, recorded or produced an international hit record.

Other than being five or ten years my senior, these guys appeared no different from me. They grew up banging out songs in their parents' basements while the cool kids were picking up girls and playing sports. They came from small towns, with no connections, and had parents who, like mine, were less than thrilled with their career choice. And somehow, thanks to talent, cockiness, hard work and thick skin, it had paid off for them. I took that to mean one thing: if I kept my eye on the ball, some day I would be one of those ordinary guys with a hit record.

And I was no fool, playing up the "RCA recording artist" schtick for all it was worth while never letting on that I'd released a single that stiffed. (The one advantage to being a rookie artist with a failed first single was that no one outside RCA knew about it.) My self-promotion paid off, landing me more and better-paying gigs. Matt's dad hired me to perform once a week at Seneca College, where he taught music. A sixty-dollar fee for playing for thirty minutes at the college cafeteria during lunchtime took care of my monthly food bills. The Ontario civil service paid me even more to sing twice a month during people's coffee breaks on the main floor by the elevators. And there were always plenty of club owners willing to hand out one to two hundred dollars for a five-night, three-set-per-night stint at their bar.

Throughout the summer, my infrequent phone conversations with Dad went something like this.

"Look at it this way, Dad, approaching a club owner for work as a kid with a major record deal is like applying for a teaching job with a PhD."

"Dream on, son!"

"Okay, let me give you a hypothetical—if two guys with equal talent were vying for a gig to sing and play original songs in a club and one guy had a PhD in music theory and the other guy had an international record deal, who do you think would get the gig?"

"If you're asking me, son, a third guy would pop up with a PhD in music and a record deal, leaving you playing for quarters on a street corner and the other guy teaching music in a respectable school for a good living."

I stopped phoning home. It was beginning to feel as though Dad was the last holdout in a crowd of ardent supporters.

Towards the end of the summer, I was invited to a small record company party to honour José Feliciano, an RCA artist, who was in Toronto performing. To the horror of everyone but Feliciano, I yanked out my guitar and assaulted him with a couple of my songs.

"Man, you sing with a lot of soul for a white teenager," Feliciano responded, in that habitually serious but joking manner of his that I found difficult to read. Most of his wisecracks that evening centred on his being blind, leaving me unsure as to whether he already knew that I was half-Black or not.

Leaving nothing to assumption I said, a little forcefully, "I'm not white, my skin's easily as brown as yours. And I'm almost twenty."

"Oh, well, then you're not that good after all."

Taking Feliciano's teasing as a challenge, I risked playing one final song, figuring he might relate to it. The hook, "Lord don't let this crazy world make a jukebox out of me, let the songs keep flowing strong and naturally," made him interrupt me before I could get to the second verse.

"Tell me the chords," Feliciano demanded. "I want to start performing this song!"

"Here, it's easy," I said, showing him how my fingers chorded the progressions on the neck of my guitar, forgetting in my excitement that he was blind.

"Whoaaa! Who do you think I am, Stevie Wonder?" he laughed, causing everyone else at the party to break out in applause. Before the end of the evening, he'd given me his address and phone number, insisting that I send him every song I'd ever written, as he was looking for material for his upcoming album.

It didn't take long for everyone in Toronto's gossipy music business to hear about this. Impressed as much by my chutzpah as my talent, Dr. McCauley, then the music director at Toronto's O'Keefe Centre, slipped Harry Belafonte one of my demo tapes. Belafonte promptly flew the McCauleys and me to Manhattan for a meeting.

Meeting Belafonte was as strange as it was memorable. I'd sung along with his records since my parents played me "Day-O" on my little turntable in Newmarket. As I came into the office prepared to meet my childhood hero, my newest song came blasting from his stereo. There was the man himself, singing along to my words with such volume that it felt as though our voices were joined in some intergenerational duet.

"*You make me want to be a father . . .*" Belafonte crooned back at me once this new song of mine, clearly his favourite, had looped off his tape recorder. He'd taken my sentimental opening line and breathed a whole new life into it, his voice having all the more impact now that it wasn't in lockstep with mine.

"How does a nineteen-year-old kid write a love song that romantic?" Belafonte asked.

How could I act nonchalant when I was grinning so hard that my jaw ached?

"This is a hit song, Danny," Belafonte continued. "My secretaries love it. My daughter loves it. But it's a young man's song, and I'm forty-six. Anyway, this next one on your tape is almost as good, and not quite so youthful-sounding."

And off he went, threading another tape of mine onto his recorder and then belting out my next song.

"I could definitely use you as one of my songwriters. I'm about to do some more musical theatre and need a ton of new material."

Several hours later the McCauleys and I were stepping off a plane back in Toronto, trying to make sense out of what had just happened.

"This is the situation," Matt explained as we drove into the city. "Both Feliciano and Belafonte are a lot more impressed with your writing ability than your singing."

"Or maybe they just want to have first dibs on my songs. Because if I release them first, Feliciano or Belafonte won't be the ones introducing them to the public."

"Possibly," Dr. McCauley, who was a great deal less opinionated than Matt, conceded. All too often he deferred to Matt's observations as though Matt were the father and he the child.

"Don't get too conceited," Matt said. "Dad played your songs to Tony Bennett and he didn't think they were all that hot."

"Yeah, and every label in England passed on the Beatles before they finally got signed."

"Right, Danny, and you think you're as good as Lennon and McCartney put together," Matt chided.

"The two of you are missing the point," Dr. McCauley said. "Getting signed isn't your problem. Getting unsigned is."

"Leave RCA," Matt said. "They don't know the first thing about how to produce your songs. Let me produce your album. My parents and I have already talked about this—you can sign with us, and we'll sell the record to the highest bidder. What do you have to lose? You've already wasted a year at RCA and all you've got to show for it is a single that stiffed."

"Because the production was so terrible," Dr. McCauley added, backing Matt's claim that I didn't have a chance without his son's production help.

I didn't answer them right away. I needed time to take it all in: the round trip to New York City, Belafonte singing my songs, the McCauleys suggesting I break with RCA and sign with them. It was all coming at me so fast.

CHAPTER 13

Dad's Career Gamble

Brrrinnnggg. It was the first call to Dad's new business number, and he barrelled across the kitchen like a fullback, determined to get to the phone before Larry or I did.

"Daggum, my new line just got put in yesterday and already it's ringing off the hook!" Dad said.

"It's the sound of family history in the making," I cracked.

"Shhh, look at how excited he is," Larry whispered.

"Daniel G. Hill and Associates," Dad's voice thundered into the phone's mouthpiece.

"The caller's going to think he dialled the wrong number and got God on the line." Turned out I was half right. The caller had been hoping to order some takeout Chinese food.

"Larry, time to get to work. Take a look at the blurb I've put together to go on my new business brochures. See if there's anything I should add."

Feeling like I was getting in the way of a bustling work day—I was the only Hill family member not working part-time for Dad's new firm—I left the kitchen and started putting on my shoes in the front hallway. Catching Mom walking down the stairs with a stack of Dad's latest press clippings, I asked, "Don't you think it's a little weird how Dad can get so crazy excited over a phone call and then fold up with disappointment if it's a wrong number?"

"It's clear you haven't been around much lately, Danny."

"Huh?"

"Your father's always been labile. And anyone easily wound up can just as easily feel let down."

"That means changeable," yelled Larry from upstairs.

"You mean Dad's like a little kid?" I asked Mom, ignoring my smarty-pants brother.

Mom smiled as if to say, *Is that so bad?*

I knew I was nitpicking. Surely I wasn't miffed because I was the only Hill not asked to work for Dad. I barely had enough time to manage my nine-to-five job and all my musical commitments. But still, Dad could have at least approached me with some kind of minor work offer—if only so I could proudly remind him of how busy I was.

Once more, I felt like the odd one out, drifting further away from my family, seeing Larry from time to time, invariably to engage in yet another silly running competition—not as much fun lately as he'd become faster than me—and staying in touch with Karen and Mom with a twice-weekly phone call.

Mom kept me up to date on Dad's array of new jobs: teaching courses at the University of Toronto while acting as special advisor to the university's president, providing consultation services to the likes of the Nova Scotia Human Rights Commission, the *Toronto Star* and the City of Toronto. His was the first human rights consulting firm of its kind in Canada, and to some the very idea that he was being paid as a private businessman to break down racial barriers—rather than receiving an annual government salary—appeared if not mercenary then certainly opportunistic. This couldn't have been farther from the truth.

Because Dad's true passion was Canadian Black history, the majority of his time was spent writing the groundbreaking book *The Freedom Seekers: Blacks in Early Canada* (published by Stoddart Publishing in 1981) and forming, along with my mother and some close friends, the Ontario Black History Society. These twin endeavours, realistically speaking, earned very little. Running a consulting firm reminded me of the upside-down world of being a working musician. The important stuff, projects that in the future might be of significant value, be it songwriting or book writing, didn't pay that well, or if they did, the resulting money could be several years away. On the other hand, the fluff jobs, making a quick five hundred dollars for sleep-singing through Chicago's "Color My World" during a wedding, or producing a series of general recommendations for fairer hiring practices in, say, the Ontario Department of Agriculture (recommendations that would look good on paper but likely go unimplemented), promised little lasting value but paid a lot of bills.

"My parents were very concerned about me leaving the security, the pension of a government job," Dad told me a few years after setting up his business. To be sure, for a man raised in the Depression, this abrupt change of profession represented a major gamble. But thrifty though Dad was, a big salary had never been important to him. Furthermore, his twelve years at the OHRC had earned him a comfortable pension.

Dad would be forced to draw on some of those savings in his early days as a consultant. He'd expected, somewhat naively, that significant work would pour in from the Ontario government, but he'd underestimated the egos he may have bruised when he vacated his job. When the government work didn't immediately materialize, he took it personally. And there was another blow to his ego. Self-promotion, marketing, advertising, billing and following up on clients slow to pay were all part of running one's own consulting firm. For a man such as my father, who'd spent the last twelve years dealing with people approaching him, hustling up work represented the ultimate act of self-abasement.

Dad was fifty years old, an age at which most people take stock of their accomplishments or lack thereof. Perfectionists tend to ignore their triumphs, downplaying any past successes while dwelling on their failures, real or imagined. In a sense Dad was, once more, ahead of the curve. Nowadays there are legions of fifty-year-olds launching their own businesses. This was not the case in 1973, when fifty was considered too young to retire and too old to be sustained by dreams that could take years, if not decades, to achieve.

That Dad's children were closing in on adulthood, with Larry and Karen but a few years away from university, marked another milestone in Dad's life. While he and I were on civil terms (meaning we weren't fighting because we rarely saw each other), I knew that the thought of Larry and Karen leaving home saddened him. All these life transitions left him dislocated and out of sorts, which in turn dimmed his usual spark, the very thing that had always made him such a whirlwind force. His work suffered.

One day, Mom, in her double role as wife and bookkeeper, came into his office and told him that he wasn't bringing in enough money. Mom had never minced words with any of us, and although Dad consistently absorbed Mom's barbs with an equanimity that bordered on the heroic, her warning that he had to work harder left him, in his own words, "shocked and deeply ashamed."

Dad removed his ovoid, black spectacles and stood up from behind his sprawling mahogany desk. He closed the office door, looked Mom in the eyes and said, "Donna, I won't let you or the family down. Wait and see, I'm going to land more contracts. I'm going to make you proud of me."

Dad told me this story more than twenty years later with tears in his eyes. If his candour left me unhinged, his response to Mom's "buck-up" talk confirmed what I'd always known. Dad's internal emotional wiring had undergone little or no change since he was a boy. There could be no greater disgrace than to be regarded as an underachiever.

Within a year, Dad landed the biggest contract of his consulting career: an exhaustive report commissioned by the attorney general of Ontario on the practices of religious cults, sects and mind-development groups. It would take him more than eighteen months to complete and span close to a thousand pages. (In keeping with Dad's philosophy on free speech and freedom to embrace any belief, religious or otherwise, so long as it was legal, Dad's position was that cults and sects should enjoy the same rights as mainstream Christian, Muslim or Jewish groups.)

As had been the pattern throughout my adolescence, Dad's work made only a glancing impression on me. Except that now every press clipping or review that mentioned me also mentioned that I was "son of Dr. Daniel G. Hill, former chairman of the OHRC." Would I never be able to separate myself from my father, or at least be viewed by the world as my own person?

However indifferent I pretended to be about Dad's ever-growing body of work, I never stopped studying and analyzing him as a man. And as a husband. Now that I was living on my own, what I missed most about Dad, or rather Mom and Dad, was their continued devotion to one another.

When Karen and Larry left home for school, my parents had a home largely to themselves for the first time in twenty years. I'd seen more than a few married couples drift apart once their children left. The opposite happened with my parents. Dad missed Larry's frenetic darting in and about the house (he was always rushing, late for something) the same way he missed Karen's calm, dependable presence. But that didn't prevent him from soaking up the extra mothering that started flowing his way once his children weren't around to lay first claim to it.

"Dan, honestly, what have I told you about walking around the house without shoes on," Mom would tut. The two of them would be sitting on the corner of their bed, Dad's humongous feet dangling across Mom's tiny lap. All too aware that a diabetic's first weak spots show up where the circulation is most easily compromised, such as the extremities, Mom would carefully clip the calluses off Dad's big toes, wielding the nail clippers with the dexterity of a surgeon, hollering at him to stay still.

"Danny, don't distract your dad," Mom would command without looking up, when I'd make one of my surprise visits. "He refuses to believe how easily he could lose his toes to infection—and his doctor's too busy singing his praises to bother with keeping him healthy."

"He's a human rights doctor!" Dad said, the boom in his voice making it clear that he was responsible for converting his doctor to the righteous cause. I'd mumble an apology for dropping by without warning, feeling as though I'd interrupted some primate grooming session.

"Not at all, son," Dad said. "Your mother's trimming back all the dead skin on my toes. It's from years of marching in the U.S. Army in the steaming hot south, with boots two sizes too small for my big Black feet."

I stood watching the two of them, trying to hold on to this all too rare relaxed moment we were sharing. Lately Dad had become slightly more approachable. But even our more pleasant visits were invariably torpedoed by one of his "innocent questions."

"So tell me, son. What's all this foolishness I hear about you thinking about leaving RCA Records and signing your life away to the McCauleys? Is this your idea of a step up in what you call the music business?"

Should I tell Dad the truth? That I was learning from the best? He'd gambled with his career, leaving the status and security of a big government job to strike out on his own. Was that any different from me leaving RCA Records to join forces with the McCauleys? One day Dad would connect the dots between him and me. Or so I hoped.

CHAPTER 14

The Story behind "Sometimes When We Touch"

I was sitting in the office of Barry Keane, RCA's new A&R man now that Bayers was back in the States. In the thirteen months that I'd been signed to RCA, I'd come to really like Barry; he'd grown up in Scarborough, just a few miles from my Don Mills stomping grounds. One of those nauseating types who happened to be extremely gifted in many areas, Barry exuded a quiet confidence, rarely talking about himself or his considerable range of abilities. Regrettably, my exposure to Barry's talents came the hard way: through being blanked by him in a one-on-one basketball game or attempting, and failing, to follow his complex drum patterns during one of our "casual" music jams. (Having turned down an offer to try out for a professional baseball team, Barry eventually went on to perform and record with Gordon Lightfoot.) Now, as our first official A&R meeting kicked off, I was discovering that Barry possessed yet another aptitude that most musicians lacked: a shrewd grasp of business.

"I've reviewed all the paperwork and budgeting with the president here, and we've agreed to go ahead and produce an album with you," Barry announced, the stack of demo tapes and finished masters crowding his desk making it clear he had little time for chit-chat. "Considering you have no track record—let's pretend your single never happened—the fact that I've been given eighteen thousand dollars to make your record should tell you that everyone here believes strongly in your potential. Along with this big budget we have free, unlimited studio time, since RCA is the only label in Canada equipped with its own in-house studio."

Although not the jump-up-and-down, "that's the greatest mother-fucking song I've ever heard" type, Barry's confidence in my writing and singing was pretty apparent. I was being offered something that, frankly, any of the countless thousands of singer-songwriters trying to be heard in Canada would have died for. This was all the more incredible considering the sorry fate of my RCA single. (Unlike today, in the 1970s record com-panies were willing to stick with artists they had faith in through several failures, partly because it was less costly to nurture a "baby artist" back then.) So why did I find myself hesitating? Desperate to stay in Barry's good books, I prevaricated and told him I was more than willing to go ahead with the album. I figured it would buy me some time while I took RCA's offer to the McCauleys, curious as to what they'd come back with.

Flattering as it was to have options, my indecisiveness left my career in a kind of limbo, forcing me to return to my government day job while chasing down various paying gigs in the evening. Had I sold a few songs to Belafonte or Feliciano I could have avoided the nine-to-five grind, but I wasn't prepared to do that. As a cocky teenager, I likened selling off my precious songs to chopping off one of my arms for cash. And without my best songs to draw from, once I got down to the business of record-ing my first album how could I hope to compete on the pop charts? But hubris didn't pay the bills, and all my so-called potential and growing recording options still weren't resulting in any money. Paradoxically, my biggest problem with my forty-hour workweek was that I didn't find it a problem. I liked my day job. Too much. And I was afraid that might take the edge off my hunger to succeed as a musician.

"You've got it made in the shade here," Lloyd, my on-and-off boss over the last two years at the Ontario civil service, clucked. I was leaving work early for yet another audition. "Your old man's a big wheel in government; you couldn't get fired from this place if you sat on your ass and played guitar all day."

"But my dad doesn't even work in government anymore."

"Doesn't matter. If not for your dad pulling strings to get you in here, you wouldn't have made it through the first week without getting tossed. Us regular stiffs in the mailroom take bets every morning on how many personal phone calls you'll be getting that day or whether you're gonna bother making it into work before 10:00 a.m."

Lloyd had recently emigrated from Jamaica and, despite his tough talk, got as much a kick out of me as I did out of him. He claimed to be sleeping with half the women in the building, and whether or not this was true, his tales of conquest were highly educational. In turn, he lapped up my music-business stories, always offering enthusiastic, if misplaced, advice such as, "Get a fucking gun and shoot that sonofabitch Bayers!" He'd seen me quit (whenever I thought I was finally pulling in enough money gigging to say goodbye to straight work) half a dozen times, only to come back on bended knee once the gigs got short and the bills got tall. And he always took me back after a lecture, delivered in an Island accent that cracked me up: "Wait for a sign from God. He'll let you know when you can quit this job for good."

"What kind of sign might that be, Lloyd?"

"When every woman in this building wants to fuck you, instead of me."

Spoiled as I may have been at the civil service, my life had become jam-packed. A typical day would have me leaving my job at 5:00 p.m., scrambling to make it on time for my three-hour solo stint—5:30 till 8:30—at a gay bar called the Carriage House on Jarvis Street, and then dashing to a coffeehouse gig in Yorkville from 9:00 till 1:00, collapsing onto the filthy mattress in my closet-sized bedroom sometime between

2:00 and 3:00 a.m. with several cheques folded into my wallet and close to one hundred dollars in tips bulging out of my pockets. When I wasn't performing after work, I'd go straight home to my guitar and start writing songs. Dad's constant warning, "Son, if you're not careful, you're gonna live out the rest of your life toiling away at the civil service making a buck eighty-nine an hour," was all the motivation I needed to keep composing, performing and demoing. Knowing that with either RCA or the McCauleys I'd be soon recording my first album, I'd nod off to sleep still writing, my dreams awash with unfinished lyrics and herky-jerky melodies, startle myself awake, jot something else down and then nod off again. The following morning on the subway, the words and music from the night before would spin round and round, chasing me out of Wellesley station and into the elevator that led me down to the second basement of the Mowat Block.

A morning of sorting through intra-governmental mail would be followed by an afternoon of making deliveries to the dozens of ministry departments. As I made my rounds through the complex of interconnected government buildings I'd run into enough budding singers, actors, authors and comedians to power a lifetime of variety shows. Most of these creative types had started working for the government in their late teens. But after five, ten, twenty years they were still there, still talking about an upcoming audition, showing me their latest publicity photos or bragging about a friend of a distant cousin who knew someone in New York who was "seriously connected." Recently, *Chatelaine* magazine had picked me out as one of Canada's next generation of singing stars, mentioning Belafonte's and Feliciano's interest in my work. If that was true, what was I doing trapped in this fractious double life, running halfway across town to score Jamaican patties for Lloyd during lunch hour? Would I be showing this wrinkled and faded *Chatelaine* clipping to fellow workers half my age twenty years from now, while they regarded me as some pathetic relic?

Between straight work and music work, switching residences as casually as changing clothes, and spending what little free time I had flying to

Newfoundland to visit Cynthia, I managed to avoid, for as long as possible, dealing with the decision of my life: RCA versus the McCauleys. But I couldn't stall any longer.

"Other than the Guess Who, and they're dinosaurs now, and one fluke hit single by the Stampeders, RCA's track record at breaking new artists has been disastrous," Matt argued, as he and his parents sat with me in their Don Mills living room. Mrs. McCauley served tea and cookies as Dr. McCauley concurred, "You and Matthew are a great combination. Your songwriting and singing style is perfect for orchestration. You can hear it in your chord progressions."

"Your best songs have always been your ballads," Mrs. McCauley cut in. "RCA's strong suit is rock music—they don't know what to do with you. What makes you think RCA is capable of producing an album of yours any better than the hatchet job they did on your first single?"

Now the three of them were talking at once, with Matt's voice cutting through the din: "Look Danny, what RCA Canada is best at is distributing all the hits that their U.S. parent company gives them. The advantage to making an independent album with us is that we control the master. When it's finished we can lease the rights to different territories rather than being stuck with the same label worldwide."

Lease, distribution, royalty flow, ownership of masters—it reminded me of all the boring stuff I could never quite concentrate on in high school. Wasn't becoming a musician supposed to free me from all this?

"Just give me a bit more time to think about what you're saying," I said.

"Danny, if no one ever hears your songs, what good is your talent?" Matt asked as I got up to leave. "Lightfoot, Joni Mitchell, James Taylor, Dylan—they all had records out by the time they were twenty-one. You're going to be twenty soon. And so am I. That's old in this business. I can't wait around for you much longer."

With the help of one of my parents' lawyer friends, I found a legal loophole in my RCA deal (something to do with RCA failing to release a certain number of singles within the contracted time frame) that enabled me to get out of my obligations. Because Barry Keane was as soft-spoken as Bayers had been abrasive, his disappointment was palpable.

"I don't want to talk to you about this, Danny, except to say that you've strung me and RCA along for months. I'm going to hang up now, before I say something I regret!"

I was developing an unfortunate habit of misleading people, while secretly weighing, cross-referencing and cataloguing any and all career options. Over the years, my calculating approach would become second nature, my way of navigating through the ever-challenging record world.

The McCauleys, relieved that I was no longer bound to RCA, relented slightly in pressuring me to sign with them, understanding that getting out of my contract meant that I was, for all intents and purpose, teaming up with them. As a gesture of faith, they gave me a shot at writing the lyrics to a piece of music Dr. McCauley had composed for a big-budget Canadian film titled *Between Friends*. I nailed the words while slurping down my morning cereal, recorded the vocal for the theme song and was rewarded with five hundred dollars. Because of my ability to write on assignment and sing with confidence under studio pressure (which is entirely different from performing live), I was tossed a few more movie songs. Some I co-wrote, some I simply sang, socking away the studio experience, as well as the dough, for when I would really need it.

For a nineteen-year-old pulsing with creativity, energy and confidence, it was a wonderful time to be a singer-songwriter. Along with Lightfoot's international success, a new generation of Canadian performers was finding a voice on Canadian radio: Bruce Cockburn, Murray McLauchlan, Valdy, as well as behind-the-scenes songwriters and producers like Gene MacLellan ("Snowbird") and Daniel Lanois. I studied these artists the way my father read up on master sociologists like W.E.B. Du Bois and Thorstein Veblen. Beyond their obvious talent, how did these singers transcend the throngs of almost-made-its? Why did so many of these top-flight Canada-based writers appear to shun love songs? (Lightfoot and Leonard Cohen notwithstanding; I suspected this may have pointed to one of the reasons for their greater international success.) Was it about appearing hip and cool? And, if so, did that make me the lamest of anti-cool?

"I'm sorry I'm not as romantic as my co-headliner," a singer I was sharing an engagement with at Toronto's Riverboat said to the audience, implying that this was why I was enjoying a better reception. (The truth was, I'd stacked the audience with dozens of my friends.)

Part of my "problem" was that, unlike most teenage males, I'd always loved romantic songs. Raised on Sinatra and Sarah Vaughan, I later took to so-called mushy soft-rock groups like Bread and the Association, while other boys my age reacted to their requiems for lost love by making armpit farts to announce their disgust.

Now, as I found myself edging out most of the competing local singers, the grumblings of "wimp" were getting louder, and there was nothing I could do but suck it up and move on. Besides, some unexpected perks came along with my growing love-him-or-hate-him reputation. Women were starting to pay attention to me—lots of women. This was certainly not something I'd experienced in high school.

"Better keep up with all your long-distance running, Danny," advised a sexually rapacious older woman, who appeared to take delight in shocking me out of my Don Mills prudishness.

"Why's that?" I asked.

"Your way with a love song tells me you're right at the beginning of a long and juicy career in fucking."

Was I shocked more by her crudeness or her harsh insight? Somehow, in the period between scaring Cynthia out of my house with my very first love song and catching the ear of international stars, I'd changed from a Don Mills virgin to a young man being seduced by generous numbers of women.

Distracted (not to mention supremely thankful) as I was by this turn of events, I rationalized any twinges of guilt by reminding myself that this tumbling in and out of women's beds inspired and informed my songwriting.

"It's all research, Danny," my boss, Lloyd, explained.

"I don't know, Lloyd, that sounds pretty darned cold."

"It's the other way around, Danny. That's what makes it so hot."

Wonderful as all this lovemaking was, it did come with what I came to call the "sex tax." This sex tax manifested itself as stress, a constant, subterranean emotional tug that it was all too good to be true. There had to be some kind of catch.

"It concerns me, Danny, that you may be objectifying these women," Mom said, spotting the hickey that glowed on my neck.

"Ha, ha, ha!" roared Dad, before saying, "Donna, you got it wrong, it's our son who's being objectified. Not only are these women gobbling Danny up, they leave their mark. Take another look at that love tattoo over that boy's Adam's apple. Golly day, it's a territorial brand."

For me to really understand the gist of what Dad was saying, I had to rid myself of all my previous misconceptions about women and sex. First, that women didn't crave sex as desperately as men; actually, from what I was discovering, they craved it more. Second, that for women, sex and heartfelt emotions were inextricable; actually, the women I kept running into were just fine with recreational sex. It was men (like me) who weren't fine with women being fine with it. To wit, the first three women I became sexually involved with, I fell hard for. For me at this time, monogamy was automatic and absolute.

"Why would you assume such a thing?" While these three women each had her own way of asking me this, the message amounted to the same thing. For them, monogamy was praised by everyone but practised by no one. Woman Number Two was the one who had blithely predicted that, despite my protests to the contrary, my "career in fucking" was about to begin. A month later she informed me that she was going back to her ex-boyfriend, an Olympic rower. Woman Number One had left me for "Jack the Acrobat" (a bruising hint that my imagination, or rather my bedroom technique, lacked variety). I was starting to feel like Woody Allen's poorer, less talented brother.

Then came Woman Number Three—my third and most mortifying strike. Any lingering notions I still clung to about sex and emotional attachment being the same were thoroughly shredded by Helena, who, at twenty-two, possessed enough worldly sophistication to make Erica Jong (her heroine) look like the Flying Nun.

Helena also happened to be a competitive athlete ("Donna, Danny's taken to dating Canada's entire female Olympic team!" Dad had remarked), which was why, she explained, she felt so natural about her body. "Natural": how I came to hate that word. For Helena it was a code for being free to do whatever she wanted with whomever she wanted. One day she'd be swooning over the physical perfection of a professional football player she was having her way with, only to replace this "boring jock" a week later with a suave, older professional photographer who "discovered" and took pictures of her. Oh yes, she was cruelly, unfairly beautiful. She knew this about herself and understood that this enabled her to dictate the terms of her relationships.

One night, curious as to Dad's reaction to this woman, I decided to take Helena to my parents' house for dinner. What I hadn't counted on was Helena's reaction to my father. Later that night as she led me into her bedroom, she launched into an elaborate description of my dad's perfect looks and how, well, if he wasn't my dad . . .

"Helena," I interrupted, "what are you saying? I mean, he is my dad. And besides, he's like, fifty."

"Lose the Don Mills prig-boy act, Danny, it's getting kinda old," Helena yawned. "Although I must confess," she added, "you're kind of sexy when you're shocked."

I left Helena's flat later that night dizzy and weightless from angry, aggressive and delirious lovemaking, and determined to write a song that would make her realize she was destroying me with her callous, shove-it-in-my-face appetite for other men. I knew I was losing her. My status as a "young, inexperienced novelty fuck" was, as she would put it, "getting old."

There was something irresistible about her coldness, her spare-no-details stories about her other, better-looking, better-built, better-off men. And it didn't hurt that the one time she wasn't cold, or selfish, or superior, or condescending was when we made love.

Barely a week into our affair, Helena had asked me if I loved her. I had understood that anything I might say in response—yes, no, kind of, maybe—Helena would find a way to use against me. Her question provided me with the perfect opening line to a new song: "You ask me if I love you, and I choke on my reply . . ."

From the moment I met Helena to the day I completed my new song, twenty days passed. When it was finished, I played it to her over the phone.

"Has anyone ever told you that you're way too fucking intense?" Helena asked, before hanging up on me.

The next day she phoned me from the Toronto bus terminal to say goodbye. Her pro-football-playing friend (whose "boring jock" manner suddenly didn't seem all that bad compared to my teenage angst) had been released from the Toronto Argonauts, and she'd accepted his invitation to spend the summer with him in Texas.

"He's half Black, like you," she added.

"I feel better, knowing that."

Click. Helena's brisk goodbye was the first of many unintended consequences of "Sometimes When We Touch." Already, within hours of being written, it had started to change my life: mercifully driving a woman I was powerless to resist hundreds of miles out of reach.

At the time, no one seemed too impressed with my new song. Too heady, too heavy, too wordy, too real—it was always *too* something-or-other. And so, between brooding over Helena's abrupt departure and writing at a song-a-day clip, I shelved "Sometimes" and jumped into pre-production for my first full-length record. Two weeks before I was to start recording my album, I flew to St. John's to spend some time with Cynthia.

Conveniently, I never thought to connect my first three girlfriends' faithlessness to my deep and growing bond with Cynthia. Because Cynthia and I had remained platonic, I saw no reason to conceal my relationship with her from Helena or anyone else, taking great pains to explain that what Cynthia and I shared transcended traditional romance—blah,

blah, blah. Was I really too immature and narcissistic to understand that blathering on in this manner would be enough to send any self-respecting woman running in the opposite direction? I suspect a part of me wanted to drive all other women away. That, even though I could not admit it to myself, I'd always held the hope that one day Cynthia and I would have it all, that rarified love that an increasing number of my songs extolled.

As far as I could tell, Cynthia was confronted with similar relationship problems out east: getting to a certain level of closeness with some "perfect male candidate" (her description never failed to unnerve me) only to have the relationship mysteriously fall apart. "Maybe it's 'cause you refuse to sleep with them," I suggested, trying to trip Cynthia into divulging just what had transpired with her constantly changing "candidates."

Cynthia pointed out that I was living proof that, "sex or no sex," we both seemed unable to make a relationship last more than several months. Sly as always, she had an unfair advantage; our tetchy talk was taking place during ninety-second breaks between eight-hundred-metre repeats, leaving me too dizzy to think clearly.

"Well, how far do you actually, ah . . . you know . . . take it with these boyfriends of yours?"

"Not too far. Just far enough."

"Meaning?"

"Oh, Danny, let's talk about something else. Like that new lyric you sent me. Mom and I both agree it's the best title you've written. But what does it mean? *Sometimes when we touch, the honesty's too much?* I have to admit, that girlfriend of yours, well, she sure didn't seem very nice."

As Cynthia took off with me in pursuit I tried to convince myself that I was hearing, for the first time, a hint of jealousy in her voice. "Just looking out for your best interests, Danny," she giggled, reading my thoughts as she leaned into the first turn on the cinder track. I loved the way she could always read my mind. I hated how much I loved that about her.

The two weeks I spent with Cynthia seemed to go by in one long, extended training run. What better way to avoid getting physical than by being physical in every way but "that way"? I watched Cynthia's wildly curly hair bob off her glistening neck when we ran the neighbourhood streets at midnight, spiking our quarter-mile jogs with fifty-yard dashes, and a part of me wanted to never return to Toronto.

"What have you written this morning?" Cynthia would ask first thing every day, when she brought a pot of coffee down to my guest room.

"Well, I started this song, but . . ."

"Finish it. You played me the first verse and it's beautiful. This could be the one, Danny. Your lucky song."

Cynthia's belief that I was strong and talented enough to take on the RCAs, the Bayerses and the hyper-talented Matt McCauleys of the world came at just the right time. And, I would discover, she wasn't just referring to music-business hurdles.

Dad's voice came through the phone receiver at high volume: "You've worn out your welcome with Cynthia's family. By now they see you as a mooch. Or some charity case. Nothing's worse than having people feel like they have to take care of you. If they feel sorry for you, they're never going to respect you."

Dad's voice had been so typically loud that Cynthia had been able to make out everything he'd said. My issues with Dad had been the one thing in my life that I'd attempted to play down with Cynthia. But now, feeling outed as the family fuck-up I really was, I could feel myself getting emotional. Leaving Cynthia was bad enough without letting her in on my highly guarded secret: Dad's disappointment in me.

Cynthia wrapped her arms around my neck and shoulders, something she'd never done before.

"Danny, your dad didn't mean it. You know how parents are. They know just what to say to make you feel awful. Really, what I think is your dad misses you. He loves you and he's hurt that you're not around more. But he's a man. He's never going to come right out and tell you that. Now, I'm going to let you in on a little secret. Mom and I were crying last night at the thought of you going home. We wouldn't be shedding tears over a charity case."

"I think I'd better get packing," I said. "My flight takes off in a few hours and I have to organize all these lyrics and chord charts before I lose track of everything."

Cynthia brushed back my long, matted hair—I'd let it fall over most of my face to cover my gloom—and blew me a kiss as she turned to leave my room. The last thing she said stayed with me on my return flight to Toronto.

"Wait till your father finds out that the McCauleys are going to invest all that money in your first album. I'd love to be there to hear what he has to say about that."

"This is Matt's bar mitzvah present," was all Dad chose to say about the McCauleys' twenty thousand dollar investment. That the McCauleys were obviously not Jewish gave Dad's wisecrack even more sting. My professed talents were nothing more than a cute present for Matt to toy with, while I, just an ornament bought for the sole amusement of this rich Don Mills family, continued to waste my life and imperil my future. Incredible, I thought, how Dad could so totally demean not only me, but the entire McCauley family, in one short sentence.

At twenty, I still knew and cared precious little about the business side of the record business. But despite my self-righteous attitude that "artists" should never bother with such lowly concerns such as money, my instincts—about the McCauleys versus RCA, as well as the type of deal I was entering into—were anything but naive. The bottom line was that, all things considered, the McCauleys and I had stumbled onto a reasonably fair (by industry standards at that time) deal. By that I mean I'd been offered a better contract than artists like Bruce Springsteen and Billy Joel, who had, unlike me, signed away all their publishing (which represents half of a songwriter's prospective royalty stream) to managers and production companies.

The contract I signed with the McCauleys granted them the life of the copyright and a little over twenty-five percent of the potential future income for all of the songs I'd written up to that point as well as any written over the next five years. They would also own, in perpetuity, the masters to all the albums (a minimum of five) that I'd record over the next five years.

In the summer of 1974, Matt and I, along with Fred Mollin—a local musician whose love and command of every facet of pop music was as boundless as it was infectious—recorded the bulk of my first album. To an outsider, it may have seemed foolish to break a recording contract with RCA only to sign a new contract with a family who, in theory, would be approaching record labels for the same kind of deal I'd just walked away from. But after my experience with Bayers, I liked the idea of making a record without any creative or business interference from a major label. Sure, Matt and I had had our disagreements, but we'd grown up together, understood each other and had a fundamental sense of how to play off each other's strengths and weaknesses.

It was mesmerizing and humbling to watch Matt conduct a twenty-four-piece orchestra consisting of musicians twice his age. I sat there, staring in disbelief, feeling the goose bumps tingling across my skin as my songs took flight. One track at a time, Matt's Wagnerian strings sailed over my guitar and vocals, leaving me feeling a combination of elation and envy. I knew his swirling swath of violins, violas and cellos, not exactly a typical sound on most pop records, would give my songs the extra commercial kick—and, dare I say, class—they needed. Still, I feared his ambitious arrangements might upstage my songs, especially at the volume he wanted them featured in the final mixdown. I couldn't appreciate that this album was his child as much as it was mine. Fred Mollin's role as de facto referee and studio prankster soon became as valuable as his knowledge of radio and its constantly changing tastes. Once, when Matt and I were lost in a battle over which of us should sing which background vocal, Fred arranged for a friend to barge into the studio perfectly disguised as a Toronto cop, right down to the mirrored aviator sunglasses and forehead-concealing cap, and scare the daylights out of me. (At the time I had some grass hidden in my guitar case.)

"Stop your snivelling," Fred laughed, when I complained that he'd taken his practical joke too far. "Nothing like a good fright to give your vocals that edge."

Meanwhile, relieved that I wasn't going to have to call Dad to bail me out of jail, I forgot about Matt's and my latest clash. Still shaken, I ran to the bathroom to flush my modest, illegal stash down the toilet. By the time I'd returned Matt had finished his background vocals on two of my songs. Only needing to hear my phrasing once, he could blend his whispery tone seamlessly with mine, catching the rise and fall of my rhythmic tics in three minutes: as long as it took for the song to play back over his headphones. Unwilling to admit that he'd deservedly won the background vocal contest, I played him a song I'd written the night before.

"Great hooky chorus," Matt allowed, before qualifying: "Sounds perfect for a Salada tea commercial. I wish I could write songs that people could relate to. Problem is you have to think like normal people to write songs normal people like."

Much as I felt threatened by Matt's mathematical understanding of harmony, formal composition and original string arranging, it was how his parents treated him—like the second coming of Beethoven—that both amazed and, on occasion, unsettled me. One night Matt dreamed that a certain stock shot up in value, and his father, interpreting this as yet another sign of his son's mystical, otherworldly vision, invested a fortune. When he subsequently lost it, I couldn't help but feel a guilty rush of *schadenfreude*.

Our contrasting relationships with our fathers may have been another reason why Matt and I clicked. While Dad's denouncing of my musical ambitions gave me focus and drive, Matt's parents' blind faith in all he said and did gave us the keys to the recording studio and opened the purse strings for the orchestras, the cream of Toronto session musicians, the photos and press kits—in short, all the prohibitively expensive tools necessary to get the undivided attention of the key music industry insiders.

The McCauley parents, months before the recording of my first album, had quietly approached my parents to offer them an equal partnership in my publishing and record royalties, provided they take on fifty percent of the McCauley investment. That my parents politely rejected their offer was not surprising. Mom later explained it this way: "Your father and I didn't want to be in the uncomfortable position of having a business investment with a loved one, for fear of how it might taint our relationship." Two sets of parents (and Matt) managing to keep this from me was nothing short of miraculous, and an act of impressive discipline, given Dad's garrulous tendencies. Had I known about it at the time I would have been mortified.

The summer and fall of 1974 flew by in a mad and exhilarating rush of eighteen-hour studio days, making it easier for me to forget, for a while anyway, that Dad and I hadn't spoken in almost six months. But then I started to miss him. A lot. By refusing to go along with Dad's definition of who I should be, I'd been forced to define myself, set my own goals and stick religiously to them. Our scores of skirmishes had toughened me, leaving me well-equipped for the daily conflicts I was now encountering with Matt, with some bass player over whether his part was too busy or with some Yorkville club owner over a broken contract.

Still, when the following phrase, supported by a lilting major-to-minor chord sequence, came to me as I killed some time during a studio lunch break, I had no idea where it came from. How long had I been filing these thoughts away, somewhere safe, until I was brave enough to face them?

"This is just a song to say, that I'm proud for what they are, and I hope my world can take me half that far. Way back in McCarthy's day, my parents left the USA ..."

Whereas most of my songs were written within a few hours, "McCarthy's Day," as I eventually called it, would take eight months. It was something I couldn't have written without leaving home.

"Hi, Dad," I said, deliberately casual, once he'd picked up the phone. My newly finished song was my best shot at puncturing our unofficial wall of silence, while still saving face.

"It's Danny, Donna," Dad called out.

"I know it's been some time, Dad, but I got this new song, one that you and Mom might find interesting. It's pretty different for me. I thought you guys might want to hear it."

"Hold on, son," Dad said, handing the phone over to Mom to make the arrangements.

The following evening I sauntered into my parents' living room, carefully avoiding Dad's censuring stare and brushing aside Mom's typical questions: Was I eating enough? Did I make my dentist appointment? Was I planning on going back to work full-time?

I pulled out my guitar, slid it onto my lap, closed my eyes so they couldn't see how nervous I felt and sang them my new song. Once I'd finished the final lines, I busied myself packing up my guitar, not daring to look at them, embarrassed by the rush of emotion I was feeling.

"That's a very good song, son. I didn't know you had it in you."

I kept fussing with my guitar case, shuffling pages of lyrics around, stuffing capos and guitar strings into its tiny rectangular compartment. When I finally snapped the case shut, stood up and glanced in the direction of Dad's subdued voice, he was nowhere to be found.

"Can you show me the lyrics, Danny?" Mom asked, as if it would be a huge imposition for me. I handed her two crumpled-up pieces of paper, and she read them out loud—in a voice at once faltering and disbelieving. Still, when she reached the lyrics' coda, I thought I could pick out the subtlest hint of pride.

Way back in McCarthy's day, my parents left the U.S.A.
Young, rebellious lovers
They left behind a nation far too proud and powerful to say
That love, oh love transcends all colours
Some Black men turned against my father
Some white men turned against my mother
Each race has its place, they all would say
But with a past so battle worn

And a future begging to be born
They found a life that's growing still today

And glancing through the years and living through their fears
I hope they can accept my goals, a bit confused, a bit unclear

And all the years behind me now, seem like a book I've read
And yet somehow, I still don't understand the words
And all the Black and all the white, that rest in me
That make me fight, remind me, of all the knowledge left
to earn
Still some Black men turn against my father . . .

And glancing through the years, and living through their fears
I hope they can accept my goals, a bit confused, a bit unclear
This is just a song to say, that I'm proud for what they are
And I hope my world can take me half that far

I didn't ask Mom why Dad had left, or where he went. It was
enough for me that he sat through my performance. And, heartening as
it was for Dad to say, *That's a very good song, son,* what really melted me
was when he said, *I didn't know you had it in you.* Coming from Dad,
those were powerful words of praise.

CHAPTER 15

Sweeping Changes

Strange and beautiful as Cynthia's and my long-distance friendship was, we were making it up as we went along. It was extraordinary that we managed to pull it off, our bond, our whatever it was, for so long. It's impossible to gauge just how much denial factored into our growing physical attraction. Cynthia had this saying: "It's always harder to go back than move forward." We knew that if we acted on our attraction, we would surely be doomed to take it all the way.

How did it happen? What did it feel like? Where were we? What did we say afterwards? Does it really matter? In the end, like someone after a trauma, I could barely remember how we crossed the line into a physical relationship. And though that event itself wasn't traumatic, the way everything unravelled afterwards—slowly at first, one deception at a time, until it finally ended in one horrific bang—most definitely was. But it's always harder to go back than move forward.

The start of my romantic relationship with Cynthia coincided with a series of sweeping changes in my life. My album finished, I returned to work with the Ontario government, where I found myself working the night shift tracking licence plate numbers, often as a means of catching suspected criminals for the Ontario Provincial Police. Saturday and Sunday nights I usually had a high school concert lined up.

I was on the move every second, vaguely aware that all this non-stop activity was somehow connected to, indeed set in motion by, Cynthia. It seemed that by becoming intimate with her I'd achieved the impossible. Accordingly, all other previously insuperable life challenges—record deals, hit singles, international fame, even Dad's admiration and respect—were not only possible but inevitable.

Matt, however, feeling the weight of his parents' un-recouped investment in my album, did not share my optimism.

"We've blown my parents' life savings, and what do we have to show for it? A bunch of form rejection letters from just about every record company out there."

"Be patient, Matt. There are still lots of companies out there we haven't approached. Once this record hits radio—"

"It can't get to radio without a record company releasing it first. And all the labels think you're too soft and mushy. No one wants some teenage Frank Sinatra these days. I told you we needed more electric guitar and up-tempo songs."

Four months had passed since we'd completed the recording of my album. Since then, a day hadn't gone by without Matt making me feel as if I'd burned through his family's money to support my dope addiction. Making things worse was the fact that I kept finding agents who promised the McCauleys they'd land us that magic record deal. But after thousands of dollars of expenses, these same agents came back armed with rejection slips and invoices. Columbia Records already had too many singer-songwriters; A&M thought the singer-songwriter thing had run its course and they were looking for the next Supertramp; Arista was cutting back on its roster.

Fed up with agents and their big bills and promises of that dream contract right around the corner, Matt and I decided to dispense with the deal brokers and talk to record companies directly. Though we steeled ourselves for more rejection, the labels turned out to be surprisingly complimentary, curious as to why we'd chosen to make such a "different-sounding" record.

But flattery was a far cry from a record company slotting me into its well-oiled marketing, promotion and distribution network. Most labels we talked to had this to say: "What you're offering is a luxury item. Your kind of music is very expensive to promote and produce." Sure, Elton John was big, but the Brits had more eclectic tastes, whereas Canada liked more straight-out, balls-to-the-wall rock 'n' roll. Along with my quaintly luxurious sound, it appeared that my "look" was also working against me. More than a few execs confessed, "We played your album to all our secretaries and asked them what they thought you might look like. They loved your songs and imagined you as a blond, blue-eyed, California surfer type. Your look is, ah, well, let me guess, are you Turkish, maybe, or Greek?"

I'd gotten to the point where I joked about dying my hair, bleaching my skin and posing in leather with an electric guitar. Matt was more direct about his disillusionment: "I don't think I can sit through many more meetings where A&R guys are trying to tell us that our record is too good to be released. Most of them are so deaf they can't even hear that their speakers are out of phase."

Ten meetings over two weeks had covered every label worth approaching save one. Expecting one final rejection, Matt and I met with Ross Reynolds, president of GRT Records, at the time Canada's most respected and successful independent record label. We were surprised Ross had even agreed to meet with us, since one of our former agents had wined and dined him in a bid to sell our album, only to come back empty-handed. When Matt mentioned Ross's earlier rejection, thanking him for agreeing to give our album a second listen, Ross shook his head.

"Take this any way you want, guys, but that agent you're talking about never played me your record. He's never tried to pitch me anyone's record. We've said hello at one or two industry functions, but that's it."

I did my best to ignore Matt's scornful stares. Okay, so I blew a ton of his parents' money on an agent who seemed to have invented record company meetings and expenses, but on the positive side, that meant a handful of U.S. labels that had supposedly rejected my record hadn't actually heard it.

"I think you have one potential hit single in here," Ross said, after glancing through the notes he'd written beside my song titles on the tape box. "Although I don't hear a lot of other obvious hits among these songs."

"Well, I have a few new songs I could tack on to this record that are really commercial," I said.

"Who's gonna pay for the recording, Santa Claus?" Matt hissed, beneath his breath.

"We can always discuss the option of adding some new songs if your first single takes off. These days, everyone holds back on their album release till a month or two after their single's been shipped to radio."

"So you're offering us a record deal?" Matt asked, the surprise in his voice making me want to smack him.

"What I'm offering is to buy rights to a first single. With the contractual understanding that GRT Records has first rights to lease and release your album if your single's a hit."

Everyone in the Canadian music business knew that GRT wasn't simply another northern branch of a U.S. multinational, and that Ross Reynolds had a reputation for standing by his Canadian acts, turning an unusually high percentage of them into household names. And if first impressions counted for anything, Yale-educated Reynolds was smart without acting arrogant, optimistic without being hyperbolic, quick to emphasize that overnight successes usually disappeared the following morning. He took great pains to point out that sustained discipline was what separated the stars from the chumps.

"Are you willing to put everything else in your life second to your career? Not for the next month, or the next year, but for the next twenty-five years?"

My answer, an unqualified yes, felt like an understatement. Hard as it was to imagine where I'd be next week, let alone next year or the year after, one thing was beyond imagining: a life that did not completely revolve around music. Such an existence seemed like no life at all.

Matt and I signed with GRT Records in April of 1975. GRT scarcely waited for the ink to dry on our contract before shipping my single out to Canadian radio in early May. I was still a month shy of twenty-one, and everything—my career, my life, my entire identity, even (if Matt was to be believed) the McCauleys' financial security—now hinged on the fate of one song, my make-or-break first single, "You Make Me Want to Be (A Father)."

It was the perfect choice, perhaps too much so, as my go-for-broke opening line, after impressing Belafonte the year before, had also made an impact on one of Nashville's most powerful country record producers. My fellow guitar player on the recording of "You Make Me Want to Be," Don Potter, had returned to Nashville in the fall of '74 and raved to Tammy Wynette's record producer, Billy Sherrill, about a killer song he'd played on. When Potter sang Sherrill the opening line, Sherrill said, "That's one of the best damned titles I've ever heard," and proceeded to write "You Make Me Want to Be a Mother," an instant country hit for Tammy Wynette. (There's no copyright on a song title.) By the time my song was released, I was accused of nicking the title from Tammy Wynette. (Ms. Wynette more than paid me back ten years later, when she scored a top-five country hit with a song I'd co-written.)

Despite my indignation at being accused of plagiarism, my single immediately started receiving heavy radio airplay throughout the country. That point demarcated my life: before my voice hit radio and after my voice hit radio. In the seventies, a pop singer's career lived and died based on Top 40 airplay. TV appearances and coast-to-coast rave reviews could give your career a boost, but nothing compared to the galvanic whoosh, the one hit song and you're off to the races propulsion, delivered by radio play.

Within weeks of my song sweeping the radio, I signed with one of Canada's most powerful management teams: Finkelstein/Fiedler. The McCauleys had done their job, financing and producing my album and then procuring a record deal, and were now, in effect, passing the baton to the next team up my career ladder. It was up to my new managers to help put a face, an image, on to what, at this point, was little more than a new voice on Canadian radio. Procuring tour dates, finding the right media exposure and securing international record deals; this second stage of my career was every bit as crucial as the five or so years Matt and I had spent learning the craft of record making.

I could have searched the world over and still not have uncovered two more unlikely relay partners than the McCauleys and Finkelstein/Fiedler. The McCauleys, still smarting from the agents I'd introduced them to, regarded my new managers, both named Bernie, as necessary evils at best. It was a culture clash so monumental that it would have been amusing had I not been caught in the middle. The Bernies' every second word was "fuck," Finkelstein was wildly unkempt—the remnants of his last tomato-and-egg sandwich were frequently lodged in his caveman beard—and Fiedler was an unapologetic Lothario. Finkelstein, brilliant as he was formally uneducated, worked tirelessly for his beloved acts, Cockburn and McLauchlan, regarding every other up-and-coming singer as the sworn enemy. Anyone caught singing along with, say, Springsteen's "Born to Run" was treated as a defector, and quite possibly a spy working for the other side.

Fiedler, who owned the legendary Riverboat coffeehouse in Yorkville and had booked the likes of Joni Mitchell and Jackson Browne before they became superstars, saw the music business as one extended riotous party, frequently travelling for weeks at a time with his high-rolling friends: everyone from Jack Nicholson to Gordon Lightfoot and music-biz heavy hitter David Geffen.

These two Bernies had been power figures in the Canadian singer-songwriter scene for years, and I was as flattered as I was star-struck to be managed by them, willing, sometimes against my better judgment, to defer to their advice. The Bernies' clout, along with the growing momentum of my single, led me to tour across Canada and the United States as an opening act to established pop stars (Gino Vanelli, Maria Muldaur and Murray McLauchlan, to name a few). Finding myself the subject of tons of positive media attention, I took everything that was written about me too seriously, not understanding at the time that if you unblinkingly accept the media's praise you are bound, ultimately, to absorb their scorn.

I couldn't have been happier. After all, I'd plotted and schemed my entire life for this, and now I was living it with gusto: energetically bopping from photo shoot to interview, to tour bus, to recording studio, to penning out new lyrics on airplane stationery, to three hours of shuteye. Then repeat. Little wonder that pop music is a young person's game; its numbing pace would do in all but a few adults over thirty. All the while I believed I was emotionally mature and intellectually shrewd enough to handle this new and exciting world that was laying itself before me. But I wasn't.

"So, what else is going on in your life, son?"

I was talking to my parents in their bedroom. There was something instantly reassuring about seeing them in bed, snuggled under the covers. I'd just finished bragging to them about the deal I'd signed stateside with 20th Century Records and the impressive promotion and marketing campaign it was launching to gear up for my record's release in America.

"Your mother and I would like to know what you're doing to stay balanced. Are you reading any new books to expand your mind, like your brother and sister?"

"Dan, kindly don't drag me into this," Mom said, picking up a magazine from the nightstand.

I wanted to say something quasi-pithy about balanced lives being a luxury lost to people with demanding careers, but really, that would have been exactly the kind of defensive outburst Dad would have expected from me.

Now that he could no longer take me to task over my career choice, he was bent on uncovering a new potential weakness: my career obsession. *Fine,* I thought, *but where, pray tell, have I picked up the curse of this tunnel vision?*

I headed downstairs. In my wake I could hear Mom slowly getting out of bed, and Dad weakly objecting to her abandoning him. "No one's preventing you from getting up and joining me," Mom answered.

"Would you like me to fix you something, Danny? I've picked all these raspberries from our garden," she asked, minutes later.

"No thanks. You know me—a visit home can't be complete without me rummaging around in your fridge."

Mom was about to say something but was distracted by the sound of Dad's snoring.

"Christ, that's loud. Sounds like Dad's cutting my hair with a lawn mower."

"You've got to hand it to your father. Even when he's sleeping he manages to dominate the conversation."

I walked into the foyer and picked up my car keys.

"Here, Danny."

Mom handed me a small container of fresh raspberries, and I could see a reddish-pink stain of raspberry juice tainting the tips of her fingers. Dad had stopped snoring, leaving the low hum of the fridge motor the only sound in the house.

As I opened the front door to leave, I gave Mom a few posters advertising my new album.

"Maybe you and Dad can think of them as my university diploma substitutes," I said.

"Don't tell him I told you this," Mom said, "but in the morning, the first thing your father does is turn the clock radio to the rock station, hoping he'll catch your song."

There's a delicious delay between the time that the media and your record label align to spring you on an unsuspecting public, and the public's eventual response. I felt like a pebble in a slingshot with the sling stretched back taut, to the breaking point, just before its release. In the seventies, thanks in part to recent Canadian Radio-Television Commission regulations, it was a lot easier than the public realized to become an "overnight celebrity." Canada was starved for its own celebrities, even if, once a homegrown star was established, the media and public couldn't quite decide whether to love or hate its latest, fresh-faced hero. When my mug was suddenly plastered on the cover of Canadian magazines, when I could be seen regularly performing on television, when my voice was saturating Canadian radio, I believed it had everything to do with my undisputed genius as a singer-songwriter. I didn't understand that celebrity was mysteriously unequal parts timing, serious marketing dollars, good luck, cultural mood and, above all, that certain *je ne sais quoi.*

What I did understand was that an entirely different set of rules—and frequently no rules at all—applied to so-called celebrities. At the beginning, I quite enjoyed the spectacle of well-adjusted adults abandoning every vestige of civil behaviour upon spotting a "famous person"; the WASP reserve vanished, giving way to staring, pointing and animated whispering. Damned if now that I finally had some money, I found it almost impossible to spend it. Store clerks started giving me merchandise for free. Bartenders and waiters refused to take my brand-new credit card, instead offering me more food and free drinks. Where were these generous souls when I was broke? Cops, who used to regard my long, bushy hippie hair and hard-to-pin-down racial origins as a surefire indicator of lawlessness, would now stop me for speeding, amble over to my car and then, upon recognizing my face, reach in and shake my hand. Then they'd tear my ticket in half and bashfully ask me to autograph it.

On my twenty-first birthday, in between sets at the Riverboat, the McCauleys gave me a thousand-dollar advance on my royalties. I'd never seen a cheque that big. My parents gave me twenty-one silver dollars. Those shiny silver coins felt like the gift of a lifetime. I kept rolling them around in my hands that night as I lay wide awake in bed, as if to convince myself that they were real, that any of it—this new and alluring stardom, the concerts, the radio airplay, the outpouring of female attention—was real. Twenty-one silver dollars. It was the type of gift a kid might receive. With all that was happening, it felt comforting to be still regarded as a child by my parents.

"Take care of my boy, now. Keep him safe and out of trouble," Dad warned my new managers.

"Of course, Dr. Hill," they said.

What kind of trouble was Dad referring to?

"You're on your way, son," Dad told me a few months later, solemnity creeping into his tone. I'd just brought him ten advance copies of my first album. I already had a second single, "Growing Up (In the Shadow of the USA)," moving up the charts, and GRT was gearing to get my album out the next week, while my voice was still dominating the airwaves. Dad and I were sitting on the front porch, his favourite spot when the weather turned warm. The streetlights turned on, reminding me of earlier years when streetlights meant curfew time.

"Danny, now that you're making money, I expect you to contribute to your brother's and sister's college educations." College education. Nothing like those two words to bring me crashing back to the present. After all the years of Dad predicting I was never going to make a dime in music, now he was casting me in the role of financial provider, at twenty-one, with two songs on the radio. I took this to mean that, in some fashion, he was finally blessing me with his approval. That was all that mattered. I had no idea that my newfound money-making skills would ultimately open up an entire new realm of conflict between Dad and me.

CHAPTER 16

Dancing on a Slippery Slope

Throughout my teenage years, I'd been driven by two overlapping goals: to win the heart of a seemingly unwinnable girl, and to live a life of fame and fortune as a singer-songwriter. These two goals fed off each other, creating a positive cycle: my obsession to get the girl sparked my songwriting, which played into my career, which then made me more desirable in the eyes of that unwinnable girl. Incredibly, these once-impossible, overlapping dreams of mine, hatched at roughly the same age, were now being realized at the same time.

My constant radio airplay, reinforced by coast-to-coast touring and continuing media coverage, catapulted my first album, titled *Dan Hill*, into the position of hottest-selling record on GRT's roster. And Cynthia had moved from St. John's to Toronto, transferring to York University, where she'd received a partial athletic scholarship. Gone forever were the days of me sharing a house with six other guys. Now Cynthia and I were living together.

Aside from the seventy-two hours I'd spent lost in a sexual frenzy with Helena, I didn't have a clue how to go about living and sharing my life with a serious girlfriend. Furthermore, anything I'd learned about women through my past relationships could most certainly not be applied to Cynthia.

My earlier girlfriends had treated sex as a statement, rather than the beginnings of a deepening emotional bond. ("Whom I choose to share my body with is no one's business other than mine," Helena would say, in the midst of clunking me over the head with every unsavoury detail of her last encounter.)

But Cynthia embraced our new intimacy with the same commitment she brought to everything else in her life. Sex meant a permanent monogamous relationship: approaching it any other way was disrespectful to the act itself and cheapened both participants. Cynthia didn't expect other people to share her beliefs, and she was the first to poke fun at her old-fashioned standards. But of course, I wasn't "other people"; I'd officially become her life partner.

According to Cynthia, our new status as lovers, when factored in with all those years growing up apart yet together, was now incontrovertible evidence that we were and would always be the perfect pair. So then, what was the problem? This was what I'd always wanted. Why was I complicating things?

Did I love Cynthia? Absolutely. Could I imagine any woman other than Cynthia in my life, for the rest of my life? Not a chance. Did that mean I could remain faithful? Well, I was working on that one. However, as a work in progress, it was proving to be a challenge.

"Where are you? Don't fade away on me," Cynthia would implore whenever she caught me drifting, lost in an unfinished song or second-guessing something imprudent I might have said in a recent interview. Her wake-up call, reinforced by a playful nudge of her chin against my shoulder, always brought me back. In that way that befitted the narcissist I was becoming (nothing like a quick shot of fame to make the self-involved that much

Dan Hill

more so), I loved how absolutely Cynthia seemed to know and understand me. At least the part of me I was willing to open up to her. She never failed to find the right words to put me back together following a crisis. And the music business was essentially a series of crises: you solve one only to confront the next one that's popped up in its place. Upon my cry-babying over a particularly vicious review, she'd giggle, mimic my stricken expression and say, "Danny, can't you see, that critic really likes you, he's just afraid to admit it. Look how he accuses you of writing the kinds of songs only fourteen-year-old girls can relate to. That's a compliment. Do you know how hard it is to get the attention of a fourteen-year-old girl?"

Did the critic really like me? Doubtful. Did Cynthia really believe what she was telling me? Doubtful. But that didn't matter. What mattered was that I believed her.

In turn, I did the same for her: calming her down when she'd stress over her ever-tight hamstrings, convincing her to ease off on her training so her body could recover. Ice, heat, massage, ice, heat, massage: one or two nights a week were spent with me trying to coax some life back into her beaten-down legs as she lay moaning in pain on her stomach, reading for some psychology course. To the outside world, we must have come across as an insufferable advertisement for perfect love. Indeed, more than a few people found it nauseating to be around us. But we may well have been so demonstrative on the outside, smooching and stroking, giggling and caressing, to compensate for serious problems on the inside. Because beneath our shared glow, our permanent smiles, the inside jokes, the knowing back-and-forth looks, the cutesy glances and exchanges that tended to make everyone else feel excluded, we were the furthest thing from the perfect couple.

Cynthia, while becoming close with my mother, had a more difficult time with Dad, not knowing what to make of his teasing manner or his homey, off-colour humour.

"What were you two up to last night?" Dad asked, the morning after Cynthia and I had slept over in the basement bedroom.

"I'm sorry, did we have the TV on too loud?" Cynthia responded.

I stared into my cereal bowl, knowing what was coming.

"What I was hearing didn't sound like the TV," Dad said.

"I don't understand," Cynthia maintained.

"Ignore him, Cynthia. Dad's being—"

"Son, haven't you told Cynthia about the air vents in that basement bedroom?"

"Dad, enough already."

"Dan," Mom echoed.

Knowing that once Dad got started any discouraging words from Mom or me would only egg him on, I grabbed hold of Cynthia's hand under the table. Then I braced myself.

"The thing about those old air vents of ours," Dad explained, "is that they carry every single basement moan to every room in the house."

"Why would your father deliberately embarrass me like that?" Cynthia asked, once we'd made a hasty exit.

"Relax, we didn't even fool around last night. Once Dad realizes he can't get your goat he'll stop teasing you."

"That's what hurts. That your father wants to get my goat in the first place. Why? Is it about my family being religious? I know he thinks that means we're all narrow-minded. And he's always commenting on how rich my family is."

It was hard to say what was worse, Cynthia crying or Cynthia losing her temper. Neither had happened all that often until she'd moved to Toronto. But now, as I unrolled the car window so that her raised voice had a place to go, I spoke without thinking.

"Cynthia, you have to admit your dad's one of the richest guys on the east coast. And you could hardly accuse him of being a liberal thinker."

"You and your dad. You're snobs. You're always making digs about my dad being Mr. Straight, after he's been so generous to you. But you're no different than he is."

"Okay, so first you accuse me of being a snob like my dad, and now you're telling me I'm a dead ringer for your father?"

"You're both businessmen who never went to university. You both have a product that you're obsessed with selling around the world."

"So what are you telling me, that you've fallen in love with your father?"

"You know what? You can let me out at the next stop sign."

Cynthia had disconcertingly efficient ways of putting an end to unpleasant conversations. The abrupt hang-up. The storming out of restaurants. The sudden, silent exit from a movie theatre. Now Cynthia scrambled out of the car before it had come to a complete stop. Her final words as she slammed the door were "I want out, now!" leaving me to think she meant out of Toronto. Out of her life with me.

Cynthia returned several hours later, apologizing for overreacting. I matched her apology for apology, pretending not to see the truth. That we were turning into the last thing we'd imagined: a cliché. What could be more predictable than a couple getting into a fight over the in-laws?

As teenagers, our quick long-distance visits had granted us a shared escape from our immediate worlds; we were each other's vacation from life as we knew it. Now we were confronted with the overwhelming permanence of being a couple. No longer were we escaping reality; we were reality.

The things that had fuelled our friendship and correspondence through our teenage years were starting to trip us up as a couple. It had been easy for me to defer to Cynthia in St. John's and for Cynthia to do the same with me when visiting Toronto, but now that we were living together neither of us felt comfortable being in the other's shadow.

Even the thing that had once been such a source of connection for us—my music—was now threatening to divide us. My songs no longer served as our personal immutable bond; they'd blossomed, or rather, bastardized, into something hugely public, taking on a life of their own. And the greatest insult was that, for the first time, people were only interested in Cynthia because of her relationship to me. She'd uprooted her life and moved halfway across Canada for this? To become the *girlfriend of the star*? Although Cynthia got along well with my Toronto friends, I was on the road a lot, leaving her lonely and homesick in this sprawling, impersonal new city.

More and more Cynthia began to blow up at me over minor incidents rather than the real, overarching problem. My absent-minded eccentricities—such as confusing a pot of tea for maple syrup in the much too early morning and pouring it on my pancakes, causing the plate to overflow and drench the floor—started to grate on her nerves. I was always talking too loud, usually about something risqué, in an intimate restaurant; or getting lost while driving her to a track meet, which made her late, which cut into her warm-up time, which resulted in another round of strained hamstrings. It seemed I could do nothing properly. Had I told my parents the story about one of Cynthia's girlfriends trying, unsuccessfully, to seduce one of my musician friends (the more Dad roared with laughter, the angrier Cynthia became) because I was insensitive? Or worse than that, was I a chip off the old block, going out of my way to upset her for my own warped amusement?

Most of the time Cynthia wouldn't reveal why she was angry, and would deny being angry at all, leaving me scrambling to apologize while feeling clueless about what, exactly, I'd done wrong. But how could Cynthia articulate the source of her anger when she didn't really understand it? I understood it: more and more, I was being seduced by my own stardom.

I blamed it on the power of radio. On writing those cursed romantic songs, delivered in that raspy, too-Black-for-folk, too-white-for-R&B voice. On being a solo singer, my guitar as my backing band, which made me appear vulnerable and approachable to audiences weaned on rock 'n' roll bands big enough to form an army. Given a chance, I could come up with a million reasons why it wasn't my fault. Only it was my fault.

I was becoming secretly addicted to sex on the road. Even though I managed to limit my one-night stands to while I was touring, Cynthia, on some visceral level, must have sensed what was going on.

I found myself straddling two worlds—acting the swashbuckling pop star on the road while setting up a quiet domestic life with Cynthia at home. What was astounding was just how well, superficially speaking, I managed this double life, tucking it discreetly out of view: from Cynthia, from my family (whom Cynthia and I, despite Dad's incorrigible antics, spent most of our free time with) and even from my closest friends. All those years of pulling the wool over my father's eyes had left me adept at covering my tracks.

In my determination to savour the best of both worlds, I found little enjoyment in either. At home, I'd alternate between feeling guilty over my road sex and longing for the next adventure. On the road, I'd swear that each new woman would be the last, and, as morning greeted my escape from a college dorm or some coffeehouse dressing room, or as I exited some cramped bathroom encounter during a red-eye flight, I hungered for home, convincing myself that I was finally cured, that I could start fresh with Cynthia.

Somehow, through all of this, the positive cycle that had resulted in everything magically falling into place for me at twenty-one was beginning to reverse itself. I was in the process of gradually and methodically destroying all that I'd managed to achieve. (Even though my career kept gathering momentum, my rate of songwriting was slowing down, which was certain to erode the consistency of my future albums.) If I didn't know when, exactly, things in my life would start coming apart, I did know how: sooner or later my watertight compartments would give way to the rising pressure and flood into one another, all the separate parts finally whooshing together and washing the life, or lives, I was expertly juggling down the drain.

When the truth finally tumbled out, what would happen to Cynthia and me? I felt a constant gnawing pressure squeezing at my insides the way it used to when I was a boy and Dad trapped me upside down in one of his wrestling lock-ups. Only now it was me, no one else, who was tying the deepest, darkest part of me up in knots.

CHAPTER 17

1976: Mom's Breakdown and Karen's Breakthrough

In 1976, Mom was checked into a downtown Toronto hospital for what was supposed to be routine surgery to repair a bladder damaged by childbirth. During Mom's stay, the hospital misplaced her medical chart and she was mistakenly taken off lithium, the drug that had kept her manic-depression in check over the last decade. In less than forty-eight hours, it felt as though she'd been yanked back to that horrible winter of '66 when she'd come so terribly undone. Now, as then, she came across like someone possessed: hallucinating, hearing voices, talking gibberish. Only this time her descent was even more rapid and extreme.

With Larry away studying at the University of British Columbia and Karen enrolled at the University of Ottawa, the onus fell on me to help Dad take care of Mom. At twenty-two, I was old enough to understand that if one parent fell badly ill, the "healthy" parent needed to be monitored just as closely, in the event that they buckled under the pressure and grief of seeing their loved one so infirm. Cynthia had already pointed out to me that Dad could barely make it up the stairs of his house lately without losing his breath, and that his diabetes might be a lot further along than any of us realized. The added stress of Mom being sick was sure to send his blood sugars through the roof.

My gut reaction to all this turmoil was to run as far as possible from both my parents; I was afraid I'd be dragged under, ripped away from the comfort zone of my music, derailed from my quest to kick my career up to an ever-higher international level. I'd recently won my first Juno award, for best new artist, and was deep into recording my second album. The pressure of topping my successful first release was consuming me, straining my relationships with everyone in my professional circle and causing me to withdraw from Cynthia. Resisting my impulse to flee, I visited Mom every day at the hospital during my extended lunch break from the recording studio.

Dad would always be there, usually sitting on the bed beside her, stroking her legs over the rumpled, crumb-lined (courtesy of Dad's daily gifts of food) blankets. Dad's tenderness towards Mom left me feeling all the more secretly resentful. *She's your wife,* I'd think to myself, *you deal with her. I can't afford to lose my focus. I can't afford to care.*

Ashamed of my cold attitude, I did my best to cultivate a shining picture of smiles and good cheer, praying my parents wouldn't twig to what I was really feeling—that I was frightened to be with them, impatient to get back to my music, anxious that I might catch whatever illness Mom had. My fear turned to helplessness, then sadness whenever I spotted the concern blotting out the usual mischievous glint in Dad's eyes or detected that extra edge in his voice when he asked me to meet with him and Mom's psychiatrist.

"Danny, it's hard for me to stay on top of all the drugs they're throwing at your mother. You and I need to let her doctor know that there can be no more screw-ups in her medications. Next time, it could kill her."

Ten years before, any fear and grief Dad felt over Mom's hospitalization had been lost on me. When you're twelve, dads don't feel fear. Dads can fix anything. Now I was too lost in my own terrors to realize that Dad's response to Mom's breakdown was pretty much the same as it had been ten years earlier. It was me who'd changed. I was torn between the two opposing principles that Dad had instilled in me. One: Hill males must be unconditional successes in their chosen profession. Two: Hill males must take care of their family, especially the females. But what happens when you have to choose between those two imperatives? What if seeing Mom daily undermined my ability to make a great record? To consider, even for a moment, that there was a choice—Mom's well-being versus my career—made me feel so torn with guilt that one day I simply stayed in bed, abandoning both my studio commitments and my mom. Unable to live with myself, I made it into the hospital later that evening, cynically timing my visit so that visiting hours would be over an hour after my arrival.

"Oh Danny, you're going to sing for me!" Mom said, her face lighting up when she saw me. I'd taken along my guitar, knowing that if I strummed and sang I wouldn't have to think of the proper things to say or how to react if Mom said something peculiar. I could also close my eyes when singing. As long as I could avoid looking at her, really looking at her, the better chance I had of pushing away those memories of ten years ago. As things turned out, I was stronger (or, as Dad had written back then, more "resilient") than I realized. As was Mom.

She recovered very quickly. She asked that I bring my guitar every visit. Sometimes I sang for her and a slew of other patients in the hospital's large social room, humbled at how something as natural as live music appeared to soothe them, and me.

I'm not sure if my music helped in Mom's healing. It was Dad who was always Mom's magic healer. But something about me singing beside her, and listening to her sing along as if she hadn't a care in the world, had a way of breaking down my dread of being swept into her vortex of madness. But more than that, Mom's straight-from-the-heart singing reminded me of how deeply I loved her. And of how much she loved me.

"You behaved just as a son's supposed to behave," Dad told me one night once Mom had returned home. "It meant the world to your mother that you went to the hospital every day."

Dad would never know how close I had come to bolting.

"Where is she?"

"She's upstairs sleeping."

"How are you doing, Dad? You look pretty worn out."

"You know, Danny, any number of external events can throw off your mother's body chemistry. Even a big social outing or a little dinner party."

What this had to do with how Dad was doing, I wasn't quite sure.

"I know that, Dad. But sometimes it feels like life and stress go together."

"Well, son, there's stress and then there's stress. When your mother's body chemistry goes haywire all of her meds become useless. That's when she can go off. Just like that." Dad clapped his hands together, the hollow smacking sound reminding me of him setting me straight in earlier days.

"Try not to excite her too much, Danny. Even funny stories that make her laugh a lot, anything that arouses her emotions suddenly, can throw her off."

Dad was letting me in on how he was doing after all. He was petrified of losing Mom. How does a husband's terror at losing his wife compare to a boy's fear of losing his mother? I could only imagine.

Since childhood I'd been exposed to myriad medical experts, all of whom took great pains to define mental illness as a disease, a specific malfunctioning or misfiring of the brain, frequently reinforcing this explanation with complex, colour-coded illustrations of two minds: one healthy, one wacko. I imagine that they thought this destigmatized the illness for me. It didn't. *Well, cancer's also a disease,* I'd think. *So what?* How does that make it any easier for the cancer victim, or the victim's circle of loved ones? Did these doctors think I was some moron? That I believed mental illness was some punishment exacted on my mom or my aunt Margaret by the likes of Satan or, worse still, God?

But the truth of what the doctors were saying clicked in within days of Mom's release from the hospital. I found it as discomfiting to see Mom go from totally crazy to totally rational as I had the reverse. That the brain could come unglued and then refasten itself so quickly forced me to realize just how fragile we all were.

"Danny, my God, are you listening to a thing I'm trying to tell you?"

Mom had been letting me have it for showing up ninety minutes late for a family dinner. And while I had been listening to her accusations, backed by a few choice examples of my selfishness, I'd also been thinking about all the different "Moms" I'd been exposed to over the years. I'd come to the conclusion that I liked this fiery and ferocious Mom most of all.

There she stood, close to a foot shorter than me, straining her neck so that her glare would catch my eyes just so, and snapped, "Can you kindly tell me what you find so amusing about keeping all of us waiting like this?"

I mumbled something about being caught up in a final mix of my soon-to-be-released single, "Hold On." Matt and I had just gone through our typical ego flexing about the level of my voice in respect to the level of his orchestration.

"It's not just dinner. Cynthia was waiting to run with you, and when you never showed up she was left to jog through that Donalda golf course in the dark. Your father would never have allowed me to be all alone in an unlit stretch of park like that at night."

"I'm really sorry, Mom."

That's all Mom was looking for. Once you'd apologized, her anger vanished and the atmosphere felt light, deliciously fresh and clean.

It had gotten to the point where no one, other than Cynthia and my family, would dare take me to task over one of my many acts of thoughtlessness. Managers, agents, publishers, recording engineers, sound and lighting crews: they all depended on me to keep touring and recording and writing so that part of whatever I earned would trickle down to them. Taking me on directly would have been like picking a fight with the boss. My growing throngs of fans treated me like some cult leader, confusing my ability to write about things they could relate to with an indication of saintliness, of existing on some higher moral plane. Still, part of me welcomed this deification, even as I understood how dangerous it could be.

Consistency. That's what I craved more than anything from my family. If I didn't love hearing Mom scold me for, among other things, spending too much time on the road and too little time with Cynthia, I did love that she wasn't in the least cowed by my recent success. With my helter-skelter schedule and the feeling that every phone call represented another surge in my career, I found myself turning to my family more and more to stay, in Dad's word, "balanced."

Dinner over, Cynthia had gone to the basement to study, Larry had busied himself packing for his return flight to UBC and Mom and I were doing the dishes.

"You're gonna laugh when you hear this, Danny, but sometimes your father and I worry that success is coming to you too fast."

"My entire life has consisted of Dad predicting I was on the road to ruin. Now you're telling me I've peaked too soon. You realize what you're saying, right? That no matter what I do or don't do, somehow I'm letting you guys down."

"I never said anything about feeling let down by you. And parents worry, that's just the way it is."

It was a relief to be back in our old familiar patterns. God forbid my parents should ever say, "Congratulations. Everything about your life is humming along perfectly. Don't change a thing." Now, that would be a lot of pressure. But even as I expected my family to keep me grounded, Dad, in his unflagging way, constantly reminded me not to confuse staying grounded with getting too comfortable.

"Don't listen to your mother," Dad warned, in reference to Mom's caution that I was working too hard. He was walking Cynthia and me out to the front porch and closing the door, so as not to be overheard. "This is the time in your life when you have to work harder than ever. You've got to strike now, while the iron's hot."

Larry, more than anyone else in my family, acted as if my success was a forgone conclusion, and that I was just being my ever-predictable self. We'd always been smart enough to make sure that our overweening competitive natures came out only in meaningless sports competitions. We knew better than to compete where it truly mattered: writing in its various forms. We understood that our talent as storytellers, whether manifested in song or prose, should never be turned into a contest, as there was simply too much Hill pride at stake. This allowed us to be each other's cheerleader; I could assume Larry would one day be a hugely successful author and he could confidently predict my future success as a singer-songwriter without either of us feeling threatened.

I'd never realized how much I'd taken my family dynamics for granted, complaining from time to time about our collective and individual foibles while coming to expect and be comforted by these same traits. Of all the members of my family, I was the one most resistant to change. I had always gone out of my way to do whatever I wanted, and my recent success made it easier to continue to ignore the stuff I had little patience and aptitude for. Karen, meanwhile, welcomed change as enthusiastically as I avoided it. This made sense. The same Don Mills that had proven to be such a surprisingly fertile environment for me—thanks to my assortment of über-motivated friends—had been a washout for my sister, a dreary desert of airless shopping malls, golf courses and female classmates whose conversational repertoire rarely deviated from shoes, purses and boys.

Eager to put Don Mills behind her, Karen had managed, given her excellent grades, to get accepted into the University of Ottawa after grade twelve, rather than the standard grade thirteen. She immediately attached herself to a new, more progressive college crowd. Attending university hundreds of miles from Toronto also gave Karen some much-needed distance from Dad. Living under Dad's roof could feel like living with a celebrity, mostly because Dad acted the part. Larry and I, thanks to our respective passions, learned as best we could how to cope with the looming shadow of Dad at an early age. Karen began to cope when she moved to Ottawa. And then, just as she started coming into herself, I became a "star," leaving Karen to feel smothered all over again.

Not that I'd clued into any of this when I met Karen for lunch in an Ottawa café the day after I'd performed two sold-out shows at the National Arts Centre. Scarcely aware of my sister's suffering when we were growing up together, my enlightenment was about to begin.

"It's a real drag a lot of the time, Danny. Everyone always coming up to me saying: 'Are you really Dan Hill's sister?' Like I'm some non-person."

Unsure of how to respond, I handed Karen the one menu allotted to our table. Barely glancing at it, Karen elaborated, "I'm sick of everyone pretending they want to be my friend, when all they want is to get to you through me."

The last person in our family to show frustration or anger, Karen's surprise reaction to my fame hit me like an unexpected blow.

She dropped a recent photo spread of me draping my arms around Prime Minister Trudeau and his wife, Margaret, next to my napkin.

"You don't even vote for Trudeau," Karen pointed out.

"What was I supposed to do? Turn Maggie and Pierre away? They showed up at my dressing room surrounded by Mounties."

"They were just using you for a photo-op."

Whew, college life was making Karen a lot more opinionated. She even looked different, sporting an outfit that looked like something Dorothy Parker might have worn: sexy yet severe, as if she was dressing for herself and not for some ogling male jerk. Her white V-neck sweater made her brown skin glow, while making me think of Dad reacting to the low neckline. She had a vivaciousness, a crackle about her, no doubt an offshoot from feeling so gloriously unshackled. For the first time, I felt guilty about being famous, as though it had crept up and bitten Karen on the backside, chaining her to our family once more. Our facial features were so similar that we could be mistaken for twins, making her instantly recognizable, to any fan with a discerning eye, as my sister. Looking for a distraction I waved the waitress over.

"Danny, I haven't even looked at the menu."

Ignoring Karen, I instructed the waitress to buy a bottle of wine for two girls sitting directly across from us, pointing and giggling in my direction. I imagined they were first-year college students away from home for the first time, with all the attendant possibilities.

"Boy, you're really enjoying this being famous thing, eh?" Karen mused. The girls' giggling increased as they toasted us. "That's pretty sexist, Danny. You know, patronizing male plying pretty young students with drinks. Do you think Cynthia would approve?"

"Fine, Karen. I'll just tell the girls that you bought the drinks."

"'Women.' That's what females over twenty are called nowadays, Danny. Unless you see them wearing bibs and being fed by their mothers."

As Karen reached for another cigarette and popped it in her mouth, daring me to disapprove, it struck me that she was the true family rebel.

"Hey Karen, when the food comes, how 'bout I swap you half my Greek salad for half your fries?"

"Since when did you become so civilized and proper? In the old days we'd just reach across the table and grab whatever food we wanted from somebody's plate."

"Not in front of Dad, we didn't."

"I'm not talking about home. But at restaurants it was a free-for-all. Now that you're hanging out with the prime minister I don't expect you'd remember our family outings."

Because Karen loaded up and fired off one of her zingers so rarely, when she did, she always hit her mark. I opted for my usual defence tactic. Teasing.

"Dad tells me you've got lots of boyfriends now." What Dad had really said was that, because the Ottawa college campus was less colour conscious (due in part to a high population of Haitian and African students), for the first time Karen was "enjoying the company of men."

"Hmmm. So you and Dad are still the family gossips, eh?"

Good deflection, I thought, before posing what seemed a fairly neutral question.

"Are you coming home for Christmas?"

"No. I'll be staying with Edmond and his family in Trois-Pistoles, Quebec."

"Have you told Dad yet?"

"Don't start with Dad, okay? He's fine with you and Cynthia living together, but the thought of me shacking up with Edmond for two weeks over Christmas has him up in arms. I'm passing along *The Female Eunuch* and de Beauvoir's *The Second Sex* for you to give to Dad once you're back in Toronto."

"I've had the hots for Germaine Greer since I wrote a book report on her in grade eleven. Though she lost a bit of her sex appeal when she wrote about how liberating it was for a woman to taste her own menstrual blood."

"You have to turn everything I say into a joke, don't you? And who don't you have the hots for?"

"Whoa there. I'm being what I've always been. The family clown."

I might have considered Karen's unlikely burst of temper a healthy sign, except that the slight wobble in her voice suggested more than just anger. Or was I the unstable one? To the point where I couldn't bear my sweet little sister growing up and offering an opinion?

Karen, competing in an ongoing Hill family movie bursting with four overbearing leads, was clearly having none of this "cute little Lena Horne" crap anymore. So much for family dynamics remaining unchanged. Certainly, Karen was hardly the first student to enter college and suddenly view the world through a new, radicalized lens. Was I jealous, threatened by her superior education, her curiosity and determination to, as Dad might put it, "expand her horizons"? But the way she swung from Malcolm vs. Martin, to separatism vs. federalism, to Dad's vs. my chauvinism as though, if I didn't fall into line with her views, life might just as well be over, reminded me of the one other person who used to carry on in such an intense manner, before she . . . I didn't dare finish the thought.

"Karen, I'm not about to be drawn into an argument with you on the reasons why Zora Neale Hurston's books aren't included in any college curriculum. By now you know I try never to participate in a contest I might lose."

"Christ, Danny. You're even patronizing like Dad."

"What do I have to be patronizing about? I know nothing about nothing except singing and writing songs."

"You've always known what you've wanted. You with your famous killer instincts, unable to see past your next guitar chord. Growing up with you was like living with a ghost."

Ahhh. That's what felt forced about this lunch. About this new, tougher Karen. Not so much that she was opinionated and angry. But that she was angry at me.

"Danny, you dropped out of our family long before you'd physically left home."

I wanted to tell Karen that I wasn't as tough and selfish as I made myself out to be. That I loved her. At the moment, however, I was having a tough time warming to her.

"Lunch is on me, Karen," I announced.

As the two of us approached the cash register the waiter announced that there would be no charge for our meal.

"You mean it's on the house?" Karen asked enthusiastically, as though she'd just won something. How refreshing, to see her so excited by something so trivial.

"Nope. The two young ladies paid your bill."

Karen greeted the news with a smirk.

"You're something else, Danny."

I grabbed hold of Karen's hand and we headed to her apartment. Glancing down at our interlocking fingers, I couldn't get over our contrasting skin tones. There it was, staring back up at me, the defining difference between us. Not only that her skin was several shades darker than mine, but that she thought much more deeply about her skin colour, its emotional and psychic ramifications, than I ever did—at least consciously.

"What is it, Danny? Was it all my teasing? I'm only getting you back for all those years you tricked me into eating insects."

"Actually Karen, it was grabbing hold of your hand so automatically. It made me think of Dad, always carefully steering Mom out of whatever restaurant they'd finished eating at."

"If you really want to know, Danny, this is how Dad takes Mom's hand. I know 'cause he grabs mine the same way." As Karen demonstrated, her smile returned, bashful and adorable.

Watching Karen leap up the stairs, tossing "See ya, brother!" over her shoulder as her front door swung shut, it finally dawned on me that Karen had always been independent, much more so than I. I simply hadn't bothered to pay attention. My wilful blindness (and deafness) had started around the time Karen was thirteen, when she said, "I wish I'd been born Blacker. Then people would know my race. I hate all the questions about whether I'm East Indian or half this or part that."

How dare she? It was okay to talk about what it meant to be Black from a political standpoint. But to even allude to any personal feelings or ambivalence about your own racial background (your own inherited and individual shade of colour at that) was wholly unacceptable. You were who and what you were without question, speculation or uncertainty. Dad had never come right out and explicitly said this, it was just one of those things he'd made clear, in that so obvious it didn't have to be explained way of his. There I was, hiding beneath my stocking cap as Karen brazenly announced to the family that she wished she lived in a country where biracial backgrounds were far more commonplace— a country where one-eighth or one-quarter or one-half or one drop Black meant, unequivocally, all Black.

I for one wasn't going to admit that I sometimes wished for the opposite miracle, that one day—presto—my skin would be Donny Osmond white, my eyes Paul Newman blue, my lips Sean Connery thin. Unlike me, Karen had the guts to take the political out of being Black and make it personal. Which put pressure on me to own up to my very contradictory feelings, when I was just a confused adolescent who wished all this race stuff would simply disappear in a pretty cloud of guitar chords and love songs.

So where did all this leave me now? As I strolled along the Rideau Canal, nodding at people who recognized me, I wondered if I was a complete fake, playing the part of the great new Canadian singer-songwriter who'd sidestepped the whole race thing by flinging himself into making his mark on the world. Did I really think that pop-star success meant a free pass on the inner contortions of racial angst? While Larry's university fiction sparkled with the influence of Richard Wright and James Baldwin, my singing voice came closest to resembling Don Henley or Elton John, much as I longed to sound like Marvin Gaye or Donny Hatahway. Had I become the family's white sheep? Was this part of Karen's anger at me? Was this part of my anger at myself? There was no easy answer. My solution was to shut out the questions, the way I'd tried my best, as a teenager, to shut out my sister's ideas, confusing my refusal to listen to her opinions with her not having any opinions at all.

CHAPTER 18

Hit Song and Heartbreak

n the fall of '76, my second album, *Hold On,* was released internationally. My earlier concerns about running into a "sophomore slump"
proved to be ill-founded; within a few months the record's sales
exceeded that of my first album, soaring past gold status in Canada (over
fifty thousand units) as well as steadily building up a solid fan base for me
around the world.

The quick success of *Hold On* meant that I was now selling out
two-to-three-thousand-seat concert halls across Canada—the same
venues I'd played less than a year before as an opening act. Between
my performing income and my record and publishing royalties, I was
making more money that I could possibly spend, even if I'd had the
time to spend it. Because I'd recently incorporated, the cheques weren't
even written in my name, making the money seem all the more unreal.
"Out of Control" (the name of my company, after a line from my first
hit), the royalty statement would say, with enough zeroes following

the first number that I had to read it over a few times to determine the amount.

There was little doubt that Dad's conflicted attitude about money had rubbed off on me. In the following letter he wrote to his father in 1957, I can almost picture him twitching with pride as he talks about his raise, all the while trying his best to sound nonchalant:

> I shall be making well over $6,000 (annually) starting Jan 1, and though I do not consider myself wealthy, I do feel it is enough to support my family adequately . . . our needs and tastes are simple. We are not great entertainers, liquor buyers, or fashion plates. We [realize] credit buying is a necessary economic evil in our society—we treat it as such and buy through it sparingly. I think that there is little doubt that Donna and I are both committed socialists.

Reminding his parents in a letter written six years later that his attitude about frivolous spending hadn't changed, Dad complained that he took Mom's father, George Bender, "out to dinner at a rather high class place—flaming desserts and all that—and ended up with a $37.50 dollar dinner and wine bill . . . No damn meal is worth that much."

By the age of six, I'd taken to modelling Dad's miserly ways, inspiring Mom, in a 1960 letter to Grandma May, to write: "Dobbie received the five dollars on his birthday and decided to save it in his piggy bank . . . he gets a small allowance now—5 cents a week—which has made him very money conscious. He hordes it like a little miser, then finally decides to buy something—like a popsicle! So he'll hang on to the $5 for a good long time."

At twenty-two, still very much the miserly son of a self-proclaimed socialist, I tried to ameliorate any traces of guilt by spending extravagantly on everyone but myself. Five-star dining, colour TVs (Dad believed it wasn't déclassé to own a colour TV if you received it as a present), boom boxes the size of a small planet, jewellery, impulsive cash handouts—all my generosity bought me a new sense of power. The financial arrangement my managers had set up provided me with the comforting illusion that whatever I was spending, or making, had no real bearing on me. Every penny I earned flowed through them. After they took their twenty-five percent gross commission, they paid all my bills and gave me spending money in the way that a parent might dole out a weekly allowance to a ten-year-old.

"An artist shouldn't be distracted by such common tasks as writing cheques, balancing bank accounts and reading over Visa statements," they'd explain. Sounded good to me—especially the "artist" part. That my managers and I shared the same accountant and lawyer made eminent sense according to their logic, since no one but music-business insiders could properly grasp the arcane intricacies of such dramatic cash flow and the related need for tax shelters.

The early years of pop music stardom follow a cookie-cutter pattern: each rising star, while believing he or she is undergoing a highly unique and individual process, is living through a set sequence of events so similarly ordered and graphed as to be largely interchangeable with the next star's career. More to the point, in pop music, any window of opportunity is extremely narrow and the resulting success is usually fleeting. This means you have no choice but to squeeze out every drop of fame before it runs dry, taking on the workload and pressure of a dozen people. In my case, that meant hitting two hundred markets a year, performing and media touring, all the while coaxing enough songs out of my addled brain to meet my recording and music publishing commitments. Saying no to any work opportunity wasn't an option. If my managers told me to do something—fly to Saskatoon on a moment's notice to do a highly publicized benefit concert, tape for ten consecutive sixteen-hour days at CTV over Christmas for some middle-of-the-road music special, perform two weeks at L.A.'s prestigious Troubadour while absorbing a loss of several thousand dollars in expenses—I obeyed. Believing that at any moment my inexplicable success could be stolen from me, that one reckless "no" might topple everything I'd worked so long and hard for, I frequently pushed myself until my voice gave out. My body was telling me something that I was otherwise incapable of admitting: there's only so much you can do before everything starts to break down.

And then there were the occasions when back-to-back contrasting gigs proved to be more psychologically discombobulating than physically taxing. Nothing scrambled my ego more than selling out Toronto's Massey Hall only to fly to Boston the following night for a week of opening for singer-songwriter Ronee Blakley, in a tiny coffee-house called Passims. (As well as being an esteemed and quirky singer-songwriter, Blakley was a successful actress who had starred in Robert Altman's classic *Nashville*.)

What planet have I landed on? I'd wonder, staring out from my tiny stage into a hostile crowd of highly vocal lesbians. "You make me wanna be a father..." I'd croon, expecting, as only a cocksure twenty-two-year-old with a couple of gold records under his belt could, that my voice would convert these women into swooning Doris Days. But instead I'd be welcomed by hisses—and "Get off the stage, loser" or "Shut the fuck up, dickwad."

I found the occasional nightmare gig easy to laugh off, since my career remained on a steady upswing. Tomorrow meant another city, another adventure, leaving yesterday to be moulded into another "road story." Sure, I worked my ass off, but I also managed to have a hell of a lot of fun.

The most fun I had was phoning Dad from the road and breathlessly informing him of my latest cheque, or gold record, or sold-out concert. If some high-rolling performers could never buy enough crap, I could never tire of strutting and preening for my dad. I felt compelled to win him over anew every day. Interestingly, Dad's studied and cynical analysis of North American society, with all its class stratifications, consumerist brainwashing and racist underpinnings, didn't extend to pop music success—at least not to his son's pop music success. And I loved that about him. Dad honestly believed, as I did, that I'd continue to earn huge whacks of money and bang out hit records indefinitely. Dad's fixed musical point of reference was sustainable geniuses like Basie, Ellington and Ella, from a different, less confectionary and disposable era, unlike typical current hit-and-run pop acts like the Bay City Rollers or David Cassidy. While my career was flying, Dad never spoke of his former, decade-long dismissal of my musical dreams. Nor did I. Now was the time for me to play the big wheel and for him to respond in kind—advising me of my corresponding financial and moral commitments to the family. Not that I needed any convincing. I'd offer him five grand if he lost twenty pounds and hand the cash over to him once he did (though he gained it back quickly); fly his sister Doris and her husband into Toronto to surprise him and Mom on their twenty-fifth wedding anniversary (along with whisking my brother from an Algonquin canoe camp by private plane); donate countless thousands to the organizations he believed in, like the Canadian Civil Liberties Association; and stage costly benefit concerts for whatever left-wing cause or minority group he felt most deserving.

I leaned on Dad for support once the local music critics started nipping at my heels. He, of all people, knew what it felt like to be burned by the press. "Don't worry, Danny," he'd say when I'd complain about some reviewer describing my songs as "callow," "most people don't even know what 'callow' means."

But more than Dad's new enthusiasm over my recent success, it was his naïveté, his total lack of understanding of this new world I'd become a part of, that I found most reassuring. To my boast that I'd sold out two shows a night for two weeks straight at New York's Bitter End, or gossiped with Elton John who'd shown up to say hi between a couple of my musical sets at the University of Guelph, Dad's response would always be something like: "And your album's sold out at the Don Mills Plaza. I promised the people working at the record store there that you'd drop off an autographed poster for them." Elton, Margaret and Pierre—that kind of craven name-dropping was lost on Dad. I may as well been talking about touring on Mars. Don Mills, however, was something tangible, something real and immediate.

In the spring of 1977 I was in Los Angeles meeting with my label, 20th Century Records, and my publishing company, ATV Music, before recording my third album. At the time, the U.S. president of ATV Music was Sam Trust. Closing in on forty, Sam had a severity about him, his thick eyebrows perpetually set in a half-scowl as he walked by you, his face buried in some royalty printout. He'd signed me through the McCauleys (since they published my music) in 1976, paying healthy cash advances to administer my songs internationally. One Friday morning in early April, a few days before I was scheduled to return to Toronto to start cutting my new record, Sam summoned me into his office.

"Dan, I've just signed Barry Mann and Cynthia Weil to a publishing deal. Along with Gerry Goffin and Carole King, they're one of the most successful songwriting teams in the history of American pop music."

This was why I'd had to get out of bed so early, to hear Sam talk about other songwriters?

"Let me be straight with you. You're an incredible lyricist. And Barry writes better melodies than anyone. I'd like the two of you to try writing together."

I agreed, but Sam could tell I wasn't terribly enthusiastic with his suggestion. Up to that point, all the songs I'd recorded I'd written on my own. From where I sat, I didn't need to write with anyone. But as I glanced over the endless list of hit songs Barry Mann had co-written— "You've Lost That Lovin' Feeling," "On Broadway," "Kicks," "We've Gotta Get Out of This Place," "(You're My) Soul and Inspiration"—I knew, if nothing else, it would be worthwhile meeting him.

"Barry loves your voice," Sam added. "And your song 'Hold On,' which is getting lots of airplay on the soft rock station here, is one of his favourites right now."

The next day I met Barry at the ATV offices on Sunset and Vine. ATV was situated on one of the top floors of what was then referred to as the Motown Building or the Black Tower. Motown Records, along with dozens of other record labels, publishing companies and various music business enterprises, had offices there. Many times I'd ride the elevator standing next to Michael Jackson's dad, who'd be cussing the *National Enquirer* or *Herald* for inventing something about his son, his flagrant fury reminding me of my dad fuming about being slammed in the *Globe and Mail*. On my way to meet Barry Mann, I ran into my old nemesis from my RCA days, Tim Bayers, who was then working Bing Crosby's movie song catalogue. Bayers was all smiles now, aware of all I'd accomplished in the last few years. I extricated myself from Bayers's torrent of compliments and escaped into the ATV Music offices, where I found Barry Mann waiting for me in a tiny music room stashed at the back of a long hallway.

After the obligatory "You're great," "No, you're great" compliments, Barry got down to business. As he puffed through three packs of cigarettes, he rattled off dozens of criss-crossing musical ideas intended for me to write lyrics to, seemingly on the fly. I had no idea people wrote like this, hurled together in blind-date fashion, mixing words and music into a finished song like mad chemists. I still clung to the notion that songwriting could only come from a pure, inspired place—sexual torment had always worked for me. Feeling as if I'd stepped into the wrong party, I told Barry I wasn't experienced at writing on the spot and, by way of excusing myself, handed him a lyric that I spotted lying on the bottom of my guitar case.

"I'm not sure if it's any good. I never wrote any music to it," I lied, afraid that if he knew it had once been an entire song he might think I was giving him one of my castoffs and take offence. "If you can do something with it, great. But don't feel any obligation if you hate it."

Then I wandered into the reception area to call a cab. By the time I was off the phone, Barry was standing in front of me, smiling. "I think I got something for the chorus," he said, almost apologetically. I followed him into the hovel-like piano room and stood just behind him as he sang, plangently, his new melody and chords to "Sometimes When We Touch."

I was so used to my original music that Barry's melody sounded overly ornate, like something Barry Manilow would come up with. (In fact, Manilow recorded "Sometimes" and released it as a single in 1997.) "Yeah, Barry. That sounds really, ah, nice," was my stammered attempt at diplomacy. Barry, disheartened, nonetheless told me he'd finish writing the music to my verses and bridge and get back to me.

The next day, Barry tracked me down by phone at the posh Polo Lounge in the Beverly Hills Hotel, where I was breakfasting with my managers and the president of my U.S. label. "Phone call for you, Mr. Hill," announced one of the perfectly attired waiters, approaching me (in my jeans and ratty lumberjack shirt) as though I were a visiting dignitary. He fussily handed me over to another, white-haired, septuagenarian waiter, who escorted me to their plush private phone room. *Surely, this is someone's idea of a practical joke,* I thought.

"You gotta hear this, Dan," Barry said. Then his finished music flowed out of the Polo Lounge's candy-floss-pink guest phone. The song was starting to grow on me. "I've doubled up the chorus," Barry told me, as I hemmed and hawed on the other end of the phone, nervous that any comment I offered about his music might sound unworthy of all his effort. "So you need to add three lyric phrases to go along with the second half of the chorus."

"Okay," I said, like a student promising his English teacher that he'd fill in the gaps of a half-written essay. I had no idea what had just transpired. My original music to "Sometimes" had been funereal, making it impossible for a listener to wade through my turgid chord changes and actually hear—and, more importantly, feel—the lyrics. But Barry's gripping verse melody, offset by the light, ingeniously singsongy release of his chorus, gave these same words a kind of soaring majesty that made them instantly (and to some ears, excruciatingly) memorable.

"Before we got together to write, I studied your first two albums," Barry explained, when I dropped by his newly purchased Beverly Hills mansion the next day to record a work tape of our new song.

In effect, Barry was telling me that he'd done his homework on me. His assignment had been to analyze my range and what melodies and series of notes brought out my vocal personality to its best advantage. What I thought had taken Barry a few minutes to write had really taken him hours of preparation. Those hours of preparation had further benefited from twenty years of writing and rewriting scores upon scores of hits (and at least ten times as many misses), learning through the process how to refine and improve his natural gift. And here I'd always thought genius was a genetic fluke, a secret switch turned on in your brain at birth that made you mysteriously and effortlessly superior.

In a most unexpected way, Dad's constant warning that I would need higher education to succeed in life proved to be absolutely true. But neither he nor I could have known that my advanced studies would come from collaborating with songwriters whose abilities were far more developed than mine. Had it not been for Barry Mann, and the impact of our first collaboration, I would never have been embraced by and informally schooled by a world of elite songwriters, artists and producers. But that came later. In the immediate future, my first collaboration with Barry would become my first international hit single, and it would be all I could do to ride the wave, barely holding on as it swept me around the world.

From strictly a pop star point of view, 1977 and 1978 represent the zenith of my career. They also happened to be the darkest, saddest years of my life. If the sudden explosion of my career was in fact the culmination of ten years of steadily writing songs, singing and practising guitar every day, and performing in front of anyone who would listen, then the flip side was also true; the stunning evisceration of my personal life that appeared to take place over one terrible night was really the result of a decade of separating sex and romantic love without understanding where that would lead me.

In the fall of 1977, I showed up at my parents' front door in the middle of the night, my face swollen and covered with tears. When Dad answered the door, bleary-eyed from being awakened, wearing his red-and-blue checked bathrobe, I declared that I was moving back in with them.

"Don't worry," I began, a picture of false courage. "You'll hardly know I'm here. I'll be on the road touring for the next year."

"Tell me what happened, son."

"Cynthia and I just broke up."

As Mom tread cautiously down the stairs, Dad led us into the kitchen. For the next couple of hours I spilled the unseemly details. It had all started, or more precisely, ended, six hours earlier. I'd just finished playing Cynthia a new song I'd written, where the narrator had discovered that his lover had been unfaithful. When the song ended, Cynthia looked as though she'd been ambushed.

"I'm sorry," she whispered.

"What do you mean?"

"Oh nothing . . . really . . . I just meant that—"

Cynthia, assuming that my latest song meant that I'd somehow caught on to her affair, had just blown her secret. She stumbled badly through a few flailing minutes of reflexive denial, but it was an obvious stall, a chance for her to buy some time before our dialogue reached the inevitable "How could you, and for how long, and how many times?" stage.

"It only happened once. When you were performing in Whitehorse. We went up north to his cottage for the weekend. Afterwards I swore to him that this could never happen again."

"Oh, that's reassuring."

"He told me that you've probably had hundreds of women on the road. That there isn't a singer alive who'd be able to walk away from all the temptation out there. Danny, you can tell me. Whatever you've done, it's only natural."

"Tell you what? Just like you to try to turn this back on me."

"Don't yell. You're starting to scare me."

What did she expect? For me to throw her and her new lover—Jesus, I'd introduced them—a party of congratulations?

"Danny, it's your turn now to talk. You don't have to lie anymore."

Did she think that we could casually swap our stories of unfaithfulness, cancel out our wrongs and start over with a clean slate? No way I was going to make it that easy for her.

"C'mon, Danny. It's not like you to clam up like this. You're the one who always taught me to open up, to not hold back."

Cynthia's voice trailed off, giving way to what appeared to be a sympathetic smile. I was dimly aware of being somewhere else. Lost, in a totally unfamiliar state: shaking, hurting, beyond angry, all I wanted was to strike out.

"Fourteen."

"What?"

"That's how many there've been since we've been together. Fourteen."

Cynthia laughed, thinking at first that I was joking. I remember when her smile faded. When it finally hit her that this was no joke. How her face turned hard and cold. Good, now she knew just what it felt like. And that's when things got ugly. The kind of ugly that I'd never known was possible.

As Cynthia's accusations bounced off and fed into mine, I was dimly aware that we were effectively dismantling, insult by insult, confession by confession, eight years of our lives. Not only had we lost each other, we'd lost something fundamental within ourselves.

It's hard to know how long we carried on like this, our name-calling exchanges interrupted by demanding, and recounting, specific details of the most masochistic nature. It was like being in a prolonged car wreck, or waking up after being knocked unconscious; the time spent in that kind of altered state is impossible to calculate once you've come to and realized you're actually still alive.

There was only one question left for me to ask.

"Do you love him?"

"Yes."

I picked up everything in the living room I could get my hands on—books, framed photographs, records, chairs—and started throwing them at the wall. When there was nothing left to hurl, with my voice screamed out, I emerged from whatever spell had possessed me to see Cynthia crying, cowering, covering her head, in the corner of the room. The living room looked like the scene of a botched robbery, objects scattered and shattered everywhere. That was when I knew it was over. I'd loved Cynthia for eight years. As a teenager, I never dreamed she'd love me. As a young man, I never believed she could fall out of love with me.

I was wrong on both counts.

I stood up from my parents' kitchen table and helped myself to a glass of water. Dad had barely stirred as he'd listened to me. Mom, aside from clasping Dad's hand and issuing the odd gasp of disbelief, had remained unnervingly still.

"Well, you can't accuse me of being boring. Just think, Dad, had I followed your advice and gone to university, how much simpler life would be for me right now."

"How much simpler life would be for all of us," Mom corrected.

This was the first time I'd ever opened up to my parents about my personal life. Had part of my intention been to shock them, to expose what I believed was the vilest part of me, in the hope that they would still find it in their hearts to accept me? But they didn't appear surprised, only sad. Had they somehow known all along that sooner or later I'd be showing up at their front door in the dead of night, broken and crying, assailing them with what I considered to be the worst story of all time? I pointed out to Mom that at least my cheating had been on the road, with strangers. Cynthia's transgressions had taken place with a person I'd known for ten years. Surely, I rationalized, that was way worse. Mom cleared her throat, released Dad's hand and said, in a wry tone, "That's the way it always is, Danny. Couples cheat with someone within their social circle, not total strangers."

Mom's slap-in-the-face logic was the last thing I wanted to hear.

"Is there something wrong with me?" I asked, directing my question at Dad, pretty much pleading for his exoneration, as Cynthia's accusations of "sex freak" gonged in my head.

"No, son, there's nothing wrong with you," Dad answered, adding impishly, "At least you weren't the dog that my old roommate Calvin Jackson was. He'd sleep with anyone—could've been as big and ugly as a pickup truck. Wouldn't have made a damned bit of difference."

"Dan, really, what does that have to do with anything?" Mom asked, now upset with both of us.

Dad sided with me. What twenty-three-year-old, red-blooded male touring the United States with a "sexy as all get out" hit record would be immune to the sudden clamour of female attention?

"Trust me, son. This is a stage you'll grow out of."

"I certainly hope so, Danny, for everybody's sake," Mom said.

"Whatever you do," Dad warned, "don't apologize, cry and beg forgiveness. It'll make you look weak. And, anyway, talk about the pot calling the kettle black," he said, his face tightening. "She's in no position to take the moral high ground."

Mom took Cynthia's side. If I'd spent more time at home and been less obsessed with music, neither she nor I would have been exposed to so much opportunity and temptation. Now it was time for me to show Cynthia that she came first, not my career. The one thing my parents agreed on was that Cynthia and I, given our eight-year history, would probably get through this mess.

Throughout the fall, I ignored Dad's advice and followed Mom's: pleading, sobbing, threatening suicide (Cynthia phoned my manager one night and demanded he go into my hotel room and take away my sleeping pills) and unwittingly doing everything in my power to drive her away. Following a brutal phone conversation with Cynthia after a concert in Moncton, New Brunswick, Bernie Fiedler tracked down Gordon Lightfoot by phone, persuading him to extend me five thousand dollars credit so I could lease his Learjet that night. I had it in my head that my only chance of reconciliation with Cynthia would be to see her immediately. I should have listened to Lightfoot's immortal advice after he wished me a safe flight: "I'll lend you the money, Dan, but take it from someone who knows, there ain't no woman alive worth spending five thousand dollars on."

Several hours and a thousand miles later, stoned on sleeping pills I'd stolen back from my manager's toiletries, I dragged myself up the stairs to Cynthia's apartment. Though I'd officially moved out weeks before, I still had a key. Had I phoned her in advance or banged on the front door, she would never have let me in. After giving Cynthia the fright of her life, I collapsed into a strewn-out mess on the floor, apologizing, promising anything that flooded into my jangled brain: I'd change; I'd never so much as look at another woman again; I'd stop touring—all the crap that people say (and actually believe, at that moment, anyway) when they know they're on the way out. Cynthia wasn't buying any of it. It wasn't until I threatened to throw myself down the stairs that she relented and said she'd take me back. We spent the next forty-eight hours together, scarcely leaving the bedroom. We both knew it was over.

Then I flew back to the Maritimes to resume my tour. Aside from two extremely unexpected and awkward run-ins, I never saw Cynthia again.

That September night in 1977, as I fell apart in my parents' kitchen, I reached out for their help, their understanding, their forgiveness and their love as though my life depended on it. And quite possibly it did. I look back at that night of awful truth, of confession and counter-confession with Cynthia, as the defining moment, the major turning point in my life.

Trying night after night, month after month to make sense of what had happened to me, to Cynthia, to us, only left me more confused, convinced that nothing in life mattered, because when you boiled it all down, there was no logical pattern or purpose to anything. What did those five years of letters and visits, of shared dreams and longings, followed by two years of living together, mean? What did anything mean?

Of course there are times when you learn things even as you throw up your walls and pretend that nothing's seeping through. I was learning what my dad had learned, back when he was eighteen and about to be drafted for goofing off at work. That there were consequences.

Not unlike Dad and his first, botched marriage, I pretended that Cynthia and I never really happened. Furthermore, in keeping with the Hill family tradition of certain subjects remaining taboo, it was tacitly understood that no one was to mention Cynthia's name again. This made recovery easier for me in the short run, while in the long run I remained haunted and torn for many years.

From September 1977 till August 1978, whenever I wasn't touring I lived with my parents, finding refuge and healing in our old Don Mills home. From a career perspective, those eleven months were the busiest and the most exhilarating I've ever experienced. I won three Juno awards, was nominated for a Grammy and received a publishing advance big enough to retire on. I bought a house for $150,000 (where I continue to live to this day) writing out the cheque as casually as if I were buying a new pair of socks. Three days of the week, I toured with Art Garfunkel as his opening act. The other four days I'd perform two-hour shows all over North America. Often the schedules were so wacky—New Orleans one day, where it was ninety-five degrees and humid, Winnipeg the next, where it was thirty below zero—that Fiedler and I would show up at private airports and bribe pilots into flying us from one town to another. I'd complete a show in Chattanooga, Tennessee, fly to New York, swing over to Europe on the Concorde, blitz the media, perform live on shows like *Top of the Pops* (getting Andy Gibb's starlet girlfriend's phone number while poor Andy was on set singing), and then Concorde back to New York and catch a flight to Cleveland, barely in time for my weekend shows with Garfunkel.

One memory, however, stands out more than everything else during those eleven months: returning to my parents' home for a three-day break and finding a huge square of white bristol board glued to my bedroom door. Written on it in sloppy block letters was "Welcome home Danny, we're proud of you. Love, Mom and Dad." The innocence, the simplicity of those words stood in such contrast to all the awards and adulation. I stood in front of my bedroom door and stared at that note for a long time. This was Dad's work.

I didn't reach out to Dad for support and advice till I'd hit my twenties. Till I was rich and famous, and badly damaged. But I more than made up for it after that. I'd lost my heart. But I'd gained a father.

CHAPTER 19

Guns and Lawsuits

"The McCauleys didn't pick up your option. Do you know what that means?" Bernie Solomon, my entertainment lawyer, was asking me a question that he was clearly dying to answer himself. He was sitting sandwiched between the two other Bernies in my life, Fiedler and Finkelstein.

"Bingo. You're free," Solomon declared, like some Supreme Court judge summarily dismissing all charges. "Now you can make direct record deals with labels without the McCauleys scooping half your royalties. You can set up your own publishing company so that you own your songs and don't have to give away such a huge chunk of your songwriting income."

"Why wouldn't the McCauleys pick up my option when I owe them one last album?" I asked. At this point, 20th Century Records was funding all my recording costs, leaving the McCauleys with the enviable job of raking in the considerable publishing and recording royalties that this fifth and final album in their contract would generate.

"It's simple," Fiedler explained. "The McCauleys forgot to renew your contract. This proves what I've been trying to tell you over and over again. They're incompetent."

"Their forgetting to pick up your option speaks to the core issue here," said Finkelstein, the brightest and most volatile Bernie. "It shows they're in way over their heads with you. Constantly messing up and late on your royalty statements, begging us to help get money owed them and you from the record and publishing companies. We're sick of doing their job. We've been carrying them for too long."

Solomon, knowing that Finkelstein couldn't talk about the McCauleys for more than a minute before losing his temper, took over. "The McCauleys buried themselves here. They're the ones who didn't renew your option—it's not like you tried to find a way out. They handed it to you on a silver platter."

Finkelstein's bloodshot eyes bore down on me as he coolly summarized the last five years of my career: after four years of remarkable success, I was now, in 1979, caught in a freefall, in danger of losing all the momentum I'd taken such pains to build. Russ Regan, the man who'd signed and championed me at 20th Century Records, had parted ways with the label and then, a month into the release of my long-awaited follow-up single to "Sometimes When We Touch" (my self-penned "All I See Is Your Face," the lead song to my fourth and upcoming album), 20th Century had fired all its radio promo guys. After bulleting to number forty-one on the Billboard Hot 100 singles chart (and selling a few hundred thousand 45s over that month), "All I See Is Your Face" had quickly nosedived. Although the song hit the top of the U.S. adult contemporary charts (known as the middle-of-the-road or MOR charts in the seventies), generating plenty of airplay dollars and an ASCAP award for one of the most-played songs of the year, it did little to alter the perception of many in the music industry that my career was finished. Finkelstein wrapped up his doom-and-gloom scenario accordingly: "The only chance you have to save your career is to ditch the McCauleys and buy your way out of 20th Century Records— which may mean close to a million—and sign with a huge major, hoping their advance will cover your cash buyout."

"A million?" I echoed. That I could be bought and sold for a fixed amount of money bothered me even more than the amount of money in question.

Solomon smiled and opened up a box of expensive cigars, offering them around like Belgian chocolates. Then he said, "Danny, this will be the wisest investment of your life. 20th Century is a sinking vessel. If the Beatles signed with them and released a comeback album, 20th would find a way to fuck it up."

Finkelstein mashed his unlit cigar into a flattened mess in an over-sized ashtray before saying, "As it is now, Dan, no major label with the heft of a Columbia or Warner Brothers Records is gonna touch you if you're still signed to the McCauleys' production label. Too many people in the mix. Too many fingers in the pie, diluting the profits. And without a major label behind you, you're history."

As I shifted uncomfortably in Solomon's thousand-dollar leather chair, Fiedler leaned over and slapped my back. "Danny, my buddy, the McCauleys have made a ton of dough off you. Their great-grandchildren will continue to be cashing your royalty cheques long after you're dead and buried. But once your contract expires with us, a year from now, we'll never see another dime from you. Even though we're the ones who've worked night and day to break your career wide open."

"I was the one who introduced you to Sam Trust and got you signed to ATV Music," Solomon said, forgetting that he'd already told me this dozens of times. "Then Sam teamed you up with Barry Mann and now you have a song you can retire on."

But without the McCauleys financing and producing my first album, ATV Music would have never heard my music in the first place, let alone signed me and introduced me to Barry Mann. I knew better than to mention this, as it would have been akin to dropping a lit match into a vat of gasoline. The meeting finally ended with Fiedler, the Bernie I felt closest to, getting in the last word: "Young Danny, what's the financial incentive for us to continue working with you if you don't walk away from the McCauleys?"

When it came to musical decisions, which lyric over which chord progression, which song to select as that crucial first single, I never hesitated. Business choices were another matter. Feeling as though my brain were being squeezed with a clamp, I'd make a decision, change my mind, get flustered, shift positions once more and continue in this manic fashion until all my options circled around in my head, leaving me all the more indecisive. Five years earlier, when I'd been forced to choose between the McCauleys and RCA, I'd hemmed and hawed for several months, even though I understood in my heart that the McCauleys were clearly the only choice. Now I had to make a far more difficult decision within the next twenty-four hours, one in which there was no hard and fast correct option.

Much as I wished otherwise, the McCauleys were not some faceless corporation like RCA, where a contract loophole could be exploited with cool objectivity. And the more I tried to examine every point of view and agenda, starting with the McCauleys' perspective, and then the Bernies' (collectively and individually), the more I could see that everyone had legitimate frustrations and grievances.

Nothing got under my managers' skin more than the McCauleys owning my copyrights. I was the only act the Bernies had signed that hadn't given up his publishing, or at least part of it, to them. This drove them crazy. But though they were loath to admit it now, I'd actually approached the Bernies for management in 1973, before I'd signed with the McCauleys—and they'd turned me down. It wasn't until eighteen months later, when I was all over Canadian radio with "You Make Me Want to Be" (a song the Bernies had heard back in '73, in demo form), signed to GRT Records and published by the McCauleys that they'd offered to manage me.

Connections are a funny thing: too slippery to pin down to just one contact here or critical business decision there. Countless elements and people have to coalesce in order to hatch a hugely successful pop music career. As I traced out on a piece of paper who was responsible for my steps up the career ladder, I realized just how complicated and multifaceted the star machinery process was: (1) a family-financed record led to (2) a Canadian record deal, resulting in (3) a Canadian hit single, which brought in (4) high-powered management, who set up touring and media exposure and created the buzz for (5) a dream U.S. record deal, which opened the door to (6) a huge publishing deal, which produced (7) a mega-hit song, a song so big that it threatened to become a standard.

And before I could say "jackpot" I'd become the latest pop star. And before everyone in my circle could say "royalties," anybody connected to me, whether tangential or indispensable, came out of the woodwork to claim sole credit for my "sudden success" and demand financial compensation.

From 1975 to 1979, as my records and publishing continued to generate greater and greater income, the angrier the Bernies became at the McCauleys—and, consequently, the more paranoid and resentful the McCauleys became of the Bernies. Naturally, if the McCauleys were out of the picture, the Bernies' commissions from my royalties would increase. Better still, from their point of view, it might allow them access to my publishing. And if the Bernies were out of the picture, I might be more open and malleable to any future recording contracts the McCauleys might offer me, as well as being more susceptible to their influence on everything to do with my career.

Throughout the seventies, as my career had soared, I'd formed an unhealthy dependence on the Bernies. And now that I was in the midst of my first career setback, my dependence had turned to clinginess. Much as I'd fought hard to resist my father's dominance, I found standing up to the Bernies extremely difficult. Always going out of my way to avoid confrontation, I'd spent most of my life getting whatever I wanted in a roundabout, undercover manner. But it was difficult to be sneaky with the Bernies, since everything in my life, be it money, bills, mail, phone records, transportation arrangements, even my driver's licence renewal, was handled by them. As a teenager, I was able to stand up to my father because if I didn't, my music career would have never seen the light of day. But I saw my situation with the Bernies as being the exact opposite, meaning that I was afraid if I stood up to them they might lose interest in my career.

On a personal level, I had far more in common with the McCauleys than the Bernies. I'd played hockey with Matt, I was the first person he'd phoned when he'd "gone all the way" with his girlfriend (even though I'd hated him for telling me this at the time), he'd been the one who solved my studio stage fright by placing a photo of Cynthia on my music stand when I'd been struggling to sing "You Make Me Wanna Be" with the right passion. Sure, Matt and I sometimes felt as if we hated each other. But only because we'd invested so much—our dreams, our talent, our future—in each other. That my dad was the only other person I was known to sometimes hate as deeply as Matt spoke volumes about the intensity of our relationship.

This is not to suggest that my relationship with the two Bernies was strictly business. Fiedler had been there for me after my bust-up with Cynthia, watching over me like an anxious mother as I threatened to go bonkers under the combined stress of sudden international stardom and a shattered heart. On more than a few nights, he had sat at the foot of my bed as I lay rocking in a tight ball under the hotel bedsheets.

"Danny, my buddy. You'll get through this. You won't always feel this bad."

London. Amsterdam. L.A. Frankfurt. Few and far between were the cities where I didn't wake him, begging to talk, unable to cope with the pain I was going through alone, in some strange hotel room, in yet another foreign country. Fiedler would always listen.

There was also much to admire about Finkelstein. No one worked harder or fought more fiercely on behalf of his artists. Like Bayers, he blew up if you disagreed with him on anything. But unlike Bayers, he passionately believed in what he was doing and whom he was doing it for. And he backed up his passion with results.

Beyond the hand-holding, I viewed the Bernies as the gatekeepers to my career, the ones in charge of taking me further or at least sustaining my current level of pop stardom. I lived day to day, minute by minute, with the Bernies. That I was as good as married to them left me terrified at the thought of losing them. I'd already lost Cynthia, and that it had been entirely my fault didn't leave me feeling any less abandoned.

My mom's brief breakdown during the recording of my second album had touched on one of my great unspoken fears—of never knowing when the most important person in your life might abruptly leave you to fend for yourself. I remained determined to hold on to the one thing in my life that I thought I could depend on. My career.

Had I possessed more maturity and confidence, I would've seen Fiedler's threat of abandoning me for what it was—a big fat bluff, never to be acted on so long as I continued to reel in large amounts of money for everyone.

As for Matt and me, our habitual quarrelling had lately become more biting, as quarrelling invariably does when the stakes are high, and contractual details between production company and artist can be interpreted in as many ways as there are lawyers hired to interpret them. Further complicating matters, Matt had broken up with his long-term girlfriend around the time Cynthia and I had parted ways. Which left Matt and I both overly enthusiastic bachelors, with predictably sordid results: the two of us occasionally locking horns over the same women. Whereas Fred Mollin (or in a real pinch Dr. McCauley) could defuse Matt's and my creative rivalries, no one could save us from this, the oldest and dumbest rock cliché in the book: who gets the girl. Our mutual resentments hitting an all-time high, Matt and I sometimes carried on like an old married couple; the more we felt bound to each other, the more we resented each other.

Except that now, the theory was, Matt (or rather the McCauleys) and I no longer had to stay bound to each other. I could be free. All that was left for me to do was to give the Bernies the go-ahead to do the dirty work. The next day I phoned the Bernies and gave them permission to inform the McCauleys that their contract with me had expired. And then all hell broke loose.

In retrospect, I understand that my managers were simply doing what managers do: making as much money for their client (and thus for themselves) as possible. I can't judge them, I can only judge myself. They weren't the ones severing a relationship with their best friend. Their oldest friend. At twenty-four, I was streetwise enough to have picked out the incongruities and hidden agendas wrapped up in the Bernies' disaster scenarios and to have looked beyond my hunger for over-the-top success. But the unvarnished truth was that, having sipped at the cup of one worldwide hit single, I was desperately thirsty for more. In my efforts to live up to my father's exacting standards of "Hill superiority," I'd forgotten another less ballyhooed but equally valued characteristic of my father's: loyalty. Not only to one's family but to one's friends. It was by no means coincidental that my early twenties marked both the most successful and the most singularly selfish period of my life.

The decision to act on the lapsed option renewal set into motion a series of events that stalled my career and put me on the brink of bankruptcy. Even more disturbing, I'd single-handedly destroyed my two longest and deepest relationships, driving away Cynthia and Matt (along with their respective families) within a span of eighteen months. But whereas Cynthia and I were able to make a chillingly clean break, the same would not be true for Matt and me. No longer creatively "married," we were now cast in the role of a divorced couple with several demanding children. Our offspring came in the form of the hundreds of my songs that Matt's family published, and my four internationally released albums to which they owned, in perpetuity, the master rights.

The McCauleys launched a two-million-dollar lawsuit against me for alleged breach of contract, and they also sued the three Bernies. What no one had noticed was that the McCauleys had failed to pick up my contractual option several times. The fact that we'd continued to work together despite these lapses could be interpreted as a precedent and suggest an implied contract between us.

Over the several highly expensive years it took for the McCauley lawsuit to run its course (all the royalties from my songs and recordings were held in escrow until the case was settled), I remained busy. But no matter what I did, no matter how hard I worked, things had a way of backfiring on me.

Following the advice of my managers, I bought myself out of my contract with 20th Century Records for $330,000 U.S. (That the buyout was a third of the original million-dollar estimate was an indication of my eroding market value.) Not long after my buyout 20th Century went under, declaring bankruptcy. That meant I'd just spent big money to get out of a deal I might have been out of for free, had I simply sat tight a while. Due to 20th Century's demise, hundreds of thousands of dollars of record and publishing (mechanical) royalties owed to me went up in smoke. When GRT, my Canadian record label, declared bankruptcy the following year, it meant another six-figure loss in royalties for me.

My laissez-faire attitude about money meant that, for the time being, I didn't fret very much about the millions of dollars that had come and gone from my life. Desperate to prove to the world that I still had what it takes, I took it upon myself to finance my next record to the tune of $250,000, planning to sell it to the highest bidder. Unmoored from the two major lifetime ties I'd severed, I reached out even more to my parents. And they were there for me, never questioning the choices I'd made. Nor did they refer, except in passing, to my ongoing lawsuit.

I kept busy writing, demoing and recording new songs in preparation for my future records, as well as work-for-hire songs for the odd Hollywood movie and TV specials, and performing all over the world. With the instruction of my musical collaborator and close friend, John Sheard, I took up the piano, practising several hours a day. Finding it a natural instrument for me, I quickly started writing keyboard-based songs, which gave my songwriting more range and musical depth. Seeing the notes spread out in front of me over eighty-eight keys, rather than bunched up within six strings and their corresponding frets, gave me a keener insight into Barry Mann's and Michael Masser's (both keyboardists) melodic mastery, seamless modulations and constantly shifting chord roots. I was back in school, my kind of school.

Self-discipline had always defined me, playing a major role in whatever success I'd managed to cram into my twenty-four years. But since childhood I'd always been aware of the other side of me. The part that thrived on breaking all rules, losing myself to my impulses, the wilder the better.

Now that I was single I found myself less interested in sex for its own sake and more interested in settling down. A month didn't pass without me picking out some woman hanging around backstage following one of my concerts, or working at a radio station where I was being interviewed, or even slinging drinks in some smoky bar in Timmins, and thinking, *She could be the one I could spend the rest of my life with.* Most of the time, after as little as ten minutes of conversation, the arrangements were made. A woman I knew virtually nothing about would be flying wherever I was performing, staying in an adjoining hotel room, all expenses taken care of. Although all these fly-ins resulted in one disappointment after another (for the woman as well as me), I must have done this twenty times over two years. I always fooled myself into believing that, through some random encounter, I could capture what I'd come so close to realizing with Cynthia. That all it took was a plane ticket, a fancy hotel room, sex in a Jacuzzi, followed by some meaningful conversation and I'd be happily settled down for the rest of my life.

I was very, very lucky. I shudder now to think of how easily any of those encounters could have gone out of control. I wasn't only playing with my life, I was upsetting other peoples' lives, wandering into their worlds like a wrecking ball, turning everything upside down for a silly, juvenile fantasy. There were a few nasty consequences. Late one night, I was returning to my Winnipeg hotel when my touring partner, John Sheard, stopped me in the darkened parking lot.

"Turn around and start walking, Dan," he warned me.

Earlier that evening, I'd stood up a woman I'd been casually dating. Known for her violent temper (she booked strippers for a living and concealed weapons for the Hells Angels), she'd been waiting for me in the shadows of the parking lot, gun in hand, intent on teaching me a lesson. Only John's calming words had caused her to reconsider. Nevertheless, John thought it would be prudent to stay clear of the hotel for a while, in case the woman had a change of heart.

"Hey, when you've grown up with three sisters, you learn how to diffuse a temper," was John's modest reply when I got around to thanking him.

Because I was in the process of coming a little undone, I sometimes found myself drawn to women who appeared similarly broken. Some of these women ended up in jail. Some dead. Two things (beyond luck) saved me from a similar fate—a preternatural survival instinct and family.

It was my twenty-fifth birthday. Mom and Dad had just finished singing "Happy Birthday," and I'd blown out the twenty-five candles in one quick breath.

"Daggum, boy, all that singing's given you a lot of lung power." Dad pulled a candle from the cake and licked off the chocolate.

"Hey, I thought you weren't eating that stuff anymore."

"I'm glad I'm not the only one nagging your father about his sweet tooth," Mom said. "I'm going to let you two fight it out while I go upstairs to finish wrapping your present."

Once Mom had gone, Dad's smile faded.

"Son, I hear you got in a bit of hot water during your tour through the Prairies."

"What did Larry tell you?"

"Just enough. Son, you're twenty-five now. The same age your mom was when she married me."

The thought of Mom settling down at twenty-five made me think of just how out of control my life had recently become. After slicing himself a sliver of chocolate cake over my protests, Dad said: "You gotta watch yourself when you're on the road. There are some nuts out there who'd love nothing more than to bring you down."

"I know, Dad. Why do I keep getting myself messed up with these crazy women?"

"You're just swinging to the other extreme. That Cynthia took a lot out of you, son. But that doesn't mean you can keep running around with women who'll love you one minute and turn around and shoot you the next."

"Sometimes I think there's something wrong with me."

"There's nothing wrong with you that a little hard work won't fix. When are you back in the studio?"

"Next week. Roy Halee, Simon and Garfunkel's producer, gets into Toronto on the weekend and we'll make our final decisions on which songs I'll be cutting."

I wanted to ask Dad how and when he came to realize that he didn't want to be wild anymore.

I knew I was running from my slow-burning pain over losing Cynthia, from the surreal fear of being sued for two million dollars by my former best friend, from spending close to half a million Canadian dollars to free myself from a bad American record deal. But most of all I was running from myself. How could I have had everything, beyond everything, at twenty-three, yet feel as though suddenly now, at twenty-five, everything was being ripped away from me? I felt so old and used up. I didn't want to run anymore. But how do you stop? How did Dad stop? Was it meeting Mom? Could it be that simple? Could anything be simple for me? Or would I always have this habit of complicating everything, turning even the smallest occurrence into some twisted, high drama? My life had become my greatest creative expression. The last thing I'd wanted to happen.

CHAPTER 20

Granddad Dies

The first time I saw my father cry was the day his father died. I was twenty-five and in the middle of recording my fifth album. Mom called with the news early Sunday morning that Granddad had died, and I was at my parents' house within fifteen minutes. When I walked up to their bedroom, Dad was alone. He had the phone cradled between the crook of his neck and his shoulder, on hold with the airline, waiting to book a flight to his parents' home in Washington, D.C., while he neatly folded clothes into one side of an open suitcase on the bed. The tears streaming down his cheeks seemed detached from the rest of him. His physical movements were as purposeful as ever, and his voice, though slightly clipped, was steady. I stood frozen in the doorway. He looked at me impatiently and motioned for me to come in.

"I have to get all this crying out of my system so I can be strong for my mother," he said, as if he was deliberately plotting out the sequence of his emotions for the next few days. With his right hand he started jotting something down on a pad of paper. With his left hand he continued packing. He was on to his socks, all black, and his various diabetes paraphernalia.

When the flight reservations person said there were no flights available, Dad replied, "But my dad just died." In that second, he lost his bearing, if only slightly. The puzzlement in his voice threw me off more than seeing him cry. Dad's voice could express any number of emotions quite vividly, but puzzled was rarely one of them.

Dad hung up the phone and continued packing. I could tell that he needed to keep busy, the more banal the task, the better. I kept expecting him to run out of tears, but it was as if a tap that had been shut off for as long as I'd known him had now been opened, and as the endless tears continued glistening down his face, I felt that familiar urge to protect him. More than anything, though, I wanted him to stop crying.

"Can I get you a Kleenex, Dad?"

"What for?"

Perfect. Now that we could both proceed as if his weeping was a kind of mirage, I asked where Mom was. After explaining she'd gone to the drugstore to pick up more insulin for his trip, he asked me to go down to the kitchen and bring him back some cheese and crackers. I could hear him talking when I walked back up the stairs. I wasn't sure if he was carrying on a conversation with himself, booking his flight on another airline, or simply trying to tell me something, until I saw him standing in the adjoining bathroom fixing his tie in the mirror. When he caught me staring at his reflection he fell silent, as if he was waiting for me to respond to something he'd asked.

"Sorry, Dad, I didn't hear you."

"I was telling you that your granddad lent me five thousand dollars to help me buy this house in 1965. It cost eighteen thousand. Your mother was convinced we were getting in too deep. Dad only charged us one percent interest. I paid him back in two years. Paid off the whole mortgage just a few years later."

Although Dad had told me this before, I knew he was telling it again for his own benefit. He'd always possessed an ability to boost his spirits by recalling one of his past feats. As he talked his way through the various raises he was awarded while at the OHRC and his dad's corresponding praise, he seemed to regain a semblance of his trademark pluck. I got the feeling Dad didn't want me to say much of anything. Or maybe it was that I didn't want to risk saying the wrong thing. He just needed me to be there.

"I don't expect your brother or sister to make it to your granddad's funeral. They're up to their ears in exams right now. But I'm counting on you to represent the family, Danny."

"Of course, Dad."

(Larry ended up attending Granddad's funeral after all.)

Driving home, I thought of all the musicians I'd flown to Toronto to play on my record. I would have to pay their salaries and expenses, as well as the prebooked recording studio, to sit around idle for the next several days while I was at Granddad's funeral. It was easier for me to think of the details of my day-to-day life than to come to terms with these larger, inconvenient and messy events: Granddad's death, Dad's corresponding grief. With Granddad gone, I felt one step closer to losing Dad.

As I prepared to fly to Granddad's funeral, I distracted myself by conjuring up every recollection I had of Granddad, starting from my earliest. In 1959, Dad had chosen me, not Larry or Karen or even Mom, to accompany him to Washington, D.C., where we'd be visiting my grandparents.

From my four-year-old perspective, it felt as if Dad had just handed me the world's greatest prize. (Dad, in his take-charge way, had instructed Granddad, in a letter shortly preceding our visit, to "kindly re-arrange your schedule so you can spend considerable time with Dobbie and me.") Our car trip was to take sixteen hours. Imagine, sixteen hours with Dad all to myself. I'd have been thrilled to have driven to the end of the world and back with Dad, never leaving the car.

As the two of us drove up to my grandparents' beautiful red-brick home on the magical-sounding Chainbridge Drive, I could hear their welcoming cries before they'd even opened the front door.

"Get a load of this, Mom and Dad, your grandson here is the perfect travel companion, he made sure I stayed alert through the entire trip." Dad rested his hand gently on my shoulder.

"Didn't that poor boy get tired?" Grandma May asked reprovingly.

"Nope. Danny was brave as could be."

Granddad reached in with one arm and scooped me out of the passenger seat of Dad's rusted Plymouth. In one smooth motion he had me flopped over his shoulder—I could feel one of his knobby bones sticking deep into my stomach—and carried me, as I kicked and shrieked with joy, into his home. "No, Granddad, don't drop me. Don't put me down, keep me up—up high."

"Welcome home, grandson," Granddad said, pretending not to hear my pleas as he deposited me on the floor of his study. He reached into the breast pocket of his white dress shirt and pulled something out. It was shiny.

"For me, Granddad, for me?" I squealed greedily, reaching for this small, silvery toy. Granddad stepped away from my grasping fingers and placed his mouth against the sparkling thing, like he was going to eat it. Thinking he wasn't going to share his toy, I started to cry.

"Listen, Danny." Then Granddad blew and amazing and unfamiliar sounds filled the room. For the next hour there was no one but Granddad and me, as he improvised, sucking and blowing out music on the spot. Each thirty-second solo would segue into Granddad singing some wonderfully loony, improvised verse, concluding with "I'm going to play my harmonica, cha-cha-cha."

I laughed till my sides hurt. "Again, Granddad, again," I'd demand whenever he paused for a breath. It was the first time I'd witnessed spontaneous musical creativity. It was like standing in the middle of a magic trick, only better. When Granddad eventually tired—"My mouth is weary son, it needs a rest"—he handed me his harmonica and patiently showed me how to blow into it: "Easy now, no hurry, the harmonica isn't going to run away on you," and suck out, "Release, slow, that way the music lasts longer."

Now it was twenty years later, and I was walking into the same gracious Chainbridge home. Long-forgotten smells of homemade almond butter and apple jelly left my legs feeling hollow as I plodded into the hallway, suitcase in hand, following the muffled cries of Grandma May. Grandma's bedroom door was open wide. She was lying on top of her bed, her straight black wig pushed halfway off her head to reveal a patchy greyish scalp, as she sobbed and sobbed into her pillow. A radio was playing softly on the night table beside her bed. Dad was going through the closet, silently removing Granddad's clothes and packing them into large cardboard boxes. He was speaking gently to his mother, calm and in control, taking charge. Throughout the day I rarely took my eyes off him, following his lead, not only so that I could conduct myself properly over the next few days, but also for later, hopefully many, many years later, when I'd be going through Dad's closet, and trying my best to comfort my own mother.

I have no idea what was going through my father's mind as he busied himself in his parents' home and the funeral parlour, propping up his family in the days following his father's death. I like to imagine that he made it through by summoning his own special memories of his father. Like the ones so lovingly detailed in a letter he wrote home when he was nineteen, in the U.S. Army.

Dear Dad:

I went to church today, and heard a good sermon from Chaplain Gross . . . the only thing wrong with him is that he is too much mouth. You see Dad, I'm so used to you and your intelligent viewpoint to everything, that if a man or minister does not measure up to you in my eyes, then I either immediately put him down, or I completely ignore him . . . Last week after four days on the rifle range sleeping in snow and mud, I picked up a rifle, shot for record and made 160 out of a possible 180, which is sharpshooter. The medal is supposed to be awarded to

me soon. I don't give the army credit for that, not a d—— bit.
That credit goes to you. Remember when you bought me a BB
gun and showed me how to hold my breath, squeeze the trigger
and get a correct sight picture. I've never forgotten.

CHAPTER 21

Slow Dancing with the IRS

I flew home from Grandad's funeral, thinking I was fine, that I was ready to jump right back into recording my album. Driving into the city from the Toronto airport, I spotted an old man covered in two dirty green garbage bags, passed out by a bus stop on a downtown street. It was a bitterly cold night, well below freezing. I parked my car, approached the sleeping man, tried unsuccessfully to wake him and then signalled a cab, asking the driver to call an ambulance.

A policeman soon showed up and found me kneeling beside the still-unconscious man. I'd thrown my down jacket over the man's small, shrivelled frame, and something about the way it covered him so completely reminded me of a sheet spread over a corpse. That thought, along with a blast of northern wind, made me shiver. And in no time, my shivering had given way to sobbing.

"What's wrong?" The policeman was standing over me.

"That man is going to die," I said, "unless he gets shelter."

"Are you Dan Hill?" the policeman asked. I glanced up at him and saw that familiar look of wonder spreading across his face. The look I once craved. The look I now detested. Admitting that yes, I was *the* Dan Hill, I gestured towards the frozen old man, now curled into the fetal position. It scared me that the cop had yet to really notice him.

The policeman offered me his notepad to sign. Was I in some *Monty Python* meets *Candid Camera* sketch? That's when I started laughing. The wind had made a cold mishmash of my tears, and the policeman stepped away from me, the way one gives a crazy person lots of space. I waited until the ambulance came and then drove home.

It wasn't only Granddad who had died. It felt as though everything around me was slowly dying. Everywhere I turned there was loss, turmoil and rejection. I'd always dealt with pain by turning to songwriting, but for the first time in my life, music wasn't opening its arms to me. It felt like music was causing me more hurt than healing.

Over the three years following my break with the McCauleys my career bottomed out. Epic, a division of Columbia Records in the United States, purchased the finished master of my fifth record in 1980, in the process signing me to a multi-label record deal. They paid me $450,000. This was to reimburse me for the cost of my self-financed record and fund my follow-up album (to be cut and released eighteen months later), and to ease the financial burden of me buying myself out of 20th Century Records. But with twenty-five percent of Epic's money commissioned by my managers and another ten percent going to my lawyer, combined with the astronomical travel expenses incurred sealing the deal, I would eventually be deeply out-of-pocket. Two poorly selling records later, I was dropped from the label. How quickly things had changed: at twenty-five, I was considered so valuable that I'd spent a fortune to get out of a U.S. record contract; at twenty-seven, I couldn't pay a U.S. label to sign me. For my career to turn so cold, so fast, left me devastated.

A pop singer's rise is public. A pop singer's fall is also public. And for much the same reason that people are obsessed and moved by success stories, a celebrity's descent is equally, if morbidly, transfixing. Someone else's misery, particularly a famous person's, makes us feel better about ourselves. Our own personal failures and disappointments feel a little easier to swallow.

Fortunately, Dad's salient father-son lesson—*Get tough in my household or get eaten alive out there in the real world*—served me well through the mid-seventies and early eighties. I spent the early part of my twenties subjected to adoration bordering on deification, only to spend the second half of my twenties stumbling through a big Canadian media backlash, as my star exploded and just as quickly faded, to give way to the next breaking story.

Since I had revelled in the perks of stardom, it seemed only fair that I should suck up the ridicule that came with falling out of stardom, take my public lashing and move on. "Remember what Kennedy said," Dad used to tell me when he caught me feeling a little too sorry for myself, "don't get mad, get even." And my revenge would come by proving to myself that I could take it.

For me, as a fading Canadian celebrity, no place offered the sensation of a brand-new start more than Los Angeles. In the early eighties, no other city in the world hosted as many internationally successful songwriters. No one in Hollywood cared about your "cool factor", whether you wrote alternative or wimpy songs; everything in Hollywood boiled down to money. Thus, the L.A. songwriting community regarded me objectively: I'd co-written one of the biggest hits of the seventies and had recently co-penned another R&B/adult contemporary crossover smash, titled "In Your Eyes," for George Benson. I found L.A. to be an amazing blend of the superficial and the unabashedly honest. If you can write or co-write a hit, you're welcome everywhere. And I felt welcomed.

Still, hit songs take time. Not just time to write, but time to demo—each instrument, each vocal part, recorded perfectly and expensively. Then time to place (if you're really lucky) with the *right artist*. Then time for that *right artist*'s record to come out. Then time to see if that *right artist* chooses your song as one of a handful of singles. Then, if your song is so fortunate, time for it to become a hit. If you beat the odds and score with a hit, then you wait for over a year to see any royalties. If you don't get screwed, that is. Thousands of talented writers have grown old in L.A. chasing down hits. The standard industry joke goes like this: What did the songwriter say when he won the ten-million-dollar lottery? Answer: I'm going to spend it all on demos until my money runs out.

With the royalties to "Sometimes" still tied up in escrow till the McCauley lawsuit was resolved, I felt a lot like that lottery-winning songwriter. I was running out of money. Finkelstein, figuring (with good reason) that my singing career was pretty much over, split with Fiedler. Bruce Cockburn, whose career had always been as solid as mine had been mercurial, stayed on with Finkelstein, and Fiedler and I agreed to continue working together. Finkelstein's departure was a signal to everyone in the Canadian music business that, short of a miracle, my reign as one of the country's top pop singers was over.

But then another, far more serious problem surfaced. In 1982 the U.S. Internal Revenue Service sued me for tax avoidance. The Canadian backlash, okay, that came with the territory. My frozen royalties would in time be released. Being treated like a pariah by corporate record companies, well, I could always keep writing for the hot acts of the moment. But the IRS? That made no sense. Never a big spender, raised by parents who'd taught me that people with healthy incomes should pay more taxes, I'd always assumed tax avoidance charges happened either to the amoral super-rich, or to ignorant celebrities who had been bilked by their accountants and managers. Which category best described me?

And so, with my career a shambles and my royalties tied up indefinitely, I swallowed my pride and did the one thing I'd always sworn I'd never do. I went to my mom and dad and told them that I could be on the verge of losing everything.

It's a six-mile uphill run from my house to my parents' house, straight up Victoria Park. The run is not particularly aesthetic; strip malls give way to mega-malls, which then give way to faded, poorly maintained apartment complexes, occasionally interrupted by very small, always empty parks. Cars and buses rushed by within inches of the sidewalk, polluting my lungs with exhaust and leaving my face grimy, my eyes itchy and stinging with dust and sand and specks of gravel. But the run felt mandatory, at once exhausting and exhilarating. Pieces of my past life drifted by with each step. At the two-mile mark I spotted the pancake house where Dad used to take us on special Sundays, once our chores were completed. Now it was a McDonald's. A mile later, an insurance company advertised its services in the same cubicle-like building where I started taking guitar lessons at ten. The Zumburger, just south of Eglinton, where I used to go as a teenager to spend the five bucks I'd earned from a gig at an old folk's home, or when I'd been kicked offstage at a downtown bar once the manager realized I was below the legal drinking age, had become a used-car lot.

As I turned off Victoria Park and cruised the final half-mile to my parents' house, my knees started to ache, making me wish I had Brian Maxwell's endurance. The last time I'd run this course was with Brian two years ago, after he'd qualified for the 1980 Olympics, which Canada then boycotted. We had both been struck by the similarity of our quick success and even quicker setbacks. We'd promised each other that we wouldn't give up, that we'd keep fighting, because fighting back, whether against Olympic boycotts or uninterested record companies that believed you were past your expiry date, was the only thing that made sense.

"Donna, look, that crazy Danny has risked his life running all the way from his house to ours! Daggum, boy, you smell like a barn. Let me get you one of my old sweatshirts to change into."

I wandered into the family room. Strange, how this very room where Dad had grilled me so effectively when I was younger had, over the years, turned into a kind of safe haven, the place where the three of us would gather whenever I was in some kind of trouble and in need of their support. Mocking me from the top of an oversized bookcase that housed hundreds of Dad's old sociology texts was all the memorabilia of my past success, from international platinum records to Juno awards, to ASCAP airplay awards, to my Grammy nomination. I'd never felt comfortable keeping all those awards at my house. Bad luck. But even here, my gaudy career showpieces felt out of place, as if they belonged to someone who no longer existed, who never really existed in the first place. Childhood memories intermingled with pop star memories, as the cold currents from the air conditioning vents pressed my sweat-soaked T-shirt into my chest, causing me to shiver.

"Look at him, Donna. That boy's almost twenty-eight and thinks he can run all the way from his house to ours as if he's still a teenager."

When I made a flip remark about how running was the only constant left in my life, Mom knew something was up.

"Are you all right, Danny?" she asked.

I tried to think of how I could lead up to the IRS quagmire. Where to start? *Hey Mom, how's Larry's job at the Winnipeg Free Press? Oh yeah, by the way, guess what kind of notice I received in the mail? Talk about a rock star stereotype. Next thing I'll be arrested for exposing myself on stage.*

"What is it, Danny?" Dad asked, my unlikely silence making him nervous.

Better get this over with, I thought.

"The IRS is suing me. I've been told they think they can set a kind of precedent with my case."

"The IRS?" my parents repeated, aghast. "KKK" notwithstanding, that was about the worst three-letter abbreviation I could spring on them.

Knowing Dad's impatience for bureaucratic details, I tried to simplify a complicated story. Back in 1976, the two Bernies, on the advice of the third Bernie—the attorney—suggested I take advantage of my dual citizenship and get an American passport. This would make it easier for me to tour in the States. The result was me being "dual taxed," meaning that if I earned fifty thousand dollars for a three-night stand at Ontario Place, on which I paid taxes to the Canadian government, the IRS demanded a similarly huge chunk. With my accountant and tax lawyer charging me a fortune to untangle the U.S.-Canada tax overlap, I was advised to revoke my American citizenship, as well as my dual status, immediately. In 1979, I'd laughed at the question posed by an American official in the U.S. consulate in Vancouver: "Are you sure you want to do this, Mr. Hill? We don't take kindly to high-profile U.S. citizens revoking their citizenship."

The American official was doing his best to warn me that I might be waking a sleeping giant. Meaning that the IRS viewed me as a rich (as in generous-tax-paying) celebrity. For me to revoke my U.S. citizenship would be seen as an insult, and the IRS would not take kindly to a slap in the face by some nouveau riche pop star.

The official's warning was lost on me. I was smugly proud of how my response—"Sorry, I must have the wrong address. Guess I stumbled into the Russian embassy by mistake"—pissed him off.

Months later, I received invoices and threats from the IRS claiming that, as an individual, I couldn't claim a corporate tax rate. Since I'd incorporated in 1975, my earnings over the last five years had been reassessed. Based on this assessment, I owed $200,000. Plus penalties, fines and interests growing daily. My entertainment lawyer hired a top Toronto tax lawyer on my behalf, who in turn hired a top tax firm based in Manhattan. Now my fast-mounting legal fees were threatening to eclipse what I allegedly owed the IRS.

It took a great deal to surprise my parents. They shared the grim expression of students attending a class in music-business economics— music-business economics gone awry.

Finally, Dad said, "This is exactly what they did to Joe Louis. And Jack Johnson. This is the story of every Black celebrity who makes it in America."

"Not just Black celebrities, Dan," Mom corrected, "and who's this 'they' you're talking about?" My parents continued their familiar jousting, part of which was the way they naturally communicated, and part of which was a performance put on for the purpose of distracting me from my business woes.

Now that I'd finally come clean about the collapsing state of my career, I felt as though I'd come out of a ten-year coma only to find myself back where I was when I was eighteen: broke, unemployed and unemployable, and dependent on my parents.

"It's not as though you blew all your money on jewellery and drugs and fancy cars," Mom said. But I could see that my lack of superstar spending left her all the more confused as to how I could have blown through so much cash, so fast. Wanting to say something to make me feel better, she added, "And you've always been more than generous with all of us."

I told my parents that I'd lived without much money before and I could certainly do it again. Singing was never about money in the first place. *So then, what was singing about?* If my singing was about impressing Dad, as much as anything else, where did that leave me now?

My tax imbroglio meant that, in a worst-case scenario, every future penny my songs or my concerts earned, in fact anything I earned, could be garnisheed. Usually I could read Dad's face, but not this time. Probably because he, like Mom, was pondering so many things, reviewing all this strange, shady information, still not sure what to make of it all. Then he scrambled to his feet, all smiles, like he'd just thought of something that would solve everything.

"Donna, why don't we get out our RRSPs and bonds, so Danny can take a look at what we've got." Dad motioned for Mom to head upstairs with him.

"Dan, you don't even know where all our financial statements are. They're not up in your office, they're in the basement in the boxes underneath your father's old desk. Honestly, what's going to happen to you if I die first?"

Cheerfully arguing about which of the two of them would be the first to go, they disappeared downstairs, their lively voices fading into the steady, dull tumble of the washing machine. I considered taking off before things got really humiliating, but then I remembered that I'd run over. I had no car and no wallet. Brushing aside the symbolism, I tried to comfort myself with the reminder that since leaving home as a teenager I'd never received a cent from my parents. They came back as I was putting on my shoes to leave. *What the hell, it was a downhill run home. This could be the start of my new austerity program.*

"Daggum, son, one more step of running today and you're likely to break something." With Dad playfully standing between me and the front door (reminding me of earlier years when he refused to let me out of the house at night), Mom painstakingly illustrated how much money they'd saved. They'd never shown me their savings before; somehow by revealing, right down to the penny, their life's worth, they appeared all the more vulnerable.

"Whatever money you need, we'll help out as best we can. Your mother and I know you'll find a way to pay it back. You're a survivor. You've never been afraid of hard work."

I was waiting for the inevitable "Now might be a good time for you to go to college," when Dad said something that made me feel even more exposed, because it was so unlike him.

"We love you, Danny. We'll always be proud of you. You don't think Sinatra, or the Count, went through ups and downs like this?"

I turned down my parents' offer of money. Then I left their house. Other than the day his father died, Dad had always led with his strong side. At least in front of me. Now it was up to me to return the favour. Having reassured my parents that I'd do more walking than jogging on my way home, I ambled down their driveway. Even without turning around I could feel them standing side by side on the front lawn, watching me head up the sidewalk.

When I knew they couldn't see me any longer, I attempted to run. But my legs were too sore to even hobble. Clearly, running wasn't the constant in my life after all. It was family.

CHAPTER 22

Marriage and Healing

"You don't need a wife, you need a harem."

That was Dad's only comment when I told him, in the summer of 1982, of my plans to marry Beverly Chapin. Why all the skepticism? If Dad could transition successfully into married life, why wouldn't he expect the same from me?

Throughout my childhood, women never stopped oohing and aahing over Dad: "He's sooo handsome, like Sidney Poitier," "Donna, your husband is sooo strong, is there anything he can't do?" "Would you mind if I borrowed him for some household chores?" Even as a little boy, I understood that race played a factor in all this gushing. A Negro in sexually repressed Newmarket or Don Mills in the fifties and early sixties—even without Dad's good looks and coyly underplayed intellect—would have easily fed into many people's goofy fantasies.

Despite all this female fawning, however, nothing indicated to me that Dad was interested in other women. Besides, there was enough sexual energy crackling between my parents to power Las Vegas.

Dad had married Mom when he was twenty-nine. I married Bev when I was twenty-eight. By the time Dad and I had reached our late twenties, we'd both been exposed to all the delights, and drudgery, of single life. What irked me most about Dad's "harem" crack was that I'd always been inspired by my parents' marriage and, despite—or perhaps because of—my copious (and from Dad's viewpoint, endlessly amusing) romantic capers, I knew that I longed for a relationship as sustainable and loving as theirs.

When my career had gone crazy in the mid-seventies and women started to take notice of me, I had flattered myself into thinking that their sudden interest had little to do with my rising fame and everything to do with my personality. But when my voice vanished from radio, the women, for the most part, vanished as well.

"Lucky for you, or you'd be dead now." It was Larry's tone, so matter of fact and without judgment, that gave his words such grave impact. And there was another positive consequence of having my celebrity wings clipped: when a woman appeared interested in me, it was easier for me to trust that her interest was genuine.

When I first I met Bev in the summer of 1980, I could hardly be considered a catch. Not only was I running short on cash, but my once infamously wild hair was falling out in clumps, leaving Dad to chortle that I was going bald faster than any Hill in history.

Bev and I met at a cottage weekend in northern Ontario. Due to lack of sleeping space, she and I, along with two other friends, shared the same bedroom. Finding that my chances of attracting a woman were better if she wasn't aware of my past life as a famous singer—"Oh no, you're *that* guy! I liked you a whole lot better before"—I cringed when Bev mentioned that she'd seen me perform a year earlier at a concert. Fortunately, Bev did not hold my iffy status against me. The attraction between us was as instant as it was powerful. But beyond the "hmmm, we're up north, sharing the same bedroom, and I've got to have her" reflex, I felt something deeper, something strange and discomfiting. Yes, she was gorgeous, while at the same time acting as though her appearance were nothing special. But I'd met other women who came across as unaware of their looks, only to find out later that this was part of their pose. Bev's sense of humour, however, enlivened by her quick, unaffected mannerisms, recalled the zaniness of Lucille Ball, only sexier. Beauty and madcap wit—I hadn't come across anything like that before. Bev's rolling laughter could take over the room, causing everyone else to laugh so hard that by the time the room finally quieted down, no one could remember what had sparked the laughter in the first place. If someone (invariably me) said something wickedly unsuitable, Bev would howl, her shock and disapproval (and, based on her flushed red face, glee) registering throughout her body.

Everything about Bev seemed honest to the point of being raw; her opinions, her reactions, her forthright body language left no doubt as to how she felt about whatever was being discussed. So why, then, did she seem so hard to categorize? This was supposed to be a specialty of mine: sizing someone up so that I could better manipulate, or at least influence, them.

That night, she lay sleeping in the bunk across from mine, wearing an oversized Toronto Maple Leafs hockey jersey and white tennis shorts. Alone in my wakefulness, I found myself replaying the last few hours, wishing that I'd cut back on my grandiose storytelling and asked more questions. Had I confused Bev's natural enthusiasm for life with an enthusiasm for me? Would she return to Toronto lumping me in with the cottage experience: a fun way to spend the weekend but nothing memorable? Hearing Bev shift onto her back, I snuck another look. Even fast asleep she appeared scary-smart, and yet there was something so heartbreakingly innocent about her. And here I was as jaded as I was uneducated.

Raised in the blue-collar village of Long Branch, the middle of three children of a socially conservative family, Bev was studying law at the University of Windsor. Her visible embarrassment at having to share a small bedroom with another woman and two men didn't mean she wasn't also tickled pink at the idea. Even at her shyest she sparked with sexual energy.

The next morning Bev and I swam out to the raft on the lake, where we spent most of the day diving into the sun-speckled water and lying on the gently swaying platform, gazing up at the sky. Once more I talked way too much while Bev listened. I'm not sure why I felt the need to let her in on all my varied catastrophes. Maybe I thought I was giving her fair warning. If, despite my checkered past, Bev still agreed to go out with me, at least she'd be proceeding with open eyes.

But it was how Bev listened, so intently and with such empathy—showing equal concern for both Matt and me when I talked about our stormy past, expressing sympathy for Cynthia without condemning me for sleeping around on her—that really affected me. Here I'd assumed, in my world-weary way, that I'd be shocking Bev. And the reverse had happened. What shocked me most about Bev was her kindness.

That fall, Bev returned to Windsor, Ontario, for her last year of law school. Our relationship built cautiously over the next two years. It took me a long time to shed my ghosts, my many shadowed selves, my fears of hurting someone and being hurt. Surely Bev would ultimately come to her senses and find a man with a more suitable background, a more stable career and a more grounded personality. Because I'd resigned myself to being the "fling guy," I frequently did everything in my power to drive Bev away—my skewed version of a pre-emptive strike. But rather than being scared off, Bev would fight back, challenging my behaviour, picking my thoughtless actions apart with the thoroughness of a cross-examination. That I could be a slippery witness, ducking and weaving behind my creative and convoluted rationalizations, meant that we fought incessantly during those first two years. But rather than drive each other away, we always emerged from these battles a little bit closer.

This kind of relationship was completely new for me. I'd never been involved with a woman who would announce her unhappiness or disapproval over something I did immediately following (if not during) my transgression. Bev taught me that two people could fight without it signalling the end. Through fighting we came to understand that we shared something worth fighting for—a potent and uncontrollable connection we weren't likely to find anywhere else.

I imagine that Bev saw in me what I saw in her: a compelling, seductive opposite. I simply had to look at my parents to understand this phenomenon. Beyond Bev's and my chemistry, and the invisible pull of our temperamental differences, it was a litany of unexpected and unrehearsed little things that caused me, one small surprise after another, to fall in love with her.

Bev's quick, ribald jokes would be followed by an unconscious sidewise glance, as if she felt concerned that I might disapprove. For an exceptionally attractive woman pulling down As in law school, with a coruscating wit that could as easily maim as delight ("Here's a prick for your prick, prick!" Bev once scowled, handing her girlfriend's philandering husband a sewing needle), she betrayed moments of insecurity that rivalled my own. But her occasional lack of confidence was offset by her courage, her fearlessness when jumping into unfamiliar, possibly dangerous territory. Thanks to me she'd already been exposed to lunatic L.A. songwriters, the nuttiest of whom had showed up unannounced at my door one Saturday afternoon, suggesting group sex almost before he extended his hand to Bev in greeting.

Hate mail to Bev from deranged fans who—yikes—had somehow clued into the news that I finally had a steady female partner, the odd songwriter who alternately made passes at and felt threatened by Bev, my fading pop star status currently overshadowed by two enormous lawsuits: all this baggage made me look down at my feet when I finally asked Bev, in an apologetic tone, "Will you marry me?"

"How about this August, before I start bar ads?"

My first thought was *Damn, this woman does not scare easily.* My second thought was *This woman's almost as crazy as I am.* And my third: *Danny, whatever you do, don't blow it this time.*

Before marrying Bev, I'd always believed that a couple's relationship was conducted in a vacuum, irrespective of anyone else. My attitude came out of growing up in a household where the in-laws lived in another country, at a time when airline travel was as costly as it was rare. Bev grudgingly went along with my request that our wedding be short and civic, with only family in attendance. But soon after Bev and I announced our wedding plans (springing it on our dumbfounded families only two weeks before our date at City Hall), I discovered that I still had a lot to learn about family relationships. And about Bev. A lifetime of attuning myself to the slightest sign of female fragility had left me exaggerating Bev's vulnerabilities. When the situation called for it, Bev was wilful, driven and—if someone crossed her—brutal. She gave to her friends and family completely. If they, in turn, disappointed her, they would be sure to hear about it in the bluntest manner. So it was only a matter of time before Bev and my father clashed.

Much as I wanted out of my former life, replete with fierce ambition, fractured friendships and instability, some people preferred my life to remain dramatic and entertaining. Frequently the people who love you the most are the ones most likely to confuse your needs with their own voyeuristic tendencies. The idea that I might be willing to put my gallivanting behind me and catapult myself, body, heart and soul, into married life, didn't sit well with Dad.

"You're different, son," he would often tell me with a perfidious smile, refusing to elaborate. There was no doubt that Dad wanted to believe that I was "different." It was easier than admitting that my relationship with Bev could possibly compromise my relationship with him. Throughout the five years following my 1977 breakup, Dad and I had enjoyed a closeness we'd never experienced before. When Bev and I announced our wedding, Dad realized that our interdependent relationship would once again be shifting.

Furthermore, if I thought getting married would smooth out most of my life's rough edges, a phone call I received ninety-six hours before our big day suggested otherwise.

"I'm Mario Kassar, co-owner of Carolco Pictures and executive producer of a movie called *First Blood,* starring Sylvester Stallone. We'd like to hire you to sing the movie's title song. This is a big-budget film and we're willing to pay you a lot of money. Can you be in London, England, tomorrow, ready to cut your vocal at Abbey Road Studios?"

"What do I have to lose?" I asked Bev.

Bev reminded me, in colourful language, that we were getting married in four days.

"No problem. I'm booked to return home early morning the day of our wedding."

"Who are you kidding? Since when do you sing songs you didn't write? Now you're flying to England to sing a song you haven't even heard? You could be gone for a week."

Bev, who had spent the last few days trying to convince her traumatized parents that she wasn't making the mistake of her life by marrying me, was already at her breaking point. She was convinced that once I set foot in England, I'd reconsider this whole "marriage thing" and promptly disappear into the forests of Europe, never to come home.

I decided it was best not to admit to Bev that I'd promised Mr. Kassar that I'd remain in London for as long as it took for me to nail the title song's vocal to everyone's satisfaction—be it a day or a month. I made a big show of packing only a day's worth of carry-on luggage.

The movie's title song, "It's a Long Road," was, technically speaking, a pop singer's worst nightmare. Jerry Goldsmith may have been one of the world's most successful film composers, but judging from this song, he had little understanding of the human vocal range. Singing, beyond coming naturally to me, was something I'd worked hard on, particularly since I'd started making records. Stretching the high and low end of my voice considerably over the last few years, I'd developed a finely tuned understanding of exactly how far I could push the outer limits of my voice. But I could have been blessed with the multi-octave range of an opera singer and still have been unable to hit the top notes of "It's a Long Road." Because the track had been cut in England before anyone consulted me as to the right key, the only solution was for the recording engineer to slow down the tape, making the top notes at least a quarter-tone lower.

All the studio tricks in the world, however, couldn't solve the fact the song's lyricist, Hal Shaper, believed I should sing his lyrics one way—theatrical, with a big Ethel Merman vibrato and lots of deathbed sighing and gasping—while Jerry Goldsmith demanded the opposite approach—raw and real, something between Wilson Pickett and Tom Jones. On one of the many occasions that Mr. Shaper led me out of the vocal booth to demonstrate how his lyrics should be sung (imagine Ed

Sullivan trying to do Mick Jagger), I let it slip that I was getting married in seventy-two hours.

"Your wife-to-be is going to have to learn that show business always comes first. The sooner she accepts that she's married a famous singer, the better. I hope you told her we spent a bloody fortune to fly you over here."

"Have you ever been married, Mr. Shaper?"

"Many times. Why do you ask?"

Before I could say something cheeky, Mr. Shaper announced that he was late for a tennis and tea date with Margaret Thatcher's daughter.

"Great, he's gone," laughed Jerry Goldsmith over the studio speakers once Shaper made his exit. "Now give me your best Wilson Pickett!"

A combination of fear of missing my own wedding, and the knowledge that if I had to listen to Mr. Shaper babysit me through my vocals one more time I'd be imprisoned for murder, meant that I managed to record all the vocals and background vocals to "It's a Long Road" in ninety minutes.

"Great job, Dan," Mr. Kassar exclaimed as he walked me to the Rolls-Royce that would be taking me to Heathrow Airport. He reached into his pocket, pulled out a stack of U.S. hundred-dollar bills and stuffed them into my shirt pocket. "Just some spending money to top off your fee!" he said, affecting the tone of a gambler tipping his black-jack dealer. The limo driver opened the passenger door and Mr. Kassar disappeared back into the Abbey Road Studios.

The burgundy Rolls-Royce swung into traffic. As several bills fell out of my shirt pocket, I understood that, as much as I was being paid to sing the movie's title song, I could have easily demanded three times as much. Mr. Kassar had let me know that I'd undersold myself: an unforgivable sin by Hollywood's standards.

I arrived in Toronto hours before our wedding at City Hall. Adrenalin pulled me through the five-minute ceremony, but as the family dinner dragged on, with Bev and I sitting on pins and needles waiting for one of our parents to do something that would upset the other three, I felt myself starting to fade. I wanted to go home, throw a few hundred-dollar bills around the bedroom and celebrate our honeymoon rites. Before I passed out. For a week.

"Emergency phone call for the lucky groom." Bev's sharp elbow into my ribs alerted me to the waiter and saved me from dropping my sleeping face into a hot bowl of lobster soup. Relieved that I'd managed to show up in time for our wedding, Bev was willing to overlook my nodding off. Just the same, she walked me to where the maître d' was holding the phone.

"Who would be calling you now?" Bev demanded.

Thinking there might be safety in numbers, I waited until we were back at the table before I replied, "That was the movie producer. He's insisting I fly down to L.A. tomorrow and re-record my vocals. Apparently the group Toto is re-cutting the song as we speak."

"Danny, you're newly married! You're not going anywhere. Enough is enough!" my mom yelled.

"Just say no," Bev advised in her most lawyerly voice, the one she used when she expected no rebuttal. Feeling Bev's eyes blaze through me with a Nancy Reagan–esque severity, I thought, *She's been married to me all of a few hours and she's starting to get the look of a woman who's been trapped in a bad marriage for half a century.*

Dad was trying to suppress an "I told you so" smile. Bev's parents looked at me with incomprehension, as if it were finally sinking in that they'd acquired an alien for a son-in-law. I did a quick juggling act in my head: Bev's fury versus the wrath of the IRS (which, while several motions away from possessing my house, was likely to do so if I lost my case), Mom's "time to grow the fuck up" stare versus the expensive McCauley lawsuit. Deciding that love, unlike the IRS, ultimately forgives, I flew to L.A. the next day, arriving back home the day after, my vocal chords feeling scraped raw from twelve hours of singing, but with fistfuls of hundred-dollar bills filling out my jean pockets.

The movie, better known these days as the first *Rambo,* went on to become the second-biggest movie of 1983, after *E.T.* The title song became a hit in faraway markets like Hong Kong, New Zealand, Australia and England.

Due to this overlapping of the *Rambo* song and our wedding, for the longest time Dad tended to view the two events as one and the same, expressing considerably more enthusiasm for the movie than my marriage. I didn't share Dad's view. Bev and I weren't only marrying each other, we were marrying into each other's worlds. Marriage did not mean the end of excitement in my life. No more than it meant that Bev would be tossing aside her core values or her future as a lawyer to live a debauched rock 'n' roll life. She would still practise Christianity, start up, in a few years, a law firm called Chapin and Chapin with her father and, eventually, raise a family with me. The fusing of two lives and personalities as disparate as ours would prove to be fraught with conflict and passion, compromise and monumental stubbornness. But we soldiered on because, beyond a million other reasons, we really, really loved each other.

After a few years, realizing that my marriage wasn't a temporary act of madness, Dad's perspective mellowed slightly, and he began saying things like, "You surprised me son, you're really behaving yourself. You've always had an unpredictable streak." Just as Dad had, thirty years earlier, I'd recovered from a relationship gone horribly wrong, learned a thing or two and then, upon spotting the right woman at the right time, done everything I could to hold onto her.

Among the many disappointments throughout the second half of my twenties, my marriage to Bev stood out as a brilliant stroke of luck. It was the one choice I made as a young man that turned out better, much better, than I could have ever hoped.

Bev healed something that was, if not broken, certainly wounded, still bleeding, deep inside me. The results began to show within weeks of our wedding. At Bev's urging ("Dan, my guess is that Matt wants to settle as badly as you"), I contacted Matthew McCauley, whom I had last seen while I was being cross-examined by his lawyer in a courtroom packed with spectators and journalists.

"Hello, Matt?"

"Danny!" I'd braced myself for Matt's voice to be brimming with anger and betrayal. But all I could hear was incredulity.

"Look, Matt, I think we should get together for dinner, see if we can figure out a way to settle this thing."

"When and where?"

"Matt, I'm really, really sorry about your mom."

"Thanks, Danny. The letter you sent meant a lot to me. It meant a lot to all of us."

Mrs. McCauley had died recently from a complication during a simple surgery. The last time I'd seen her, we'd found ourselves in the same elevator en route to a music-business function. The McCauleys and I were receiving ASCAP airplay awards (as publisher and writer) for two of my songs. Dr. McCauley managed a polite, if strained, hello, but Mrs. McCauley looked right through me with an icy gaze that I couldn't shake for months.

Now, Matt and I were having dinner at Noodles, an overpriced, well-known music-business restaurant where artists and A&R men went to advertise how much money they were hauling in. From the moment "You Make Me Want to Be" had landed on radio, five-star restaurants had become a regular part of Matt's and my lives, one of the many extras that came with being toasted by the so-called movers and shakers.

As Matt and I looked at the filet mignon and lobster on the menu, I felt a longing for a cheeseburger and a chocolate milkshake. I wanted to be swivelling on the creaky stools at the Donwood Plaza's greasy spoon, stealing Matt's fries and threatening to stab his fingers with my fork if he tried to steal them back.

"Remember when the Greek restaurant owner with that uneven moustache used to demand to see if we had enough money before he agreed to serve us?" I asked Matt.

"No," answered Matt, "but I do remember when you asked me if my girlfriend would help you out with your sperm sample problem."

"It was very gallant of you to grant me permission to ask her. Even though you had broken up with her during my time of need."

"Well, Danny, I knew she'd reject you."

"I still remember how she answered me, hands on her hips, smacking her gum like some moll: 'I don't think so, Danny . . .'"

"Should I come back to take your order, gentlemen?"

Once again I'd been talking way too loud. Matt and I began laughing so hard that little bits of half-chewed bread roll sprayed out of my mouth and the poor waiter did an about-turn, scurrying over to a table of executives from Capitol Records. It felt good to laugh. It took a bit of the pressure off being alone together for the first time in three years, without litigation lawyers in black gowns, a judge and a packed-to-the-rafters courtroom between us.

Even though it felt strange, really strange, to be seated across from each other, talking like geezers about the good old days, strange sure beat the hell out of surreal and costly. If our courtroom proceedings continued to stretch out for several more weeks, we'd be looking at hundreds of thousands of dollars in lawyers, court costs, witnesses and unwelcome publicity, since the media was claiming the case was the first of its kind in Canada.

As Matt talked to me about life in L.A., his new marriage, his new baby, I was struck by how happy I was to see him. With little effort, I could pretend that we were still a couple of Don Mills kids, lost inside his basement studio, the world ours for the taking.

Before we'd finished our appetizers, we'd settled our legal differences. McCauley Music would own the record and publishing royalties on my next album, which meant, from a business standpoint, we were back to square one. What a waste of time and money. And those were just the tangible losses. What had it achieved to walk away from a contract and turn my back on a family who'd believed so totally in my talents?

"My litigation lawyer's gonna be crestfallen," I joked. "He was counting on squeezing another six figures of legal fees out of me."

Matt smiled wanly. Since parting ways in 1979, we'd both gone on to make more records. Neither of us had come close to the success we'd had back in that swell season of the seventies when we were working together, when everything seemed to jell.

"When was the last time you ate here?" Matt asked, once we'd split the lobster and steak evenly between us. I told Matt the story of how, in 1978, I'd brought a British pop star here after three consecutive days of shooting what was turning out to be a horrendous TV special. I'd slept with her the night before and immediately regretted it. Towards the conclusion of our dinner at Noodles, she'd demanded I sleep with her again that night. When I said no (a word pop stars don't hear all that often), she'd passed out. Since she was given to throwing hugely dramatic scenes on set, I assumed she was faking it and half carried, half dragged her out of the restaurant as patrons looked on.

"No wonder you haven't been back here since," Matt said, sounding more concerned than entertained. "So what happened next?"

"I managed to get her back to her hotel. Once I tucked her into bed she seemed to wake up. Thinking she was fine, I got the hell out of there. But when I arrived at the TV studio the next morning I found out she'd been rushed to the hospital, due to a near-lethal combination of booze and pain-killers."

Matt had stopped eating. I'd forgotten how his face turned dismissive when he heard something, usually an out-of-tune vocal or a lazy lyric, that he didn't like.

"Why are you telling me this, Danny?"

"You mean, other than the fact that you asked me about the last time I ate here?"

"You know what I mean."

When was I going to learn that not every experience could be reshaped into a rollicking anecdote? That a funny story could not excuse callous behaviour?

When Matt and I agreed to split the cheque, we both laughed awkwardly. We knew why we were laughing again. But really, the symbolism felt more poignant than amusing.

"How did it go?" Bev asked, when I came home that night. She'd been sleeping when I walked into the bedroom. She rubbed her half-open eyes in a way that filled me with tenderness.

"Thank you," I answered.

"For what?"

"I don't even know. It's too much for me to think about right now. Just thank you."

New Ombudsman's ready to roll with punches
He'll fight for little guy

CHAPTER 23

The Ombudsman

B ev and I chose to spend the greater part of 1984 in L.A. The previous year had been a year of mixed blessings. It had started with a thud, thanks to the twin failures of a poorly selling album (despite massive radio airplay and surprisingly good reviews) and my poorly received novel *Comeback,* released by Bantam/Seal books in Canada. But 1983 had ended positively, with a recent co-write of mine ("One Giant Step") being covered by the platinum-selling Spanish singing star Camilo Sesto. As well, "In Your Eyes" kept landing on more and more best-selling records: a couple of George Benson greatest hits packages and enough soft rock and R&B compilations to fund my ongoing legal battle with the IRS.

"How do two songs I write in a total of thirty minutes rake in a ton more royalties than a novel I slaved over for a year?" I asked Bev, who'd been calmly flicking a cockroach out of her tea, courtesy of L.A.'s hot climate and crappy hospitality apartments.

"Did those two songs really take you thirty minutes, or fifteen years of writing several hundred songs to set you up for those fifteen minutes?"

"So I have to write fiction for fifteen years before it can stand up to my songwriting?"

"How old's Larry?"

"Twenty-seven."

"How long has he been writing fiction?"

"About as long as I've been writing songs."

"*Res ipsa loquitur.*"

"I hate it when you pull that legal Latin stuff on me. Okay, you win. I'm sticking to songwriting. It pays better and it's more fun."

It sure hadn't been fun having my book castigated by the Toronto papers. And it was pretty embarrassing when *Maclean's* magazine warned readers that my novel resembled soft-core porn.

"Soft-core porn? How dare *Maclean's* write that about my first-born son!" Dad had fumed, after he'd updated me on my latest media spanking. "You ought to sue for slander. That book wasn't the slightest bit soft-core—it was hard-core all the way."

I was still smiling at how Dad had sucked me in for the nth time when the answering machine clicked on: "Son, it's your pappy checking up on you. Still don't understand why you two are risking your lives in earthquake country. And where's that letter you promised to write your mother and me?"

"Get to the point, Dan!" Mom squawked.

"Shhh, woman, get a hold of yourself!"

I could picture the two of them, Mom giving Dad that exasperated scowl, Dad acting as though he had no idea what she was going on about.

"Anyway, Danny, I'm calling to tell you that I've been selected as Ontario's new ombudsman. I expect you and Bev to be here for the official swearing-in session next week."

I listened to the crisp sound of the answering-machine tape rewinding and thought of that old *Mission Impossible* scene, where the message self-destructs after one play.

"That's so exciting!" Bev said, having overheard the message.

"Yeah, I guess."

"Can't you hear how thrilled he is? Be happy for him."

Ahhh, if life could only be so simple.

When Bev and I flew into Toronto for Dad's swearing-in ceremony, it felt like we'd arrived to pay homage to a rock star. Weird enough that I'd landed in a time warp, but the eras kept moving around. Was I revisiting the late seventies, when I played the big pooh-bah, or the sixties, when I'd watched people swarm Dad after one of his enthralling speeches on human rights? *Let go of the knee-jerk father-son comparisons,* I repeated, silently, to myself. *Stop analyzing everything and just enjoy watching Dad shine.*

Without question, this new job represented Dad's crowning achievement. The media was abuzz with praise over Dad's ombudsman appointment and, in a rare display of solidarity, all of the provincial party leaders enthusiastically supported Dad's posting.

There was, however, more to my uneasiness than the feeling of déjà vu. At sixty, Dad's undimmed charisma fooled people into believing he was robust and healthy. But the combination of decades of diabetes, no exercise, poor diet and low-level dysthymia meant that his body was on the verge of giving out. A five-year posting as ombudsman would add one more ingredient to Dad's growing health problems: stress. And while too much stress is toxic for everyone, regardless of age, it is exponentially worse if you're older and diabetic.

Bev and I took a cab straight from the airport to my parents' home. I could hear Dad's footsteps before we'd made it through the front door. *Clomp, clomp, clomp*—"Donna!"—*clomp, clomp, clomp*—"Donna!" For a big man he moved disconcertingly fast, pacing in ungainly circles in the kitchen. Any nagging rivalry I may have felt evaporated the moment I saw his face.

"Son! You got here just in time. This is—"

Larry and I jumped in: "Family history in the making!"

"Donna! Daggum, I can't find my gold cufflinks. You must have moved them."

310   Dan Hill

"Dan, Jesus Christ. I'm coming with your blasted cufflinks. You handed them to me five minutes ago."

"What about my acceptance speech? Did you take that too? Come on, woman, hurry! Danny, get over here and help me with my tie."

"I can't help you with anything if you don't stop with the pacing."

Gone were my worries about how Dad's health would hold up over five years; he looked like he might spontaneously combust within the next five minutes. Meanwhile, Mom's constant refrain, *Dan, calm down*, clanged like an alarm clock that couldn't be turned off. It took all four of us—Larry, Bev, Mom and me—to escort him to the car.

"If this is another Hill succumbing to mania, I swear I'm gonna fly straight back to L.A. and assume a new identity," I whispered to Bev, as she, Larry and I wedged into the back seat.

"It's just all the excitement, mixed up with his diabetes," Bev diagnosed, adding, "Has anyone checked his meds today?"

"Why is Dad driving?" Larry asked.

"How about because we're a family bent on mass suicide by car wreck," I said.

"Shut up, you two," ordered Mom. "You know how driving always settles your father down."

Actually, I'd never known that. As we wound down the Don Valley Parkway, en route to Queen's Park, the group of us settled into a stolid silence. The grimace on Larry's face led me to believe he and I were thinking the same thing: that Dad should turn the goddamned car around, floor it until we were out of Ontario and act as though this whole ombudsman appointment had never happened.

By the time we'd driven up to the front steps of the legislature, Dad's behaviour had gone from agitated to erratic. None of us knew until later that Dad had snuck one of Mom's Valiums. Mistaking his slurred speech for a dangerous blood sugar crash (insulin injections can sometimes cause a diabetic's blood sugar to plunge to the point where they lapse into a coma), I urged, "Take some deep breaths, Dad," quickly reached over Mom in the front seat, popped open the glove compartment, grabbed one of his dextrose tablets and pressed it into his mouth. The car sat idling.

"Dad, listen to me, try to relax for a minute before everyone starts swarming."

Uh oh. Dad had that same glassy-eyed glaze as Cassius Clay during his first, 1964 pre-fight weigh-in with Sonny Liston. As Mom was getting out of the car (presumably to run interference for Dad, who was already late), Dad confused the brake with the accelerator, leaving her to flail about on the legislature's front steps like a child tripping over her feet. Perhaps it was Mom cussing Dad out in language not exactly suited to the occasion that snapped him out of his fugue. He somehow pulled himself together and within an hour was delivering his acceptance speech in his typically congenial and homespun style. He spent the rest of the afternoon soaking up the attention and congratulations as if he'd been born in the spotlight.

Dad's fluctuation between breakdown and celebration was a telltale glimpse of how he would live his next five years. That final half-decade of his working life more or less destroyed what remained of his health. For Dad, wired to believe that success was everything, sacrificing an extra ten or twenty possible years of retirement in exchange for five tempestuous years as Ontario's ombudsman seemed a bargain.

"To me, an ombudsman's office is the incarnation of human rights," Dad explained during his swearing-in speech. "I really believe this is a human rights agency." Speeches such as these, steeped in easy-to-grasp comparisons, are usually written to inspire rather than be taken literally. It says something about Dad's naïveté and his passion that he honestly believed that he could pattern the provincial Ombudsman's Office (OO) after the Ontario Human Rights Commission (OHRC). Regrettably, he would discover that these two organizations could not have functioned more differently.

The purpose of the OO is to investigate claims of wrongdoing within the government or government-run services and agencies. If, for example, inmates at the Don Jail were complaining about the poor quality of their food and an investigation by the ombudsman uncovered a systemic problem in food preparation and services, then the OO would recommend that the Ministry of Corrections implement an improved food policy.

Unfortunately, the visionary thinking that had served Dad so well at the OHRC was not so easily applied at the OO. For one thing, prosecuting a racist restaurant owner was far more straightforward than taking a branch of the government to task for an alleged act of malfeasance. The never-ending political layers of bureaucracy, the chummy protectiveness of certain high-up government officials and the multiple connections between civil servants left the OO frequently hoop-jumping, often with no resulting basket.

Once the ombudsman is able to spot and confirm a problem in government services then the real challenge begins: the branch of government in question must be persuaded to own up to its problem. Only then can changes be made through direct policy recommendations or, failing that, through strenuous debate and voting in a parliamentary hearing.

This new world, which seemed to foster obfuscation at senior levels, was not ideally tailored to my father's brand of one-on-one, friendly-but-fierce confrontation. Increasingly frustrated by the limitations of the OO's reach, Dad argued passionately that his office needed more power and authority to properly investigate and advocate on behalf of Ontarians wronged by their government. To his credit, Dad's strenuous lobbying managed to eventually equip the OO with more power, but that extra muscle came only after his term was over. Alas, among my father's many strengths, patience was not high on the list.

Early in his term, Dad discovered that the inner workings of the organization were a mess; the staff often seemed too caught up in their own office rivalries to have any energy left over for their work. Dad wanted no part of the internecine squabbling.

"I want to do things, I don't want to worry about staff," Dad told Eleanor Meslin, a long-time friend whom he'd hired to be his executive assistant. Dad's natural delegating skills translated into Ms. Meslin handling the interpersonal issues, administration and finance, leaving Dad to concentrate on what he'd always excelled at: innovative ideas, combined with broad-stroke, spare-me-the-details thinking.

"He had a temper," Eleanor Meslin told me, her voice dropping to a whisper as though she were revealing some long-held secret. "Every so often with a couple of the senior people, he'd discover they'd done something wrong and he would blow, like, fast." Ms. Meslin quickly went on to qualify, "And then it would be over. He had a fantastic oratory ability. Such wonderful language. And of course, that amazing charisma. So that when he got angry, it was devastating."

The despotic figure that Ms. Meslin described was perfectly in line with the dad I grew up with, so the inconsistency of Dad's aloof persona in the office with his populist image outside the office came as no surprise for me. But twenty years later, Ms. Meslin still appeared flummoxed by Dad's "contradictory" behaviour.

A master of the symbolic gesture, Dad, upon taking the reins at the OO, made a big to-do of ridding the executive dining room of all the garish displays of elitism held over from the previous administration. There was no refuting Dad's point that this gaudy show of luxury (fine linen, elegant cutlery and china, and an endless supply of expensive liquor, which Dad referred to as befitting a "princely kingdom") was hardly appropriate for a branch of the government created to serve the public. But Dad's first in-house mandate—that his office would be permanently off limits to everyone other than Ms. Meslin without prior appointment—didn't do much to bolster his image as the ever-approachable people's champion.

Interestingly, during his travels throughout Ontario, Dad's ability to connect with anyone and everyone returned. Dad was the first Ontario ombudsman to set up field offices so that the OO's services could be more accessible, forming new networks of human rights allies everywhere he went. North Bay, Sudbury, Thunder Bay, Owen Sound, Timmins—the more remote the Ontario towns, the more Dad delighted in the people he came into contact with.

The legacy of Dad's work as "travelling ombudsman" in small-town Ontario came to my attention in the late nineties, when I was performing in these same small towns. Every town brought me in touch with someone who had worked with Dad at the OO. Almost everyone had the same thing to say: "Your father was the most amazing man I've ever met. He inspired me to make things better for everyone in this community. Everybody loved him here." No matter how many times I heard this, I could never think of what to say in response.

"I can't believe it Danny, you look just like him." I would find myself on the receiving end of an intense stare, as though Dad's former employee were looking into the face of a ghost. Dad's ghost.

"Well, I'm not as good-looking as my dad," came my formulaic reply, while signing an autograph.

The reserved, well-dressed adult, usually twenty years my senior, would often start to cry, embracing me in a hug that gave me chills, as though I could feel the very soul of my dad pouring out of the stranger's arms and finding its way deep beneath my skin.

All his travelling, however, tore Dad apart physically. He finally admitted to Eleanor Meslin, two years into his term, that he'd "recently been diagnosed with diabetes"—and only because Eleanor had grown increasingly suspicious and Dad had wearied of her questions. After extracting a vow of silence, he went on to claim that it was just a minor health issue that he had under control.

The more Dad denied his illness at work, the more anguished he appeared about it at home. "The travelling is hell," he told me, after returning from yet another long trip. "This hotel in Ottawa had a fabulous after-hours buffet in one of their hospitality suites and I wandered all night through the hallways, trying to remember where it was. I finally asked a hotel clerk. He explained they had no such suite. Then I realized I wasn't in Ottawa anymore. I was so exhausted, I'd forgotten which city I was in."

"When are you going to quit that job?" his family doctor would ask, reacting in alarm to Dad's ever-escalating blood sugar readings and weight gain. I also suggested that he consider stepping down, citing health reasons. But that was as likely as me setting aside my guitar.

While Mom and we three kids were counting down the days to Dad's retirement, Ms. Meslin and many of Dad's closest friends, convinced that he was retiring too soon, urged him to carry on. That if he wanted, he could conceivably extend his ombudsman's term beyond the usual five years. True to form, Dad had managed to project an air of invincibility to everyone in the workplace.

It's easy to imagine Dad caught in the middle of these two opposing forces, his friends and work associates telling him he had a moral imperative to keep working—"The mandatory retirement age of sixty-five was a travesty for your dad," was the statement most often bandied about by my father's friends—while his family demanded that he retire before he was carried off in a coffin.

"Thank God for those five years as ombudsman," Dad would always say when he'd finally retired. "That big, fat salary and pension is paying for all my extra medical bills."

I didn't have the heart to tell him what he already knew, that all his costly health problems—enlarged prostate, collapsing bone structure in his feet due to badly compromised circulation, glaucoma, macular degeneration—came as a direct result of those same five years as ombudsman.

To this day, Eleanor Meslin insists that Dad's diabetes didn't affect his ability to work, and that it was really Dad's retirement, more than anything, that damaged his health. She told me that once Dad had retired, "The community wanted to do tremendous things in his honour. Give him awards and dinners. To fete him. He wouldn't have any part of it." Ms. Meslin had loved Dad too much to openly criticize him. And it was this very affection that left her so disappointed when he appeared to withdraw from public life. Refusing to sit on committees or be part of arbitrations was one thing. But Dad appeared to take pleasure in turning down the lifetime contribution awards that "hounded" him after retirement, viewing them as little more than political grandstanding.

"Son," he'd snort, "the only reason that mean s.o.b. Harris [Ontario's ultra-reactionary premier at the time] wants to give me some bogus human rights award is because he thinks it will reflect well on him. That the public will be fooled into thinking he's a champion of people's rights."

What Dad left unsaid was that he believed any kind of lifetime recognition ceremony suggested his best work was behind him—something he couldn't bear to consider.

"I'll be taking your mother on lots of vacations now," Dad would tell me in his increasingly gravelly voice. "My pappy always promised my mom he'd take her to Europe after he retired but he never did. He was too weak by then. I promised your mother I wouldn't make the same mistake with her."

And they did go on vacations. Alaskan cruises. Month-long stays at quaint little Portuguese inns. Villas in Spain. But Dad far preferred the idea of a European vacation to the event itself. He'd hole up in his little room, rarely venturing outside. In fairness, Dad's foot was far more irreparably damaged than either he or Mom understood at the time. Not only was walking excruciatingly painful, it exacerbated his injury.

Work addicts do not make good retirees. I've known lots of successful performers whose wives begged them to go back on the road when the sight of them muddling about in a cloud of inactivity, or slowly dying in front of the TV, proved far worse than the loneliness of being separated from them.

A therapist once told me, "People like you all end up the same, super-achieving your way into that final heart attack."

But what's the alternative? Is playing bingo and being coddled through a senior's art or stretching class really preferable to falling dead onstage at Carnegie Hall?

This put me in the unusual position of understanding, perhaps more easily than most sons, what Dad was dealing with now that he'd retired. Once you're out of the public eye, regardless of the profession that catapulted you there in the first place, you're no longer viewed as special. At least when I crashed out of my brief superstar orbit I was in my twenties; there were countless creative stones still left for me to turn. Dad was sixty-six when he officially retired. He knew his physical health couldn't stand up to the stress of any more work, just as he tacitly understood that his mental health would suffer if he stopped working.

Dad slipped in and out of various stages of melancholia for the last thirteen years of his life. His father had also drifted in and out of his own deep blue moods once he'd retired, a paralyzing sadness that followed him to his grave. It's fine when you're king of your imagined domain, but sooner or later you have to step down. And once you do, the black dog is always there, patiently waiting.

I knew, all too well, the deep, seemingly irrational sadness so often connected with diabetes, the sum total of which felt more dark and overwhelming than its individual parts. I could spot the slightest flicker of depression in a stranger a football field away. And so, if I quickly developed a knack for distracting Dad from his moodiness, it was born out of pure selfishness. I couldn't bear to feel the sadness spilling out of his soul and leaking into mine.

CHAPTER 24

Berlin

"Karen, stop! What are you doing?"

I was in a literal life-or-death tug-of-war with my sister's right arm. Without warning, she'd tried to lunge into the middle of a busy West Berlin street at rush hour. When I yanked her to safety on the sidewalk, Karen gave me a reproachful look.

"Karen, even if you don't care about your own life, think of the poor driver who runs you over. He's going to be devastated."

For a moment I didn't realize the shrieking voice competing with the cars honking at my sister was mine. It was February 1985, and I was once again trying to keep someone I loved from being pulled under. As I felt my sister's numbness wash over me, I turned away, wanting no part of her latest mood swing. The idea that Karen was in no state to think of anyone or anything else, that her desire to put an end to her blackness blotted out all other considerations, was terrifying precisely because a part of me could understand how she felt. It wasn't my father's recent melancholia that it called to mind, but the women in our family. It killed me to look into my sister's face and see the shadows of my mother's suffering. 1966. 1976. Wasn't I supposed to have another ten months before the family crazy cycle repeated itself?

"It's your turn, son," Dad had announced in that inimitable way of his. "Your sister's very, very sick. Larry just returned from three weeks in Berlin. Your mother and I were there for almost a month before that. Now it's time for you to step up and be strong for Karen."

If God's voice had thundered out of the clouds to issue some awful, irrevocable command, I thought, he would have sounded like Dad—only less aggravating.

Larry had thoroughly prepped me for my Berlin trip, writing out a list of questions for Karen's psychiatrist, along with choice trigger terms to drop on the hospital bureaucracy if she needed to be committed again, quickly.

In addition to our concern for Karen, Larry and I were worried about the domino effect: the harder Karen fell the more likely that Mom would be dragged down with her. We'd witnessed a variation of this in 1981, immediately following a suicide attempt by Mom's twin sister, Dottie. Although both Mom and Dottie recovered, the memory of Mom, incoherent and unreachable, still rubbed raw, as though it had happened just the week before and could happen again at any time.

As Larry and I discussed Karen's situation we caught ourselves sneaking glances at each other in that critical, appraising way. Was Larry talking too fast? Was I interrupting too much? Which one of us would be the next to go? Despite fundamentally different personalities, there were times when Larry reminded me so much of myself that it was almost impossible to be around him. His intensity, his inability to relax, his unrelenting drive, all the more pronounced by his outright dismissal of his accomplishments, smacked so much of my self-denigrating style that sometimes I'd hear him seemingly steal my yackety-yack phrases seconds before they tumbled out of my mouth. Nevertheless, Larry wasn't manic. Just brainy and high-strung. Like me. But I'd stumbled across my technique for emotional survival a long time ago. The same was true for Larry. He'd recently finished a successful stint as a reporter for the *Winnipeg Free Press,* where they'd honoured his stellar writing with a huge poster that read "Dan Hill's smarter brother." Dad, finding the poster as hilarious as I found it most unfunny, had taped it across our Christmas tree.

But it wasn't Christmas in snow-white Don Mills any more. It was West Berlin in February, and the sky was dark and polluted with a mixture of low clouds and the thick belching smoke of coal heating. Karen lived in the northeast part of the city, in a working-class area called, ironically, Wedding. The buildings, grey and tall and as close to the road as they were to each other, stretched so high that it was impossible to see the sky unless you craned your neck to the breaking point. The same Karen who, just moments ago, had come close to flattening herself underneath a speeding Mercedes was now bounding up the steepest stairs I'd ever climbed. "Cycling," her shrink called it when her moods plunged down, then flipped up as though her brain were hitched to a roller coaster. By the time I caught up with Karen she was in her hut of a kitchen, her back to me, fumbling with something. Stiffening at the sound of my footsteps, she turned around to face me.

"Karen, don't eat the fucking salt."

Karen squinted at me as though I were overreacting and it were a perfectly acceptable dietary regimen to scoop up a fistful of salt that had hardened in the bowels of some neglected pantry container and then cram it into her mouth like some tightly balled-up snow cone. *It's the meds,* I told myself. *All the anti-psychotics mixed with lithium mixed with thyroid pills—next thing she's gonna be biting off her arm.*

Karen giggled as I continued to mouth silent, soothing messages to my brain. Then she narrowed her eyes, like I was the real nutcase, and, as if to humour me, let the leftover salt that had been squeezed in her fist sprinkle soundlessly to the floor. To make sure she didn't get any more bright ideas, I primly picked up the container, still heavy with salt, and walked back to what I considered—why I don't know—my side of the kitchen.

Karen started opening and closing all her cupboard doors as if to protect the rest of her foodstuffs from my thieving ways. Task accomplished, she looked back at me and licked her salty fingers clean, one digit at a time. How did she get this way, so freakin' out there, so suddenly?

"Would you like me to get you a wet cloth for your hands, Karen?"

"No thank you, Danny."

How oddly formal.

I took in the round loveliness of her face. For the first time I could see Aunt Margaret in Karen's high cheekbones, Margaret's dimples curling around the edges of Karen's full mouth. Even Karen's intelligent, quick-moving brown eyes, at odds with the excruciating slowness of her physical movement, recalled the lonely, sad Margaret who taught me, as an eight-year old, the meaning of "suicide attempt." Hard to believe that Margaret was then just a few years older than Karen was now.

It would be better to compare Karen's situation to Mom's. After all, since Dad had become ombudsman, Mom had remained emotionally solid, even unflappable. And if Mom (by Dad's reckoning) consistently bounced back because she was married to the world's most wonderful husband, then the same reasoning might be applied to Karen. Because Karen had married a Caucasian German who loved her as ferociously and protectively as Dad loved Mom.

"Hey Karen, when's Thomas getting back?"

Karen had padded to the living room to tend to her coal oven, the apartment's heat source. As the stove came to life, spewing noxious sparks of orange dust everywhere, her tiny apartment started to get that rotten-egg smell. Karen listlessly poked at the oven with a fire tong for a few more minutes before curling up on the living-room floor and instanty falling asleep. I grabbed a pillow, pounded some of the dust out of it and tucked it under my head as I lay down beside my sister on the grimy—what was that sticky stuff?—floor.

Try as I might to slow down my thoughts, I couldn't get Dad's latest command—*Get your sister home, fast*—out of my head. Or Larry's: *Danny, make sure you never ask Karen to come home, it'll turn you into the enemy.*

But Karen is home, I thought, as I did a quick survey of the photos on her living-room wall. Thomas with his parents, the wedding picture of Dad kissing Mom, a blurry snapshot of the seven kittens that had briefly turned our house into delightful mayhem. So much love on those walls, among the sadness and the filthy floors and the stink of the coal heater. *Sleep when she sleeps, try to stay on Karen's schedule. That's what Thomas has to do, when he doesn't have our help.* Trying to absorb Mom's advice, I found myself doing that open, shut, flutter thing with my eyes. *Maybe Karen will just sleep for the next seventy-two hours,* I thought, too exhausted to relax, too lazy to drag my jet-lagged ass off the floor. As I drifted in and out of consciousness, I fantasized about my sister waking up in the middle of next week to find that she'd slept the whole bipolar thing off.

Karen had moved to Germany five years earlier, in 1980, at twenty-two. The official reason was that she'd fallen in love with Thomas while travelling. Karen had taken off to Europe within forty-eight hours of graduating from the University of Ottawa. But it would take more than crossing the Atlantic Ocean to escape what Karen later termed "the ghost of Dad."

Thomas, according to Dad, was a "permanent student" (code for "underachiever"), even though Dad could have been accused of the same thing at Thomas's age. Originally from Frankfurt, Thomas had been studying in Berlin for a good half-dozen years, stacking up degrees the way a short-order cook piles up pancakes.

"That Thomas is a lazy so-and-so," Dad had complained, hours before I flew off to Europe. "I think Karen's supporting him. And he's paying her back by putting crazy ideas in her head."

Even if that were true, what did Dad expect me to do about it? Enact some kind of gallant Don Mills–style intervention, as if I were rescuing Karen from a deranged German cult?

"Thomas is against everything. He's a radical. An anarchist," Dad said. "And disorder is the last thing someone like your sister needs. Your mother and I agree: Thomas is the reason why your sister's so sick!"

Thomas was unlike any anarchist I'd come across. (Then again, the streets of Don Mills weren't exactly paved with revolutionaries.) Thomas didn't like socializing, preferring books to people. In fact, beyond reading and listening to obscure blues records, Thomas didn't appear to like very much of anything. He was one of those rare people who take delight in hating things, whose purpose in life springs from the three Cs: criticizing, complaining and, most of all, correcting. So why did I like Thomas? Because Dad wanted me to hate him? Partly. But despite himself, Thomas was entertaining. One of the reasons it was so easy to get a reaction out of him, to piss him off, was that he cared, deeply, about everything—most of all, my sister. An intellectual snob nonpareil, he reminded me of another dominating, know-it-all husband.

Slam! The sound of the door startled me out of my sleep.

"Look at the two of you! Huh!"

Thomas, pointing disparagingly to Karen and me spread out like a couple of drunks across the living-room floor, had said hello in his mocking fashion. He had arrived home from an afternoon researching medical illustrations (his part-time job) in the library, dressed in black, looking considerably older than twenty-eight. When I rose to shake Thomas's hand, he strong-armed me into the kitchen.

"No wonder your sister's borderline catatonic," Thomas began. "She's overawed by your family. Talking to her you'd think your dad is Martin Luther King Jr., your brother is Langston Hughes and you're fucking Bob Dylan."

"Well, you know Karen, always downplaying her family's achievements," I said. "And nice to see you too, Thomas." It appeared as though everyone thought they knew the reason for Karen's out-of-the-blue undoing, while remaining a little less certain of the cure. Oh well, if this was how a husband stood up for his wife, by castigating her family, I was willing to absorb some abuse.

"Your dad is so ashamed that Karen works as a foreign language secretary at the Max Planck Institute that he lies and tells everyone she works as an international translator. And he comes over here asking me why she's so sick."

"Thomas, you show me a parent, and I'll show you someone who exaggerates their children's accomplishments."

"Do you even know what put Karen in this hole?"

As Thomas explained that he'd repeatedly told her not to go away on that union retreat with her co-workers, I could feel his anger melting into hopelessness. Without interrupting, I gestured towards the living room, thinking that the sounds of Karen waking might slow down his play-by-play. Instead, Thomas continued: "I knew that your sister was getting in way over her head when she went to that conference. But she wanted to take on more responsibility . . ." Thomas let his unfinished sentence hang in the air, all the better for me to infer the obvious: because Karen needed to send a message to her Canadian family that she was willing to better herself at work, she had "bettered herself" into a breakdown.

"Hi guys," Karen said, now en route to the bathroom. She had the look on her face that she used to get whenever she overheard Mom and Dad fighting: pleased at hearing something off-limits while at the same time unnerved.

"Listen, Thomas, I know Karen was talking gibberish when she got back home, that despite her doctor getting her on haloperidol, you had to watch her every second for weeks before she could be committed—"

Karen walked out of the bathroom, smiling as though life were a perfect fuzzy peach.

"Hey, you two. Let's go for a walk. All these pills have me gummed up and exercise always helps."

Things were going from weird to weirder. Was it me or had the new Karen—the manic woman who'd been trying to body-block speeding cars but a few hours ago—been inexplicably replaced by the Karen of old?

"Your sister's depression always lifts in the evening. I had to explain the same thing to your brother. Her body chemistry undergoes a change at night—"

"Woo-hoo! Here I am, Thomas!" Karen said. "You don't have to talk about me as if I'm not around."

As my weeks in Berlin unfolded, it became clear that the dynamic of Karen and Thomas's interactions shifted in tandem with Karen's moods.

Morning until suppertime passed with Thomas ordering and hovering over Karen like a teacher at a girl's finishing school: "Stop staring at strangers, Germans don't like that," "Look at your brother, he's just as bad, what other bad habits of his have you picked up?"

During the day, Karen took in all this carping without offering much in the way of defence. She'd hang her head, affect a look of guilt and offer the occasional, "Okay, Thomas, I'm trying. Really." But at night, Karen, shaking off her depressed stupor, would rebel: "Fuck off, Thomas, if you don't like me clipping my fingernails in the subway then look the other way." *Bop!* Karen would cap her defiance by smacking a rolled-up newspaper over Thomas's head.

"Ow!" he'd whimper, then back off.

"Don't tell me what I can and cannot eat!" and Thomas, chagrined, would return Karen's bread roll. He may have talked like Che Guevara, but when you stood up to him he curled up like a kitten.

Anxious to have someone else to order around, Thomas would start in on me: "What do you put coffee in the fridge for? That's stupid," "You're not supposed to use the thumb of your left hand for bar chords. That's what lazy guitar players do," "Why are you reading Ralph Ellison? He's a one-hit wonder, like you. Here: read Pushkin. I'll bet you didn't know that he was Black."

Karen had fled to Europe to escape Dad, only to replace him with a pastier, more didactic and—hard as it was to believe—bossier version. Thomas was also attentive like Dad: keeping track of Karen's medications, making sure she made all her doctor's appointments, cooking and cleaning, ensuring she had clean clothes to wear. He was her sense of structure and stability, something Karen needed as much as she loathed.

And most importantly, I suspected that Thomas was in it for the long haul. As for his perpetual crankiness, who wouldn't be a little frayed around the edges by living with a woman who, before being committed the previous October (why on earth had they released her?), was convinced that the curtains tied into neat knots hanging out the window of her Vietnamese neighbour's apartment were a sign from God that she was pregnant. After all, everyone knew that knots symbolize embryos.

Spared Karen's delusional ravings (thanks to her recently improved and newly prescribed pharmaceuticals), I was exposed, head on, to her long jags of morning sobbing. When these began, she was inconsolable. She just wanted to die, so all the pain would go away. All Thomas or I could do was take turns holding her and wait it out. The guttural sound of her crying seemed to me like the very definition of bone-racking despair. It made me sick. It made me hate her sometimes. And it made me hate myself for hating her. But most of all it left me very, very sad.

"Your sister needs solidarity, friends and family around her, keeping things calm."

"How about increasing her haloperidol?" I asked, glancing suspiciously around the doctor's office for signs of his credentials. He was dressed as sloppily as Thomas and me, and looked a good ten years younger. Fuck. When did I start to get this reactionary? I had to get home before I turned into Brian Mulroney.

"You Americans and your drugs," the doctor said. "Anything to take the pressure off human responsibility."

"America's run by the drug companies," Thomas added, helpful as always.

"Above all, your sister needs rest. No conflict. Give her lots of support. And lots of time to build her strength up. I hope you're planning to stay with her for a while."

"And if she tries to kill herself again?" I asked.

"Your sister is improving. Think of her crying sessions as her way of letting out the poison. She's made it clear that she doesn't want to go back into the hospital. So long as she's slowly recovering, her wishes need to be respected. That's part of the healing. We need to see the hospital as a last resort."

"What about antidepressants?" I asked.

"Antidepressants are not advisable for manic-depressives, as they can trigger uncontrollable highs."

"I'm talking about for me. I could use some uncontrollable highs."

While I cackled uncontrollably at my advanced wit, the adolescent-looking doctor, sweeping the boyish flop of hair off his forehead, dismissed us.

"How much longer will you be away?"

"Bev, honestly, I wish I knew."

"It's already been more than two weeks."

"Well, Larry was here even longer. And it was way worse for him. Karen's getting better now. Finally."

"So then why can't you tell me when you're coming home?"

"Because I don't know."

"You sound really down. Do you need me to fly over there? Are you depressed?"

"Not at all. Why? Are you depressed?"

"Look, for your own good, you've got to get home. Soon."

Karen's mood gradually started to lift earlier every day. Her crying jags took up less time, washing through her in a matter of minutes rather than a couple of hours. We'd frequently go swimming after dinner, then walk for miles, occasionally darting into cafés, where we'd gobble up thick cream doughnuts and wash them down with heart-thumping German coffee. Wedding, in February, was dark and rainy. The sidewalks were deserted except for old ladies who'd lost their husbands in the war. Karen, still mood-coasting, would break unhurriedly into a Bonnie Raitt song, her tone so pure and airy that I wished she'd never stop singing.

It was wonderful to feel my sister return, little by little, from the darkness. Now that she seemed more stable, I found myself worried about her future. About the possibility of her slipping back.

"Karen, have you ever considered moving back to Toronto?"

"Why would I ever want to leave here?" Karen asked. And in that moment, she really appeared to love her life, her husband and this distinctly un–Don Mills city with its coal-smudged skies, constant drizzle and mounds of poodle poop. I swallowed, not trusting myself to say the right thing.

"Danny, tell me the truth, did the family send you here to try to bring me home?"

I decided I'd wasted too much time sugar-coating my every thought. Maybe all this Hill male tiptoeing around the females had contributed to my sister's "issues."

"I don't know, Karen, why would you want to leave West Berlin? I mean, other than the fact that you're suffering from life-threatening mental illness, that Thomas is so judgmental and controlling that he makes Dad look happy-go-lucky, and that the people you work with are willing to make you some sacrificial lamb, leading the fight for some union cause you barely understand, even if it kills you."

"Danny, you sound just like—"

"Don't take the easy way out, Karen. Did it occur to you that on the subject of you living in Berlin I also happen to sound an awful lot like Mom? And Larry?"

"Easy to be judgmental when you're rich. It wouldn't matter to you that it costs nothing to live in this city. Nobody cares about money here. Not like Canada, where everyone lives to work."

What I hadn't understood was that Karen felt accepted in Europe; that there were pockets of culture, tucked away beneath the mainstream, that thrived in Berlin and that appreciated her vibrancy, welcoming her rainbow of racial origins, as well as sharing her distaste for all things status quo. The time had come for me to leave Berlin. Karen knew better than any of us where she belonged.

When Karen left Thomas, a year or so after recovering—"She finally decided to rebel against Thomas's dominance as a way of rebelling against your dad," was Mom's interpretation—he was crushed. Though I didn't blame Karen for fleeing Thomas and, ultimately, Europe (she returned to Canada for good in the late eighties), I found myself feeling sorry for him. In his overbearing way, he really, really loved my sister. That kind of love, regardless of all the attached, nettlesome baggage, was pretty damned hard to find.

CHAPTER 25

Bev versus Dad

My experience with Karen had finally driven home a hard lesson for me, one I'd resisted most of my life: I wasn't an island. Much as I gravitated, in my moody creative fashion, towards solitude, I was at best a half-hearted isolationist. I was part of a family, and if one person suffered, we all suffered. Being an adult, whether famous and rich, or struggling and poor, offered no protection, no licence to look the other way. But this realization didn't leave me feeling warm and fuzzy, or noble. Quite the opposite.

When I returned from Berlin, still feeling the detritus of my sister's depression grinding beneath my skin, Bev had a surprise in store for me.

"I didn't want to tell you this while you were away, but when you were in Germany, an IRS collection officer came to Toronto to execute on your assets, including our house."

"What?!"

My outstanding tax battle with the IRS had been dragging on for years. In fact, one of the reasons that Bev and I had spent half a year in L.A. was out of fear that if the IRS succeeded in its claim against me I'd be banned from travelling to, and working in, America. While Bev and I were a considerable business force, three years of paying an American tax firm, on top of a Canadian tax firm, along with an overworked accountant, ate up the six figures a year I was netting. Meanwhile the IRS claim—as interest, fines and penalties continued to snowball—had metastasized into almost a million dollars. Given that the Canadian government taxed fifty cents on every dollar I earned, I had to make two million dollars, fast, to get the IRS off my back. That or legally prove that the IRS didn't have a case. Bev, but a few years out of law school, remained determined to pull off what the four-hundred-dollar-an-hour tax firms swore, right from the beginning, was most unlikely to happen.

"The IRS did not allow you to claim expense deductions when touring through the States in '76/'77," Bev explained, summarizing details I'd purposely blocked out.

Still unpacking, I snapped, as if Bev were on the opposing side, "I don't get it. I mean, touring across America—with airfare, hotels and rental cars for me and everyone travelling with me—cost me more money than I actually earned."

"But your managers couldn't produce the receipts evidencing your travel expenses."

"Evidencing your travel expenses? Plain English, please!"

Bev disappeared in the middle of my sniping, returning moments later with something that looked to me like a combination art-geography project that a grade schooler might hand in. Arms spread wide, she held a big wall map of the United States, along with a stack of contracts and reviews confirming all my stateside gigs over the years in question.

"See on this map how, with different-coloured pencils and pens, I illustrated the routes you had to travel all across America performing night after night? Only a singer with wings could perform in Seattle, fly home to Toronto afterwards and then show up in Portland two days later for another concert."

I stood, entranced by Bev's colour-coded visual recreation of my touring schedule. Surely, the IRS official would never have come across a defence like this before. Continuing to look over the different hues of lines and circles connecting some one hundred American towns and cities I'd hopscotched throughout the seventies, I mumbled, "How long did it take you to do this, honey?"

"Don't ask. But don't you want to know what happened next?"

Bev gave a lottery winner's smile, still stretching out her proud creation, as she detailed the negotiation that followed. After a long and careful examination, the IRS official allowed my travel expenses to pass, reducing my outstanding bill to a "measly" one hundred thousand. Determined to return to his tax bosses with something, he reminded Bev that this amount had to be repaid before he caught his evening flight to Washington, D.C. Bev, usually cautious by nature, decided to go for broke, informing her adversary that during my dual citizenship period I'd overpaid the IRS twelve grand. (Bev had mailed several letters informing the IRS of this overpayment, to which there'd been no response.) According to IRS interest tables from the time of the overpayment right up to the present day, that wiped out the hundred thousand I still owed. Frowning, the official countered that if Bev could produce my "alleged" cancelled cheque and hand it over to him by early evening, before he left his hotel, he'd consider my claim.

Rising to what was meant to be an impossible challenge, Bev taxied to my parents' home in search of the hundred-thousand-dollar smoking gun: my cancelled cheque to the IRS. A few hours later, after fumbling through reams of papers, documents and old fan mail piled into several boxes in the basement laundry room, Bev found my cancelled cheque, taxied back to the official's hotel and presented her evidence.

"Your husband's one helluva lucky man" was the taxman's way of announcing I was, finally, free and clear of all the IRS's claims.

How did I respond, jet-lagged and still unhinged from seeing my sister struggling to fend off the oldest Hill family scourge, upon arriving to such amazing news? Not the obvious "hooray, we've dodged bankruptcy and the spectre of moving in with my parents" reaction. Instead,

I had the surreal realization that I'd married a woman who would go to the ends of the earth, to hell and back, to protect me.

What gave me the right to be on the receiving end of such utter devotion? All my life I'd believed I had to earn, through formidable achievements, whatever kindness I received. Cynthia had always been a magnificent friend, but in order to win, to earn, her heart, I had to write five years of letters and prove that I was on the verge of becoming a singing sensation. A variation on this principle could apply to how I eventually gained my father's approval. But I didn't have to achieve anything to "earn" Bev's love; it simply poured out of her.

While I happily shared with Bev every drop of royalties, property, money, etc., I owned and would continue to earn (she'd offered to sign a pre-nup, and I'd scoffed at the idea), money and material things had always been easy for me to share. But it was never about money and possessions for Bev. It was about being loved in return. The kind of devotion Bev longed for and deserved could never be purchased. Bev needed to know that, when push came to shove, I'd choose her over everyone else. And "everyone else" meant one person: Dad.

"A man may be married to several different women over the course of his life. But he'll only have one father."

Whenever Dad made this statement, he would argue that he meant it generally, with the implication that if I took it personally, that was my issue, not his. True to form, Dad's reservations about Bev did not interfere with his swooning over everything she appeared to symbolize. "My son married a top-notch attorney!" was how he described her to his friends. For someone as scrupulously class-conscious as my father, Bev's intelligence, bearing (Bev's grasp of etiquette rivalled Grandma May's) and law degree, should have put him over the moon. Except that Bev the perfect wife caused my dad great concern as Bev the daughter-in-law. Because all of Bev's kindness and grace couldn't make up for one fatal flaw: she'd married Dad's oldest son.

I was plagued by conflicting loyalties; it wasn't as basic as me loving Dad in one way and Bev in another. I kept feeling as though I were being forced to quantify which love was stronger and more significant. As in many families, the tensions, between Bev and Dad, between Bev and me over Dad, between Dad and me over Bev, were never dealt with directly, coming out from time to time in petty observations.

"Why isn't Bev drawing a paycheque yet?" Dad would ask.

"She's starting up a business, Dad. Any money she and her father are making is being invested back into the firm."

"Well, how long will it take before she can help out with all your fancy restaurant bills and holidaying?"

This was a pointless discussion and one that I'd quickly put an end to. Dad, like most people, assumed lawyers walked out of law school and straight into high-salaried jobs. (Similar to the public's view of a pop singer with one song on the radio.) But this wasn't about Bev's money-making abilities.

Still, money was largely the point of contention between Bev and my dad. Dad felt that I should give, or loan, money to various members of our family, no questions asked. Bev disagreed. A lot of this revolved, as usual, around control. But it went deeper than that. Dad, coming out of a family where it was a moral obligation for a brother to financially support an ailing sister, or any other relative in need, couldn't understand Bev's point that singers (unlike university professors or top-echelon government employees) make and lose huge pots of money at unprecedented rates, often ending up, when it's too late to stage a comeback, desperately broke, if not in debt. As a lawyer, Bev had seen many businesses surge and then fail. Dad's demand that I needed to give, no questions asked, no paperwork necessary, an advance on, say, a cousin's down payment on a house, because that's what Hills do for other Hills, was galling to Bev.

As always, I muddled through, trying to please both parties and usually accomplishing the opposite.

"It's better to have Dad's respect than his admiration," I'd explain to Bev, spinning things in my typical manner. "I mean, your mom took a long time to warm to me. In fact she couldn't stand me."

"And she still doesn't respect you!" Bev joked (an encouraging sign).

"The key is not to take it personally," I added.

But the thing about Dad was that, despite himself, he remained, to all of us, unavoidably and unabashedly lovable. And when you love a person as much as Bev loved Dad, everything little thing he says and does has a way of getting to you.

Furthermore, when Dad judged Bev, however unfairly, it felt as though he was judging me. Still, I knew better than to point out that Bev, by cutting out all sorts of middlemen who'd been siphoning off my royalties, by making the IRS go away and by advising me to settle with the McCauleys, was earning us plenty. These things were too corporate, too impersonal, for my father. Money, as in big money, along with big money complications—like publishing lawsuits and tax claims—was boring, arcane and maybe even a little bit frightening.

It wasn't until the summer of '86, when Bev took on one of the most powerful men in the music business on my behalf, that Dad's respect for her started to cross over into something approaching genuine affection. A one-on-one confrontation, especially one so seemingly lopsided, was something Dad could relate to.

Halfway through recording my "comeback" album that year, my record producers (Hank Medress and John Capek) realized they were way over budget. The only person willing to confront my executive producer, legendary music mogul Charles Koppelman, with this news, and dare to ask for more money so we could finish the recording, was Bev. Koppelman was known to throw around lots of cash when he chose to, but it tended to be on himself. When he'd visited Columbia Records in Toronto the previous spring to sew up the Canadian portion of my record deal, his rented white limo had been too massive to manoeuvre into Columbia's parking lot. Everyone inside the Columbia building had stopped work to gawk out the window at the monstrous vehicle stranded on Leslie Avenue like a whale washed ashore. The president of Columbia Canada was rumoured to have been so taken with this spectacle that he decided, at that moment, to give Koppelman whatever he was about to request in terms of co-financing my record deal.

While I appreciated Koppelman's influence and power in securing my international record deal (which led to a string of hit singles in America), I hated his penchant for keeping me on a tight creative leash when I was in the studio. During the final recording stages I'd have to report to him each morning so that he could hear the previous night's mixes. Koppelman would always demand changes that I believed were dated.

"Dan, you write great fucking hooks, so why do you keep changing your chorus melody at the end of the song? Go back in and sing each fuckin' line exactly the same."

When I'd cite recent examples of pop hits with ever-changing final choruses, like, say, Don Henley's "Boys of Summer," he'd hop out from behind his grand piano–shaped desk, his outlawed Cuban cigar popping in and out of his mouth as he spat out the same command: "Stop fucking around and just do it!" Then he'd snap his W.C. Fields suspenders hard against his puffed-out chest, causing a swift, sharp *bwack* that signified my dismissal.

Koppelman, a former songwriter, was not unlike a lot of hugely wealthy, megalomaniacal record execs who revelled in micro-controlling the artists signed to their roster.

So when Bev volunteered to meet with Koppelman on my behalf to negotiate a bigger album budget, I felt as though she were about to be fed to the lions. But Bev returned from New York City with the extra money we needed.

"What's the big deal?" Bev asked my flabbergasted dad. "Charles is a businessman. He's not going to pull the plug on a close-to-finished project. He's invested a fortune in Danny, he plans to make it back and then—"

"Charles?" I parroted. "No one calls Koppelman by his first name!"

"Daggum, girl! Tell me once more how you got that rich old so-and-so to part with his loot! Donna, I should have used Beverly to negotiate my ombudsman's salary."

Dad was finally seeing the light. Bev was a fighter, just like him.

CHAPTER 26

Comeback (of Sorts)

A s my father made the difficult transition into retirement, I was trying to come to grips with issues of retirement as well. Had the time come for me to call it quits as a singer? Despite enjoying songwriting more than performing, I had continued to release records for the simple reason that people make more of a fuss over a successful singer than a successful songwriter. To use the movie industry as a parallel, if Tom Hanks is standing next to the writer of *When Harry Met Sally* at a movie premiere, how many people are going to approach the writer and say, "How did you think up that restaurant orgasm scene with Meg Ryan?" Maybe two. The other 498 are going to be swarming Tom Hanks.

By the mid-eighties, the music industry had become more about business and less about music. The ever-burgeoning importance of image and packaging, something largely overlooked in the seventies (if Joni Mitchell's name is mentioned you think of her songs; if Madonna is mentioned you think of her cone-shaped bra), started nipping at my heels in the eighties. My new U.S. manager seemed more concerned about my quickly receding hairline than the quality of my songwriting and kept at me to get a hair transplant. I scheduled several appointments, putting down a thousand-dollar deposit each time, only to chicken out at the last second.

Shortly before my "comeback" album was to be released in the summer of '87, I was subjected to serious scrutiny by Mary, my annoyingly young, saturnine product manager at Columbia Records in New York City.

"You have a problem," she told me. "Everyone who hears your new record loves your voice. But they picture a powerful, virile man behind that voice."

"Yeah, I've heard that before," I said.

"Really, Dan, you look more like a college professor than a singer. You're going to have to hire a trainer and beef up. It's time you lose that hippie, granola image. As Springsteen's product manager, I made sure he did a serious weightlifting program before we launched the promotion to *Born in the U.S.A.* That butt shot on the album cover probably sold more records for us than all his combined radio airplay."

As a high school kid, I'd embraced pop music as a heroic way of rebelling against convention. What a joke. The music business is rife with more "be cool or die" pressure than the most exclusive high school clique. And the bottom line—make the company a quick profit or get the hell out—is no different from any other profession. Except that the music business, disingenuously, sells itself as a daring, sexy alternative.

Part of the reason I put up with the record industry's ever-increasing obsession with image over musical substance was that I knew I'd finally recorded an album that contained a straight-down-the-pike, no-brainer smash. Columbia Records had readily acknowledged that the duet I'd recorded with Vonda Shepard, "Can't We Try," sounded like a number-one hit. The catch was that Vonda had recently signed to Columbia's archrival, Warner Bros. Records. The last thing Columbia wanted to do was help Warner Bros. by igniting Vonda's career, especially since it had passed on signing Vonda months earlier. Columbia had already tried taking Vonda off my record and replacing her vocal with Ronnie Spector, formerly married to Phil Spector, and lead singer of the sixties girl group the Ronettes.

On the day of the recording, I had been instructed to stay away from the studio. "You're not to go within a mile of where Ronnie's recording," Koppelman ordered. "You'll just intimidate her."

Two hours later Koppelman tracked me down again: "Get into the studio right now. Ronnie needs direction. You're the only one who can sing the melody for her."

I spent all afternoon coaching Ms. Spector through her vocal, praying that she would sing the song either wonderfully or terribly. If her performance landed somewhere in the middle, Columbia was sure to replace Vonda's vocal with hers, which, I believed, would doom the single's shot at success. Spector gave the song her best efforts, laying down dozens of takes.

"Try singing it like this," I'd suggest, changing the song's melody to better play into Spector's limited vocal span. "Less air and more tone—think Gladys Knight."

"Don't you dare mention another female singer in front of my artist again!" warned Spector's manager, a woman who wore a black suit and punctuated her threats by blowing thick clouds of cigarillo smoke in my face.

But it was obvious that my multi-octave song was beyond Spector's range. Once Spector and her manager were gone, I combined the worst of Spector's vocal takes into one spectacularly out-of-tune "finished" track. Still, I wasn't confident that Columbia Records, blinded by the meretricious flash of marketing possibilities, would choose Vonda's recording over Spector's. Spector had made waves recently with a cameo vocal part on an Eddie Money smash, "Take Me Home Tonight," which had left the execs drooling over the potential of a Tina Turner–like revival. I would have to wait three sleepless weeks for the suits at Columbia to render their verdict.

It was amid all this turmoil that I got out of bed one night, unable to sleep, and wandered into my living room and turned on the TV. I aimlessly surfed the channels, trying to find something that would take my mind off my career. I settled on David Letterman. He was in the midst of announcing his infamous top-ten list. Tonight it was the worst records of all time. Numbers five through two fell into the novelty category, consisting of over-the-hill actors like Leonard Nimoy massacring folk-rock classics like "Blowin' in the Wind."

I had a sinking premonition of what was coming next. There was a drum roll, which echoed the rumbling I felt building in my stomach, followed by Letterman contorting his face into his patented pained expression.

"And here it is," he groaned, "the number-one worst record of all time: the New York City Gay Men's Chorus, live from Carnegie Hall, singing 'Sometimes When We Touch.'"

My seventies recording was turning into the perfect send-up song, enjoying more ridicule as it became further ingrained in popular culture. And indeed, there were times when no one hated that song as much as I did. I could tolerate people slamming it. So many pop stars recorded it (to list them would fill two pages), and so many movies, TV shows and commercials featured it, that, in a sense, it didn't belong to me any longer. It was bigger than me, bigger than life.

"Bring on the criticism," Dad would proclaim, "so long as your cheques keep rolling in." Unlike typical hit songs, my song kept earning more each year. BMI had informed me that it would soon be among the top one hundred most-played pop songs of the last fifty years. No wonder people hated it, they'd heard it too many times; the damned song was like a dripping faucet that couldn't be turned off. *Be my guest, people, hate it all you want,* I'd think. What I couldn't tolerate was people telling me how unbelievable the song was: leaving me to infer that I'd peaked, that everything else in my life would pale in comparison. I promised myself that, whatever else I did or didn't accomplish, I would record at least one more U.S. hit record before I packed it in.

In a way I have to thank Tina Turner for shaming me into writing and recording my eventual, and long time coming, follow-up U.S. smash, "Can't We Try." (Bev contributed to the song's lyrics.) After taking in Turner's show at Toronto's Imperial Room in the early eighties, I was spotted in the audience by the room's booking agent, Gino Empry, who insisted on dragging me back to the star's dressing room.

"I heard the song shortly after I broke up with Ike," Ms. Turner told me, after I thanked her for recording "Sometimes" on her last album. "I woke up to it playing on my hotel clock radio. It was exactly what I was going through at the time. I knew right away I had to record it." Ms. Turner slathered her face in cold cream as she talked, moaning over the sorry state of her aching muscles and stiff joints, while shivering in a housecoat. It was as though, en route from the stage to the dressing room, she'd gone from being the sexiest woman alive to my great-aunt Mabel.

As she continued talking, I flashed back to the time Barry Mann had first played me Tina Turner's version of our song. We'd both listened, shell-shocked. Her tough-driving vocal veered into S&M territory: when she sang the bridge—"At times I'd like to break you, and drive you to your knees"—I'd found myself almost covering up, as if the primal power of her voice could have snapped me in two.

"I told everyone I know about your record," Ms. Turner continued.

"I really appreciate that, Miss Turner." Never had "appreciate" sounded so underwhelming.

"I went out and bought every record you made the day I heard that song." She paused to look at me, taking me in with those dark, soulful eyes, like she was trying to find something deeper beneath my skin—some clue that there was more to me than I was choosing to reveal. "You know something, Dan, you really let me down. There was nothing else on any of your records that came close to that song. Why was that?"

There was no trace of condemnation in her voice, only puzzlement, as if she needed me to clear up this mystery of my colossal inconsistency so she could put it behind her. I stood up, shook her hand and backed out of her dressing room, feeling like a bright but underachieving creative writing student.

When "Can't We Try" was listed as *Billboard* magazine's number-one U.S. adult contemporary single of the year in 1987, going on to spend more weeks on the Hot 100 than "Sometimes," I thought of how Tina Turner had unintentionally embarrassed me into recording at least one more hit song before I called it quits. But there was one person I needed to impress even more than Tina.

"You wrote a classic, son. That song will haunt you till the day you die," Dad would laugh, referring to "Sometimes" whenever I was about to play him one of my new records. Finally, after a decade of Dad telling me I was pop music's Roger Maris (who broke Babe Ruth's home run record one year, only to never again come close to matching this feat), I loped into his house one day in late 1988 grinning triumphantly.

"I've got something to show you, Dad," I huffed, handing him a copy of *Billboard* magazine. I'd folded it open to the page listing the top-three adult contemporary singles in the United States for 1987. "Can't We Try" (the Dan/Vonda version) was number one, beating out Whitney Houston and Michael Jackson. Dad smiled, shaking his head.

"Trust me, son, 'Can't We Try' is a good song but 'Sometimes When We Touch' is your masterpiece."

I prissily reminded Dad that a week hadn't gone by over the past four years when I hadn't had at least one, and usually two, songs on the Billboard AC chart. (My streak had started with Jeffrey Osborne's "In Your Eyes" in early '86 and ended four songs later in late '89.)

"Danny, maybe with all those royalties you could think about being a little more generous with your own flesh and blood. And besides, if 'Can't We Try' is as good as 'Sometimes,' then how come Vonda refused to sing with you on Johnny Carson?"

Dad, typically, had lasered in on one of my career sore spots. When "Can't We Try" became a hit, Vonda, caught up in recording her own album (and perhaps feeling the same pressure from Warner Bros. as I'd felt from Columbia about not helping an artist from a rival label), had refused to perform with me. With offers pouring in for me to sing "Can't We Try" on numerous television shows, I needed to find a female singer. In the summer of 1987, a visibly nervous and timid teenaged girl walked into my house to audition as Vonda's replacement. Unable to speak a word of English, she looked as though she were ready to skedaddle out of my house with stage fright when I reached out to shake her hand.

"It's okay, this should only take a few minutes. The important thing is how our voices blend," I said, in a mishmash of words and gestures, already expecting her audition to be a bust. But then she opened her mouth and started singing. Her name was Celine Dion.

The following year I decided to include Celine, still unknown outside Quebec, on a duet called "Wishful Thinking" for my next album. My new executive producer, Don Rubin (Koppelman, having just signed Tracy Chapman, no longer had time for me or my backtalk), nixed the idea, believing the song sounded better as a solo. My only recourse was to sneak Celine into the Right Track Studios in New York City and record her vocals when I was supposed to be mixing. Celine's shimmering performance turned Rubin and Columbia Records into believers. A few months later I found myself playing the duet for Dad, thrilled by the blend of Celine's voice with mine.

"That's a pretty good effort, son."

"Pretty good effort? That's all you have to say?"

"Who's this Celine Dion, anyway? Why does she sing with that French accent? Tell your old man the truth, boy, what happened between you and Vonda? How come she isn't singing with you anymore?"

"Forget about Vonda, okay, Dad? And I already told you, Celine's from Quebec. French is her language. Her accent is part of what makes her voice so authentic."

"Whatever you say, Danny, you're the music expert. But if you're asking me, 'Wishful Thinking' is an okay song, but it's no 'Can't We Try.'"

"You always do this!"

"Quiet down! Just because you've got a few hits under your belt doesn't entitle you to raise your voice to me."

"I'm not raising my voice. I'm a singer—I project."

"Joe Williams. Billy Eckstine. Those are real singers, son. You're a pop stylist."

"Listen, Dad, when I played you 'Can't We Try' last year, you said the song was no 'Sometimes When We Touch.' That was after you asked me why I didn't have a Black woman singing with me. Remember? You said Vonda sounded too vanilla. So next year, when I play you a new song, are you going to tell me it's no 'Wishful Thinking'? If I have a new singer featured with me, are you going to ask what happened to Celine?"

"If you don't want my opinion, then don't bother asking for it. Anyway, what do I know about modern music? I'm just a broken down ol' sociologist."

Despite my run of chart-topping songs in the late eighties, my heart simply wasn't in it anymore. I'd become a human jukebox, saddened that I'd predicted as much during my RCA days when I'd impressed José Feliciano with my lyric, "Lord, don't let this crazy world make a jukebox out of me."

Singing and performing, non-stop, for a quarter-century had left me burnt out, wrung out, stressed out. Being signed to Columbia Records out of Manhattan brought me, everyday, face to face with my label mates: Springsteen, Barbra Streisand, Michael Jackson, Billy Joel, George Michael and up-and-comers like Celine Dion and Mariah Carey. Such a stacked roster reminded me that no matter what I achieved, it would never be good enough, commercial enough, whatever enough, to launch me into superstardom. Dad had raised me to believe that I had to be the best. Lower-case stardom—strings of million-selling hit singles without the corresponding Springsteenian album sales—was only second-best. And second-best was failure.

Much as artists love to blame their record label for their commercial frustrations, it wasn't in my nature to do that. And to Columbia Records' credit, they spotted my strengths as well as my weaknesses. As a performer I was a product of, and perfect for, the seventies. So perfect, in fact, that I was not suited for any other era. But because I came of age when melody and lyric meant everything, I was perfectly positioned to write songs for other, more charismatic and enduring artists, who may not have shared my gift for words, for memorable titles, for the nuts and bolts of storytelling. Columbia Records, sizing up the situation, started pestering me to write for several of its top artists.

"Neil Diamond's having a bad dry spell," my A&R man, Mickey Eichner, would tell me. "He needs songs, badly. Do you have anything that he could sing?" Then the promo guys at Columbia got into the act: Streisand needed a triumphant power ballad (somehow "power" and "ballad" struck me as a contradiction), Michael Jackson was looking for a message song in keeping with his current hit, "Man in the Mirror," etc.

But I wasn't yet ready to accept a backstage role in pop music. What had started as my greatest strength twenty years ago was now holding me back. My identity as the singer of my own songs was so ingrained that shifting gears in the way that, say, a pro athlete retiring as a player becomes a coach was anathema to me. This eventually left Columbia Records with no other option than to drop me.

Though I was slow to realize it, Columbia did me a great favour by liberating me from adult contemporary hell. The stylists could dress me up in padded suit jackets, thrust a shiny electric guitar in my arms and teach me faux dance moves to get me through singing one of my lacklustre up-tempo songs on *Late Night with Arsenio Hall*, or cast Vonda Shepard as a Roger Vadim–ish sexpot in the video for "Can't We Try," lying sprawled across a four-poster bed, but the whole exercise was phony. Worse than a clown, I felt like an imposter. If I didn't believe in what I was projecting, why should anyone else?

CHAPTER 27

Fatherhood: From Both Sides Now

Back in 1982 when I'd lost my first major U.S. record deal, I was about to get married, leaving me feeling as though one lifetime dream had been interrupted and replaced by another dream. In 1988, mere months before Columbia dumped me, I'd become a father. Would it always be like this, one without the other? Career or family? At some point, was I going to have to make a choice?

"Don't do this," Bev warned. "Don't start disappearing into yourself. Your son isn't going to care whether or not you have an American record deal. Your son needs a father."

Just like Dad, I couldn't be happy unless everyone viewed me as a supreme success story. That wasn't the way I wanted my son to live. No one should have to live like that.

"That boy has matinee-idol good looks," Dad effused upon laying eyes on our baby boy less than twenty-four hours after his birth. "Donna, take a look at how alert he is. He's a Hill, no doubt about that—he's gonna be a genius, just like all the other Hill males!"

When our son was born, I decided he'd come to fill the void; I'd lost my career and gained a son. Financially speaking, the timing was pretty good. Because my hit songs were all ballads, their shelf life on adult contemporary radio could easily span decades, which translated into a trust fund–like royalty stream. (Hit rock songs, unless they're classics, burn on and off rock playlists like a paper fire, thus earning fewer royalties in the long run.) So long as I didn't spend money like Mike Tyson, I could unofficially retire, spend some much-needed time at home and throw myself into being a full-time dad. At least, that was the plan.

Dad's enthusiasm for being a grandfather took a hit when he found out his first grandson wasn't going to be named Daniel Grafton Hill the Fifth. Someone in the media, piqued that I hadn't returned calls about what we'd named our first child, decided to invent a name: Elvis. The Toronto media jumped on this misinformation, criticizing Bev and me for such a high-profile name choice. My "screw the media, I refuse to let their lies affect me" response was not shared by my wife. Exhausted and emotional from a long labour, the last thing she needed was to be inundated with calls from relatives and friends congratulating her on our one-day-old son, Elvis.

"I never even liked Elvis," Bev lamented. "We have to come up with a name, right now. How can they lie like this about our baby?"

"All I know is we're not naming him Daniel Grafton Hill the Fifth."

"Why not?" Bev asked.

"Let him be his own person," I answered. "Let's call him David."

"How about David Daniel? That way he gets Daniel as his middle name."

Bev had come up with the perfect compromise.

But Dad didn't see it that way. To him, the string of Daniel G. Hills had been coldly cut short at four. Thanks to Bev. He wouldn't accept that David's name had been my choice. What red-blooded Hill male would dare break the chain of successive Daniel Hills?

Here I was, defying Dad once again, at a time when he would have felt it most acutely. Too proud to show outward concern about his deteriorating health, and—his greatest fear—how Mom would fare once he was gone, he chose instead to fret over seemingly trivial matters, steadily becoming more and more anxious: the house was overheated in the winter and too air-conditioned in the summer (a waste of electricity); Mom called her sister too frequently (expensive long-distance bills); the weeds in the front were getting out of control (a potential sign for robbers that the house might be abandoned) and the squirrels and raccoons were savaging the back garden. Dad was seeing disaster everywhere.

By the same token, retirement appeared to be softening Dad in ways both beautiful and shocking. The slow slide from omnipotence to vulnerability had made him more approachable, more humane, less obstreperous. Twenty years earlier, Dad might have carried the hurt about David's name for a very long time. But it was as though Dad knew that time was running out. It was too precious to be wasted on bruised feelings.

Whenever Bev and I brought David over to visit, Dad would melt into a cooing, adoring grandpappy, reminding me that his inborn love of babies was one thing that would never change.

"Songwriter or sociologist? Are you going to take after your celebrity dad or your broken-down ol' grandpappy?" he'd say. "Look at you, wiggling and squirming, constantly in motion. You can't wait to set the world on fire, can you?"

The warmth, the hint of self-mocking, the pure joy in Dad's voice meant that he could have been saying anything to his bundled-up grandson and it would have come out sounding like music. Indeed, Dad's gigantic and now liver-spotted hands, tenderly drawing his tiny, squiggling grandson to his chest, seemed to be the very definition of love.

Watching Dad purr and growl as David yowled in return, drooling and then gumming on his grandpappy's forearm, I could almost feel at peace. What could possibly be more perfect than this? I stood close to my father, hoping that his natural affection for babies, that get-down-on-your-knees-and-coo, the dancing and mugging, the tossing in the air and catching, all the stuff Dad had loved to do when he was a young father, would now rub off on me. And so it did, slowly at first, improving with time. When I stumbled, or felt as though David could sense that I was acting at being affectionate, I did what I always did when all else failed: I picked up my guitar.

I sang to my son constantly, showing him how my fingers danced across the neck of my guitar. I could tell when he wanted me to pick up the tempo and would kick it up a notch, gawking at the sight of him bopping along happily to my uneven rhythms. Whenever he tired of my strumming and singing he'd lean across the tray of his high chair and jam his little hands into my mouth. "No more singing, Daddy," he appeared to be saying, "I want all of you now." As the guitar left my hands, David would fill the space between my arms and chest, gurgling his own songs. Who would have thought that the day would come when I'd prefer the warmth of a ten-month-old's gyrating body to the cool contours of my Martin D-35?

I tended to speed-write and record on the road and slack off in Toronto, so when I was home I'd spend as much time as possible with David, taking him to my parents, bundling him up in his stroller for long winter walks along the shore of Lake Ontario, or taking my regular turn as duty parent at his playschool. Still, I had to work at being a father. How does anyone adjust to a new bundle of life dropping, as if out of the blue, into your ordered world, turning it into a helter-skelter commotion of feedings, diapers and all-night rocking to soothe three full months worth of colic? Bev and I went through the stuff all parents go through, feeling at the time as though no one else in the world had ever been subjected to such a delirious, frightening and exquisite life change. Like all other parents, we adjusted.

As an artist I was used to everything revolving around me. The time that Bev and I spent together was always at the mercy of my touring and recording schedule, our relationship defined by the vicissitudes of my career. If my singing voice was strained, she understood that I wouldn't talk to her, or anyone, until I was totally healed—which could take a week—and Bev's law practice was constantly being interrupted by any number of "career emergencies" of mine that she had to smooth out.

All that changed once David entered our lives. It took a while for me to fully step up, to be a man and admit that my music could no longer come first. My son and my wife came first. But when I finally understood this and began living my life accordingly, I became a better person, a more complete person. I have the birth of my son to thank for that.

"You're spoiling that boy, Danny. Is he toilet-trained yet?"

"For Christ's sake, Dad, he's not even eighteen months old."

"Don't baby him, son. Don't you and Bev go running to him every time he opens his mouth. He's gotta learn some independence. If you ask me, he was breastfed for too long."

"He was only breastfed for six months."

"You didn't last on your mother's breast for more than two days and you've made out just fine. How about letters and numbers? Can he recognize them? Is he writing anything down yet?"

Grimacing at Dad, I needed every last ounce of willpower to follow my mental script: *No, I'm not going to fall into the trap of exaggerating my son's abilities—"yup, Dad, David's writing full sentences already"—just to satisfy my ego, or my father's. Let David be a baby. It's over so fast.*

As David moved into the toddler stage, he appeared to share a lot of my childhood qualities: aloof, often impossible to engage and perpetually lost in his imagination.

"Look at how that toddler buries himself in his projects," Dad would remark as David lay across our kitchen floor, painting his version of some fantasy animal on acres of construction paper. "For heaven's sake, Danny, I've never seen a kid so small stay on task for so damned long."

Ah, but with that intense focus came the unavoidable fallout. David, like me as a tot, would connect with someone only if, and when, he felt like it. Once David grew out of that cute, adorable baby stage, Dad's interactions with him dropped off.

"Why is your father suddenly so uninterested in David?" Bev asked.

"Because David's not interested in him," I said.

"Stop making excuses for your father. He's the adult here."

"Yeah, and so?"

"So, he should be making the effort to connect with his grandson, not the other way around. Listen, if you don't talk to your father about this, I will."

But Dad wasn't the kind of guy who was going to take lessons from Bev on how to interact with his grandson. Dad wasn't the kind of guy you could really give lessons to, period.

Despite the regular hiccups and transitions of life the bond between Dad and me remained strong. As the nineties rolled in, we were pretty much in the same place career-wise, despite our thirty-year age difference. We were two professionals who, for different reasons, had already realized a major part of our life callings—something that neither of us could entirely accept. The thought that nothing we might do in the future would ever impact our respective worlds as powerfully as our past accomplishments was too crushing to consider.

"I've got a few books left in me. And some important articles I need to write," Dad would say, the odd time he'd come over to watch a boxing match with me on TV.

"Great, Dad. I've just signed a new record deal with Quality Records out of L.A. The only downside is that they insist I wear one of those Hair Club for Men hairpieces."

"Congratulations, son, you still may have a few years left as a sex symbol. Ha ha ha."

We were quite the pair, Dad with his dreams of publishing more seminal material on Black history and me always chasing that elusive hit record. The two of us seemed to be becoming more alike, or was I just better recognizing our sometimes disquieting similarities? Unlike my younger but more mature siblings, Dad and I both excelled at teasing people, either through practical jokes or irregular and invasive questions designed to put them on the spot. I'd inherited a touch of Dad's mean streak, along with his ability to cloak it beneath a warm and humble persona. We wasted little time worrying about whether or not people liked us. Our problem was wanting people's worship, respect, even adoration, which had nothing to do with being liked per se. Unlike Larry and Karen, we had become increasingly detached from people outside our immediate family, avoiding, as best we could, social events, parties or even small outings with friends. Dad and I had sleepwalked through so many business dinners, conferences and work-related soirées that the mere thought of another cocktail party was enough to put us in a foul mood. Family was the only place where we could relax and interact without feeling as if we had to perform.

After Dad retired, Larry and Karen often joined him and Mom on vacations, something I could never bring myself to do, especially when stories of Dad's ever-escalating money neuroses made their way back to me.

"Hang on, I changed my mind. Let me pay this in traveller's cheques," Dad would say to the peeved cashier when checking out of a hotel—after his Visa card had been processed. Then, as soon as the clerk had stashed away his traveller's cheques he'd declare, "On second thought, I've decided to put this on my American Express."

"We don't take American Express," the clerk would answer, snippily.

"Donna, I've decided to pay this bill in cash. I don't trust those bloomin' credit card companies." Dad's cash was Canadian but the bill would be in American dollars, leading to testy negotiations about the exchange rate. Fifteen minutes later, as the line of impatient hotel guests grew, Dad would be still changing his mind, finally deciding to split the hotel bill evenly between his Visa, his cash and his traveller's cheques.

Trying as it was to go on vacations with Dad, however, accompanying him to America for family funerals, which started happening with increasing regularity once Dad entered his seventies, represented a whole other level of torture.

"As usual, Dad took over everything," Larry would report upon his return, "throwing out commands like a drill sergeant to anyone within earshot."

"That's precisely why I avoid going to family funerals," I'd say, my flip manner camouflaging my guilt.

I was always pretending to take things lightly, often slipping back into the guise of family jester. Karen was all kindness and affection. Larry, Mr. Responsible. It would soon take the combination of all three of our roles to buoy Dad's worsening moods. But even with our collective love, along with Mom's round-the-clock devotion, Dad's spells of sadness came and went of their own accord, like some default biological rhythm that resisted all external stimuli.

Dad knew that his body was falling apart. An incremental, year-by-year demise would mean a lot of extra health care. And not the kind of care that would be covered provincially. Whatever his pressing concerns about the future—did he have enough saved to pay his growing medical bills, or to provide a decent quality of life for his wife (and for Karen, should she need assistance) after he was gone?—he tried, as best he could, to conceal them. If not from me, most certainly from Mom. The last thing he wanted was for his wife of over forty years to worry, especially about her own well-being. And so really, when Dad constantly reminded me of my financial responsibilities to my relatives, he was trying to ask me this: would I be there to look after him, and more importantly, take care of Mom when he no longer could?

Because Dad was too proud to talk directly about his financial concerns, he redirected and disguised them. And I was too close to Dad to see it at the time. Knowing that Dad had plenty of money, between his savings and his pensions, to take care of all their needs for a long time caused me to miss what was at the root of Dad's fear. His self-esteem had plunged, distorting all his other perceptions. No matter how much money Dad had saved, he remained convinced that he didn't have enough. This man who had lived to control everything now felt out of control. No wonder he was sad.

I've always held the superstitious belief that everyone's born with a finite supply of energy and passion, and the faster we burn it up the less there is to draw on later. No doubt my superstition was reinforced by watching Dad, from the mid-nineties on, slowly fade. Would this also be my fate? In 1996, at age forty-two, I was diagnosed with diabetes—the same age Dad had been when he was diagnosed. The night I was confronted with the reality of my precipitously high blood sugar level (my doctor was astonished that I hadn't already fallen into a coma), I dreamed I was lying beside Dad in bed. I was cooling his fevered forehead with a damp cloth as he told me, with a proud sense of finality, "Son, we are both doomed to die young." In my dream, we were eerily indistinguishable and our death sentences represented some badge of honour.

Growing up, I was always the first of my peer group at everything: first to hit puberty, first to know what I wanted to do once I finished high school, first to make a lot of money, first to lose it. It only stood to reason that I would be the first to wither up and disappear. As Dad started his slow, inglorious unravelling, my natural response was to hurl myself into my music, so I wouldn't have time to consider the unthinkable: that Dad, the strongest man I'd ever known, was dying. That I would soon be without a father.

CHAPTER 28

Singer or Joker?

W atching David fly through those early years from baby to toddler to playschool both thrilled and alarmed me. He was already in kindergarten, inhaling life, changing by the second, and I was standing still. Caught between two generations—David growing older and stronger, Dad growing older and weaker—I felt as though I was treading water. I was retired, kind of. I was a singer—wait. No, I was a songwriter. A little of both, a lot of neither. So what did that make me? Restless, for one.

By the mid-nineties I'd been in and out of so many record deals that I was beginning to feel like the musical equivalent of a journeyman NFL player. But rather than admit that I might well be singing on borrowed time, I set up my own record label in the States and continued to shovel my songwriting royalties back into my singing career. *If I can score with one more hit record,* I kept telling myself, *the hundreds of thousands of dollars I'm investing will roll back into my life in the form of several million.*

An independent label such as mine, however, was in no position to compete with the major U.S. labels for radio airplay. A typical radio station may have only one or two slots open each week for adding a new song to its playlist. If WXYZ in Kentucky was promised backstage passes and comped tickets to a Billy Joel concert provided it added his latest single to its playlist instead of mine, it didn't take a Vegas odds-maker to figure out which record the station was going to choose. The only favour I could offer radio stations for choosing my new single over someone else's was to perform, gratis, for a community event sponsored by the station. Soon I found myself spending every weekend performing free concerts for radio stations across small-town America. My duet remake (with Rique Franks) of "In Your Eyes" made it to number ten on the U.S. Radio and Records adult contemporary charts. Compared to my top-three single of just two years before, "Fall All Over Again," it was a troublesome sign that I was working harder for less gain. In fact, I was committing the cardinal sin of all labels that end up bankrupt: spending two dollars in order to earn one. But rather than fold up my fledgling company, the rational choice, I started taking on more and more quick-money gigs to offset my expenses.

The general rule with fast cash performances is that the greater the sum of money involved, the weirder the gig. If nothing else, my 1992 Grey Cup halftime performance taught me, once and for all, that there was no such thing as easy money. I must have been delusional, agreeing to lip-synch the words to my latest single while floating high over a Toronto stadium in a hot-air balloon.

"Have you forgotten that you're scared of heights?" Bev asked. "You won't even climb a stepladder for fear of fainting."

She had a point. Never great at lip-synching to begin with, as I mouthed along to my record on live TV my nervousness gave way to terror. I lurched about in the very small and jiggly hot-air balloon, staring down at the football field one hundred feet below, fighting nausea as the heat from the gas fire lofting the balloon curled down over my shoulders.

"You're a real pro, son, I can't believe how you pulled it off," Dad told me the next day. Then he added, "You've got a mighty fine grip."

"Huh?"

"For God sakes alive, you were holding on to the handles of that hot-air balloon so tight that I could see the splotchy white of your knuckles glaring through my little TV screen."

I assumed that singing the national anthem at a Toronto Blue Jays playoff game would be less stressful; for one thing, I'd be standing on solid ground. Dad, ecstatic that my pre-game anthem would be televised across North America, had called all his relatives in the States, demanding that they watch his son sing "O Canada."

"In the interest of Hill family history," he'd stressed, as if any relative who had more important things to do than watch me sing at a baseball game was turning his back on a critical world event.

But as I looked out onto the pitcher's mound I wasn't thinking about family history. My thoughts were on the lyrics to "O Canada," which I'd pre-recorded. (The arrhythmic, ricochet acoustics at Toronto's SkyDome make it impossible to sing the anthem live.) Because I so infrequently sang other people's songs, I'd developed a mental block when it came to memorizing anyone else's lyrics. If I was spotted lip-synching the wrong words to "O Canada," I was going to be crucified.

"You want me to walk out there all alone?" I asked the head of media relations for the Toronto Blue Jays, who'd informed me that it was time to go out to the pitcher's mound for my performance.

"Well, you *are* the only one singing," Mr. Media Man answered.

"Aren't they gonna think I'm some wacko who's just waltzed onto the field?"

"Everyone knows you're Dan Hill."

The media guy nudged me towards the diamond. The players, their backs to me in a tight circle, had blocked the way. Tiptoeing up to where they were huddled, I tapped on the back of one of the players. He turned around, gave me a slow once-over and then stepped slightly to his left. I squeezed between him and another uniformed monolith and made my way to the mound. When I grabbed hold of the mic stand and looked up at the crowd of fifty thousand people staring down at me, I felt this blip, then a few blips, turning over, deep in my stomach. I hadn't eaten a thing all day. Not a good thing to do if you're unknowingly diabetic. The mound started moving, imperceptibly at first, then swaying beneath my feet, as if I were balancing on a swimming platform during a storm. A weird sensation of breathing but not getting any oxygen into my lungs came over me. I was on the verge of fainting. I imagined myself out cold, splayed face down on the pitcher's mound, as my voice continued to serenade the SkyDome and the entire TV-watching world, including my horrified Dad and all our relatives. I was about to become Canada's answer to Milli Vanilli.

Just then my pre-recorded voice clicked on like a rescue siren. I sang along, lips carefully obscured by the microphone, and made it through the song without bringing shame to myself or, more importantly, Dad.

After singing one more national anthem (in Philadelphia, during the Jays-Phillies World Series in '93), just to prove to myself that I wasn't a total wuss, I vowed never to perform at sporting events again. Happily, there were private corporate events and weddings that paid well, and if I died a slow death during a performance, there was no risk of the media feeding on my carcass. I rationalized that my experiences as a B-league celebrity-for-hire made for killer stories.

Then there was the time when a wealthy stockbroker wired crazy cash into my bank account and flew me on a private plane into Manhattan where I was to appear beside his horse and buggy in Central Park and serenade his fiancée with *that song* while he proposed. But as I started singing she thought I was a busker and told me to get lost. Her fiancé had to convince her that I was the "real Dan Hill" and not some impersonator. I even had to show my driver's licence.

The fact that all singers do these kind of gigs didn't make the realization that I was whorishly cashing in on the old "famous for being famous" syndrome any easier. I was running faster and faster while sliding backwards. Using work as my drug instead of facing the real issues: that my father, the most powerful and influential figure in my life, was on the road to becoming as weak and helpless as toddler; that due to my steady weight gain and frenzied work pace, I could easily end up just like him within ten years; and that my singing career had devolved into a series of hollow after-dinner stories. I'd make more money if I just hung it up, stopped playing at being the pop star, sat back and let my two decades worth of royalties stream into my bank account. I could spend my time with the human being who needed me more than anyone. My son.

But then I wrote a song that would, once again, change my life.

"Seduces Me" (co-written with John Sheard) was intended for a new album on my own money pit of a U.S. label. On a hunch I played this track to my former Canadian product manager at Columbia Records (now Sony), Dave Platel, who had become part of Celine Dion's management team. Dave loved the song and said he'd like to play it to Celine. "Seduces Me," with its European-style 6/8 waltz tempo, combined with its foreboding, classical minor chord progression and its ultra-suggestive lyric, was a perfect "cast" for Celine. But knowing that a lot of politics and relationship building went into landing a song on a major international artist's record, I didn't hold my breath. Two weeks later, Dave woke me up in the middle of the night with a transatlantic phone call.

"Grab your guitar, Dan," he said.

Even half-asleep, I knew not to ask questions.

"I love your song," was the next thing I heard.

"Who is this?" I yawned.

"Sorry, my voice is hoarse. I've just finished a long night at Hammersmith, here in London." Before I could reply, Celine started singing "Seduces Me" like she'd been singing it all her life. Within seconds, over the static hum of a buzzing long-distance line, we were trying to figure out what key she could record "Seduces Me" in.

"What on earth?" Bev groaned, raising her head from her pillow.

"Shh."

I slid the capo up and down my guitar, making the song higher, then lower, keeping in mind that Celine's voice would have greater range and suppleness once she'd taken a break from the road and was rested and ready for the studio. I convinced Dave, who then convinced Sony, to allow me to produce "Seduces Me" for Celine's new album, on spec. I would pick up all the recording costs, knowing that if she included the song on her album, I'd be reimbursed and then some.

"But what if Celine doesn't include your song on her record?" Bev asked.

"Then I'm out at least fifty grand."

"After all the money you've wasted on your U.S. label, do you really think that's wise?"

Fair question. After all, there were few purely vocal-driven artists left to pitch songs to. Radio had turned edgy with groups like Smashing Pumpkins, Oasis and U2, who wrote their own material, which left everyone from Jon Bon Jovi to Stevie Wonder to Elton John vying to get a cut on Celine's new record. And that wasn't including the hundred hit songwriters scattered across the world, all of whom had banged out more number ones than I had.

To Bev's credit, she listened while I explained why, despite the steep competition, I had a good feeling about "Seduces Me": Celine already loved the song; René Angélil (Celine's husband and head manager) and Dave Platel loved the song, so I was in the door. All that was left for me to do was nail the arrangement and recording of "Seduces Me."

Bev, who had stood loyally by my career choices, did so again. But I couldn't afford any more blunders. And in the mid-nineties, unlike the sixties and seventies, it wasn't enough to have a great song. Production, instrumentation and the ever-vexing "hip factor" were equally important. I knew plenty about singing and could back up my ideas simply by dashing into the singer's booth and laying down a few sample tracks. But I was no technician. When it came to recording great drum sounds or conducting a horn section, I faltered. So I delegated, hiring John Jones, an old Toronto friend and excellent musician (who'd worked extensively with George Martin, the Beatles' producer), and Rick Hahn, a classically trained musician, to assist me in turning a great song into a great Celine Dion record.

In every business there's politics. This is especially true in the music business, where a song can earn millions of dollars, and a hit album many times more, in a remarkably short time. Vito Luprano, Celine's

A&R rep at Sony who'd been with her from the beginning, expressed doubts about "Seduces Me" (Dave had played it to him after Celine had jumped on it), angry that I hadn't sent him the song first.

"I want you to send me your new version of 'Seduces Me' now!" barked Vito, when news got back to him that I'd almost completed the recording for Celine and Sony.

To play it safe, I didn't send my recording in progress anywhere, waiting until my two co-producers and I arrived at the Hit Factory in Manhattan to present the new arrangement to Celine.

If I were the type to feel intimidated, I would have folded up my tent the moment I walked into the legendary studio. One room was block-booked for the entire month by Jim Steinman, Meatloaf's producer, another room taken over by David Foster. As I walked into my assigned studio I spotted Aldo Nova (a former platinum-selling rock artist out of Montreal who'd been writing and producing hits for Celine, as well as many other international artists, for years) leaving yet another studio. He looked pale and beaten up. *Sheesh,* I thought, *if Aldo's freaked out by the competition, I should be petrified.*

But I wasn't. Perhaps because Celine, her body clock turned upside down from international travel, had insisted that she cut her vocals to "Seduces Me" at 2:30 a.m. I could night owl with the best of them and after flying back and forth between Toronto and L.A. a half-dozen times, cutting this track in three different keys to make sure I had the perfect key for Celine's voice, I was prepared to do anything that helped Celine sing better. Because above all, it was her performance that would determine the song's fate.

Celine arrived an hour late, along with a film crew that would be shooting our session, and an entourage of relatives, friends and Sony reps.

God help me, if she's gone Hollywood, I'm in serious trouble, I said to myself, smiling nervously in Celine's direction as she walked into the studio, confident and focused, oblivious to the small nation of people trailing behind her. *Am I even allowed to look at her?* Some stars I'd recently written with forbade eye contact from anyone considered not to be of equal standing.

"I'm so glad we have a chance to work together again," Celine said, grasping my hand affectionately, as she used to do when we'd meet to perform on various TV shows. "We had so much fun back then."

That's when I knew for sure that Celine had every intention of putting "Seduces Me" on her album. But even the greatest of singers can have an off performance. Fortunately, Celine brought her best voice to the Hit Factory that night. In the past, Celine had appeared to be encumbered by the magnificence of her engine, like an amateur driver behind the wheel of the world's most powerful car. Now, however, she'd learned how to harness her explosive talent, when to let up and allow the song to sing itself, when to crescendo and let it rip, when to use her breaths between key lyric lines as a seductive tool, when to remain silent and let the space do the talking. Celine was also tireless, demanding that I roll the tape over and over, never pausing to sip water or stretch. She'd listened very closely to how I'd sung the original version, taken what was best about my performance and made it into her song, her experience. I fed her a bit of advice, steering her clear of the odd "Celine-ism," where she'd twirl the end of her phrases a little too predictably (imagine a toned-down but still grating Mariah Carey) which she accepted without any "I'm a superstar, who the fuck are you?" attitude. She just looked at me and said, "Okay, got it, hit me with another take." So I did what a good producer always does: I shut up and let the tape roll. The session was over in three hours.

Afterwards, Vito Luprano approached me. Earlier, he'd scolded me for not presenting Celine with flowers. Apparently I'd breached some kind of studio etiquette. I flinched, wondering how many things I'd said during the session that Vito had taken offence at.

"Great song, Dan," Vito said, shaking my hand and looking straight into my eyes. I blinked. Weird. Vito wasn't known to be one of those "look you in the eye" types. "I was wrong. 'Seduces Me' is a perfect fit for Celine."

That impressed me. In the music business, it's very rare for someone to own up to a mistake.

Two weeks after my session with Celine, I was informed that "Seduces Me" would be included on her new album, to be released three months later, in March 1996. But there was one potentially catastrophic complication. No one at Sony Records knew that an artist in England, Bill Tarmey (a major star in the internationally successful soap opera *Coronation Street*), had already recorded "Seduces Me" and that it was slated to be released on EMI Records at the same time as Celine's album. There was no chance Celine would include "Seduces Me" if she didn't have an exclusive on it.

Should I bluff it and hope that Celine and Sony don't catch wind of the other recording? Even as the thought occurred to me, I knew this was not the time for games. There was always a consequence that came from playing two sides, and usually it was me who ended up squashed.

Forty-eight hours later, I was sitting in a pub in London, England. My loyal British music publisher, Eddie Levy, was hovering beside me, too nervous to sit, tapping his fingers on his pint of beer.

"How come you're not drinking, Dan?" Bill Tarmey inquired, politely signing autographs for the people milling around our table.

"Lately I've been trying to cut back." I had an urge for a double martini.

"Grab your Perrier then, Dan, so we can toast 'Seduces Me.' Did Eddie tell you that we're looking at your song as my first single?"

Then a strange thing happened. I told the truth. There was an agonizing pause. Then Bill Tarmey said, in a voice as gracious as it was resigned, "I get the picture, Dan. I'll have your song removed from my record. What the hell, I'd ask the same thing of you if our positions were reversed."

When more money flowed in from Celine's recording within the first year of its release than I had earned from nearly all my recordings over the last ten years combined, I finally got the hint. Why should I bother competing as an artist with the Celines of the world when I could work alongside them, albeit in the background, as a writer-producer? In the past, when my record sales were being whomped by other performers, I'd felt disgraced and untalented. But at forty-two, I was finally mature enough to accept that it was far more complicated and impersonal than that.

Dad's warning from my childhood was finally sinking in: "Stop your foolish dreaming, boy. It's time you got that thick head of yours out of the clouds." It had taken me a mere thirty years to heed his advice.

The first thing I did after I picked up the mastered version of Celine's "Seduces Me" was play it to Dad over the phone.

"What happened to that woman's French accent, son? Now she sounds just like any other American singer."

After I hung up, I realized that David had picked up the phone in our bedroom halfway through my playback, just in time to catch Dad's twist of the knife.

"Daddy, why was that lady copying you?"

"She's not copying, David. Celine's the singer and I'm the writer."

"Why aren't you the singer, Daddy?"

"Because I'm not going to be singing anymore."

"How come?"

"Because I've decided to join the international songwriting sweepstakes."

"Can I join too, Daddy?"

At seven, David would have happily joined any club that gave him a chance to spend time with his globe-trotting father. David hung up the phone and ran downstairs to me. *Does he think we'll be part of some circus?* I wondered.

"Answer me, Daddy!"

The more I hemmed and hawed, the more David's wiry body stiffened, preparing for, and then resigning himself to, the one word he hated more than any other. Especially coming from me. "No, David." Regardless of how I softened that no, despite whatever qualifying words I tacked on afterwards—"maybe next time"—David always saw it for what it was: rejection.

In 1997, Celine Dion's *Falling into You* won a Grammy for album of the year. This meant that the various producers of this album, myself included, won a Grammy as well. International sales of this CD would ultimately climb to thirty million. Never one to take awards seriously, I felt even less deserving in the case of my '97 Grammy, believing that I was a freeloader, piggybacking on the Celine Dion gravy train. That's not how the music business saw it. Out of nowhere I was fielding calls from A&R men, producers, recording artists and songwriters wanting to work with me. In a business where it's almost impossible to get that one huge break, I'd been given a second chance. Twenty years earlier, the trappings and temptations of pop stardom had caused me to lose my focus. Older and wiser, I would not make the same mistake again. Sure, the public didn't care about songwriters and neither did the media. But my bank account cared. And the behind-the-scenes movers and shakers, the powers that create the future Madonnas and Britneys, sure as hell cared.

My wife and son cared too. For different reasons.

"David's in grade one now," I rationalized. "That means a lot of his time will be taken up with school, with homework, with new friends." I chose not to remember how, when I'd started grade one, I'd turned even more insecure, even more dependent on Dad's strength to get me through the tumble of rowdy boys, snobby girls and critical teachers.

So when Nashville came calling I conveniently viewed it as the perfect compromise between staying at home and travelling for long stretches at a time. Whereas a trip to L.A. consumed an entire day, it was just a ninety-minute plane ride into the heart of what music-biz insiders called Music Row. This also made it easier for Nashville-based writers and singers to fly to Toronto, where we could record whatever we wrote in my basement studio. Besides, according to Keith Stegall, one of Nashville's most successful songwriters and producers, my total ignorance of country music would work to my advantage.

"Just be you, Dan," Keith drawled laconically, when he picked me up in his blazing-red pickup truck. "I bought your first two albums when I was studying theology at Centenary College in Shreveport. I used to perform 'Hold On' and 'You Make Me Wanna Be' while playing bars to pay my way through school."

"Jesus, am I that old?"

"Country music likes old. Experience makes for better storytelling."

Had I glanced over Keith's songwriting resumé, I would have known that he was as ancient as I, despite looking like one of those perfect Marlboro men. Before discovering, producing and writing hits for Alan Jackson, Randy Travis and Terri Clark, Keith had made his name as a pop writer, penning Al Jarreau's "We're in This Love Together" and Dr. Hook's "Sexy Eyes." Very few songwriters possessed his musical range and flexibility. And he came by it honestly. His father had supported his family playing guitar for Hank Williams and Johnny Horton.

Still, predicting how Keith and I would fare as collaborators based on our past hits was about as scientific as sizing up a potential mate on the Internet based on their hobbies. To my amazement, our first two co-writes became number-one country hits. Our third, "I Do (Cherish You)," yet another country number one, enjoyed a second life as a pop hit for the Motown boy group 98 Degrees.

As country music continued to turn more pop-sounding, and L.A.-based songwriters, finding themselves shut out of the pop world by rap, moved to Nashville, the inevitable backlash occurred. But if the price of admission was earning the scorn of country music purists, I could afford to pay. Especially since the songs that Keith and I wrote continued to be recorded by dozens of country stars: everyone from Reba McEntire to Sammy Kershaw to Alan Jackson. Typically, the criticism that hurt most came from the old familiar place.

"That's racist music, son," Dad would chide. "Name one successful Black country singer—and don't start with Charley Pride. He's older than I am. That hillbilly music appeals to southern bigots and backwater Republicans."

I would counter with something about country music no longer being racist, unlike Dad's stereotypes about country music and its audience. After enduring a brief lecture from Dad about the difference between "classist" and "racist," I'd point out that, as in any musical substructure, there were different types of country music—ranging from old-style Merle Haggard to contemporary singer-songwriter, à la Gordon Lightfoot. There I was, prattling on like some didactic musicologist, trying to convince him of my worthiness. As I'd get up to leave, Dad would inadvertently reveal the real reason he was so upset about my constant commuting to Nashville.

"You've made enough money now, son. Stay home with your family before something bad happens to you. America's a dangerous place."

Now that Dad was seeing calamity around every corner, he always felt safer and calmer when I was in town, only a phone call and a twenty-minute drive away. But on my next Nashville trip, something happened that made me wonder if I hadn't been a little too quick in dismissing Dad's criticisms of country music. And of the small part I was now playing in it.

"Do you mind telling me what your background is?" a famous country singer asked me, after we'd been introduced at a popular bar in Nashville.

"Canadian."

"I mean, what race are you?"

"My dad's Black and my mom's white," I said. Two things stopped me from dumping a beer over Mr. Country Star's head. One: Keith was producing his new record. Two: I had a feeling he, like many people in Nashville, packed a gun. As I seethed, Mr. Country Star, who'd had a few too many Budweisers, continued to stare. *Not this again.* It was shortly after 9/11 and lately I'd noticed a lot of people giving me the evil eye. Meanwhile, a dozen musicians, songwriters and producers fell silent to take in this exchange.

"Well let me tell ya something, Mr. Dan Hill. You may look like a Black man but you sure as hell sing like a white man."

"Oh yeah, well let me tell you something," one of the posse watching cracked. "He may sing like a white man but he sure as hell's hung like a Black man."

As everyone around me belly-flopped with laughter, I felt like I'd been hit with the perfect one-two knockout of stereotypes.

"Come home, Danny. Your family needs you."

That was all Mom had said on my hotel voicemail. What she meant was that Dad needed me. I started to get that boxed-in feeling again. I skipped to the next message.

"Dad, it's David. Stop leaving home. Stop leaving Canada to always go to America. Choose a country."

Ouch. Like so many Hills, my eleven-year-old son had a scary way with words. "Choose your love," David was saying. "Is it music or family?" It brought back the image of him, at four or so, looking balefully out our living room window, searching, as he did every day when I was gone, for his jet-setting father. Bev had described this wrenching scene many times to me over the phone, but until I saw him there, as I pulled up our driveway from yet another songwriting journey, I hadn't understood. There he was, his small face squished up against that big bay window, waving excitedly in my direction.

On my flight back to Toronto the day after David's message, I couldn't get one particular song of mine out of my head.

Memories of when I was a little boy, four years old,
Waiting for my daddy to come home
Now I look into the eyes of my own son
Wondering what he's thinking of
Waiting at the window, when I come home
Watch his eyes fill up with joy and wonder
He reaches out his tiny hands, I feel the bond between boy
    and man

Memories of my mom crying, my daddy gone for weeks
    at a time
Not knowing how to comfort her
Face in my pillow, pretending not to hear
Now I write this letter to my little boy, I'm far away
Not knowing really what to say, except I'm sorry, oh so sorry

I don't wanna make the same mistakes my daddy made with me
Still his voice rolls off my tongue when I say boy, protect your mom

Memories of my wife crying on the phone
Wondering when I'm coming home
My voice sounds detached and cold
Reminds me of someone that I knew
He had a funny attitude, when I needed him to be
All the things only a daddy could be to me

I don't wanna make the same mistakes my daddy made with me
Still his voice rolls off my tongue when I say not now, I'm busy son

Memories of lying in bed with my wife and son
Overwhelmed by so much love, trying to explain how a man
   can cry
Yet still be happy
Thinking of all the dumb mistakes I've made
Now I understand my father's pain
He did the best with what he knew, I love you daddy
I watch my son fall asleep, and wonder what he'll think of me
When years from now, he sees his son
Reaching out his tiny hands, for love

I Am My Father's Son

CHAPTER 29

Diving for Shells

D ad is in his wheelchair. His good leg is propped up on a support attached to his chair. His stump, where the other leg was amputated just below the knee, is extended beside it. It is 2001 and Dad has been battling diabetes for almost forty years. As warriors go, he's a tough cookie. But diabetes is sneaky, patient, steady. Unlike Dad's other adversaries—racist army sergeants, stonewalling politicians, a back-talking eldest son—diabetes can't be outfoxed, out-boxed, or enlightened. It just keeps coming at you, gaining, sucking up the small blood vessels first, the ones that feed the extremities—toes, feet, fingertips, eyes—then it spreads, slowly, implacably, infections choking the life out of your ankles, then higher, deeper.

But Dad's still fighting. His weapon of choice these days is surrounding himself with the things, the people, he cherishes. Right now he's in the living room listening to Count Basie, inhaling the funky bass lines and sassy piano riffs like it's his oxygen, his morphine. The Basie beat takes me back to my childhood, memories of laughing hysterically as Joe Williams wailed about his lover being as welcoming as leftover mashed potatoes and Dad cracking up when I'd sing the song back, picking up Joe Williams' phrasing flawlessly, only two octaves higher. Music, Dad's kind of music, always put him in a boisterous mood. Dad's still listening to the same half-dozen records he listened to then. But instead of clapping his hands and swaying along to the feel-good rhythm, he sits very still between the stereo speakers.

There's something that I've been meaning to ask Dad. I've been putting it off. But I can't much longer. I'm not sure how many more chances I'll have to speak frankly with him. Much as I think I've come to understand my father, some of his past behaviour still confuses and hurts me. I don't always want to carry this anger, this sadness inside. David's almost a teenager, alternating between rebelling and reaching out for me more than ever. I suspect that my moodiness, my there-but-not-there presence when I flit through the house lost in my lyrics, is as wounding to him as Dad's overbearing presence once was for me. So I smile at Dad and take the plunge.

"I'm curious about something, Dad."

"What's that, son?"

He's looking up at me. Glad I've come to visit, but wary.

"Why were you always on my back when I was a kid? Why did you always tell me to be aware of my limitations? What made you so sure I was 'never gonna be a Bruce Cockburn,' to quote you?"

"I never said that."

"Yes, you did."

Mom yells from the kitchen, "Cut it out, you two," her voice caught between a plea and a threat.

Dad waits for a signature Basie piano riff to fade before speaking. "Before you'd turned sixteen, you were already talking about dropping out of school and taking to the streets with your guitar. I was protecting you from yourself. The world's a cruel place. It was my job to prepare you for the world. Even if I was a little mean sometimes." Dad hesitates here, knowing he's made a major concession. "You always had food to eat, a roof over your head, shoes on your feet. It's not like you weren't looked after."

Ahhh, there's the old warrior talking, I think, oddly reassured by Dad's vehemence. If he truly thought he was putting me down for my own good, then there was a chance that his criticisms had come from a place I hadn't recognized: love. Dad, fidgeting with a lever on his wheelchair, peers up at me. The emotion is rising in me so fast that I can't talk. I'm fifteen again, using every ounce of self-control to hold myself together.

Seeing me struggling, Dad turns reflective: "I underestimated you, son. The kinds of things that you accomplished in your musical career . . ." His eyes aren't as sharp as they once were, but I'm sure he can see the tears in my eyes. Lowering his voice to a murmur, he says, "That just didn't happen to kids I knew when I was growing up."

I underestimated you, son. I realize that is all I've ever wanted Dad to say.

Josie, one of Dad's round-the-clock health care workers, treads gently into the living room, presenting Dad with a fresh glass of water. She tenderly guides a straw into Dad's mouth, holding it in place until he's finished drinking. Once Josie mops the tiny specks of dribble from Dad's chin, she pads back into the kitchen to tell Mom that Dad's blood pressure is dropping again—"I can tell by touching his skin, it's too cold." Mom, unfazed, reminds Josie to start preparing Dad for dialysis. *One more expensive consequence of suffering through advanced diabetes,* I think, as Josie, moving with some urgency now, heads to the family room to turn on the machine.

Dad, unconcerned by all this activity, has nodded off, his head hanging forward, his snoring coming and going in spurts and stutters. I sit and watch him for a few minutes, knowing that if I stir even slightly, he'll open his eyes and ask where I'm going. Unlike me, Dad has always been blessed with the ability to fall asleep anywhere, anytime, often in mid-sentence. But these days his sleep is like a shallow, grey shell—every few minutes he'll let loose with a fearsomely loud snore that startles him awake. Then he'll look around accusingly, gulping in air, for the source of this rude, intrusive noise.

As I take a chance and get up quietly from my chair, I realize how difficult it must have been for Dad to concede that he may have made some mistakes with me. I hadn't meant to turn my afternoon visit with him, a guy reeling from infection to infection, who'd recently lost half of his right leg, into an inquisition. As I creep out the front door undetected, I'm haunted by the kind of guilt one feels after provoking a competition with a hugely disadvantaged opponent.

On the drive home, I blasted the radio, compulsively punching up stations, trying to find some song that would galvanize me the way "Satisfaction" or "A Hard Day's Night" did back in my childhood. In today's world we're bombarded with pop-idol reality shows. We're besieged by ever-younger singers, known only by their first names, whose greatest talents often seem to be their frightening determination, their killer abs and their illusory kid-next-door accessibility. If the prevailing propaganda in sixties America was that anyone could be president, today's dream has changed to something more realistic. These days, anyone can be a pop star. But when I was a kid, telling your parents you wanted to be a pop singer was about as comforting as telling them you wanted to join the circus and get shot out of a cannon. How could I not have seen it from Dad's perspective? According to all he'd experienced, there was no precedent of success for a moony-eyed, mixed-race, suburban kid bent on throwing away his education to risk it all on his musical fantasies. Dad must have thought I was mad. And I suppose I was. But I was also lucky.

I'm a hypocrite. Not long after Dad and I had our talk, David and I were on a flight to New York during Christmas break. He insisted that I watch a film of him rapping one of his songs in my recording studio. He held the dime-sized screen of his video camera a few inches from my face and then—*bang!*—his voice, bursting with an unlikely amalgamation of suburban and underclass, street-thug drawl (imagine J.D. Salinger crossed with Biggie), came blasting out at me and the rest of the first-class section of the airplane. Unaware of the commotion he was creating, David scrutinized my face for the slightest reaction, unconsciously mouthing along to the words of his songs. I had to make a conscious effort to hold myself in check and resist the urge to tell him to turn down that "racket" (Dad's favourite word for music he loathed) before other passengers started complaining about the litany of swear words and various ingenious, and to my ears offensive, rhymes for "nigger" bouncing off their champagne flutes.

As David's rapping and songwriting started to take over every facet of his life, I advised him to expand his talent to prose writing: articles, short stories, film scripts. (Was it so long ago that my high school English teacher took me aside to say my real future lay in journalism, anything but music?) I reminded David of when he was voted valedictorian of his elementary school, based on a graduation speech he had written. Then I pointed out, in much the same way Dad did with me, how unremittingly competitive the music business—especially rap— is. When he gave me that "times have changed since you made records" roll of the eyes, I reminded him that one of his heroes, Jay-Z, had said that statistically, it's ten times harder to make it as a rapper than as an NBA player.

I neglected, however, to share with David my deepest concern: that perhaps he didn't possess the innate sense of rhythm (not to mention street cred) needed to excel as a rapper. I knew telling David this would wound him deeply. Though he pretends not to be affected by what I say, I know he carefully calibrates my every word and observation. Besides, wasn't it better for David to pursue a dream without achieving success than to abandon it and fall into idleness, which carries with it other, unforeseen dangers?

Roughly a year later, David played me a demo he'd recorded. It stopped me in my tracks. His timing was dead on. The earnest, pleading tone of his voice gave his words a distinct and hypnotic spin. I had underestimated him.

Mom's kissing Dad. Exactly the way he used to kiss her. *Smack, smack, smack:* three loud smooches on top of his bald head. "I'm right here, honeybun," she says. Lying on his back on a rented hospital bed that takes up most of the family room, Dad's hooked up to his dialysis machine. He wants more ice. He opens his mouth wide, like a baby bird anticipating feeding. Mom delicately places a few ice chips in his mouth. Dad's seventy-seven. He's fighting off an infection in his remaining leg. I'm here to comfort him, but I'm even more concerned about Mom. I don't want to tell her that I'm worried Dad may be facing yet another amputation. Mom, seeing the gloom on my face, decides I'm the one who most needs comforting. Dad's decree that the strong take care of the weak has flipped. The weak are now taking care of the strong.

"Do you know what your father wanted when he returned home from the hospital after his leg was amputated?" Mom asks.

I shake my head.

"He wanted me to crawl into bed with him. So we could get reacquainted."

It takes a moment before the full impact of what Mom is saying sinks in. *Get reacquainted.* I want to take a sliver of comfort from this, but it makes me even sadder. I try to follow Mom's example, take strength from her strength. I realize that Mom will not fade, or even falter, so long as Dad's here. Because Dad's life is her life. She devotes herself to his care. She doesn't complain. Through it all, the health care costs keep rising: the home hospital bed, the rented dialysis machine, twenty-four-hour home care and Wheel-Trans. All Dad's stories about saving for a rainy day, which I'd always dismissed as neurotic, Depression-era talk, have now come true. More and more, Dad's lessons, as unfathomable as they struck me at the time, have turned out to be rules to live by.

And so the battle went on: death inching closer to Dad one day and retreating the next, as if daunted by Dad's determination. *I'm not going anywhere for a good while—I'm sticking around to take care of my wife and to make sure you keep behaving yourself.* But always in the air were the macabre calculations of how long he had left to live and how much money he had socked away.

"Son," Dad said, as I heard Mom untangling the phone line and telling him to aim his lips at the mouthpiece, "you and Bev need to get over here to review your mother's and my finances! On the double." Click. It was the week after Christmas 2002, the time of year Dad knew Bev wouldn't be busy with work.

"Is this a good sign or a bad sign?" Bev asked, after I'd relayed Dad's demand.

"Whenever Dad's ordering me around it's a good sign," I answered, "because he's still fighting."

As a lawyer, Bev had rushed into hundreds of family emergencies where a husband or wife was dying and affairs needed to be put in proper legal order, often within forty-eight hours. Afraid that this could be the situation with Dad, she'd balled her right hand into a small fist and pressed it against her mouth, a sign that she was fighting back tears.

Minutes later, we were in the car, Bev on her cell phone trying to exchange gifts during the madness of Boxing Week sales.

"Did I ever tell you what Dad told me twenty years ago, when I explained to him that I was putting you in charge of managing our money?"

"Make this a fast story, okay? I'm on hold with the Bay."

Doing my best imitation of Dad, I boomed, "Daggum, Danny, it's high time to let your wife know who's boss! Who's the man of your house, anyway?"

"Good thing you didn't tell me that at the time," Bev said.

"I'm telling you this now because our dropping everything—to drive over to his house 'on the double'—well, this is a big deal for Dad."

"In the middle of all this holiday stuff—which I have to do because you can't stand doing any of it—we're summoned over to meet with your dad 'on the double' and this is *big for him*? When we jumped into the car I thought your dad was in . . ." Bev caught herself here, knowing talking any more would leave her too emotional.

This was the trouble with talking about Dad to Bev. No matter what I ended up trying to say, it came out wrong. Still, I needed her to hear this: "Dad doesn't want me to look over all his savings. He knows I'm clueless about money stuff. He's reaching out for you. Your guidance. He just wants me to be there so he can pretend he's asking me."

"It's been twenty years, and I still don't always know when you make up crap, just to please me, and when you actually mean what you're saying."

Bev turned off her cell. Maybe she believed me this time.

As I gathered snacks in the kitchen, Mom started laying out mountains of paper on the living-room carpet. I returned with a platter of crackers and cheese to find Bev sitting cross-legged on the carpet, patiently breaking down what all the hieroglyphics spread across dozens of sheets of paper—everything from investments to bank statements to various pensions and life insurance—represented in real dollars.

"Your mother took perfect care of my books and accounts for almost half a century," Dad boasted, reaching out from his wheelchair to stroke Mom's arm. "But the big money decisions were always up to me. And for a broken-down old sociologist, I did a pretty good job."

Dad, like the proverbial grandfather who prefers to keep all his cash savings under a mattress, never truly believed the dollar figure on his financial statements.

Dad always liked to see and feel, even smell, his cheques. He would hold them up close to his face before Mom yanked them away for deposit, to be printed out as cold, detached numbers.

"You see, Dan," Bev said, her estate lawyer voice on full display, "you and Donna have nothing to worry about. You have enough saved to take care of both of you for years to come."

Bev had scribbled the total of all of my parents' savings on a small piece of paper and was pressing it into Dad's curled and crooked fingers. He looked up at Bev, beaming.

Dad, in his abstruse way, really did love Bev. The only snag was that it had taken him twenty years to feel that way. You could be angry that it had taken him so long, or you could claim that its long incubation period made it all the more precious.

There were moments that evening when Dad, basking in his role of supreme breadwinner, was able to relax and enjoy watching Bev and Mom calculate what represented, to him, his life's work. I stood behind him throughout most of the goings-on, as lost as he was among all the number-crunching, offering the odd, "Hear, hear. Whaddya know about that. Take a look at all that loot!" Just as Dad used to say to me when I showed him my newspaper route savings. All the while, I gently rocked him in his wheelchair.

"Can you hold these for me, Danny?"

"Sure, Dad."

He's lying on the hospital bed in the family room. His brown arm is extended towards me, his hand twitching as if conducting an imaginary orchestra with an invisible baton. His hand is empty.

"What is it you want me to hold, Dad?" Playing along with him makes this seem less depressing.

"My keys, son. Don't lose them. Your mom's gone to get my jacket."

What is it this time that's thrown Dad's mind out into space? The toxins that his atrophied kidneys and liver can't process? The morphine that dulls the pain of yet another amputation? No, that was last week. This week it's Percocet or something. He's on so many different meds that it's a miracle he can string a sentence together.

"Where are you guys going, Dad?"

"I'm taking your mother for a walk. Where's my wallet? I had a ten-dollar bill so we could do some shopping."

His voice takes on an accusing edge, as if perhaps I've taken it. In his confused state he could be fifteen years younger. Maybe younger still. It's been a while since ten dollars was enough spending money. "Son, I can't afford to go to Mushmouth's funeral. I need you to get his wife on the phone for me."

"It's okay, Dad, I've talked to her already. She understands."

Mushmouth's wife is long gone. Mushmouth died forty years ago of cancer. Dad's ravings can go on like this for hours. Often he'll voice regrets—that he didn't visit his parents enough, that his sister Margaret would be alive today if she'd lived with us, instead of dying all alone—the kind of concerns and wide-ranging guilt that I never knew he felt.

My offer of forgiveness comes in the form of wiping his cheeks and neck with a cool, moist washcloth. This calms him. His skin is still so smooth, so perfect. "Like honey," Bev always says, in a kind of admiring disbelief. I gently glide the cloth along the side of his head. What few tufts of hair remain there are full and dark.

"Thank you, son." He's come back.

"You're welcome, Dad."

Dad doesn't appear to be the least bit afraid of dying. Still, it's clear he plans on hanging on to life as long as possible. The closest he comes to broaching the subject is to say, in what sounds like a cross between a last request and an order, "Promise me you'll take care of your mother." One beat later, he always adds, "And your sister." I follow his lead and never allude to the fact that he's dying. For one thing, every time he seems to be hanging by his final thread, he bounces back.

I disappear to get him a glass of water. When I return he's got some of his old spirit back. "I suppose people think I'm gonna recant on my deathbed and embrace Jesus," he jokes, in between loud, satisfied, straw slurps. "Trust me, Danny," he says, once he's watched my eyes widen, "that ain't gonna happen." It almost sounds like a boast. Or a dare.

Later that evening, rattled by Dad's audacity, I tell David, barely fourteen: "I'm taking you to visit Granddad tomorrow. You don't know how much longer he's going to be around."

David replies, "You always say that, but he never dies."

Even though I've had plenty of time to steel myself for Dad's death, it's started to take on the shape of a distant, amorphous threat—an idle bluff, not unlike a repeated warning of punishment from your parents that you always knew, as a child, they'd never enforce. Even with the loss of both his legs, even with him sleeping as much as twenty hours a day, Dad still vibrated with life. Besides, suffering in silence was not Dad's style.

When Josie, Dad's favourite nurse, announced that she was pregnant, Dad made no attempt to hide his annoyance.

"Dan, Josie can bring her baby to work with her," Mom offered.

"Absolutely not," Dad yelled. "No babies! I'm the only baby here." Somehow he managed to strike a perfect balance between bravery and neediness, chutzpah and vulnerability.

It became increasingly unbearable to live each day never knowing if it was going to be the last day of Dad's life. *What if, when I'm out of town, he . . . ?* There was a part of me that wanted him to be set free, so that I'd be set free.

Leaving Dad was always the hardest part of my visits. I'd slowed down on my songwriting so I could see him more often, usually two or three times a week. But when I headed home, he'd feel rejected. It got to the point where I'd sometimes put off visiting him because I couldn't bear his anguish once it came time for me to leave. I made the mistake of telling him, once, that I had to rush home to record a vocal on a new song I'd just written. He could still pick out my fibs almost before they fell out of my mouth. He gave me one of those "yeah, right" looks and said, "You just wait, son, pretty soon diabetes is gonna destroy your singing voice, like it destroyed my kidneys." He still had the power to rip me open with little more than a single sentence.

I gathered my stuff, breathed in and bent to kiss his cheek. As the stubble of his face gently scratched my lips I drew back, wondering, as I looked down at him, what was the point of life, of living, if in the end it all came down to this.

It hurt so much to see his face start to buckle. To see his tears. It was the kind of hurt that took over all of me, leaving no fibre or cell unaffected. I was afraid of what would happen if the hurt plunged any deeper. Afraid that if I allowed myself to hold him in my arms I would simply come undone, never to be put back together again.

As I walked to my car, I spotted an old suitcase in the garage. It looked just like one I hauled off to summer camp back in 1965. This took me back to yet another memory of the Hill competitive disorder, which managed to cheer me up. I'd taken part in a contest to see who could pick up the most shells by diving to the bottom of the lake. I would win this competition if it killed me. It almost did. Sure enough, I was trawling along the bottom of the lake, stuffing the inside of my swimsuit and hands with shells, long after everyone else had surfaced. But it wasn't enough for me just to win. The margin had to be huge. Then everything started to slowly swirl from grey, to indigo blue, to black with white spots. I made it to the surface just as I was passing out, still clutching my winning shells.

All my life I'd been diving to the bottom of that lake, scooping up the most shells, damned near killing myself, like Dad. Could I carry Dad's passion in me without allowing it to destroy me? How could I take the best of all the things he'd taught me, and yet not succumb, like him, to catheters and dialysis and revolving caregivers? Was that the never-ending riddle? When do you drop the fucking shells and come up for air?

CHAPTER 30

Dad's Final Challenge

"You gotta hold on to what you believe in." I've brought my guitar to the hospital. Dad has managed to make a fist and he's shakily punching the air above his chest as he sings the lyrics to a song I wrote back in 1976. I'm playing the chords, muffing as many notes as I'm nailing, my fingers weak and clumsy from lack of practice. I should feel proud that after all these years, Dad is singing my words. Instead, I feel vaguely dislocated, as though I'm standing outside myself, watching and condemning everything I say and do.

I joke that he sings my songs better than I do.

"Sure, son," Dad's laugh stretches into a loud smacking yawn, bringing smiles to the nurse and the man lying on the other bed. I bite into a doughnut I'd purchased at the hospital snack bar.

"Whatcha got there, son?" Dad's eyes brighten as I offer him a bite. As usual, every move I make, every sidelong glance, registers with him. Whatever I'm eating he insists on sampling. I shouldn't be eating this crap. Dad's a living example of what will happen to me if I'm not careful. But lately I've been gulping down booze, desserts and sleeping pills in large quantities. I go extra crazy on desserts whenever I'm visiting Dad.

"What have you been up to, Danny?" Dad's question lifts me out of my haze of self-recrimination. I mutter something about a new song of mine that the Backstreet Boys have recently recorded. Right now they're the biggest-selling group in the world. Dad, bless his jazz-loyal heart, has never heard of them.

"Your infection's starting to clear up. I'm proud of you, Dad, you're a fighter."

I'm using a carbon-copy of the same rah-rah-rah speech he always gave me when I was rallying from some childhood illness. I think back to a week before, when the toxins were so high in his bloodstream that he ripped all the tubes and needles from his body and attempted to get out of bed, thinking he had to go to work. As I adjust his hospital gown to cover up his half-exposed brown thighs, I feel my self slipping again, falling back and away, into the deep dark blue.

"D'you have any other stories for me, Danny?" he asks, with a vulnerability that slays me. Our positions have been reversed now. Challenging as it's been to be his son, at least it was in keeping with the natural order of things. If this reversal is supposed to signify the final passage in my ever-shifting journey with Dad, I want no part of it. My sadness feels all the sharper because Dad, recently, appears to be more accepting of the change that's happening between us.

I ask Dad if there's a specific story he'd like me to tell him. Since he's gotten weaker, he prefers stories he's heard before. That way he knows what's coming and can savour the build-up leading to the release much the way people crave familiar songs, or children find reassurance in hearing the same bedtime story night after night. He asks for my Merv Griffin story.

"The audiences in Canada really love you, Dan," Mr. Griffin observed to me, during a pre-show prep interview in 1977. I stammered my thanks and then asked Mr. Griffin how he'd come to know this.

"I heard a tape of a live concert of yours. Where was it you were playing, again?" Mr. Griffin appeared perplexed by the stir I was creating north of the border.

I stared back at him in his loose, beige sweatpants. Wow. Merv Griffin, in sweats. I couldn't wait to tell Mom about this.

"Regina," I finally replied. "I was performing in Regina."

"Vagina?" he asked, his voice dropping to an incredulous whisper. "You performed in Vagina?"

It seemed terribly wrong, a dreadful mistake, to hear Mr. Griffin even say "vagina." Hell, I'd probably only heard the word actually spoken once or twice. I started to pedantically spell out "R-E-G," but by the time I'd hit the "G" and noticed Mr. Griffin obediently spelling the letters along with me, I lapsed into a fit of hysterical giggles.

Dad's laughter turns to coughing, to choking and, somehow, back to laughter. He rarely laughs this hard anymore. It's as though his body is being pummelled from within. Is it possible that he could laugh himself into a fatal heart attack? Would that be so bad? When I start thinking these morbid thoughts, it's time for me to go home.

Darkness is falling when I hit Queen Street. It's a six-mile walk home. I calculate the energy expenditure—ninety minutes equals four hundred and fifty calories equals three doughnuts—and I head off.

As I watched my dad physically break down, a part of me wanted to go down with him. Bev, horrified, knew that criticizing my behaviour would make it worse. At least I was home, rarely leaving except to work out or visit Dad or track down a missing royalty payment. All she could do was hope that I would emerge from this dark place when the inevitable, the unmentionable happened. Late at night, as the wine and sleeping pills worked their magic, I'd lurch and wobble my way downstairs, gripping the banister with both hands, and stumble into the basement guest room. Dropping to the bed, I'd close my eyes to the same dream: there'd be shards of glass, my foot sliced and bloodied, and a well-scrubbed surgeon about to lop off my leg. I'd wake up dehydrated and bloated, throw on my track shorts and stagger out the door for my 7 a.m., ten-mile purge. My legs, my lungs, my heart seemed to collude so that the previous night's act of self-destruction took on the form of a pre-race handicap ritual to give my body that extra challenge.

That my extreme devotion to running verged on self-cannibalism (my latest in a series of pain inoculations—a vainer form of cross-addiction) wasn't lost on me. I'd dropped over forty pounds in the last two years. Anorexia athletica (gorging on calories and burning it off with exercise afterwards) was apparently my condition—there's a succinct little term for everything these days. Basically, I wanted to shrivel up into a ball and die a slow, drawn-out death. Alongside my father.

Dad's willpower was staggering. In the army, he smoked two packs of cigarettes a day, but he stopped cold turkey in his early twenties after realizing that the dangers of smoking cigarettes outweighed the pleasure. When we were kids, all the children in the neighbourhood would swarm him on the front porch after dinner. Smoking one Cuban cigar after another, Dad would enchant them with his extemporaneous tales of talking animals and Negro sheriffs battling it out in the Wild West. Then one day, due in part to his children's constant nagging him to stop with the cigars, he did just that.

Thinking of Dad's resolve one night, I called him at the hospital and talked about my growing dependence on sleeping pills. The nightly dosages were increasing; the half-bottle of wine from six months ago had crept up to one and a half.

"You're strong, son. I know you. You can cut that stuff out any time you want. Once you've made up your mind to do something, you don't let anything stand in your way."

"I guess if you could do it, then I can, right?"

"You've already shown me that you can do anything you want."

"Thanks, Dad."

I'm sitting in a nondescript café across the street from St. Mike's Hospital with my mom, sister and brother. We're about to go upstairs and have Dad's intubation tube removed. He endured a third amputation barely a week earlier (this time, a little higher up his left leg), something that, due to the SARS crisis, had had to be delayed for far too long. The nasty, discoloured infection that started spreading across Dad's stump over a month ago had gone out of control, sending him into what would be his final coma.

After a waitress drops off our food, a Muzac version of my old hit pipes its way through the café, appearing to chase our server out of sight and into the safety of the kitchen. Mom reminds me that at least Dad won't be needling me anymore about this being my only classic. But I'm already missing Dad's jabs. His ceaseless teasing seems quaint in retrospect, an indicator of how closely he monitored and paid attention to me.

Once Dad's intubation tube is removed it will just be a matter of time before he dies. Mom explains this matter-of-factly to the three of us as we stare down at our untouched plates of pasta. We know this, just as we know it's important for Mom to tell us anyway. "Dad's simply existing now," she says. The scans are showing extensive brain damage. The two of them have discussed what was to happen if it ever got to this point. I know that all of us, playing with our plastic forks, are sharing the same thought right now. *He doesn't have to fight any longer. He doesn't have to prove anything to anyone anymore.*

Mom, the fragile one, is perfectly calm, the only truly composed person at the table. I've never known anyone to love a man so completely as Mom has loved Dad. But I can tell she's feeling some control, for perhaps the first time ever, in her relationship with him. And that this, for the moment at least, is giving her a kind of serenity. I'm saying all the right things, making the proper gestures, trying to hold it together. I know it's silly, but I feel that as the oldest child I should set an example by remaining strong, on the outside anyway.

"You know your dad," Mom says ruefully. "He likes to boss everyone around. So he has his memorial planned right down to the last second. And Danny, he wants you to play 'McCarthy's Day' and 'Daddy's Song.'"

This shouldn't surprise me, but it does. As usual, Dad has a few tricks left up his sleeve, a few final jolts, just to let me know that, even at death's doorstep, he's still way ahead of me. Dad wants me to sing the most personal songs I'd written about him. How can I possibly make it through performing those songs at his memorial? "So you think you're a singer, eh boy?" I imagine Dad saying, in his challenging, mano-a-mano tone. "Okay then, boy, prove it!"

I suggest to Mom that it may be safer to play these songs from my CDs during the memorial.

"That's entirely up to you, Danny."

When I stopped performing and releasing records to concentrate solely on writing for other acts, I'd resolved to never again play my songs or talk about my career, except when I was working. But I broke my promise and played one last song for Dad the month before he went into his last coma.

"It's about you and me, Dad. It's called 'My Father's Son.'" I took the CD out of its casing and started to feed it into the stereo system.

"Uh oh. So now you're gonna take some more pot-shots at me? I gotta listen to another song about what a terrible dad I was to you?"

"No, Dad, honestly, no pot-shots. It's hard to explain. Just listen."

The song's intro had already started. Dad stiffened imperceptibly in his wheelchair. As the first verse kicked in, I was taken aback at how intently he was listening:

> the strongest man I ever knew
> I never was a match for you
> always wanted your attention
> never knew just how to get it, so I rebelled
> tried to be your opposite, I did it well,
> strange but true, how our lives are like a circle now
> I'm so very much like you
> you were my unsolved mystery
> always barely out of reach
> at baseball games when parents came

you were always missing, that's okay
you had your meetings and promotions anyway
somehow I knew, the more I tried to be so different
the more I was like you

memories die hard, love dies harder still,
I forgive you, I have no choice
'cause when all is said and done
I am my father's son

Dad was frowning slightly as my song neared the halfway mark. He looked as if he was thinking up a rebuttal, or at least a wisecrack, to throw my way. But his reaction to the third verse moved me so deeply that I haven't been able to listen to or play the song since.

the first time that I saw you cry
was the morning that your daddy died
I stood there in amazement
as you packed up your suitcase I heard you say
"son I need you here to get me through the day"
and through your tears, I saw the boy inside the man
and it was suddenly so clear

memories die hard, love dies harder still,
I forgive you, I have no choice
'cause when all is said and done
I am my father's son

. . . what is love, without forgiveness
you did the best you could
I let go of the anger, when I finally understood

How was I to know that as my voice sang through the speakers, "The first time that I saw you cry," I was watching my father cry one final time?

The day after Dad died, I went for a run. It was hot and all I wore were shorts and shoes. White dandelion seeds were floating everywhere and I pretended they were little pieces of his soul. No one would be passing me this morning. I'd see someone jogging one hundred feet ahead of me and I'd speed up, determined to overtake him in some make-believe race, imagining Dad saying, "Look, Donna, look at Danny go!" the way he used to when I was a child, doing something that impressed him. That's when the sobbing started. It sounded like someone else's voice, the way it kept leaping out of me in heaving, gulping gasps. That was the first time I'd cried since he'd died. I'd never cried like that before.

I have to get all this crying out of my system so I can be strong for my mother. As I walked onstage to sing at Dad's memorial, I clung to my father's words. He'd have been proud of his memorial, at least so far. Although truthfully, it had been pretty difficult for me to take in. I kept thinking back to that cold day in Washington, D.C., in 1979—when Dad had shown me how to be strong for your family. I'd been there, I'd watched and learned. Now it was my turn to lead so that one day David would set the same example for his own family once my time had come and gone.

The memory of Dad's strength pulled me through "McCarthy's Day." But as I slowed into the song's final refrain, "This is just a song to say, that I'm proud for what they are," I caught Dad's sister Doris's face and felt myself falter. No more looking into the audience. "Daddy's Song" was too new, too raw. I remembered how my grade three teacher got me through my first live performance. I'd been chosen to sing the solo song for the school talent night, and my parents were sitting in the front row. *Just look up at the basketball nets when you're singing, Danny. Then you won't be too nervous.*

And so, as I sang "Daddy's Song" at my father's memorial, I looked up and stared through imaginary basketball nets, hanging from the walls of the church:

> *I always knew this time would come*
> *still I'm not ready, is anyone*

as a child I believed
daddies lived on and on
I guess I was wrong

we had our moments, didn't we though
thought we'd never speak again, the day I left home
I was so much like you, tried so hard to be strong
I guess I was wrong

why when it rains, does it always pour
why does this pain feel like nothing I've felt before . . .
as a child I believed daddies lived on and on . . .
I guess I was wrong

daddy your love, for my mother your wife
moves me more deeply, than all else in my life
on the hospital bed, she holds you till dawn
love's all that lives on
as a child I believed daddies lived on and on
perhaps I'm not wrong

I stood up, clutching my guitar to my chest, and left the stage. I spotted the exit to my right, pushed open the door with my shoulder and found myself standing in the warm night air. Expecting tears, I found myself smiling instead, thinking of the last gift I gave my father. A famous Italian pop/opera singer had informed me that he intended to record "Daddy's Song"—provided that I rewrite the verse about Mom holding Dad on the hospital bed. When I refused, Dad treated me like a hero, sacrificing fortune in the name of artistic integrity.

Do we ever stop wanting to make our parents proud of us? Does their dying free us of this need? I'll never stop trying to impress my father.

"How much longer do you think you have, Dad?" David asks me. I've grounded him, and Bev's at the cottage, so he's stuck with me tonight.

For a seventeen-year-old on a Friday night, that's a fate worse than death. Things will get worse for David, for us, before they get better. It will take every lesson Dad ever taught me to try, along with Bev, to rescue him.

"You didn't answer me, Dad. Do you think you're gonna live a long life? Or do you think you'll end up like Granddad?"

Karen shows up before I can think of how to answer. She'd been feeling pretty low and I'd suggested she spend the night here. As I'm putting together some food for Karen and David, there's another knock on my front door. It's Karen's teenage daughter, Malaika, wanting to keep a close eye on her mom.

I try to channel Dad's way of making people feel better, especially during a crisis. I do the best I can. I let David know what will happen if he defies my orders and goes out. I keep tabs on Karen. I reassure Malaika that the chili is tofu-based. I weigh the pros and cons of telling Bev about David being grounded, and more disturbingly, why. I decide to wait till she gets home.

"When I was twelve, I asked Granddad if he was scared of dying." David, Karen, Malaika and I are talking in the living room. David, after standing over me, staring me down and announcing he's going to go out despite the consequences—"no Internet, no cell phone, no money, no girls in the house, till the end of time"—has reconsidered. "Granddad said that once you reach your seventies you're not afraid to die, you worry about the people you'll be leaving behind," David says.

"That's what happens once you become a parent," I say, sounding a little too much like a parent.

David's going to be eighteen soon. The age Dad was when he was drafted into the U.S. Army. The age I was when I signed with RCA. There's only so much I can protect David from. I find that deeply unsettling. I can only imagine how unsettled Dad must have felt about my future when I was eighteen. It will take a few very difficult and unimaginably scary years before David finds something to rescue him from himself. As Dad found sociology and I found music, David will discover writing. Prose. And he will lose himself in that with a passion similar to mine, and his grandfather's. I wish Dad could read his grandson's writing now. And maybe he can. Maybe he is. Who really knows these things?

I still dream about Dad. Every night. He's in this curiously undead state. We're together, doing regular, everyday things, nothing dramatic or extraordinary. I'm just hanging out with him, like he's still alive. We both know that to everyone but me he's dead, but that somehow he's managed to pull off this caper, defying life and death in his indefatigable Dad way. He has the same cocky, "let's keep this between us" grin that he displayed when we played football in front of the Bible class on that Sunday afternoon. We're both relaxed and quietly happy. There's an unflappable, easy closeness that we never quite shared in real life. But even in this dream, we both know that soon he'll be taken away from me.

The thing I cherish most about these recurring dreams is Dad's absolute physicality. Something about knowing that this mystifying man whom I loved and battled and sometimes despised so utterly is now gone, forever, makes the world seem, at times, inescapably cold, boring and barren.

So here I am, the first son of an atheist father, his skepticism planted deep inside me, ready for him, indeed beseeching him, to visit me once more. As I bury my head deep in my pillow, Larry's final words to Dad as we gathered round, touching him and crying over him while he breathed his final breath, come back to me. *Goodbye, Dad.* Will I ever forget that moment? Will I ever be able to let go and finally say, and mean, those two, unbearably sad words? *Goodbye, Dad.* I don't think so. Instead, I reach out in the darkness and pull my sleeping wife closer, imagining Dad doing the same thing with Mom, and murmur the closing phrase that his youngest sister, Doris, the one he was always closest to, said at his memorial: "He still holds my hand."

EPILOGUE

The Cave Rescue

"I slipped a piece of paper in your day book," Mom says. We've just returned from a trip to Oakville, where we share the same chiropodist. "It's my voluntary euthanasia declaration."

Oh no, not this again. We'd arrived at our appointments fifteen minutes late, due to my squeezing in a ninety-minute rollerblade before we left. She'd been cross with me on the way. Disappointed at my tardiness, a carryover from my teenaged years living at home when I never took anyone's time, aside from my own, seriously. Shocked that I'd hired a cab rather than drive myself. I know what she's thinking: *Two hundred dollars, wasted.*

"My right hamstring's so sore from all my running that it cramps when I try to drive," I told her. "All that on and off with the accelerator."

"Oh yes, Danny, that makes sense. You're telling me your leg's too sore to drive, but you just rollerbladed twenty miles?"

There's no worse disapproval than my mom's telling silence. Trying to atone for pissing her off, I made a big fuss out of paying for her appointment. "How much was it?" she asked.

"Forty dollars. Pretty good, don't you think?"

"That's a little steep, if you ask me."

But Mom's mood improved. Over the years, her reprimands have never had much impact on me. This may be related to a lifetime of seeing Dad shrug off her criticisms with nary a second thought. Or perhaps half a century of trying to impress Dad left me too drained to fret over Mom's responses to my often inconsiderate behaviour.

Since the seventies, Mom's been hospitalized for her bipolar condition only two or three times, all for short durations. Life after Dad, to my surprise, has shown no signs of breaking or destabilizing her. But she misses him, sometimes desperately.

As I serve Mom tea in my kitchen she starts to reminisce about him. Mom's tough, less prone to crying than she was when I was a child, and she can talk about surprisingly intimate and revealing things while appearing completely composed.

"As you know, your father and I had different ideas about how long our lives should hang on. He never wanted to have anything to do with a living will."

Mom and I have been through this many times before. I reassure her that if or when that dreadful moment comes, I'll respect her decision. That's as direct as I can be about it.

"I can't talk to Karen about his. She always starts to cry. And Larry just gets very, very quiet."

Great, I think. *And who am I? The cold, unfeeling child?*

"You know I visited your dad's grave a week ago, on the third anniversary of his death. Have you visited at all?"

I look at Mom sadly and shake my head.

"I spoke to him. Planted a few yellow flowers." Mom's eyes start to well up but the tears don't form. She talks about how she wishes his gravestone was bigger.

"Did he want something big?" God, I hate talking about this.

"No, he just wanted to be buried beside a tree."

I think back to how excited Dad was when he first planted the row of poplar trees in our backyard. It was right after we'd moved into our new home. Dad was forty-one. I was almost eleven.

"You just wait, Danny," he told me. "Over the years these poplars will grow to be huge. They'll be around long after we're gone." I blanched at the thought of either one of us being gone. I felt resentful, jealous of the baby poplars—that their lives had just begun, that they would outlive us both.

As I walk Mom down my front steps, I think of how Dad always asked if I was going to put a ramp in to the front door, for him and his wheelchair. At that point we both knew he wouldn't be coming to my house anymore. He needed Wheel-Trans, a van with specially equipped ramps and space for paraplegics, to get anywhere. Dad simply wanted to see what I'd say. I never had the ramp built. I feel guilty about that now. What is love, after all, but a series of symbols and gestures—as impractical and yet vital and stirring as a diamond ring, a painting or a transcendent song?

As I open the car door to help Mom into her tiny white Mazda, my final image of her and Dad comes back to me: how she kissed him for the last time moments after he died, pressing her mouth against his forehead and leaving it there for what seemed like the longest time: her final mark, her last impression. Mom warns me, as she turns the key and starts the ignition, that if I don't respect her "final wishes" she has a stash of pills for the moment she decides she wants to end it all.

"Hey Mom, you sure you don't feel like going for a walk or something?" The thought of her going upsets me. What if I never see her again?

"No, I should take off now, before the traffic starts to build."

As I watch her drive away, I realize that one of the reasons I miss being with Dad, and love being with Mom, is that it's the only time I can slip back into being a boy.

Another memory drifts back to me and keeps me cocooned in this blissful and secure state for the rest of the day.

Our family's gone camping in the Gatineau Hills in Quebec. My parents are taking us to visit a famous cave. At the cave's opening is a path that diverges from the main road. Larry and I tear down this lower path, his matchstick, four-year-old legs scampering in a futile attempt to keep up with me. Already, everything is a life-and-death competition between us. My parents and Karen continue up the main road, assuming the two routes will eventually meet. A few minutes later, winded, Larry and I find ourselves deep underground at the bottom of a six-foot-deep cave. Too panicked and disoriented to attempt to retrace our steps, Larry starts hollering. I squint, trying to adjust my vision—it's inky black all around me, with tiny shafts of light peeking in from above.

"There they are, Donna."

Dad has traced the source of our screams. Though he can't see us, I can see him, squatting, trying to make out our tiny figures in the shadows below. The cave's walls are too steep for us to climb, and too high for Dad to descend.

"Larry, grab hold. Danny, you're next."

Dad lowers his left leg down the cave wall while his right leg bends low to the ground for support. Larry quickly wraps his little arms around Dad's thigh, like a baby monkey hugging an oversized tree trunk. In no time, he's swung out of the damp darkness and back into the warm light. My turn. I hang on, smelling Dad's sweat, his comforting and familiar muskiness. With one giant swoosh I'm hoisted to safety.

ACKNOWLEDGEMENTS

Though this is a story that explores my relationship with my dad most deeply, I could not have written this book without my mother. Mom sat down with me for hundreds of hours, answering my questions, disputing my theories and correcting me on family details. Her memory is astonishing, and her courage and loyalty continue to inspire and humble me. Never wild about the idea of this father-son memoir, Mom nonetheless talked candidly with me about intimate and sometimes painful past events, looking me straight in the eye and delivering the goods.

My sister, Karen, was equally generous and forthright, opening up her life to me in all its horror and joy. It was an invaluable contribution and a wonderful gift.

While I spared my brother, Larry, the "Big Book Interview," I didn't spare him an early version of the book. His shrewd and thorough assessment, documented in five pages of comments, criticism and encouragement, took up residence beside my laptop, constantly reminding me that I could go further, write better and tell my story, and my dad's story, more effectively.

Beyond my immediate family, I interviewed six people: my aunt, Doris Cochran; my cousin, Adele Flateau; and four of my father's closest friends—Eleanor Meslin, Alan Borovoy, Jim Maben and Jean McFadyen. All these people opened their homes to me and spent hours telling me amazing stories about my father. I will always remember their honesty and hospitality.

My editor, Jennifer Lambert, patiently and gently kept the story focused and encouraged me to delve deeper and not be afraid. My unorthodox writing methods (like finding more "missing chapters" after the project was supposedly completed) made the pace intense, right up to the final moments. Jennifer never complained. Indeed, everyone at HarperCollins showed me incredible support and an overall belief in this book.

Managing editor Noelle Zitzer kindly indulged my last-minute changes to the text while reminding me, in the subtlest and most caring way, that there comes a time to let go.

Before I sent the original manuscript to my publisher, my sister-in-law, Miranda Hill, worked side by side with me as my editor for eighteen months. Without Miranda's expert counsel and practical knowledge about Hill family history, this book would have never been published.

For more than twenty years, my assistant, Nikki Harris, has kept me organized. Her attention to the many necessary details of life and business allowed me to stay focused on this book, just as she has enabled me to concentrate on my music for two decades.

Lawyer and agent Michael Levine shared his knowledge of business, publishing and human nature, which has been a godsend.

The people at the Archives of Ontario were phenomenal guides while I considered my father's life through the lens of his many personal letters.

I'd like to thank Matthew McCauley and Fred Mollin for teaching me so much about music. My old friend and collaborator, Matthew graciously allowed me to include in this book the lyrics to some of my early songs. Thanks to my dear friend John Sheard for teaching me piano.

Keith Stegall and John Hadfield were kind enough to read my original 800-plus-page manuscript and offer wonderful feedback and encouragement.

Finally, I wish to thank my wife and son. During the years that it took to find my way through this story, my wife, Beverly, spent many moments on the verge of strangling me—always with good reason. Still, she read and reread the various drafts, offering advice, support, patience and love. Without her, I could never have completed this book and quite frankly would not have survived the many challenges, some self-inflicted, in my life. Our son, David, read the various versions—even when I asked him not to. Indeed, David's passion and talent as a writer, as well as our own relationship as father and son, helped inspire me to tell this story.

PHOTO CREDITS

All photographs courtesy of the Hill family, unless otherwise noted.

Page v, The author and his father, Daniel G. Hill, 1957; **Prologue**, page 1, Daniel G. Hill and Dan Hill, 1954; **Chapter 1**, page 9, Donna Hill and Dan Hill, 1954; **Chapter 2**, page 26, Daniel G. Hill and his three sisters (from left: Margaret, Doris and Jeanne), ca. 1937–1939. F 2130-9-2-6.2, Archives of Ontario; **Chapter 3**, page 46, The Hill family, 1958. From left: Dan Hill (front), Daniel G. Hill (rear), Lawrence Hill, Karen Hill, Donna Hill; **Chapter 4**, page 70, Dan Hill, 1968; **Chapter 5**, page 88, Daniel G. Hill in WWII army uniform. F 2130-9-2-13, Archives of Ontario; **Chapter 6**, page 109, Donna Hill (facing camera), with family and friends, 1969; **Chapter 7**, page 121, Daniel G. Hill (middle) with friends, 1941. F 2130-9-2-5, Archives of Ontario; **Chapter 8**, page 135, Dan Hill, 1971; **Chapter 9**, page 154, Daniel G. Hill, ca. 1960. F 2130-9-2-13, Archives of Ontario; **Chapter 10**, page 170, Dan Hill, in running gear, ca. 1972; **Chapter 11**, page 180, Promotional material for Dan Hill's first release, 1973; **Chapter 12**, page 193, Dan Hill performing, 1973; **Chapter 13**, page 199, The Hill family, 1976. From left: Dan Hill, Donna Hill, Daniel G. Hill, Karen Hill, Lawrence Hill; **Chapter 14**, page 205, Newspaper advertisement for performances at The Riverboat, a coffeehouse in Toronto's Yorkville, 1973; **Chapter 15**, page 223, Dan Hill, ca. 1975; **Chapter 16**, page 233, Dan Hill (centre) with Matt McCauley (left) and Fred Mollin (right), celebrating Dan Hill's two gold records, 1976. © 1976 Arthur (Art) Usherson, www.artscelebrityphotos. com; **Chapter 17**, page 240, Karen Hill, ca. 1976; **Chapter 18**, page 253, Dan Hill with his multiple Juno Awards, including Male Vocalist of the Year and Composer of the Year, 1978. Doug Griffin/*Toronto Star*; **Chapter 19**, page 268, The album cover for *Partial Surrender*, released 1981; **Chapter 20**, page 280, Daniel Hill Jr. at Howard University, 1954. F 2130-9-2-17, Archives of Ontario; **Chapter 21**, page 286, Donna Hill, Dan Hill, Daniel G. Hill; **Chapter 22**, page 295, The wedding of Dan Hill and Beverly Chapin, 1982; **Chapter 23**, page 308, Clipping from *The Sunday Sun*, "New Ombudsman's Ready to Roll with Punches—He'll Fight for Little Guy," December 11, 1983. Reprinted with the permission of Sun Media Corporation; **Chapter 24**, page 319, Thomas Spitzer and Karen Hill, 1982. Courtesy of Karen Hill; **Chapter 25**, page 330, Daniel G. Hill and Beverly Chapin at the wedding of Dan Hill and Beverly Chapin, 1982; **Chapter 26**, page 337, Dan Hill with Rick Nowels, Celine Dion, John Jones and Rick Hahn at the Grammys. Reprinted with permission; **Chapter 27**, page 346, Dan Hill with his son, David Hill, 1989; **Chapter 28**, page 355, Daniel G. Hill, David Hill, Dan Hill, 1988; **Chapter 29**, page 370, Donna Hill, Dan Hill, Daniel G. Hill, 1993; **Chapter 30**, page 382, Daniel G. Hill receives the Order of Canada, 1999; **Epilogue**, page 393, Lawrence Hill and Dan Hill, 1957.